Doris Lechner
Histories for the Many

Historische Lebenswelten in populären Wissenskulturen
History in Popular Cultures | Volume 17

Editorial

In der Reihe **Historische Lebenswelten in populären Wissenskulturen | History in Popular Cultures** erscheinen Studien, die populäre Geschichtsdarstellungen interdisziplinär oder aus der Perspektive einzelner Fachrichtungen (insbesondere der Geschichts-, Literatur- und Medienwissenschaft sowie der Ethnologie und Soziologie) untersuchen. Im Blickpunkt stehen Inhalte, Medien, Genres und Funktionen heutiger ebenso wie vergangener Geschichtskulturen.

Die Reihe wird herausgegeben von Barbara Korte und Sylvia Paletschek (geschäftsführend) sowie Hans-Joachim Gehrke, Wolfgang Hochbruck, Sven Kommer und Judith Schlehe.

The series **Historische Lebenswelten in populären Wissenskulturen | History in Popular Cultures** provides analyses of popular representations of history from specific and interdisciplinary perspectives (history, literature and media studies, social anthropology, and sociology). The studies focus on the contents, media, genres, as well as functions of contemporary and past historical cultures.

The series is edited by Barbara Korte and Sylvia Paletschek (executives), Hans-Joachim Gehrke, Wolfgang Hochbruck, Sven Kommer and Judith Schlehe.

Doris Lechner is research officer at the Karlsruhe Institute of Technology and co-founder of the Book History and Print Culture Network (D-A-CH).

Doris Lechner

Histories for the Many

The Victorian Family Magazine and Popular Representations of the Past. *The Leisure Hour*, 1852-1870

[transcript]

Printed with the support of the German Research Foundation (DFG).

PLYMOUTH UNIVERSITY

9uu967469 9

Bibliographic information published by the Deutsche Nationalbibliothek
The Deutsche Nationalbibliothek lists this publication in the Deutsche Natio-
nalbibliografie; detailed bibliographic data are available in the Internet at
http://dnb.d-nb.de

© 2017 transcript Verlag, Bielefeld

Cover layout: Kordula Röckenhaus, Bielefeld
Cover illustration: Detail from annual cover for *Leisure Hour* 1859. Images
    published with permission of ProQuest. Further reproduction is prohibited
    without permission.
Printed in Germany
Print-ISBN 978-3-8376-3711-3
PDF-ISBN 978-3-8394-3711-7

Table of Contents

List of Tables | 7

List of Illustrations | 9

Acknowledgements | 11

1. The Victorian Family Magazine and Historical Culture | 13
   Introduction | 13
   Serialised History in the *Leisure Hour*, 1852-1860 | 24
   Structure of the Study | 29
   Theoretical and Methodological Approaches | 31

PART I: THE *LEISURE HOUR*
IN THE PERIODICAL MARKETPLACE

2. The *Leisure Hour* and the Disputed Genre
   of the Family Magazine in the 1850s and 1860s | 45
   First and Second Generation Family Magazines | 46
   Debates on Reading Matter and the Popular Press | 48
   »A New Weekly Magazine«: The *Leisure Hour* as Intermediary | 51
   New Illustrated Magazines and Changes in the Periodical Market | 61

3. History for the Working Man:
   The *Leisure Hour* and the *London Journal*, 1852 | 71
   Overview | 72
   Leisure Hour | 77
   London Journal | 87

4. Images of History: The *Leisure Hour*, *Good Words*
   and the *Cornhill Magazine*, 1860 | 99
   Overview | 102
   Leisure Hour | 108
   Good Words | 122
   Cornhill Magazine | 128

PART II: SERIALISING HISTORY IN THE *LEISURE HOUR*

5. **Serialising History into and out of the *Leisure Hour*:**
    The Periodical and Book Transfer | 139
    Non-Fiction Series on the Past in the *Leisure Hour*
    and their Book Counterparts | 143
    Case Studies (1): From Book to Periodical | 152
    Case Studies (2): Monthly Parts | 162

6. **Writing History for the Family Audience:**
    Between Popular and Academic | 179
    Writing on the Past for the *Leisure Hour*: The Contributors | 180
    John Stoughton: Between Popular and Academic History | 185
    Writing History for the Family Audience: »Shades of the Departed
    in Old London« | 192
    Continuation, Variation and Negation of Stoughton's
    Narrative Pattern | 209

7. **Conclusion** | 221

APPENDIX

Appendix A: Tables | 227

Appendix B: Excursus – Fictional Series on the Past
and Their Book Counterparts | 279

Appendix C: Contributors on the Past
in the *Leisure Hour* (1852-1870) | 283

References | 293

Index | 331

List of Tables

Tab. 1: Periodical Profiles. | 227

Tab. 2: *Leisure Hour* (1852-1870): Non-Fiction Series on the Past. | 229

Tab. 3: *Leisure Hour* (1852): Covers Relating to the Past. | 236

Tab. 4: *Leisure Hour* (1852): Series Relating to the Past. | 237

Tab. 5: *Leisure Hour* (1852): Life Writing and Person-Centred Writing. | 238

Tab. 6: *London Journal* (1852): Covers Relating to the Past. | 243

Tab. 7: *London Journal* (1852): Series Relating to the Past. | 244

Tab. 8: *London Journal* (1852): Life Writing
and Person-Centred Writing. | 245

Tab. 9: *Leisure Hour* (1860): Covers Relating to the Past. | 247

Tab. 10: *Leisure Hour* (1860): Series Relating to the Past. | 247

Tab. 11: *Leisure Hour* (1860): Life Writing and Person-Centred Writing. | 248

Tab. 12: *Good Words* (1860): Covers Relating to the Past. | 250

Tab. 13: *Good Words* (1860): Series Relating to the Past. | 251

Tab. 14: *Good Words* (1860): Life Writing and Person-Centred Writing. | 253

Tab. 15: *Cornhill* (1860): Covers Relating to the Past. | 255

Tab. 16: *Cornhill* (1860): Series Relating to the Past. | 255

Tab. 17: *Cornhill* (1860): Life Writing and Person-Centred Writing. | 256

Tab. 18: *Leisure Hour* (1852-1870): Non-Fiction Series
and their Book Counterparts. | 257

Tab. 19: *Leisure Hour* (1852-1870): Historically Themed Fiction
and Book Counterparts. | 262

Tab. 20: *Leisure Hour* (1852-1870): Monthly Parts on the Past. | 266

Tab. 21: *Leisure Hour*, Monthly Parts: »How to See the English Lakes«
(July 1857). | 268

Tab. 22: *Leisure Hour*, Monthly Parts: Shakespeare (April 1864). | 270

Tab. 23: *Leisure Hour*, Monthly Parts: »The Deadly Art of War«
(August 1854). | 273

Tab. 24: *Leisure Hour* (1852-1887): Overview of Series
by John Stoughton. | 275

Tab. 25: John Stoughton's »Shades of the Departed in Old London«,
Leisure Hour 1852-53. | 276

List of Illustrations

Fig. 1:   Annual Covers for *Leisure Hour* 1859 and 1860 | 69

Fig. 2:   Covers, Didactic Mode: *London Journal* (30 Oct 1852: 113)
          and *Leisure Hour* (18 Nov 1852: 737) | 74

Fig. 3:   Covers, Sensational Mode: *London Journal* (10 Apr 1852: 65)
          and *Leisure Hour* (23 Sept 1852: 609) | 74

Fig. 4:   Cover for *Leisure Hour* (30 Sept 1852: 625) | 87

Fig. 5:   Page from the *London Journal*'s »Lives of the Queens«
          (25 Sept 1852: 41) | 91

Fig. 6:   »Lord Macaulay«, *Leisure Hour* (1 Mar 1860: 137) | 109

Fig. 7:   »Sir John Lawrence, G.C.B«, *Leisure Hour* (5 Jan 1860: 9) | 109

Fig. 8:   »Lord Clive«, *Leisure Hour* (8 Mar 1860: 153) | 112

Fig. 9:   »Charles James Fox«, *Leisure Hour* (19 Jan 1860: 41) | 112

Fig. 10: »The Fire Escape«, *Leisure Hour* (20 Sept 1860: 601) | 114

Fig. 11: »Robert Stephenson«, *Leisure Hour* (15 Nov 1860: 729) | 116

Fig. 12: »Vancouver the Voyager«, *Leisure Hour* (12 Jan 1860: 32) | 118

Fig. 13: »The Last Prayer of Gustavus Adolphus«, *Leisure Hour*
          (12 Apr 1860: 233) | 121

Fig. 14: »The Story of Ninian«, *Good Words* (12 Feb 1860: 97) | 123

Fig. 15: »Pictures from the History and Life of the Early Church«, *Good Words*
          (11 Nov 1860: 737) | 123

Fig. 16: »John Evangelist Gossner«, *Good Words* (18 Mar 1860: 177) | 126

Fig. 17: »A Woman's Work«, *Good Words* (5 Aug 1860: 497) | 126

Fig. 18: »The Four Georges«, *Cornhill* (Aug 1860: facing page 175) | 133

Fig. 19: »The Four Georges«, *Cornhill* (Sept 1860: 271-272) | 134

Fig. 20: Narrative Model for »Shades of the Departed« | 195

Fig. 21: Cover for »Shades of the Departed«, *Leisure Hour*
          (22 Apr 1852: 257) | 200

Fig. 22: Cover for »Shades of the Departed«, *Leisure Hour*
          (18 Nov 1852: 737) | 200

Images from *Leisure Hour*, *London Journal*, *Good Words* and *Cornhill* produced by ProQuest as part of *British Periodicals*. www.proquest.com

Acknowledgements

This book is a revised version of my doctoral thesis, which I submitted to the University of Freiburg in 2015. Many people have contributed to its development, for which I am very grateful. I would like to thank my supervisor Barbara Korte for initiating this research project. She first introduced me to the research fields of historical culture and periodical studies, and this project would not have been possible without her encouragement and continuous advice. Having been taught by her for many years, I am very grateful for the numerous ways in which she has helped shape my career as an academic. I would also like to thank my supervisor Leslie Howsam for her inspiring enthusiasm. I could not have had a better teacher to introduce me to the study of the book. Our discussions of my research and her constructive suggestions helped me to further develop my ideas and draw the right conclusions.

Thanks are also due to my colleague and friend Nina Reusch. Our collaboration as historian and literary critic always provided stimulating insights, and I am grateful for her valuable feedback on my research.

This study originated in the DFG Research Group »Historische Lebenswelten in populären Wissenskulturen der Gegenwart – History in Popular Cultures of Knowledge«, and thanks are due to co-speaker Sylvia Paletschek and the research group's members for an inspiring exchange of ideas. My special thanks go to my colleagues in the junior research group »Populäre Geschichts- und Wissenskulturen – Popular Cultures of History and Knowledge«: Melanie Fritscher-Fehr, Aibe-Marlene Gerdes, Simon Maria Hassemer, Imke von Helden, Konstantin Rapp, Evamaria Sandkühler, Franziska Schaudeck, Miriam Sénécheau, Kristina Wacker and Ulrike Zimmermann. They have repeatedly read sections of my research and discussed it with me over the course of its development. Katharina Boehm, Sabine Frischmuth, Christiane Hadamitzky and Stefanie Lethbridge have also read (sections of) this book, and I am grateful for their valuable suggestions. Thanks are also due to David Heyde for his efficient and careful proofreading of the manuscript. Christine Wichmann managed the publication process at transcript.

Parts of this book have been presented at conferences and workshops, and I have benefited from conversations with Margaret Beetham, Frank Bösch, Cornelia Brink, Ian Hesketh, Brian Maidment, Matías Martínez and James Mussell. I first published parts of my research in an article in *Studies in Book Culture* and am grateful to editor of that special issue Yuri Cowan and *Studies in Book Culture* editors Marie-Pier Luneau and Josée Vincent for letting me reuse this material here.

My special thanks go to E. Matthias Reifegerste at Freiburg University Library for ensuring I had access to the books and databases I needed. I would also like to acknowledge the staff of Archives & Special Collections at the School for Oriental Studies Library; Senate House Library; and British Library. ProQuest has kindly granted permission for the reproduction of images from their *British Periodicals Collection*.

My research project was funded by the German Research Foundation. The Humanities Graduate School supported my research with a conference travel stipend.

I would like to acknowledge a number of people for the support they have provided me beyond academia and thank them for their friendship during these past years: Katja Bay, Jörg Deger, Susanne Duesterberg, Jenny Eichler, Kathrin Göb, Martin Jost, Eva Ulrike Pirker, Holger Schütt, Christine Trüg and Georg Zipp. Finally, I am most grateful to my parents Emilie and Peter Pfeiffer for their love and encouragement.

1. The Victorian Family Magazine and Historical Culture

> Dismissing the idea that the key of knowledge is the exclusive possession of the sons of genius or wealth, we shall bid the working man accompany us in our visits to the hoary relics of other times; to stand with us amid the broken columns of Tadmor, and read the solemn lessons which are written in the ashes of Greece and Rome. We shall often wander among the roots and springs of those mighty changes which issued in the creation of Modern Europe; survey those fanatic hordes who rushed under the guidance of superstition to the conquest of the East; visit the home of the printing press in the garret of Guttenburg [sic]; listen to the prows of Columbus as they cut their way through the virgin-waves of the Atlantic; mark the slow but sure progress of social enfranchisement, and hail the first shouts which announce the resurrection of mankind from the sepulchre of the Middle Ages.
>
> (H.D.: »A WORD WITH OUR READERS«, *LEISURE HOUR* 1852: 9)

INTRODUCTION

In July 1851, the evangelical Religious Tract Society (RTS) decided to »issue a popular weekly magazine« which was »to be specially adapted for the working classes and particularly the Younger members of their families« (USCL/RTS

CCM 16 July 1851).[1] The decision was made on the basis of a »statistical account of the circulation of fourteen weekly papers, some of which [were] of pernicious tendency, and ha[d] an immense sale« (ibid.). The aim of the Society
was, therefore, to counter such »pernicious«, fiction-carrying periodicals with a
magazine of similar entertaining and instructive content, yet written in a Christian spirit. In its first number, the *Leisure Hour* introduced its historical programme of »learning wisdom from the past« (H.D. 1852: 9), as printed in the epigraph above. The Religious Tract Society was, for ideological reasons, interested in the presentation of truthful stories, »believing that their power to convert
readers would be undermined if the narratives were fictional« (Fyfe 2004c: 67).
The plan to include a large portion of historical narratives within the pages of the
Leisure Hour, it could be argued, was meant to compensate for the readers' increasing demand for fiction, as historical narratives could similarly be entertaining and even sensational, while at the same time they were based on facts and
fulfilled an educating function. The historical programme laid out in the *Leisure
Hour*'s initial readers' address was obviously meant to interest both the »working man« and »the sons of genius and wealth«. The past, or at least the interest in
the past, it could be concluded, was meant to unite the two parties when the editors asked:

»Are we not one people, one great commonwealth? Does not the same blood tinge our
veins? Have we not the same sires? Are there not thousands of our lower classes who
might claim a Norman pedigree, and does not the crown of Britain grace a Saxon brow?
Have we not the same heart-stirring recollections, the same watchwords of patriotism, the
same interests in the pregnant future? [...] Yes, we are one people, the inheritors of one
mother-land and one mother-tongue; we will have therefore one literature: the same voice
shall speak in the same accents to all.« (H.D. 1852: 9)

---

1   Andrew King has »argu[ed] that we move on from the language of class when analysing cultural consumption« as »many books today that continue to use terms such as
›middle-class periodicals‹ or ›working-class serials‹ lie precisely in the contradiction
between the attenuation of such engagement while still clinging on to its language«
(King 2004: 7). This study shares King's concern, yet ›class‹ still figures as a category
of disparity in the intersectional approach to the periodicals' family audience; besides
this, I apply the term class predominantly to reflect its use within the Victorian discourse, as in the quote from the RTS minutes presented here on the intended working-
class readership the Society had in mind.

The image evoked by the editors of the *Leisure Hour* was that of a united nation – or at least that of a cross-class readership – and this image reminds one of Fernando Sánchez Marcos's observation of history as the »arena in which the present and future identity of the community is debated« (Sánchez Marcos 2009: 3).

Histories for the Many examines the *Leisure Hour*'s ›historical programme‹ in text, image and serial form. Following Barbara Korte and Eva Ulrike Pirker's understanding of ›historical programme‹ as a master discourse determining a society's historical culture (2011: 44-46), this study uses ›historical programme‹ or ›historical agenda‹ rather on the micro-level of specific media products, that is, it considers aspects like the ideological, economic or social intentions that result in a singular periodical's characteristic mix of material on the past. Thus, this study argues that the RTS operated with its *Leisure Hour* at the intersection of discourses on evangelicalism, the family magazine genre and the discipline of history. The *Leisure Hour*'s historical agenda during the 1850s and 1860s was hence defined by the periodical's design as an intermediary within Victorian historical culture: between secular and religious, working and middle class, male and female, young and old, popular and academic.

Victorian family magazines such as the *Leisure Hour* were an essential part of nineteenth-century historical culture,[2] that is, the »specific and particular way in which a society relates to its past« (Sánchez Marcos 2009: 1). Billie Melman defines historical culture as

»the productions of segments of the past, or rather pasts, the multiplicity of their representations, and the myriad ways in which the English – as individuals and in groups – looked at this past [...] and made use of it, or did not, both in a social and material world and in their imaginary.« (Melman 2006: 4)

---

2 This study originated from the DFG Research Group »Historische Lebenswelten in populären Wissenskulturen der Gegenwart – History in Popular Cultures of Knowledge«, University of Freiburg, and hence understands ›popular historical representations‹ as »presentations in textual, visual, audiovisual as well as performative forms, which present knowledge of the historical past in an attractive style that allows for easy understanding and reaches a broad audience, which need not necessarily be a mass audience« (Korte/Paletschek 2009: 13; my translation). For a further definition of ›historical programme‹ as well as a discussion of historical culture as a research perspective, see the section on »Theoretical and Methodological Approaches« below. On related concepts in memory studies, see A. Assmann (2007), J. Assmann (2007), Erll (2005), Erll/Nünning (2004; 2005; 2008), Halbwachs (1985) and Norra (1990).

Ludmilla Jordanova furthermore notes:

»Remnants of the past are everywhere, but they are not necessarily seen as ›history‹ or understood as elements in a structured account of the past. Public history involves ›history‹ in many senses: the academic discipline; the dissemination and display of its findings to wide audiences; the past itself in many different forms; and a diffused awareness of that past that varies from person to person, group to group, country to country.« (Jordanova 2000: 142)

The rich Victorian historical culture was defined by just such a »multiplicity« of »remnants of the past«, reaching across the spectrum from popular to academic renderings.[3] Historical novels as well as history (text)books, travelogues, history paintings, monuments, museums and exhibitions, jubilees, the heritage movement, dioramas or panoramas re-enacting, for instance, historical battles were all part of the preoccupation with the past during the Victorian age.[4]

---

3   Korte and Pirker (2011: 12, Fn 2) note that »[t]he term ›popular‹ is a contested term« and suggest »that no cultural product is inherently popular; its popularity depends on cultural contexts and processes that *make* a product popular.« ›Popular‹ in the Victorian discourse on historical culture was set against academic approaches to the past. In the context of this study, popular is above all understood as the common acknowledgement of family magazines as ›popular‹ media in terms of reach (implied by circulation as well as price), cultural distinction (working classes versus middle classes) and a possibly simplified style of representation (setting ›popular‹ against ›academic‹). With reference to publications of the RTS, whose periodical *Leisure Hour* is the focus of this study, Fyfe suggests: »A ›popular‹ work was one that was intended for ›the people,‹ which by the middle of the nineteenth century increasingly included the working classes. [...] In the 1820s and 1830s, midpriced reprints were often labeled ›popular‹ because their price was making them more accessible than before. By the 1840s, however, publishers who were committed to reaching the working classes were also focusing on literary accessibility, making sure that the language used was as clear and simple as possible. The changes are reflected in the changing meanings of the verb ›to popularize,‹ which came to mean ›to make abstruse and technical subjects generally accessible‹ rather than simply to make available to the populace.‹« (Fyfe 2004c: 56) See Chapter 2 for further discussion of the family magazine genre's popularity.

4   For discussions of the various manifestations of Victorian historical culture, see, for instance, Altick (1978), Bann (1984), Berger/Eriksonas/Mycock (2008), Berger/Lorenz/Melman (2012: Part I and II), Black (2000), Bowler (1989), Brundage

Besides these popular renderings of the past, Victorian historical culture also saw the increasing academisation of history as a ›scientific‹ university discipline, a process which went hand in hand with debates on the demarcation of professional (objective, scientific, factual) from popular (subjective, entertaining, fictional or fictionalised) history.[5] In 1883, during the process of founding the *English Historical Review* (1886), the historian and bishop Mandell Creighton, for instance, stated that »[e]xisting reviews will only publish popular and sketchy articles« (Creigton, qtd. in Howsam 2004: 527).[6] Accordingly, Stefan Berger notices a »greater emphasis on source criticism« and a decrease in »the Romantic mode of national history writing« until the end of the century (Berger 2007a:

(1994), Cannadine (2006), Chapman (1986), Culler (1985), De Groot (2010), Delheim (1982), Duesterberg (2015), Howsam (2009b), Hyde (1988), Jones (2006), Mandler (1997), Melman (2006), R. Mitchell (2000), Phillips (2000), Pickering/Tyrell (2004), Woolf (2003) and Zimmermann (2008).

5 Leslie Howsam notes three meanings of ›scientific‹ as regards history: »a rigorous standard – for research and for the compilation and criticism of original documentary sources« (2009b: 24); »scholarly objectivity in the interpretation of the ›original authorities‹, or primary sources« (ibid. 25); »writing for informed colleagues, not for the general public« (ibid.). On the academisation of history as well as the negotiation of boundaries between popular and academic history, see Adams (2014), Bentley (2011), Berger (2007b) and (2011), Berger/Feldner/Passmore (2003), Burke (2011), Fuchs (2011), Goldstein (1986), Grever (2009), Hesketh (2008) and (2011), Howsam (2004) and (2009b), Iggers (2011), Jann (1985), Levine (1986), Lingelbach (2011), Nissen (2009), Porciani/Raphael (2010) and Soffer (1996).

6 Creighton's example indicates the way in which these ›new‹ academic historians at times worked at the boundary between popular and academic. Ian Hesketh notes that many late-Victorian historians »were forced to embrace dual personas: the pedantic upholder of scientific standards for the world of peers; and the public intellectual disseminating his critically researched scholarship to a ›general‹ audience. These identities were not necessarily at odds but often the latter had to transcend the very boundaries erected by the former« (Hesketh 2011: 115-116). Creighton, for instance, also contributed a series of articles entitled »The Story of Some English Shires« (1885-1891) to the *Leisure Hour*, which were in 1897 also published in book form by the RTS. The biographical entry for Creighton in the *Leisure Hour*'s »Jubilee Number: Completion of Fiftieth Year of ›The *Leisure Hour*‹« (1902) noted that Creighton was »Professor of Ecclesiastical History at Cambridge« as well as »Bishop of London« (»Authors« 1902: 246). For further discussion of this boundary work, see Chapter 6 on the *Leisure Hour*'s historical writers.

38), and Rosemary Mitchell observes a development from picturesque to scientific representation of history starting at mid-century (R. Mitchell 2000: 15-18, 286).[7] This change in historical representations was also signified by the increasing demarcation of fictional from scientific history writing,[8] as well as by the work of women historians, who were still frequently relegated to the field of popular history.[9] Rohan Amanda Maitzen notes that popular representations of the past were often marked as ›gossip‹, which coded them – as well as their audience – as feminine (Maitzen 1998: 50-54). This idea, which seems to mirror Creighton's observation of historical articles in periodicals as being »sketchy«, played into the distinction between academic history as ›proper‹ history versus popular approaches as inaccurate, sensational and possibly low culture.

The past, then, was accessible to a general as well as a scholarly audience in a variety of forms, and while this did entail discussion on the »myriad ways« of its use – as entertainment, a means of education or a scholarly occupation –, R. Mitchell concludes that the Victorian

»historical awareness was a democratizing force not only in its choice of subject-matter but also in its large audience and wide impact: it was not the preserve of a social or scholarly élite. Disseminated through a dynamic print culture [...] it permeated the middle classes by mid-century and became a mass phenomenon by the end of the century.« (R. Mitchell 2000: 2)

The Victorians' huge interest in the past coincided with the emergence of a popular print culture and the formation of the periodical press as the first mass medium during the reign of Queen Victoria.[10] Mainly due to technological innova-

---

7   On the popularity/academisation of history and its changing mode of presentation from picturesque to scientific, cf. also Berger (2007a: 38); Strong (2004: 55-56, 107).

8   Maitzen, for instance, points out that by the end of the century »the blurred and permeable border between historical and fictional texts so apparent and controversial in the early nineteenth century became distinct and unyielding. In particular, history became a professional pursuit and was institutionalized, primarily in the universities« (Maitzen 1998: 199).

9   On women historians and gender approaches to history, see Burstein (1999) and (2004), Epple (2003), Epple/Schaser (2009), Felber (2007), Maitzen (1998), Melman (1993), R. Mitchell (2000: Chapter 6), Paletschek/Schraut (2008), B.G. Smith (1984) and Woolf (1997).

10 Andrew King and John Plunkett note on the emergence of a popular print market that »it was not until the 1840s that [...] the social conditions [...] enabled the technology

tions and growing literacy, the market for illustrated family magazines began to grow during the 1840s and reached high popularity with an increase in titles and also circulation during the 1850s and 1860s; the success of these periodicals can certainly also be attributed to their use of illustrations, which appealed to a larger public (cf. Anderson 1991, Maidment/Jones 2009).

Similar to the ongoing negotiations of popular and academic history, the turn towards a mass print market with its inclusion of the new working-class, female and young readerships was accompanied by debates clad in a discourse of class and gender as well as cultural distinction on the reputability of the increasingly popular print genre of the family magazine and its serialised fiction.[11] While books – also because of their higher price – were mainly consumed by the educated middle classes or specialised readers, illustrated family magazines were, with their mix of fictional and factual content, suitable for a broad general readership across boundaries of class, gender[12] and age.[13] The print genre flourished

---

to fulfil its potential. In that decade literacy amongst poorer social groups increased dramatically, especially amongst women. [...] By the mid-1850s the ›popular‹ in our definition was fully established» (2004: 166-167). On the Victorian popular print market as well as the periodical boom, see also: Altick (1989 and 1998 [1957]), Anderson (1991), Bennett (1982), Bösch (2005), Eliot (1993) and (2007), Feather (1988), Haywood (2004), Hewitt (2014), Jordan/Platten (1995), Palmegiano (2009), Palmer/Buckland (2011) and Plunkett (2003).

11 See Chapter 2 for a more detailed discussion of the family magazine especially as a disputed genre.

12 Deborah Wynne notes on the falsely presumed genderedness of the family magazine genre: »Recent critics have maintained that the ›family‹ reader is synonymous with the female reader, suggesting that men were marginalized as readers of family magazines. This was not the case: editors attempted to integrate the contents of their magazines to appeal to all family members [...]. Although features occasionally appeared which were more likely to appeal to one gender or age group than another, they were usually presented in such a way as to be intelligible to other family members« (2001: 16; see also Turner 2000: 12). On a division of factual/fictional periodical content along gender lines, which thus conforms to a perception of history as a male format (see Fn 8 above), cf. Turner (2000: esp. 26) and Schmidt (1980: 9).

13 On the periodical as a »mixed genre«, see above all Margaret Beetham (1989), who proposes that »[t]his may seem obvious in relation to those kinds of periodical, like the illustrated magazine, which mix verbal text and pictures, but even the most homogeneous types [...] are characterized by diversity of voice and authorial attribution. The heterogeneity and blurred boundaries of the genre are evident in terms of the pro-

during the 1850s and 1860s, when family magazines – previously directed at and consumed by a presumably predominantly working-class audience in a weekly publication format – transitioned increasingly into monthly publications finding acceptance with a middle-class audience.[14]

As popular media, illustrated family magazines made histories for the many. They displayed a broader variety of approaches to the past, reflecting the fact that the Victorian periodical was a mixed genre addressed to a readership spanning generations. Articles and series on the past ranged from descriptive history, life writing, travel writing and geographical sketches to essayist accounts or reviews of history books and exhibitions. They often used a social, domestic or everyday history approach, but cultural and political history were likewise presented. Articles and series on the past were often accompanied by illustrations of objects, monuments, historical figures or narrative scenes, and reached across all periods with a focus on recent history. Overall, they hence covered and reflected all aspects of Victorian historical culture while at the same time forming an essential part of it themselves.

Many of the periodicals' representations of the past came in the form of serialisation. Periodicals depended on the reproduction of successful features[15] and also included series on history in order to create continuity and bind readers. Seriality is therefore an important indicator for what was popular, and in its repetition and actualisation this serial presentation of content in a way transgressed the periodical's ephemeral quality.[16] Furthermore, Linda K. Hughes and Michael

---

ducers of the periodical« as »even one number involves several writers, the editor, perhaps the proprietor, perhaps the artist or engraver and the printer« (Beetham 1989: 97). James Mussell (2012: 10 and 37-38) accordingly identifies the periodical's title-function in contrast to books' author-function; see Chapter 5 (Fn 11).

14 As such, the 1850s and 1860s have been identified as the heyday as well as a point of transition for the family magazine; cf. Altick (1998 [1957]: 359-360), Beetham (2009), Huett (2005), Hughes (2015), Law (2009b), Maidment/Jones (2009), S. Mitchell (1989), Mussell (2009), Phegley (2004: 385) and Sullivan (1984, Vol. 3: xvi).

15 Cf. Beetham (1989: 97), Brake (2011: 9-21) and Turner (2000: 38-40).

16 On this idea of actualisation and the difference between the periodical title as serial and its presentation of serials/series as content, cf. also Beetham: »Every number of the periodical is the same in that it offers its readers a recognizable persona or identity and this is part of a recognizable pattern of contents and lay-out. But every number of the periodical is a new number which is different from all previous numbers. This means that each number must function both as part of a series and as a free-standing

Lund observe that serialisation is intrinsic to an understanding of Victorian historical consciousness:

»Focusing more specifically on historical literature published in installments, we can state that to understand history in the Victorian era meant to find oneself on a line running from the past through the present to the future; this sense of the linearity of time and its forward-moving nature was embodied in the serial form, in which readers repeatedly found themselves in the middle of a story whose past was earlier installments and whose future was ›to be continued‹.« (Hughes/Lund 1991: 60-61)

This indicates that periodicals' presentation of historical time was intrinsically linked to the medium's »dynamic of periodicity – what it means to read in a weekly form, or a monthly form, and how the significant differences between those temporal forms affect interpretation« (Turner 2005: 122).[17] As Mark W.

---

unit which makes sense to the reader of the single issue. Although it has elements of the serial, the periodical is therefore not a true serial. It is both open-ended and end-stopped. Indeed, although it may include true serials, most of the items in a single number will be characterized by closure« (Beetham 1989: 99). Following Tanja Weber and Christian Junklewitz (2008), this study uses ›series‹ (Reihe) as a superordinate term for articles printed in serial form. Non-fiction series on the past in Victorian periodicals can be characterised as a mix between ›series‹ and ›serial‹, as defined by Weber and Junklewitz (2008) regarding fictional TV series: They distinguish between ›series‹ (Episodenserie) and ›serial‹ (Forsetzungsserie), yet consider representations in serial form as hybrids on a continuum from episodic ›series‹ (with a closed narrative in each part) to continuous ›serial‹ (with action transgressing the boundary of the single part). For further theoretical discussions of the phenomenon of serialisation, see also the DFG research group »Ästhetik und Praxis populärer Serialität | Popular Seriality: Aesthetics and Practice« at the Freie Universität Berlin, Giesenfeld (1994), Hopwood/Schaffer/Secord (2010), Kelleter (2012) and Myers/Harris (1993).

17 Similarly, Beetham concludes in her definition of the periodical that »[t]he relationship to time is the central characteristic of the periodical, but this means that the form has a deep regular structure. For some readers indeed the relationship between the periodical and calendar- or clock-time may be an important regulating mechanism in their lives. [...] In general, I would argue, it is impossible to separate out the periodical from other structures in advanced industrial societies by which work and leisure have come to be regulated in time« (Beetham 1989: 98). Note at this instance also the title »Leisure Hour«; see Chapter 2 (Fn 18).

Turner points out, »the whole idea of ›time‹ was a problem for the Victorians« (ibid.), which can also be observed in their

»obsession with the past and with the making of history, but also with memory as a way of understanding and recording the past. [...] We might be tempted to think of the periodical media's organization of time in the nineteenth century as offering numerous ways of trying to create a continuous flow – but again, I think we are left with the problem that there is no single rhythm, there is always cacophony.« (Ibid.: 126-127)

Through their mix of historical presentations with other content as well as the se-rialisation of the past, resulting in pauses in the reading process, family maga-zines did not present a homogeneous but a fragmented picture of the past. Yet the choices editors, writers and illustrators made in a periodical's various repre-sentations of the past defined its singular historical agenda, recognisable to read-ers through continuous actualisation.

Commercially designed as reading matter catering to a broad family reader-ship, Victorian family magazines can hence be seen – and often understood or constructed themselves – as a democratising medium which to a large extent served to also distribute representations of the past, thereby influencing people's knowledge and perception of (national) history's meaning for society's present and future conduct. Yet while the flourishing field of periodical studies has ex-tensively researched periodicals from a print history point of view, often focus-ing on the serialised novel within its periodical context (arguably the magazines' selling-point),[18] and has more recently expanded to an interest in magazines' sci-

---

18 For recent monographs and edited volumes only, see, for instance, on fiction: Chen
    (2013), Delafield (2015), Kreisel (2012), Law (2000), Patterson (2013), Pittard
    (2011), Wynne (2001) and also the online databases by Troy J. Bassett (2015 [2007])
    and Marie Léger-St-Jean (2015 [2010]); on illustrations: Brake/Demoor (2009),
    Cooke (2010), Goldman (2005), Haskins (2012) and Maidment (2013); on journalists,
    writers, editors, publishers: Brake/King et al. (2012), Collins (2006), Finkelstein
    (2006), Fyfe (2012), Gabriele (2009), Gray (2012), Humpherys/James (2008), Ives
    (2011), King (2004), Latané (2013), Leary (2010), Logan (2012), Mackenzie/Winyard
    (2013), Morrison/Roberts (2013), Patten (2012a) and (2012b), Turner (2000) and
    Worth (2003); on periodical genres: Boyd (2003), Kirkpatrick (2013), Ledbetter
    (2009) and Phegley (2004); on print history topics: Brake/Bell/Finkelstein (2000),
    DiCenzo/Delap/Ryan (2011), Easley (2011), Fraser/Green/Johnston (2003), Haywood
    (2004), Liddle (2009), Mason (2013), Miller (2013), Mussell (2012), Palmer (2011),
    Salmon (2013) and Wiener (2011).

ence content,[19] the analysis of periodicals' factual historical representations is still a desideratum.[20] Even the *Oxford History of Historical Writing*'s volume on the nineteenth century (Macintyre/Maiguashca/Pók 2011), although it addresses

---

19 Monographs and edited volumes include Cantor/Dawson et al. (2004), Cantor/Shuttleworth (2004), Fyfe (2004c), Henson/Cantor et al. (2004) and Mussell (2007). Furthermore, note the online database *Science in the Nineteenth-Century Periodical: An Electronic Index* (2007 [2005]), which indexes science content for sixteen periodicals.

20 In her 2007 *ProQuest Lecture in Modern Book History*, Leslie Howsam asked: »What was the historical content of the various periodicals? [...] Which publications catered to the public interest in historical perspectives on current events, or to the popular taste for biographies of famous men and women of the past? These are some of the questions I would hope will enter into a research agenda, if other scholars agree with me that the history-content in the periodicals has been overlooked« (2007: 2-3). On the desideratum of research on history in popular Victorian periodicals, see also Howsam (2009a) and (2009b: 124-125), Korte/Paletschek (2009: 47). The most extensive presentation of Victorian periodicals' factual history coverage is found in Leslie Howsam's *History in the Victorian Periodical Press Online: HiPPo* (2014b [2012]), which is a comprehensive online reference work on nineteen Victorian periodicals' articles of history between 1809 and 1916. Korte/Lechner's *Popular History in Victorian Magazine Database PHVM* (2014) presents in a similar vein historic content published in 1860, 1865 and 1870 in five Victorian periodicals. Article-length analyses of family magazines' contribution to Victorian historical culture are available in Korte/Paletschek (2012) and Reusch/Lechner (2013), both of which compare British and German family magazines. Other article-length discussion of popular magazines' contributions to historical culture are Howsam (2012), which focuses on periodicals for young readers, and Korte/Paletschek (2013) and Korte (2015a), which focus on women's magazines, the former again in British-German comparison. Peter Smith includes in his study of the *Cornhill* a chapter »On the Past« (P. Smith 1969: Chapter VI); see discussion in Chapter 4 below. Nina Reusch's monograph on German family magazines' contribution to historical culture during the Kaiserreich was published in 2015. Publications on a transnational perspective of history in popular periodicals can also be expected from the Gerda Henkel Foundation research project »›Geschichte für alle‹ in Zeitschriften des 19. Jahrhunderts [History for everyone in Nineteenth-Century Periodicals]« at the University of Siegen. An earlier publication on »Serializing the Past in and out of the *Leisure Hour*: Historical Culture and the Negotiation of Media Boundaries« (Lechner 2013) is in parts accommodated, in changed form and context, above all in Chapter 5.

formats of popular history, neglects to address the vast historical output of the Victorian periodical press.

Serialised History in the *Leisure Hour*, 1852-1860

Histories for the Many examines the contribution of illustrated Victorian family magazines to British historical culture during the 1850s and 1860s as a popular medium in a stage of transition – regarding the changes in history as well as the genre of the family magazine (outlined above), and evangelical influence (see below) – by analysing how issues of class, gender, age and religion were debated within a national historical identity. Research into historical representations in the Victorian periodical press requires sound methodological delimitations. James Mussell, for instance, stresses that the abundance of text as well as agents in the nineteenth-century periodical archive demands that one »engage with it in sophisticated and reflexive ways«, as there is not only »a volume of print that can overwhelm current readers«, but the change in periodicals' programmes »over their run« and »the number of editors, publishers, printers, advertisers, contributors and illustrators« involved in creating even single issues »further complicate[]« this »excess of print« by adding to it »an excess of historical actors« involved in the production and consumption of the periodicals (Mussell 2007: 3).[21] In addition, the research object of representations of the past opens up an excess of historical topics, events, and actors treated within an excess of articles and series presented in a variety of genre approaches. This study hence analyses the historical programme of a single periodical title (in comparison to other periodicals) during a limited period of time and with attention to a characteristic textual phenomenon, namely, historical non-fiction presented in serialised form.[22]

The study focuses on the Religious Tract Society's (RTS) periodical *Leisure Hour: A Family Journal of Instruction and Entertainment* (1852-1905),[23] which the *Dictionary of Nineteenth-Century Journalism* identifies as a »seminal exam-

---

21 Cf. also Beetham (1989: 96-97), King (2004: xii), Pykett (1989: 107) and Turner (2000: 3).

22 The phenomenon of serialisation in Victorian periodicals has mainly been researched regarding serialised fiction; cf. Delafield (2015), Wynne (2001), Hughes/Lund (1991), Law (2000) and Hayward (2008). Mark W. Turner (2000: 38) considers non-fiction series as similar to fiction in their potential to unite and bind readers.

23 See Chapter 2 for a general discussion of the *Leisure Hour*.

ple[]«[24] of the popular family magazine (Law 2009b: 215).[25] With circulation peaking at 80-100,000 copies, the *Leisure Hour* not only reached a vast public, but as an organ of the evangelical Religious Tract Society it accounts for the influence of evangelicalism on Victorian society at large and on the suitability of reading matter also in terms of historical representations.[26] Richard D. Altick notes in his essay »English Publishing and the Mass Audience in 1852« – the year the *Leisure Hour* was launched – that evangelicalism set the tone for life in Victorian times and for reading habits: It »stressed the spiritually salutary effect

---

24 Further examples named in Law's *DNCJ* entry are the *Family Herald* (which was, however, unillustrated) and *Cassell's Illustrated Family Paper* (which did not feature history prominently). Law states that the genre of the Victorian family magazine originated »after the accession of Queen Victoria, when the cult of domesticity encouraged by the Evangelical revival was reinforced by widespread images in the media of the homelife of the royal family. The term ›family paper‹ thus tends to imply not only an extension of readership to women, children and the workingman, but also a particular ideological orientation with the promotion of Christian virtue, domestic economy and the avoidance of social impropriety and political controversy« (Law 2009b: 214-215). Though Law's definition is helpful, it may be too restrictive, as it disregards secular family magazines and further genre developments such as the later family magazines directed at an upper-middle-class readership, but classifies as family papers only such magazines which work on a strict domestic, evangelical world-picture.

25 Though the RTS is an agent of the Victorian print market well-known to book historians, its family magazine *Leisure Hour* has, not only in its historical presentations, received little attention. Aileen Fyfe has so far conducted the most elaborate research mainly of the periodical's initial year, while focusing overall on the RTS's Monthly Series (2004a; 2004b; 2004c; 2005; 2006). Entries and shorter passages on or passim mentions of the *Leisure Hour* can be found, for instance, in Altholz (1989), Anderson (1991), Cooke (2010), Golby/Purdue (1984), Lloyd/Law (2009), Turner (2000) and the RTS jubilee publications by Green (1899), Hewitt (1949) and Butts/Garret (2006), the latter of which includes Fyfe (2006). A helpful overview on the periodical's history and contributors is available in the *Leisure Hour*'s fifty-year »Jubilee Number« (1902). On the RTS, see also the RTS jubilee publication by Jones (1850) as well as Palmer (2009).

26 For the importance of evangelicalism during the Victorian period, cf., for instance, Altick (1989: 151-152), Young (1977: esp. 1-5) and, more specifically for this study, the various publications by Aileen Fyfe on the RTS. See Chapter 2 for further discussion of the RTS's evangelical publishing programme concerning the *Leisure Hour*.

of contact with the right kind of moral and religious literature«, which it saw as important for

»one's journey to salvation [...]. Evangelicalism had revived and even intensified the old Puritan distrust of secular literature, and so thoroughly did this distrust permeate the middle class, and the church-going portion of the lower, that it remained in 1852 a strong deterrent to the reading of ordinary literature, above all fiction.« (Altick 1989: 151)

The *Leisure Hour* was set up to counter secular, fiction-carrying periodicals aimed at the working classes. It »featured regular articles on popular science, history, biography, and poetry of an uplifting character« (Lloyd/Law 2009: 356). While the *Leisure Hour* thus displayed a typical mix of family magazine content, also including some fiction, it offered a large selection of historical material to its readers to meet the evangelical »distrust of secular literature«.

This breadth of history is already obvious when one considers the overview in Appendix A (Tab. 2) of the 79 series on the past printed in the *Leisure Hour* during the 1850s and 1860s. The *Leisure Hour* presented an average of three historical non-fiction series per year, and readers were thus almost at all times confronted with at least one series on the past (besides further stand-alone articles on the past). The series on the past in Appendix A (Tab. 2) indicate a predominance of travel writing or topographical approaches to the past, life writing or person-centred approaches as well as descriptive (historiographical) series, although many series mixed different genre approaches.[27] The *Leisure Hour* above all presented a British (or rather English) history relating to readers' national identity,[28] and given that many of the series took a geographical or travel writing approach, they mainly used a cross-period frame. Other series were predominantly situated in the recent past of the nineteenth century, pertaining to the field of communica-

---

27 Boundaries of literary genres in periodicals' articles and series were rather fuzzy, and many of the series on the past in the *Leisure Hour* mixed different popular-history approaches. Travel writing might have included historiographical reports on specific historical localities, events or actors, while life writing often linked historical actors to a specific location, and descriptive reports inserted biographical anecdotes. This blurring of genres might have made history more interesting and therefore appealing to a larger, diverse readership.

28 Many of these series focused on London and at times also included Scotland or Ireland. History of the continent, mainly in travel or topographical reports, was also present, while non-European regions were rarely treated within a historical framework.

tive memory[29] and its potential to forge an »imagined community«[30] amongst readers. Though many also addressed the sixteenth to eighteenth centuries, surprisingly few series occupied themselves solely with the Middle Ages, antiquity or prehistoric times. The past in the family magazine's series was approached from a cultural, social and – to some extent – political perspective, and the periodical also included some series on science history. Series often addressed domestic, everyday experiences and objects, thereby connecting historical actors or events to contemporary readers' lifeworlds.[31] Though the series on the past in the *Leisure Hour* were generally not set up for a specific readership in terms of age

29 Jan Assmann defines communicative memory as »those varieties of collective memory that are based exclusively on everyday communications« (1995: 126) and therefore as close to oral history; he further notes that »[i]ts most important characteristic is its limited temporal horizon«, which »does not extend more than eighty to (at the very most) one hundred years into the past, which equals three or four generations« (ibid.: 127).

30 See especially Benedict Anderson's chapter on »The Origins of National Consciousness« and its connection to print culture (Anderson 2009: Chapter 3). Anderson further observes the newspaper's potential for the creation of an imagined community, which can also be applied to other periodicals or print products: »The significance of this mass ceremony [of reading newspapers] [...] is paradoxical. It is performed in silent privacy, in the lair of the skull. Yet each communicant is well aware that the ceremony he performs is being replicated simultaneously by thousands (or millions) of others of whose existence he is confident, yet of whose identity he has not the slightest notion. [...] At the same time, the newspaper reader, observing exact replicas of his own paper being consumed by his subway, barbershop, or residential neighbours, is continually reassured that the imagined world is visibly rooted in everyday life« (Anderson 2009: 35-36). See also Howsam (2008: 1091), Jordanova (2000: 155), R. Mitchell (2000: 12) and Nünning/Nünning (2010: 14).

31 Following Edmund Husserl (1970), the research group »Historische Lebenswelten« (see Fn 2) »understand[s] lifeworld [(Lebenswelt)] as the world of experience, the ›constantly pregiven‹ world, the universe of what is, which is ever in unceasing movement of relativity for us‹ (Husserl 1970: 382-383). It denotes that which is familiar and known through everyday and/or universal experience. [...] Thus, in order for consumers to be able to quite literally ›receive‹ historical contents and open their minds to historical situations, they need elements that permit them to connect to the past. The lifeworlds typically conjured up in popular historical products (both as background and as contents in their own right) show clear instances of overlapping with the life experience of the consumers« (Korte/Pirker 2011: 48).

or gender but addressed the entire family at the same time, they predominantly approached history from a male perspective and focused on a depiction of men; accounts of women – or children – were rather rare. And while the series in the evangelical family magazine tended to view their subject under a Christian perspective, singularly religious history was surprisingly absent. This tentative inclusion of religion in the *Leisure Hour*'s approach to the past coincides with a decreasing importance of evangelicalism at mid-century. Thus, Altick observes that evangelical publishers' »conservatism was something of a scandal in their own time« (Altick 1989: 152).

With the increasing academisation of history, the changing reputation of the family magazine genre and the debate in Victorian society on evangelical morals, the *Leisure Hour*'s historical representations were hence regulated by intersecting discourses on class, gender, age and religion during the 1850s and 1860s. The RTS, with its periodical project and immersion in the past, took on an intermediary position. It operated not only at the boundary between secular and religious reading matter determined by its own evangelical members and intended readerships but also at that of changing ideas about a ›proper‹ approach to history. The way in which the *Leisure Hour* made use of the past was determined by these various discourses under the regulation of the RTS's ideological interests. And the Society furthermore had to take into account the materiality of the medium within the larger Victorian print market.

In order to consider this evangelical magazine within a larger perspective of the periodical marketplace, this study compares and reads its historical output within the network of three other popular and influential periodicals,[32] namely the *Leisure Hour*'s secular opponent *London Journal* (1845-1912)[33] – against which it was designed – as well as two more upmarket periodicals of the 1860s, the similarly religious *Good Words* (1860-1911)[34] and the secular *Cornhill Magazine* (1860-1975).[35] After all, the *Leisure Hour* stood for a specific religious

---

32 See Appendix A, Tab. 1, for an overview of the four periodicals' profiles.

33 Anderson (1991; 1992), Humpherys/James (2008), James (1982), Johnson-Woods (2000), King (2000; 2002; 2004; 2008; 2009; 2011), S. Mitchell (1989).

34 Altholz (1989), Cooke (2010), Delafield (2015), Ehnes (2012), Kooistra (2014), Lloyd (2009), Srebrnik (1986), Scott (2010), Sullivan (1984), Turner (2000).

35 Colby (1999), Cooke (2010), Delafield (2015), Harris (1986), Hughes/Lund (1991), Maunder (1999), Phegley (2004) and (2009), Robinson (1999), B.Q. Schmidt (1980), P. Smith (1969), Sullivan (1984), Teare (2000), Thompson (1996), Turner (2000), Wynne (2001).

type of family magazine, as it was published by the evangelical Religious Tract Society with specific attention to a working-class audience.

The determination of the periodicals' historical programmes and the analysis of historical articles in this study considers the interplay of editors, authors, illustrators, and readers, as well as the materiality of the medium and ways of distribution. In this regard, the study specifically attends to issues of a serialisation of the past with reproduction as an important indicator for popularity of content and mode of presentation (see Fn 15 above); it considers factual – and to some extent also fictional – historical representations in text and image in their potential of constructing meaning and identity, not only in their printed manifestation but also with regard to matters of production and consumption under the following intersecting guiding questions:

- How, by whom, for whom and with which intentions are historical representations within this popular medium used at a time of social change and debate?
- How are issues of class, gender, age, religion, and space debated within the national historical identity?
- How is an intersection of academic and popular approaches to history linked to the materiality of the medium?

STRUCTURE OF THE STUDY

This study adopts a research perspective on historical culture[36] which is informed by the cultural studies concept of the *circuit of culture* (Du Gay et al. 1997), which conforms to current approaches in the field of Victorian periodical studies[37] and is expanded by the narratological idea of texts' perspective structure[38] as well as the sociological concept of intersectionality.[39] As a means of accounting for the multiple layers that define a periodical's historical programme, the theoretical and methodological framework (as outlined in the final section of this introductory chapter) is further supported by a qualitative and quantitative

---

36 Füßmann/Grüter/Rüsen (1994), Sánchez Marcos (2009), Melman (2006), Grever (2008).
37 Cf. Mussell (2007) and (2012) for an overview; see also the *Victorian Periodical Review*'s Special Issue: Theory (Brake/Humpherys 1989b), and there esp. Beetham (1989) and Pykett (1989).
38 Surkamp (2010 [2005]), Nünning/Nünning (2010).
39 Degele/Winker (2007), Winker/Degele (2009).

assessment of historical content[40] as well as an evaluation of the RTS's archival material.

Part I of this book considers the placement of the *Leisure Hour*'s historical programme within the periodical marketplace. I here compare the *Leisure Hour* to its secular opponent the *London Journal* as well as the religious *Good Words* and the secular *Cornhill* by placing all four periodicals within the development of the family magazine genre (Chapter 2) and analysing their historical programmes (Chapters 3 and 4). Thus, before turning to an analysis of the *Leisure Hour*'s historical programme, I focus in Chapter 2 first of all on the medium and means through which the Society disseminated its historical narratives. The chapter considers the *Leisure Hour*'s history of origin by discussing the RTS's decision to publish in a still contested print genre. It sketches the stages in the development of the Victorian family magazine genre and the debates that went hand in hand with this medium. It will become obvious that the content in the *Leisure Hour* (such as its historical narratives) was regulated by a double discourse, as the RTS had to negotiate between the expectations of their intended working-class audience and those of the Society's middle-class members.

This idea of the *Leisure Hour* as an intermediary between different types of family magazines forms the basis for a comparison of the periodicals' historical agenda in the following two chapters. To determine the periodicals' historical programme, I qualitatively and quantitatively assessed articles or series on the past published during the relevant years of the comparison under categories such as their genre and format of publication (article genres: fiction, life writing, travel writing, descriptive writing; serial production; use of illustration) as well as the kind of history they adopted (type of history, historical actors, events, topics or periods, and geographical space). As a comparison of the *Leisure Hour*'s historical programme in its year of initiation 1852 to the *London Journal* shows (Chapter 3), the *Leisure Hour* aimed its representations of the past explicitly at a working-class audience in order to counter sensational periodicals with its implementation of a Christian tone.

In similar manner – albeit with a specific focus on visual renderings of the past, approaching the periodicals as »dual texts« (Cooke 2010: 212)[41] – I compare the *Leisure Hour*'s historical programme in Chapter 4 to the new shilling monthlies of the 1860s, namely to the even more religious *Good Words* and the secular *Cornhill*. While the *Leisure Hour* had to face fierce criticism during the

---

40 Berridge (1986), Bryman (2004), Corbin/Strauß (2008), Mayring (2007), Mayring/Gläser-Zikuda (2005).

41 See Fn 45 below.

1850s for publishing in a still contested print genre, the arrival of the family magazine concept in the middle classes indicates a change in evangelical attitudes, and my analysis of these specific shilling monthlies' historical programmes in Chapter 4 also serves as an upmarket foil to the analysis of the secular *London Journal* and the evangelical *Leisure Hour* in Chapter 3.

After this comparative analysis of the family magazines' contribution to Victorian historical culture, Part II focuses on issues of history in serial form specifically in the *Leisure Hour*. It foregrounds the *Leisure Hour*'s historical programme as an intermediary between popular and academic approaches to the past in connection with the periodical format, in contrast to books (Chapter 5) as well as the periodical's stock of ›historians‹ and their way of writing popular history (Chapter 6). The exchange between periodicals and books builds the specific point of entry for my analysis of the *Leisure Hour*'s historical programme in Chapter 5, which considers series dealing with the past which were turned into books or, vice versa, books on the past which informed series in the periodical during the 1850s and 1860s. The transfer between the different media allows for an assessment of the *Leisure Hour*'s historical programme, as changes in text and material realisation indicated the RTS's historical intentions. While the earlier chapters mainly focus on issues of class and religion, this chapter is more aware of issues concerning the gender and age of an intended family audience.

Finally, in Chapter 6 I assess the overall set-up of the *Leisure Hour*'s stock of ›historians‹ in terms of gender, profession and popular or more academic approaches to history, before focusing on the *Leisure Hour*'s long-time contributor John Stoughton (1807-1897), a Congregationalist minister and professor of historical theology (1872-1884). Stoughton contributed at least ten series of travel writing and descriptive articles to the *Leisure Hour*, and the chapter considers his boundary work between popular periodical production and academic history. In this regard, the chapter also analyses Stoughton's typical narrative patterns of writing history in a popular medium and links this to the *Leisure Hour*'s agenda by looking at the perspective structure of these factual representations of history. Stoughton's series were printed in the *Leisure Hour* between 1852 and 1887, and thus, this chapter also gives an outlook on the *Leisure Hour*'s historical agenda beyond the 1850s and 1860s.

THEORETICAL AND METHODOLOGICAL APPROACHES

The production of periodicals was above all a collaborative enterprise. Texts and illustrations were contributed by a variety of writers and artists as well as engravers, who had to negotiate content with the periodical's editor(s) or issuing society under the perspective of an intended multifaceted readership. A research agenda commonly adopted in Victorian periodical studies is sufficiently summarised by James Mussell:

»the study of periodicals requires the simultaneous acknowledgement that the individual number is the manifest interaction of its producers – including contributors, editors, readers and the interactions of the market – and that it is part of a series. Any discussion of the periodical press must include form, and this ranges from paper and ink, to the multilayered structure of volume, number, department, and article.« (Mussell 2007: 5)

Representations of the past in these periodicals reflected this variety of actors involved in their production and consumption as well as the material set-up and means of distribution, and their analysis calls for an interdisciplinary approach. In the *Victorian Periodical Review*'s special issue on theory, Lyn Pykett notes that »the study of the periodical press is inevitably interdisciplinary« (Pykett 1989: 100). She especially discusses »the intersection of the methodologies of historical and literary studies« (ibid.), which is also central to this study's approach to the periodical press and its dissemination of historical narratives. Pykett argues for »the close reading of texts« in periodical studies:

»First I would want to emphasize textual analysis in order to underline the importance of the redirection of attention towards the formal properties of media discourse which has come from the structuralist, semiological and linguistic analyses of texts, and from the central concern of these approaches with systems and processes of signification and representation. However, I would also want to emphasize that we should think of ›Text‹ in its Barthesian sense as a methodological field. This concept of Text, and the concepts of discourse and discursive communities, reinstate history, economics, and sociology in a new inter-disciplinary formation [...]. Such an approach would avoid the colonization of periodicals study by a purely literary or formal methodology, while, at the same time, it would challenge those historians who refuse to regard the history of cultural forms, such as writing and its particular genres, as a central part of ›general history.‹ It would require them to adopt a view of history and of writing, in which cultural practices are seen as ›not simply derived from an otherwise constituted social order‹ but as in themselves ›major elements in its constitution (Williams, *Culture*, 12-13).« (Pykett 1989: 107)

Influenced by concepts from media studies as well as cultural studies, Pykett therefore demands that the periodical text be considered within the larger context of the periodical medium, that is, the »cultural practices« of production, consumption and dissemination associated with it.

Similar to Pykett's idea of not only analysing »literary or formal« properties of the periodical text or using periodicals simply as a source of historic »evidence« (Pykett 1989: 102), du Gay et al. hence argue that

»rather than privileging one single phenomenon [...] in explaining the meaning that an artefact comes to possess, [...] it is in a combination of processes – in their articulation – that the beginnings of an explanation can be found.« (du Gay et al. 1997: 3)

In their well-known cultural studies model, they determine »five major cultural processes« – »*Representation, Identity, Production, Consumption* and *Regulation*« – which »[t]aken together [...] complete [...] the **circuit of culture** [...] through which any analysis of a cultural text or artefact must pass if it is to be adequately studied« (ibid.: 3).[42] This model conforms to Pykett's idea of studying the periodical press; and it also applies to the study of historical representations following a historical culture research perspective. As such, Barbara Korte and Eva Ulrike Pirker have coined the term ›historical programme‹, building on du Gay et al.'s *circuit of culture* model as well as S.J. Schmidt's idea of social programme (Korte/Pirker 2011: 44-46):

»A society's historical culture (with its specific historical programme) is part of that society's general system of shared social meanings. It is affected by and interlinked with other social subsystems, for instance the political landscape, and it stands in a necessary interrelationship with the system of social communication. [...] Not only can media products [...] give impetus to changes in the dominant programme of historical culture; the more products there are, the more perspectives on history are (potentially) offered, adding complexity to historical culture.« (ibid.: 45)

Füßmann accordingly defines historical culture as a research perspective that takes account of »the production, distribution and reception [...] of historical knowledge within a society« (1994: 29-30; my translation). And Fernando Sánchez Marcos even more directly claims that

---

42 For similar models in book history, see Robert Darton's »Communication Circuit Model« (1982: 68) as well as Thomas R. Adams and Nicolas Barker's »New Model for the Study of the Book« (1993). For a discussion of these two models as well as further concepts from book history, see Howsam (2006: Chapter 3).

»[t]he scope of *historical culture* is to advocate the examination of all the layers and processes of social historical consciousness, paying attention to the agents who create it, the
media by means of which it is disseminated, the representations that it popularizes and the
creative reception on the part of citizens.« (2009: 1)

Looking at historical culture in this way means adopting a research perspective
of historical discourse analysis, which Franz X. Eder understands as the study of
»practices which systematically organise and regulate statements on a specific
topic and thus determine the constraints of what can be thought or said (by a social group at a specific period of time)« (Eder 2006: 13; my translation).[43] With
historical representations as well as family magazines, these constraints are obviously linked to questions of identity in terms of gender, age, religion and class.
Periodical producers had to consider and negotiate these four categories with respect to their (intended or actual) audience also when designing historical content. As Sánchez Marcos observes:

»The *historical culture* of a society therefore includes multiple narratives and different focuses, which strive to impose themselves in social terms. Social debates on the past are extremely important because not only is mere erudite knowledge of history at stake in them,
but also self-understanding of the community in both the present and its future projection.
Listening to social negotiation of the past leads to an understanding of the social dilemmas
of the present and reveals which of them are the political and axiological questions currently in the public eye.« (Sánchez Marcos 2009: 3)

Concerns about issues of gender, age, religion and class have hence been debated in their relation to a (national historical) identity.[44] My approach in this re-

---

43 Cf. also Reiner Keller's (2008) concept of discourse analysis from a sociology of
    knowledge perspective (wissenssoziologische Diskursanalyse).

44 For the relationship between past, present and future in historical representations, cf.
    also Jörn Rüsen (2006: 3): »Human time-consciousness has two basic intentions:
    memory and expectation, *retention* and *protention*, which are substantially and fun-
    damentally interrelated. So the relatedness of memory to the past is always a matter of
    future perspective as well. Therefore the sense of history synthesizes all three time
    dimensions in a specific way, namely, the interpretation of the past serves as a means
    for understanding the present and expecting the future.« For the relationship of cate-
    gories of disparity to national historical identity, cf. Berger and Lorenz (2008a). In
    their introduction, they state that »*within* a national tradition, constructions of the na-
    tion are connected to competing conceptions of collective identity of a *trans*national

spect further benefits from Gabriele Winker and Nina Degele's model for the analysis of these intersecting categories of disparity on different discourse levels (such as structures, symbolic representation or identities) (Winker/Degele 2009: 11). They define »intersectionality as the mutual interaction between (and not the addition of) categories of disparity« within »disparity generating social structures (i.e., power relations), symbolic representations and identity constructions« (Winker/Degele 2009: 14-15; my translation). In the *Victorian Periodical Review*'s special issue on theory, Margaret Beetham similarly states:

»The reader [of a periodical] is addressed as an individual but is positioned as a member of certain overlapping sets of social groups; class, gender, region, age, political persuasion or religious denomination [...]. The periodical, then, may offer its readers scope to construct their own version of the text by selective reading, but against that flexibility has to be put the tendency in the form to close off alternative readings by creating a dominant position from which to read, a position which is maintained with more or less consistency across the single number and between numbers.« (Beetham 1989: 99)

Therefore, Sally Shuttleworth and Geoffrey Cantor, who focus on the analysis of periodicals' scientific content, stress that it is necessary

»to be highly sensitive to the politics of placement: to look at the target audience of each title with regard to political, intellectual, or religious orientation, and gender and class marketing. Furthermore, we need to take into account the individual predilections of editors, authors, and proprietors [...], [while] it is unsafe to assume that a periodical retained a uniform identity across its lifetime.« (Shuttleworth/Cantor 2004: 5)

The research perspectives of historical culture as well as periodical studies hence postulate a comprehensive research agenda similar to du Gay et al.'s model. As such, Korte and Paletschek observe that media for historical representations

»not only convey and disseminate knowledge but also configure it in a specific way. They are not only a means of presentation but also of the production of knowledge. Inquiry into the means and possibilities of different media and genres is therefore essential for the analysis of historical culture(s).« (Korte/Paletschek 2009: 15; my translation)

---

character (the so-called Others of the nation [...] [like] religion, class ethnicity/race and gender [...]« (Berger/Lorenz 2008b: 1-2).

In this regard, they pose the question of genre or medium and its influence on the way the past is represented. It is crucial to consider historical content as well as the genre of the family magazine which disseminates it. Birgit Neumann and Martin Zierold, for instance, note that »[w]ithin media studies and media history, the notion that media technologies are never ›neutral‹ but play an active role in the construction of reality has axiomatic status« (Neumann/Zierold 2010: 116). Similarly, Peter Haslinger demands of historical discourse analysis »to account for the broad impact of the respective medium, as it is last but not least the choice of text genre which will reveal ›whether an author conforms to or breaks with specific conventions of communication‹ (Fellerer/Metzeltin 2002: 280-283)« (Haslinger 2006: 42; my translation). In its analysis of representations of the past in text and image, this study therefore has a double« focus on both the historical content and the genre of the illustrated family magazine as means of dissemination.

Pykett nevertheless argues for »the close reading of texts« in periodical studies (see above). As the illustrated family magazine was an intrinsically intermedial medium, this study understands Pykett's idea of ›Text‹ as also including visual renderings. In this regard, it follows Simon Cooke's idea of reading periodicals as »dual texts« (Cooke 2010: 121), that is, keeping in mind a ›collaborative‹ perspective when considering the »dynamic fusion of image and word« (ibid.: 119).[45]

---

45 Cooke takes into account the cultural as well as the economic context of production; i.e., the (hierarchic) collaborative negotiation of actors such as editors, illustrators, authors and engravers in producing a »dual text«. The focus of previous critics has mainly been on artistic illustrations and illustrations to fictitious works. Serialised novels and their illustrations were arguably the main attraction of the periodicals. While Cooke accuses earlier criticism of approaching the illustrations merely from the perspective of fine art, he still focuses on those text/image fusions in the periodicals which can be classified as artistic and fictitious. Still, his approach to the periodicals is also helpful for the analysis of other texts and modes of illustrations, as it comes close to this study's approach of the circuit of culture (cf. Cooke 2010: esp. Chapters 1 & 4). For further discussion of the text/image relation and Victorian visual culture, see Anderson (1991), Brake/Demoor (2009), Brosch (2008), Curtis (2002), Goldman (1996), Hall (1980), Harvey (1970), Maidment (2001), Meisel (1983), Ray (1992), Reid (1975), Schwartz/Przyblyski (2004), Sinnema (1998) and Thomas (2004); on (popular) Victorian illustrations of the past, see: Haskell (1993), R. Mitchell (2000) and Strong (2004).

Looking at the construction of the past at the text/image level within the periodical, this study is informed by narratological models such as perspective structure analysis and ways of worldmaking. Carola Surkamp's notion of a text's perspective structure is similar to Pykett's demand:

»The semantic concept of perspective structure allows for a correlation between the structural properties of narrative texts and their cultural implications, thus opening up promising areas of investigation for cultural studies approaches to narrative.« (Surkamp 2010 [2005]: 424-425)

The analysis of a text's perspective structure as »[t]he sum of [its] perspectival relationships« entails the examination of worldviews presented within a text through various characters and also the narrative voice in terms of their

»knowledge and abilities, psychological disposition, system of norms and values, belief sets, attitudes, motivations, needs and intentions as well as [their] sex, gender, sexuality, ethnic identity, and the general economic, political, social, and cultural conditions under which [they] live[].« (Ibid.: 424)[46]

Thus, a qualitative assessment of historical content in terms of questions of selection, authority, homogeneity or hierarchy of specific perspectives against others in the presentation of a specific historical event, period or figure may serve to determine a text's possible »moral and ideological views« (ibid.). In the case of Victorian periodicals, the perspective structure was often guided if not dominated by a narrative voice in the first-person plural,[47] which disguised contributors under the cloak of anonymity by speaking in the collective voice of the periodical enterprise. At the same time, the ›we‹ served to create unity between narrator/author/periodical and readers or support a communal reading-aloud of the pe-

---

46 Laurel Brake and Anne Humpherys suggest a similar approach following Mikhail Bahktin: »His theories of the ›dialogical‹ (i.e. interactive) nature of utterance and of the intertextuality of written language seem to be ideally exemplified in the periodical press, while his idea of ›heteroglossia‹ – dissonances among competing languages – is particularly helpful in thinking about the concatenation of subjects, voices, and visual images of newspapers and magazines« (Brake/Humpherys 1989a: 94).

47 On anonymity and the use of the first-person plural or editorial ›we‹ in Victorian periodicals, see, for instance, Brake (1994), Buurma (2007), Easley (2004), Garcia-Fernandez (2012), Law (2009a), Nash (2010) and Secord (2000).

riodical text in the family circle. David Carr similarly observes of the narrative form of history writing:

»Where the first-person plural becomes as important as the first-person singular in social discourse, we can think of the cohesive community as a kind of large-scale individual that is the ›subject‹ of certain kinds of experiences and actions. Within such a community, persons are related to each other not merely as individuals facing other individuals, but as members of the same group. [...] It is here that the past is kept alive in traditions, legends monuments, public buildings, and folk music and art. No doubt popular history belongs here, too [...]. [T]he underlying motivation here is practical: it is values such as group cohesion and good citizenship, that guide the maintenance of the public memory.« (Carr 2006: 129-130)

Similarly, Ansgar and Vera Nünning see as an

»important function of narratives and media [...] their potential to generate or forge communities. [...] Narrative genres in particular are central to the formation of collective identities and ›imagined communities‹ sensu Anderson for the simple reason that not only a nation but ›any imagined community‹ is held together by the stories it generates about itself‹ (Arata 1).« (Nünning/Nünning 2010: 14)[48]

With reference to Nelson Goodman's *Ways of Worldmaking*, they observe that

»[a]n analysis of composition and decomposition, deletion and supplementation, deformation, ordering, weighting [...], and other formal devices for making worlds can all shed lots of light on both the question of what goes into making the cultural worlds that we live in, and the ideological implications and functions that particular ways of worldmaking serve to fulfil.« (Nünning/Nünning 2010: 17)[49]

Besides such a narratological approach to the periodical text, yet similar to the perspective structure's idea of selection and hierarchy, my qualitative assessment

---

48 On Benedict Anderson's concept, see Fn 30 above.

49 See also Füßmann's approach to a narratology of documentary representations of history, which he proposes to analyse by categories of retrospectivity, perspectivity, selectivity, sequentiality, communicativity/target audience and particularity (Füßmann 1994).

of historical content is supported by a quantitative sampling,[50] enabling me to compare the four periodicals' historical agendas.[51] This quantitative categorisation helps to determine which kind of history (type of history, historical actors, events, topics or periods and spaces) was presented in which formats (fiction, life writing, travel writing, descriptive articles; also: serialisation, use of illustration) and forms the basis for my analysis of patterns of as well as deviations in the periodicals' historical agendas during the respective years 1852 and 1860. For the purposes of this study, I identified articles on the past by reviewing every article contained within the relevant volumes, as the periodicals' annual indices do not specify historical articles, and article titles listed in the indices do not necessarily reflect the articles' content.[52] Series in the *Leisure Hour* from 1852 to 1870 were identified mainly via the periodical's annual indices, reviewed for their qualification as historical, and likewise categorised. Though there are also many two-parters, the study only considers series with three or more parts because of their stronger means of building continuation or, given the dual publication format of the *Leisure Hour* in weekly and monthly format, because series with three to five parts were often used to create thematic unity in the monthly part of four to five issues (see overview in Appendix A, Tab. 2).[53]

On the basis of this corpus, I examined the RTS archives – held at the School for Oriental Studies, London – for the 1850s and 1860s. The archives include correspondence (USCL/RTS Corr) as well as minutes on meetings of the RTS

---

50 For discussions of the approach of qualitative/quantitative content analysis as well as grounded theory, see Fn 40 above.

51 All four periodicals are available online via the *British Periodicals Collection*, yet were also consulted in their physical form at the British Library and Senate House Library, London.

52 Though my research was conducted online, I accessed the periodicals at this instance in a rather traditional way by ›leafing‹ through the pages. This approach has the advantage that it enables one to understand the periodicals' historical (as well as other) content in its entirety and also find the more overtly historical content. A digital search, given the right restrictions and parameters, would have possibly meant covering a longer time frame for the comparisons in Chapter 3 and 4, yet it might also have resulted in my finding only a selection of material or having to restrict my research to specific historical topics, events or figures. On the »opportunities and problems« of digital searches for history in periodical collections, see Howsam (2014a: 8-9). On digital approaches to Victorian periodicals, see above all Mussell (2012), as well as »Forum: Teaching and Learning in the Digital Humanities Classroom« (2012).

53 See Chapter 5 for a discussion of these monthly-part series.

copyright (USCL/RTS CCM), finance (USCL/RTS FCM) and executive committees (USCL/RTS ECM).[54] Besides providing general editorial decisions as
well as some reader feedback on the *Leisure Hour*, the minutes also include
payment lists for contributors. As most articles during the 1850s and 1860s were
printed anonymously, Aileen Fyfe rightfully notes that it is »virtually impossible
to identify the writers« (Fyfe 2004c: 194). The payment lists in the RTS minutes
only provide surnames (at times with first name initials) and state that payment
was made for a contribution to the *Leisure Hour*;[55] yet they do not provide article
titles or issue numbers/dates. The minutes proved most fruitful for the assessment of a transfer between the periodical and book publications.[56]

In the description of the theoretical and methodological framework that informs this study, I started with the analytical perspectives of periodical studies,
the circuit of culture and historical culture and then turned to the more narrow
narratological models of perspective culture and worldmaking, that is, I moved
from the broad perspective of the periodical enterprise and its historical presentation down to the level of the textual manifestation of history in the single article
or series on the past. In conclusion, I will now again move out from the level of
the single manifestation towards the entirety of the periodical enterprise, thereby

---

54 Aileen Fyfe has also made extensive use of the RTS archives in her publications. She
    notes on the RTS's organisational structure (reflected in the minutes): »The RTS was
    still [from 1844 on] run by a committee, the members of which were extremely active,
    often sitting on several subcommittees as well as the executive committee; some at-
    tended RTS-related meetings several times a week. As almost all were professionals
    with their own affairs to look after, this indicates the strength of their commitment to
    the Society and its mission. Yet the extent of the Society's operations had become
    such that not even the most enthusiastic volunteers could have run it efficiently. The
    bulk of the work was now done by the sixty paid employees, overseen by the three
    senior officers: the editor, the superintendent, and the corresponding secretary« (Fyfe
    2004c: 32). See also Fyfe (2005) on the Society's publishing practice and committee
    work.

55 Chapter 6 (Fn 2) provides a brief statistical evaluation of writers listed in the minutes.

56 Cf. also Fyfe (2005: 34, En 3): »The minutes of committee meetings often provide
    useful information about discussions relating to new projects, and may have summar-
    ies of readers' reports on manuscripts. Of course, minute books are also carefully edit-
    ed, and cannot be presumed to be full records of complete discussions«. For this
    study's approach to a transfer of texts between book and periodical, thus combining
    book history and periodical studies, see Chapter 5 (Fn 3 and 7).

explaining how this model is to be understood in determining a periodical's historical programme.

The models of perspective structure and worldmaking contribute to a qualitative assessment of historical content, that is, they make it possible to analyse a specific article's negotiation of historical identity in text and image. Starting from the single article, this may be expanded to the entirety of the series within which the article was placed. In the same manner, the different manifestations of the past in various articles or series presented in the periodical on the whole (i.e., their qualitative and quantitative assessment in terms of article format and approach to history) correspond at the next level to a »sum of perspecitval relationships« (also enforced by the possible use of the editorial ›we‹ in different contributions). And the same holds true for the level of the periodical's writers, producers or even their intended readerships, and further out in the comparison of different periodical titles' historical agenda as well as other print media such as books (or Victorian historical culture at large). All of these levels are linked in their specific perspectival set-up by the idea of intersectionality, that is, by the intercepting categories of disparity gender, age, religion or class, which regulated the discourses on history as well as the genre of the family magazine at each level, be it production, consumption, or representation – that is, medium or historical content. With this theoretical framework in mind, I hence attempt in this study to consider all of these levels in their intersection when analysing the *Leisure Hour*'s historical programme.

Part I: The *Leisure Hour* in the Periodical Marketplace

2. The *Leisure Hour* and the Disputed Genre of the Family Magazine in the 1850s and 1860s

This chapter considers the *Leisure Hour* within the larger context and development of the Victorian periodicals marketplace as an introduction to the following chapters on the *Leisure Hour*'s historical programme. By thus focusing on the medium in which the Society disseminated its historical programme, the chapter shows that content in the *Leisure Hour*, such as its historical narratives, were regulated by a double discourse, and that the Society's new family magazine took on an intermediary position between secular and religious periodicals. The RTS entered into a contested field in the 1850s by using a cross-class rhetoric with its new periodical project: on the one hand, the Society attempted to reach the working classes by publishing within a genre valued by people in these classes, yet one that was the object of middle-class disdain; on the other hand, the Society had to mould the product in such a way that it would also achieve acceptance from their evangelical middle-class supporters. The chapter briefly outlines the previous tradition of penny family magazines, contemporary debates on popular reading linked to the medium with family magazines such as the *London Journal* and the marketing strategies implemented by the RTS to reach a compromise between its two readerships during the 1850s. It then addresses the change in the periodical market with the introduction of new illustrated family magazines such as *Good Words* and *Cornhill* during the 1860s. As such, the discourse on the family magazine genre outlined here forms the basis for the comparative reading of the historical programmes of the four family magazines *Leisure Hour, London Journal, Good Words* and *Cornhill* in Chapters 3 and 4.

FIRST AND SECOND GENERATION FAMILY MAGAZINES

During the 1820s and 1830s, the field of family magazines had been defined by what is »referred to as the ›first generation‹ of penny periodicals« (Fyfe 2004c: 49),[1] such as the *Penny Magazine* (1832-1845/6), the *Saturday Magazine* (1832-1845) and *Chambers's* (1832-1956), which combined instruction with entertainment. These periodicals had a strong focus on a didactic message to the working classes. Although most of them included illustrations, an important feature for reaching a mass readership, their »mixture of articles on history, biography, and the natural sciences« mainly excluded fictional texts (Fyfe 2004c: 49).

By the 1840s, the ›first generation‹ had given way to a ›second generation‹ of penny weekly family magazines, a new breed of illustrated magazine which reacted to the popular demand for light entertainment with a commercial approach to a mass audience (cf. ibid.: 49-50). Though periodicals such as the *London Journal* (1845-1928), *Reynolds's Miscellany* (1846-1869) and *Cassell's Illustrated Family Paper* (1853-1867/1932) followed similar patterns of social and moral instruction as the first generation, their main market attraction was the featured serialised sensation novels (cf. Anderson 1991: 2-3; Fyfe 2004c: 49-50). The instructional magazines of the first generation buckled because of their inability to adjust to this market demand, while the second generation periodicals soon achieved tremendous circulations (cf. Anderson 1991: 181; Fyfe 2004c: 50).[2]

The RTS had also published in periodical format from the 1820s on to »complement the tract work« (Fyfe 2006: 21), as it realised that the young as well as a general public requested »works with a more secular tone« (Butts 2006: 8). With the *Child's Companion* (1824-1932), it had shifted its style to works with more appeal to this audience in the attempt to provide suitable reading mat-

---

1 On the idea of the development, agenda and distinction of first and second generation family magazines, see, for instance, Fyfe (2004c: esp. 48-50), Anderson (1991) and Turner (2000: 66-67).

2 Anderson observes of the *Penny Magazine*: »As taste changed and people wanted their educational fare spiced with a little fiction, the magazine did not react to this change and by 1845 its circulation had declined to 40,000«, while the *London Journal*, *Reynolds's Miscellany* and *Cassell's Illustrated Family Paper* »had by 1855 achieved respective regular sales of 450,000, 200,000, and 250,000« (1991: 181). Similarly, Fyfe notes: »The amazing circulations of these periodicals made life difficult for the older ›instructive and amusing‹ periodical« (2004c: 50).

ter for those coming out of the Sunday schools. Its *Tract Magazine* (1824-1892) had been intended for the parents of such children of the working classes, and the *Visitor* (1833-1851) was the RTS's specimen belonging to the first-generation penny weekly (cf. Butts 2006: 8; Fyfe 2006: 21).[3]

With these periodicals, the RTS expanded its mission to educate and evangelise the working classes and reform the upper classes (cf. Fyfe 2004a: 170-171). As the »largest evangelical publisher of general Christian literature in the middle and late nineteenth century« (Fyfe 2004c: 25), the RTS was one of the actors who defined the suitability of reading matter at mid-century.[4] Yet the evangelical creed at the time not only defined the content of reading matter *per se* but furthermore limited the choice of Sunday reading severely to religious books.[5] This

---

3   On the development of the RTS's publishing programme and mission, see especially the following publications: In Butts/Garrett (2006) esp. Butts (2006: 7-10) and Fyfe (2006: 21), as well as other publications by Fyfe on the RTS (2004a: 166-167, 170-171), (2004c: 10-12, 35); see also Altholz (1989), Hewitt (1949: 37-42) and Jones (1850).

4   In this vein, the RTS's *Annual Report* for 1851 related an anecdote on the »Evils of Bad Books« to stress the necessity of providing suitable reading matter for the new readers who had come out of the Sunday schools and were now applying their increasing ability to the wrong material: »A father, in one of the districts, was found in deep distress, on account of the conduct of his four boys, all of whom had been taught in a Sunday-school, but who, by reading the trashy and detestable publications issued weekly from many a press, had been induced to throw off all parental restraint, to frequent judge-and-jury clubs, and other haunts of profligacy and vice, and had become so incorrigibly bad, that he was obliged to turn them from his door. The consequence inevitably will be, that the streets and the gaol will be, alternately, their home, crime and punishment their sole occupation and doom« (Religious Tract Society 1851: 16).

5   That this idea of Sunday reading was already being debated in contemporary society was indicated in a review on the RTS periodicals *Leisure Hour* and *Sunday at Home* (the *Leisure Hour*'s sister publication, initiated by the RTS in 1854 especially to provide reading matter for Sundays) printed in the *Saturday Review*: »Perhaps the strongest point in the case against the Evangelical party is their alleged view of the proper employment of Sunday. [...] There must be not only Sunday clothes, but ›Sunday books,‹ Sunday amusements, Sunday music, Sunday conversation.« However, the critic was not against »Sunday rest« *per se*, as he concluded: »many people would think it wrong to read novels on that day«, »We know many families in which Buffon or Goldsmith would be tabooed on that day;« and, »We should not wish a child of

obviously made the enjoyment of reading difficult for the working classes, who had little time to read but on Sunday (cf. Altick 1989: 150).[6]

DEBATES ON READING MATTER
AND THE POPULAR PRESS

The increasing demand for ›secular‹, sensational periodicals simultaneous to the decline of the more instructional periodicals hence shows that at mid-century the discourse concerning moral attitudes on reading was under scrutiny. That the RTS started in a contested field becomes obvious when one looks at the debates on cheap magazines (such as the *London Journal*), which peaked at the end of the 1850s, arguably due to their serialised sensational fiction. The RTS reacted to this debate with its *Leisure Hour* in 1852 by largely excluding fiction from the pages of the magazine, yet appeared to compensate for this lack through the in-clusion of historical narratives – equally entertaining though with a didactic function. As Wynne notes, the literary market was perceived – or rhetorically constructed – as divided at least up until the 1860s between cheap literature (i.e., the penny family magazines with »their ›vulgar‹ mix« of content supposedly ad-dressed to the working classes) and the middle-class literature distributed through the circulating libraries and monthly part-issues (Wynne 2001: 14-15). This »stratification of literacy« (Margaret Shaw, qtd. in Phegley 2004: 6) and reading matter – which was classified between the dichotomies of high and low culture, male and female, working and middle classes, literary reviews and fami-ly magazines (cf. Phegley 2004: 26, table; King 2004: 24-25) – was most obvi-ously constructed through a bulk of articles and reviews debating cheap literature and the popular periodical market on the basis of a random sample of periodical

---

ours to pass his Sunday in reading fairy tales or playing at cricket« (»Pure Literature« 1856: 17).

6   Altick notes: »Only in the textile industry had the ten-hour day been won; elsewhere the usual work week was seventy-two hours or more. Shop assistants worked eighty-five to ninety hours a week [...]. The only day of theoretical rest was Sunday, but a good part of it, at least among the respectable middle class, was spent at church, and in what hours remained, one's choice of reading-matter was severely limited, in mid-dle-class Victorian households, by the Sabbatarian ban on any but religious books« (1989: 150).

issues available at the specific time (cf. King 2004: 26).[7] This debate, as Andrew King notes, took place in »comparatively high-status journalistic sources« (King 2004: 23), a context which must be taken into consideration as it means that the arena for this debate was more or less restricted to the educated middle classes, who debated amongst themselves and used this means to distinguish themselves from the ›uneducated‹, thus reaffirming their own status as cultural guardians untempted by such light entertainment.

These review articles were characterised by the overarching ignorance of a cheap literature. This is implied, for instance, by the fact that the debate only really set in years after periodicals such as the *London Journal* had been initiated and started to flourish. Furthermore, the detailed descriptions of the cheap periodicals' content, which the reviews thought it necessary to provide, spoke for an obvious unawareness of what such periodicals actually looked like.[8] They attempted to scrutinise, condemn and ridicule such outpourings of print for a presumably uneducated working-class readership,[9] buttressing the »myth that all

---

7   The reviews and texts considered in the following are: »Popular Literature of the Day« (1840), »Weekly Penny Literature« (1858), »Literature of the People« (1859), *Report from the Select Committee on Newspaper Stamps. Together with the Proceedings of the Committee, Minutes of Evidence, Appendix, and Index* (1969 [1851]), Wilkie Collins' »The Unknown Public« (1858), E.S. Dallas' »Popular Literature. The Periodical Press« (1859a) and (1859b), J. Hepworth Dixon's »The Literature of the Lower Orders (1847a) and (1847b) and Margaret Oliphant's »The Byways of Literature. Reading for the Million« (1858). For discussions of these reviews, consult above all King (2004) and Phegley (2004); see also Anderson (1991) and Wynne (2001).

8   Cf., for instance, »Weekly Penny Literature« (1858: 678-679), with a close description of the *London Journal*'s set-up, as well as »Literature of the People« (1859: 16-17). Oliphant similarly was astonished at the success of best-selling author J.F. Smith from the *London Journal*, of whose existence she was entirely unaware (1858: 211). Most tellingly, Collins already entitled his review »The Unknown Public« and observed that he would describe here »what was to me a new species of literary production« (1858: 217). King also notes the actual unfamiliarity of the Victorian critics with the criticised periodicals (cf. 2004: 28-29) and observes that the exclusion in reviews of periodicals such as the *London Journal* up until 1847 »is indicative of a blind spot towards the actual division of the [periodical] market [into interest and price groups]« (King 2004: 25).

9   King, in his analysis of Dixon's review (1847b), points towards a tradition of »ridicul[ing] the ›Notices to Correspondents‹« in these periodicals (2004: 25), as can be observed in the reviews by Collins (who used them to analyse the periodicals'

working people shared a uniformly degraded taste« (Anderson 1991: 179). This resulted in a presumptuous view that the middle classes needed to improve the working classes' taste for literature, and that – since they had only recently gained the ability to read at all – they now had to be taught the right way of reading the right kind of literature.

The presumptuousness of this criticism of cheap literature was, for instance, conveyed through the health discourse installed to describe the ›diseased‹ influence of literature in terms of bodily (mal)functions, which likened its abilities to intoxication or purification.[10] This idea specifically stratified literature along lines of class, age and gender. In 1840, for instance, the article »Popular Literature of the Day« asserted that the working classes had »no recollections of a higher or purer literature«, but apparently blindly »trusted in the truth of a printed book«, as »with an unparalleled blindness of eagerness« they were »impel[led] [...] to those sources of instruction from which they fancy aid and counsel may be derived, or to those pastimes the excitement of which shall be the most intoxicating« (1840: 242). Similarly, Dixon asserted in 1847 that the working classes were provided with and attracted by a »noxious literature, the intoxicating poisons of which tempt them to return to it again and again«, linking the consumption of such a literature to intemperance and »precocious inebriety« ([Dixon] 1847a: 3). As Kelly J. Mays (1995) has noted, women and the young were thought to be especially prone to this addiction, as being less educated and not able to judge in comparison to a variety of literature – this being mainly the only reading they did – they were most injuriously influenced.[11] Wilkie Collins

---

readership; 1858: 219), Oliphant (1858: 211), »Literature of the People« (1859: 17) and »Weekly Penny Literature« (1858: 685).

10 See above all Mays' »The Disease of Reading and Victorian Periodicals« (1995); cf. also King (2004: 26).

11 Dixon, for instance, observed: »We have good reason, too, for believing that those readers are, for the greater part, females – country girls who are in service, and children whom the excitement, suffering, and evil example of crowded and busy towns have rendered prematurely conscious of the awakening instincts of womanhood« ([Dixon] 1847a: 3). Similarly, the article »Literature of the People« noted: »It appears that the most undesirable publications are principally read by children, domestic servants, and young women employed in factories. [...] In school-children a taste for reading has just been excited, and these inflammatory stories are devoured at an age when the imagination is most vivid [...] – in short, just at the age when they are like to exert the most injurious influence« (1859: 30). Furthermore, Oliphant stated: »One can perceive pretty well at a glance that it is not instruction which the multitude demands

turned his eye on the literature of the ›unknown public‹ in 1858 by studying penny magazines such as the *London Journal* and concluded that this »largest audience for periodical literature, in this age of periodicals, must, sooner or later, learn to discriminate« between different kinds of literature, as they apparently failed to appreciate ›good‹ fiction ([Collins] 1858: 222). Nevertheless, Dixon had pointed out that the working classes would be interested in reading better literature if it were accessible to them in financial as well as educational terms, that is, »if they could procure the latter, and had the elementary education necessary to enable them to understand and enjoy it« (1847b: 2). Similarly, Oliphant observed that the regress to such literature was not only a working-class problem but also to be found amongst the middle classes: »the multitude, like ourselves, loved amusement better than instruction« (1858: 203).

»A NEW WEEKLY MAGAZINE«: THE *LEISURE HOUR* AS INTERMEDIARY

Toward mid-century, the Religious Tract Society almost appeared to anticipate this common criticism of the new periodicals when it realised that there was »a wider and more heterogeneous audience for its publications« (Fyfe 2004c: 35). Its earlier periodicals intended for working-class readers presumably ended up being mainly read by the middle classes and RTS supporters, who, as the Society concluded, »wanted to read more widely« (Fyfe 2004a: 171). Before, as Fyfe asserts, there had been two types of publications by the RTS: firstly, those intended for the conversion of »their (mostly working-class) readers«, and secondly, »those which promoted existing faith (mostly among the middle classes)« (ibid.). Yet the Society was aware of the changing conditions of its working-class target audience, which had – also with the help of the Sunday schools – achieved a »better literacy and more awareness of print and the information it could convey« (Fyfe 2006: 25). This audience was now in search of a more general literature like the secular non-fiction and »sensational and perhaps scurrilous fiction carried by penny magazines such as *Reynolds' Miscellany* and the *London Journal*« (ibid.) besides or in place of the typical RTS Sunday school literature or religious content.

---

most loudly, and that the popular mind does not by nature incline towards philosophy, even should it be the philosophy of the steam-engine, for the relaxation of its leisure hours. [...] It is that love of stories which distinguishes all primitive minds, and which has its strongest development in savages and children« (1858: 204).

The RTS hence saw the need to enter this market and provided suitable reading matter where the new periodicals failed in including Christian principles. It reacted with a new publishing programme, which included more secular writings combined with a Christian tone, »a literary style intended to create a mood of sound morality and Christian faith« (Fyfe 2004c: 101), which »had to be a balance between the requirement for Christian content and the equally strong need to avoid scaring off potential readers« (ibid.: 105); this concept was implemented to reach both audiences at once (Fyfe 2006: 25-26). The Society had, as Fyfe observes, a twin target in this regard: to extend secular information and fight the licentious press, as the »RTS expected and was expected to lead the attack on corrupting literature« (Fyfe 2004b: 74). The mass circulation of secular periodicals such as the *London Journal* and the dwindling of the circulation numbers of the RTS's earlier family magazine the *Visitor* showed that the market was in the process of changing by popular demand. The RTS minutes also outline that, faced with the decreasing demand for its *Visitor* and the increase in fiction-carrying secular magazines, the Society had repeatedly discussed the necessity of a new periodical to challenge the secular competition from the late 1840s on. The *Visitor* had proven unprofitable for quite a while;[12] publicly, however, the RTS did not acknowledge this decline, which led to the periodical's absorption into the *Leisure Hour* in 1852. The RTS's initial announcement of the *Leisure Hour* linked the new to the earlier periodical:

»As it is intended to discontinue the Society's periodical, ›The Visitor,‹ families and individuals that have hitherto supported that work, will find ›The Leisure Hour,‹ it is hoped, a not unworthy, if not a greatly improved successor.« (»Periodical Literature« 1851: 665).

The *Visitor* would have been well-known to the Society's supporters, who may, however, have been astonished that the magazine suddenly was to be discontinued. Only three months earlier in the *Christian Spectator*[13] for 1 August 1851, the Society had still stated: »The *Visitor* has completed its eighteenth volume, and still proves acceptable to thousands« (»Periodicals« 1851: 339).[14] Difficul-

---

12 Cf. USCL/RTS CCM (19 Sept 1849), (17 Oct 1849), (21 Aug 1850) and (16 July 1851); see also Fyfe (2005: 31-32).

13 The *Christian Spectator* is available via *UKPC 19th Century UP Periodicals*.

14 Half a month earlier, the RTS minutes, by contrast, had stated: »it was Resolved that the circulation of ›The Visitor‹ not being remunerative to the Society the Sub Committee recommend the General Committee to discontinue that Periodical at the close of the present year« (USCL/RTS CCM 16 July 1851).

ties in the book trade had postponed the decision to discontinue the *Visitor*, which was, however, quickly put into action after »the death of the *Visitor*'s long-time editor in mid-1851« (Fyfe 2005: 41, En 125; cf. 31-32). With the *Leisure Hour*, the RTS tried to adapt to the changing market demand while still being true to its evangelical principles. The *Leisure Hour* did include little fiction at the outset, most of which was restricted to a two-parter format (see Chapter 3, Fn 8 and 16). As Chapter 3 shows, historical and biographical articles and series were a fitting surrogate to feed a demand for narratives. They introduced a sensational mode at instances, yet were based on facts, and with the right choice of topic or historical actors they thus easily managed to include a didactic or Christian tone. Thus, as Anderson states, the RTS »recognized that religious literature must find a way to match the popular appeal of secular competition like the *London Journal*« (Anderson 1991: 167).

The new publishing programme meant that the Society had to negotiate between the intended working-class audience and the RTS's evangelical supporters in terms of the content and set-up of the periodical. Fyfe analyses this as a »balancing act« (Fyfe 2004b: 80; cf. also 2004c: 58-59) with regard to the RTS's »Monthly Volumes« book series. While the *Leisure Hour*'s focus on representations of the past in contrast to fiction might have soothed RTS supporters to some extent, the periodical project entailed the problem that not only content but also the publishing format of the weekly was unpopular with and disdained by the middle and upper classes at mid-century, unlike the book format of the Monthly Volumes (in terms of material appearance as well as its unified content). This meant that the Society had to argue more carefully when introducing its family journal. The RTS therefore used different strategies of representation for its product according to or regulated by the ideas it had of its two groups of consumers and their identity. This double-rhetoric becomes obvious when one considers how the different audiences learned about or made initial contact with the *Leisure Hour* and compares these different channels of marketing or distribution.

The Society introduced the new periodical project to its supporters via a three-page article entitled »Periodical Literature: A New Weekly Magazine«, presented on the cover of the *Christian Spectator* (the periodical directed at RTS members) on 19 November 1851.[15] The article's cover position as well as its length, which allowed for an extended argument on the urgency of the project, indicated that the Society felt it necessary to win their members' support; the fol-

---

15 A very brief discussion of this article within a different context can be found in Lechner (2013: §§3-5).

lowing analysis will hence pay detailed attention to this initial announcement. First of all, the article dedicated a full two pages to an outline of the current state of literature available for the working classes and newly literate, followed by the conclusion that a more secular approach was necessary to reach this audience, before finally introducing the *Leisure Hour*.

The article started by referring to the positive results of the education of the working classes, something the RTS and its supporters had been involved in from the beginning. However, these achievements now faced a new challenge in the (presumed) deficiency of reading matter on offer: »The principles propagated in the land through the medium of cheap ephemeral and periodical papers are often the most disorganizing and demoralizing.« (»Periodical Literature« 1851: 663) The rhetoric of the article was clear from the outset, as very strong metaphors (referring to the Deluge) were used to describe how the positive educational achievements were put to ill use through »pour[ing] forth[s] of the popular press«, a »tide of impiety and licentiousness [...] which imperils all that is valuable to us as men and Christians« (ibid.). Thus, the RTS cleverly managed to get its supporters on their side by involving them directly in the phrase »us as men and Christians«, making it also their responsibility to act – presumably by supporting what was put forth in the remainder of the article, that is, the new periodical project.

To further support this initial claim, the article then criticised three different kinds of periodicals intended for or popular with the working classes. The first criticism was directed at the radical press, which showed negative tendencies »to the hurt of public morals and the desecration of the sabbath« (ibid.: 664). The article then turned to the deficiencies of periodicals »of a somewhat higher position in the social scale«, which, however, contained

»chiefly translations from French novels, of more than questionable character; or grotesque descriptions of men and manners, which convey no moral lesson, nor instruct the mind; but rather enervate the mental faculties, and indispose them for solid information and thoughtful study.« (Ibid.)

Though the article did not mention titles, the focus on French translations indicates that the periodicals at issue here were secular family magazines such as the *London Journal*.[16] Finally, the article also attacked religious periodicals, which would most probably have appealed to RTS followers' standards but were shown

---

16 See King's discussion of the *London Journal*'s internationalism and connection to France (King 2004: Chapter 3, esp. 67-73).

to fail in their purpose of reaching a working-class or unconverted audience. The article here quoted in length from W.M. O'Hanlon's sub-chapter »The Press« in his prize essay *The Operative Classes of Great Britain: Their Existing State and Its Improvement* (1851), which had recently been published by the RTS. In the presented quotations, O'Hanlon observed a general failure of religious literature to cater to a popular audience, because »[i]t is addressed too exclusively to the reasoning faculties, and too little to the imagination« and is »cast far too much in a theological mould, and invested with too many technical phrases, to be intelligible to the common mind« (»Periodical Literature« 1851: 664). Besides these stylistic problems, religious literature furthermore rather preached to the converted, as

»its voice is to the spiritually enlightened, rather than to those who are still ignorant of the great truths of the Christian revelation. [...] [I]t cannot be expected that they will circulate much beyond the range of the religious part of the population. The themes they discuss, the information they convey, are such as few but Christians can appreciate; and, indeed, most of these periodicals are so specially devoted to particular sections of the church, that they are seldom read beyond the precincts of the denomination of which they are the avowed organs.« (Ibid.)

Here, O'Hanlon identified that the problem of such periodicals was that they were produced more to create group identity within Christian and possibly sectarian circles perpetuating Christian principles to the converted, and were thereby unable to reach out to the unconverted. The reliance on theological content together with complex language (»technical phrases«) and the dominance of non-fiction (»reasoning faculties«) over fiction or fictionalised accounts (»imagination«) did not acknowledge the demands and preferences of the new reading market and hence failed to grant them access.

In consequence, O'Hanlon demanded a new kind of religious literature,

»which, while it is not directly given to the discussion of the dogmas of Christianity, is throughout pervaded by its spirit; and which, instead of avowedly shunning religion as forbidden ground, is based upon a full and manly recognition of its Divine authority, its paramount claims and its absolute necessity, as the means of man's highest improvement and happiness, in relation both to this world and the next – a literature which shall be perfectly free from all sectarian peculiarities both in religion and politics – the literature, not of a party, but of humanity; addressing itself to the deep and universal principles of our nature, and doing this in such a form and manner as shall make it welcome to the homes of the working population, while it enlarges their comprehension, conciliates their prejudices, purifies their sentiments, and thus induces those mental and moral habits which constitute the chief feature of a true elevation.« (Ibid.)

In this passage, O'Hanlon outlined what Fyfe has referred to as the Society's concept of Christian tone (see above). O'Hanlon designed a field for a periodical situated between or at the intersection of the secular family magazines (»shunning religion«; »sectarian peculiarities [...] in [...] politics«; »noxious literature«) and the religious press (»dogmas of Christianity«; »sectarian peculiarities [...] in religion«), consoling both formats yet following the demands of the new audience:

»our inquiry at present is, not as to the best mode in which the working-classes may be brought under the influence of specifically Christian truth, but as to the best principles on which to construct such a general literature for their use, as will be calculated to take the place of that noxious literature which now circulates among them in such abundance. [...] one great desideratum of the present day is, the more extensive supply of a *cheap periodical literature*, such as shall combine the lighter graces of imagination with solid instruction, borrow its illustrations from every field of nature and walk of art, adapt itself to the varied phases of our common humanity, and harmonising with the great vital truths of the Christian revelation, shall aim at the permanent and true advancement of those to whom its mission is directed.« (Ibid.)

Having spent two full pages outlining the three failing kinds of literature – radical press, secular magazines, and religious periodicals – supported by O'Hanlon's assessment and demand for a middle-way, the Society now, on the final page of its argument, came to the conclusion that

»It is undoubtedly our duty [...] to adopt such a course as may best suit the circumstances of the times. If the periodical obtains acceptance in a vast number of instances where the treatise or the volume cannot find admittance, it is our policy to use this means, and sanctify it to the promotion of truth and piety.« (Ibid.: 665)

While the article had so far pointed out the problems with other periodicals, the RTS here showed awareness that it was also the periodical format itself which posed a problem, in contrast to the tract format (as the accepted means to reach the poor and unconverted) or to the reputable book format (as the preferred medium of the middle classes). Thus, the contested content of the weekly periodicals appeared to have stained the genre itself – an idea which is discussed in further detail in Chapter 5, where series on the past printed within the *Leisure Hour* are compared to their book counterparts. The article in the *Christian Spectator* was careful to continue as follows:

»It must be admitted that a serial literature, in which knowledge is presented in an accessible form, at a low price, and at brief intervals, offers many advantages. The stores of learning are laid open to all; and leisure hours, which might be wasted or misemployed, are improved to noble and holy purposes. In this way the good which the press is capable of yielding will be employed to neutralize the evil which, in vicious hands, it is made to inflict.« (Ibid.)

As the largest evangelical publishing house, the Society was probably right in asserting that they »possesse[d] greater advantages for the production and support of a periodical addressed to all classes than [could] be found elsewhere« (ibid.), and it hence seemed natural that they would follow their overall aim of reaching out to the unconverted and working classes by this means. The long preamble before the new periodical project is finally outlined makes clear the difficulty with which the RTS found itself faced in justifying the format and content of the *Leisure Hour* even to its members. Fyfe observes not only the Society's problem of negotiating between the two groups but also a split within evangelical supporters on their idea of the acceptability of secular or sensational content:

»The editor of the *Leisure Hour* had to perform a difficult balancing act – to avoid the appearance of ›repulsive‹ religion while maintaining the RTS's high principles and at the same time to include material assumed to be attractive to working-class readers. [...] What the RTS committee had to work out was how to balance their religious ideals with the commercial need to appeal to their audience.« (Fyfe 2004b: 80)

This negotiation also applied to the commercial enterprise of the Society. Thus, supporters furthermore criticised the new publishing programme for its commercial orientation, connected to a probable shift away from an intended working-class audience to please more of its supporters, as the RTS

»appeared to be moving its focus away from the conversion of the working classes, towards the devotions of middle-class readers. Subscribers were unhappy with the thought that their monies might be used to subsidise their own reading matter, rather than helping the needy.« (Fyfe 2006: 21)[17]

Accordingly, the *Christian Spectator* article furthermore backed up the decision as being demanded by its members, as »from the communications the Committee have received, it is evident that many of its friends would consider that it was not fulfilling its appropriate service if it were to leave this powerful agency unemployed« (»Periodical Literature« 1851: 665).

Under the subheading »The Leisure Hour: An Illustrated Family Magazine of Instruction and Amusement« (ibid.), the article finally presented the Society's new project as the obvious remedy with a programme consisting of

»[a]rticles on the more prominent topics of the day [...] mingled with interesting narratives, instructive sketches from history, visits to places of celebrity in distant parts of the world, popular dissertations on scientific questions, and the choicer effusions of poetry.« (Ibid.)[18]

---

17 In a letter obviously reacting to an inquiry into the profits the Society made on its publications, RTS secretary Davis wrote that the *Leisure Hour* »barely clears itself. We have just taken the expenses returns for ›57 & the nett profit is between £300 & £400.- so little do those without know of the facts of the case. The expense of setting up a publication of this kind is something fabulous & it is only after a certain number of thousands have been sold that a profit commences. If from our present circulation we could rise to 250,000 a week our profit would be very large, but at present we have only just reached the paying point. If our profit were large it would all be spent on our benevolent objects – the free donation of religious publications to all who are struggling in their Master's cause, & are unable to supply themselves with these instruments for good« (USCL/RTS Corr 1 Dec 1858).

18 Besides content, the article gave detailed information on the *Leisure Hour*'s materiality and title. Thus, the periodical would »consist of sixteen large pages, printed with new and clear type, on good paper« and would be »illustrated with engravings. In weekly numbers, issued every Thursday, price 1d., or monthly parts, in a neat wrapper, priced 5d.« (»Periodical Literature« 1851: 665) Furthermore, the article noted the possibility to collect the *Leisure Hour* in its annual volume format, as »[f]rom the practical and instructive character of this weekly sheet, it will be deemed worthy of preservation, in the permanent form of a *volume*, and thus be available for re-perusal and reference« (ibid.). The title *Leisure Hour*, the article stated, »indicates its leading object, to make every vacant hour the means of enriching the memory with profitable and pleasant thoughts«, as developments such as the recent »early closing movement

The periodical would therefore »supply the reader with a copious fund of entertaining information, and practical comment on all suitable themes«, which would

»render it alike suited to the parlour and the kitchen, the working man's fireside and the country cottage, and equally acceptable to dwellers in town or country, to travellers by steamboat or railway, to those resident in Great Britain, or who have sought a home in its world-wide colonies.« (Ibid.)

As the article was addressed to RTS supporters, it advertised a specific religiosity of the *Leisure Hour* when it stated: »While the tone of every article will be decidedly religious, and every opportunity will be embraced of commending ›truth as it is in Jesus,‹ its pages will comprise papers on almost ever subject which can elevate, gratify, or instruct« – and hence the periodical would be »one which the Christian parent and employer may safely place in the hands of those who are under his influence« (ibid.).

While the announcement in the *Christian Spectator* was directed at the Society's middle-class supporters, Aileen Fyfe has demonstrated that the RTS's new marketing strategies for the *Leisure Hour* were explicitly directed at a working-class readership. The Society distributed the *Leisure Hour* via book stalls, small shops and hawkers (Fyfe 2004a: 176-179; 2004c: 165-177); it published the *Leisure Hour* without the Society's imprint, as it had come to realise »that for much of the working-class audience, the name ›RTS‹ would be more likely to suggest patronising middle-class interference than trustworthy information« (Fyfe 2004c: 180);[19] and it started an advertising campaign »in the provincial papers as well as the usual London-based periodicals« (Fyfe 2004b: 79) more likely to reach the working classes – though following evangelical principles, the RTS was careful not to advertise in Sunday papers, although these were most likely to reach their intended audience.[20] Additionally, the RTS freely distributed a large number of

[…] seem to lead to a principle that EVERY MAN SHOULD HAVE A LEISURE HOUR, with the view to his mental improvement« (ibid.). On the relation of periodicals to industrial time, see Chapter 1 (Fn 17).

19 Cf. also Lloyd/Law (2009) and Fyfe (2004b: 80).

20 »Mr Jones also mentioned that it had been suggested that in order to reach the masses of working men, it was desirable to advertise the ›Leisure Hour‹ in those Periodicals most read by that class, including some Sunday Newspapers – The Committee approved of the suggested Advertisements but hinted that no Advertisements be sent to Sunday Papers« (USCL/RTS ECM 1 June 1852). While advertisements in papers most likely to reach working-class readers did not reference the RTS, to middle-class

the *Leisure Hour*'s first issue and asked its supporters for help promoting the periodical by handing out free numbers to their employees and in pubs and coffee-houses or by distributing circulars.[21]

The marketing idea of free distribution shows how important a careful set-up of the *Leisure Hour*'s first issue was, in which the editors also prominently introduced the periodical's historical programme (see epigraph to Chapter 1) and in addition presented the first article of the series »The Working Man in the Olden Time« (M[erryweather] 1852; see Chapter 3). Further, a common advertisement for the *Leisure Hour* from January 1852 onwards was accompanied by the planned contents of the first five issues. An inclusion of »instructive sketches from history« was not only briefly mentioned in the advertising text but directly outlined through the additional presentation of the titles of the initial historical series »The Working Man in the Olden Time« and »Shades of the Departed in Old London« ([Stoughton] 1852-1853; see Chapter 6) (see, for instance, »Advertisement« 1852). Furthermore, the *Leisure Hour*'s initial editorial »A Word with Our Readers« (H.D. 1852), the general advertisements for the periodical and its announcements to RTS supporters linked the periodical's title *Leisure Hour* to the early closing movement, which was directed at better working conditions for the working classes but which, being an evangelical movement, also responded to the RTS supporters (cf. Fyfe 2004c: 64; see also Fn 18 above). In this way, the title introduced the periodical as »the ideal blend of mental and religious improvement for those newly acquired hours of freedom« (Fyfe 2004c: 65) while at

---

supporters the editorship of the RTS was »a very open secret« (Fyfe 2004c: 180). The RTS increasingly created an »alter ego« for itself by using the name of the *Leisure Hour* as a trademark for other publications, such as its later periodicals *Boy's Own Paper* and *Girl's Own Paper*, which were published under the imprint of »The Leisure Hour Office«, as well as book series such as *The Shilling Books for Leisure Hours* (Fyfe 2004c: 180).

21 The RTS had already announced this to supporters in its *Christian Spectator* article (cf. »Periodical Literature« 1851: 665). On »Gratuitous distribution of the first number«, see USCL/RTS CCM (17 Sept 1851), and specifically on free circulation »in the Manufacturing Districts«, see USCL/RTS ECM (23 Sept 1851). The Society furthermore decided to print a »Prospectus, at the back of which were printed various favourable notices of the work from respectable Provincial Papers« in order to »increase the circulation of the ›Leisure Hour‹ in Weekly numbers« (USCL/RTS ECM 1 June 1852). The minutes also observed »favorable results apparent from the distribution of the Leisure Hour & Sunday at Home in Public Houses & Coffee Shops in Marylebone« (USCL/RTS ECM 9 Febr 1858). See also Fyfe (2004b: 79).

the same time challenging other secular magazines, as it prescribed how people –
above all the working classes – should make use of their leisure time, namely, by
reading the presented magazine.[22]

NEW ILLUSTRATED MAGAZINES AND CHANGES
IN THE PERIODICAL MARKET

The *Leisure Hour* proved to be successful, as its circulation of sold issues during
the 1850s averaged about 60,000-67,000 and later increased to a circulation of
approximately 100,000 (cf. Fyfe 2004c: 178 & 182; 2012: 131). While it was
specifically set up as a weekly paper, it was also available in monthly parts. The
dual publication format – though common for most weekly periodicals – again
shows the negotiation between its two different audiences. Because of their
cheap price, weekly numbers were likely to reach readers with a small income,
while monthly publications had a higher reputation and could be afforded by
»(presumably) more affluent readers« (Fyfe 2004c: 178). Beyond this commercial aspect, weekly consumption of the *Leisure Hour* and its historical content
might, as the case studies on monthly parts in Chapter 5 show, have proposed a
more fragmentary outlook on the past than a monthly reception.[23] Yet the *Leisure Hour* appears to have been popular increasingly with a more affluent, middle-class audience, as the RTS urged over its initial years that the sale of weekly

---

22 The RTS minutes themselves did not discuss the meaning of the title but show that it
    was not the first choice; however, other options, such as *Old Humphrey's Journal; or
    Christian Visitor* – which would have shown a close link to the RTS's earlier periodi-
    cal and its Christian mission, also by referencing the name of Old Humphrey, alias
    George Mogridge, a successful and favoured RTS author in the *Visitor* – or *Friend of
    the People*, were rejected for the more neutral *Leisure Hour*; see Fyfe (2004c: 64),
    USCL/RTS CCM (16 July 1851), (17 Sept 1851), USCL/RTS ECM (22 July 1851),
    (23 Sept 1851), (28 Oct 1851) and (16 Dec 1851).

23 Though the RTS had as its principle to include a reference to salvation in each of its
    publications, this was, as Fyfe points out, not necessarily the case for each weekly
    number (Fyfe 2004b: 80). The monthly parts, however, consisting of four to five
    numbers, were likely to include such evangelical content; in this way, the monthly
    parts – most likely to reach the RTS supporters in this format – would also be more
    acceptable to them in terms of their Christian purpose, thereby soothing their dislike
    of the disdained weekly periodical.

issues would need to be increased,[24] while sales for the monthly parts seemed to fare better than for the weekly numbers (cf. Fyfe 2004c: 77, 177-178).

This suggests that with its *Leisure Hour* the RTS also paved the way for the arrival of the family magazine to the middle classes in the 1860s as a new stage in the development of the genre of the family magazine.[25] That the *Leisure Hour* underwent changes to adapt to a new market was, for instance, visible in the RTS *Annual Report* for 1859, in which the RTS took stock of the origin and development of the *Leisure Hour* by throwing a retrospective glance at the journal's (still short) history:

»Few topics excited more sorrow and fear some ten years ago amongst thoughtful Christians, than the cheap periodical literature which flooded the masses of the community. Whether as a symptom of the moral state of the people, or as a means for deteriorating that state still further, it could not fail to move the Christian philanthropist deeply. The field, too, was in all but undisputed possession of the enemy. Urged by this melancholy fact, the Society commenced its ›Leisure Hour‹ in 1852 [...]; and if not *propter hoc* certainly *post hoc*, a vast improvement is said to be visible in some of the works which they [*Leisure Hour* and *Sunday at Home*] were designed to supersede.« (Religious Tract Society 1859: 4)

The RTS returned here to the controversy on popular periodicals which had led to the initiation of the *Leisure Hour*, and which still continued in the late 1850s. The idea of the »vast improvement« of other periodicals was supported by the – at least in parts – positive review of the *London Journal* by some contemporary critics.[26] While the statement in the *Annual Report* seemed to carry the message that with the *Leisure Hour* the RTS had therefore reached its aim of providing suitable reading matter and influencing its pernicious opponents, its finality also

---

24 Cf. USCL/RTS ECM (1 June 1852). A letter in 1853 specifically regretted »to find that the sale in numbers decrease, though in parts it leaps up. We should be glad however to increase the sale of the weekly numbers. We shall always be thankful for any suggestions to increase the sale of the periodical« (USCL/RTS Corr 22 Oct 1853). The minutes noted a circulation for the *Leisure Hour* of »80000 per week« in 1854 (USCL/RTS 14 Nov 1854) and an increase of 10,000 per week in 1856 (USCL/RTS FCM 20 Feb 1865).

25 See Chapter 1 (Fn 14).

26 Cf. Oliphant (1858: 209), Brougham (1858: 24-25) and »Weekly Penny Literature« (1858: 679).

indicated a change in the Society's rhetoric for its periodical as well as the RTS's acceptance of its rather middle-class, evangelical audience.

A letter by *Leisure Hour* editor William Haig Miller in 1858 hence appeared to contradict the idea supported by earlier minutes that the *Leisure Hour* had been produced for a working-class readership:

»The L[ondon] Journal is written on subjects and in a style more agreeable to the working classes than the R[eligious] Tr[act] Society can produce. [...] Supposed by a deterioration in paper, print, literary ability, &c, the Society were to produce the same quantity as the L[ondon] Journal, and a few thousands more were spread in Scotland, how would the sale be affected amongst the Middle classes, for whom it was designed as a ›Family‹ Journal‹ as much as for others? would it not in all probability fall off by tens of thousands?« (USCL/RTS Corr 31 May 1858)

Another letter in 1859 clearly stated that the RTS appeared to be unsuccessful in its fight against sensational periodicals:

»The poor take their pennies to the booksellers and buy the ›Family Herald‹, the ›London Journal‹ and ›Cassells Illustrated Family Paper‹. You might have added to the list ›Reynolds Miscellany‹ and many others. [...] the poor come and purchase largely [at the booksellers, where the *Leisure Hour* is also stocked]; but because the religious dispositions of the Masses of the poor are feeble they prefer the exciting kind of reading which they get in the Journals you have named.« (USCL/RTS Corr 23 Nov 1859)

In fact, in 1858 the RTS started plans for another periodical »for the young and uninstructed poor« (USCL/RTS CCM 10 Mar 1858), »for cottagers, labourers, and the humbler classes in general« (USCL/RTS CCM 18 July 1860), which resulted in the publication of the *Cottager* in 1861. These letters, as well as the necessity for a new periodical expressed in the committee meetings, again contradicted the message presented to RTS supporters in the *Christian Spectator* article from 1859 (quoted above) on the *Leisure Hour*'s success. Thus, the RTS changed its rhetoric »*propter hoc*« and at the end of the 1850s defined the *Leisure Hour* rather as a periodical intended for the middle classes.

During the debates of the 1850s outlined above, arguments on the genre had been clad in a class discourse which reflected prevalent middle-class anxieties of a changing society and an empowerment of the working classes. The link of the (class) controversy to the medium was still visible during the 1860s, and the introduction of a ›new‹ publishing format to the middle classes was, as is common with a change and expansion of media formats, applauded and criticised at the same time. Wynne for instance states:

»Before 1859 [...] there was a marked divide between ›respectable‹ and ›unrespectable‹ fiction, a divide which was reflected in the publishing formats of the novels: middle-class readers tended to borrow books from circulating libraries, or buy novels in monthly part-issues; working-class readers, on the other hand, consumed novels as serials in cheap magazine. [...] The years 1859 and 1860, however, marked an important turning-point in the development of the Victorian periodical press, when many new family magazines of a ›respectable‹ nature appeared on the market.« (Wynne 2001: 14-15)

That Wynne uses quotation marks for the terms respectable and unrespectable not only indicates that this divide was a constructed one; it also hints at the fact that these new periodicals were still subjected to debates on their status, a fact which has been outlined distinctly by Maunder for the acceptability of the *Cornhill* during its year of introduction 1860. In his essay, Maunder convincingly questions prevalent academic views of the *Cornhill* as an admired popular magazine of its time (cf. Maunder 1999). This can, for instance, be observed in the similarity of the RTS's introductory rhetoric for the *Leisure Hour* to what Maunder argues on the initial reception of the *Cornhill* in 1860:

»The *Cornhill*'s pages aimed to bring together classes that would normally have been separated both in life and in reading: leisured cultured gentlemen, indifferently educated women and unschooled but ambitious artisans. In doing so, Smith and Thackeray crossed the boundary between elite and popular cultures, demonstrating its demarcation. This putative violation prompted praise, but it was also a reason for members of the mid-Victorian press to degrade the *Cornhill* as popular culture. [...] These particular anti-*Cornhill* anxieties centred on the desire of an elite audience to devalue the leisure reading habits of newly literate and thus disturbingly mobile classes.« (Maunder 1999: 247-249)

Nevertheless, recent periodical critics' perception of the *Cornhill* as thoroughly respectable shows how successful the periodical was in creating this image and in contributing to a construction of the mid-nineteenth-century periodical market as a field of distinction. Accordingly, Phegley argues:

»While family literary magazines followed elite reviewers by setting up common critical binaries, they did not uphold them in practice. Rather, the critical oppositions served as a means to articulate cultural authority while the magazine actually conveyed that the divisions between the high and the low, the masculine and the feminine, were more permeable, blurred, and mutually constitutive. In other words, family literary magazines engaged with the terminology of the binary critical system while subtly refuting it.« (Phegley 2004: 28)

The class rhetoric and the stratification of literary forms in terms of gender and age were, hence, still preserved; they seemed, however, to lose some of their impetus with the increasing acceptance and favour brought to family magazines by the (upper) middle classes and the adaptation of the form to its new audience. This adaptation of a genre from the lower classes to the middle classes can be perceived as a bottom-up development, in contrast to the top-down idea of middle-class influence.[27] The new magazines resolved to follow the successful formula intrinsic to earlier journals such as the *London Journal* in their production of (educational and entertaining) reading matter for leisure times, while at the same time excluding features (such as notices to correspondents), as the *Leisure Hour* already had done.[28]

Periodical studies have commonly noted this stage in periodical production by defining the new magazines through their time of publication as well as their main attraction of illustrations. Terms like ›Sixties magazine‹ or ›illustrated periodical of the Sixties‹, however, still refer to a large bandwidth in design and format. Simon Cooke, for instance, notes that a definition of »what constitutes an ›illustrated periodical of the Sixties‹ [...] is more difficult to establish than one might expect« (Cooke 2010: 32). The overall definition he provides is thorough enough and can serve as a helpful way into further observations on the Sixties periodicals:

»In a general sense, the Sixties magazine can be explained as a literary periodical, aimed at a large middle-class audience, which uses illustration as an accompaniment to serials, poetry, histories, discussion pieces and other articles of a more general interest. Their range was from the purely literary to the ›improving‹, evangelical and doctrinaire, but

---

27 Wynne asserts that »none of the new family magazines published letters from readers. This lack of editorials or readers' comments meant that the family magazine had shifted away from the controversy and debate associated with newspapers, offering itself as a product designed largely for relaxation and entertainment« (2001: 17). See also Fn 9 above.

28 See also Maunder (1999: 250) for the discussion of a review from the *Saturday Review* which »brackets the *Cornhill* with the *London Journal*, a mass circulation magazine whose audience was ›known‹ to be the ›indifferently educated‹ and even the ›barely literate‹«.

their focus, as *The Leisure Hour* puts it, was always on ›recreation‹ and ›instruction‹. The illustrations played a central part in entertaining the eye and improving taste, and a key characteristic of all of the magazines is the symmetry of word and printed image, with equal value being given to each.

This winning formulation was embodied in a number of outstanding publications, the most notable being the mighty triumvirate that de Maré describes as the ›Big Three‹: *Once a Week*, published by Bradbury and Evans, established in 1859 and on sale for 3*d*.; *The Cornhill Magazine*, the brainchild of George Smith of Smith Elder, which sold for a shilling and was published monthly (1860); and Alexander Strahan's sixpenny *Good Words*, a magazine set up in direct challenge to *The Cornhill*. These periodicals established the tone and form, and others quickly followed suit. Characteristic examples are *The Leisure Hour*, which had appeared in the fifties, and was reissued in a Sixties format by The Religious Tract Society [...].« (Ibid.)

Cooke's extended definition contains a number of important points: the focus on serialised fiction as a »literary periodical«; the arrival of the genre in the »middle-class audience« (while previous journals were regarded to have mainly a working-class or lower middle-class following); the extensive use of illustrations not only for the serialised fiction but also accompanying non-fiction content such as history; and their overall design to refrain from controversies commonly addressed in newspapers but to focus on a combination of instruction and entertainment suitable for a family audience.

A feature which specifically made the periodicals of the Sixties attractive and highly esteemed was their incorporation of illustrations, often making use of innovative, avant-garde and increasingly well-known illustrators. As Fyfe points out for the *Leisure Hour*'s initial volume(s), the use of illustrations was necessary especially to reach the lower classes (2004c: 108), but judging from the new market for the (upper) middle classes, it was equally important to reach this audience. In addition to the *Leisure Hour*'s weekly cover illustrations, which were from the beginning in 1852 conducted by *Leisure Hour* top illustrator John Gilbert (1817-1897),[29] the periodical included a full-page illustration in every week-

---

29 The entry for Sir John Gilbert in the *Leisure Hour*'s jubilee number reads: »The late Sir John Gilbert, R.A., illustrated the first story which appeared in this magazine, ›The Accommodation Bill‹ (1852), and continued to draw the serial illustrations, including those of ›A Life's Secret,‹ by Mrs. Henry Wood (1862), for about ten years. He died in 1898 at Blackheath, where he was born in 1817« (»Artists« 1902: 257). On Sir John Gilbert, see Bucklow/Woodcock (2011), and therein on his work for periodicals especially the chapter by Bills (2011); see also Anderson (1991: 95), King (2004: esp.

ly issue from 1861. In 1862 the *Leisure Hour* was reissued in a larger format due to the abolishment of the Paper Duty, and the annual volume featured a coloured plate.[30] In 1863 a coloured plate accompanied every monthly part.[31] As the jubilee issue points out, the *Leisure Hour* also »attained its largest circulation« at this time (»Fifty Years« 1902: 181), a fact which was most probably linked to this innovation. The introduction of the monthly plates further supports the idea of the *Leisure Hour*'s constant movement away from the disputed weekly towards the more respectable monthly;[32] it was turned into a strict monthly by 1881. Retrospectively, the *Leisure Hour* addresses this change initiated by the new journals of the Sixties in its jubilee number's entry for 1881:

»Any one who looks back over the ›Fifty Years of *The Leisure Hour*‹ must include in his vision other magazines which had more or less of the same purpose. The beginning of *Chambers' Journal* is part of history; John Cassell is a name that cannot be forgotten; Charles Dickens wrought on other lines, but he had a large place in shaping magazine literature, and keeping it pure; and the high standard to which *Good Words* attained will be ever memorable. *Blackwood* still remains to remind us of the intellectual reach of the earlier magazines; and so also the *Cornhill*, the first year of which brought together some of

---

61-62) and Murray (2009). On Gilbert as illustrator for both *London Journal* and *Leisure Hour*, see Chapter 3.

30 Cf. »Fifty Years« (1902: 180), USCL/RTS CCM (7 Aug 1861).

31 Cf. USCL/RTS CCM (19 Mar 1862), (18 Mar 1863), (15 July 1863) and (30 Sept 1863). From 1866 onwards, monthly plates tended to be produced mainly as black and white images, so that by 1869 the recognition of the »List of Coloured Illustrations« added to the annual index was renamed as »in Colours or on Toned Paper«. In contrast to *Good Words*, the *Leisure Hour* index – same as the *Cornhill*'s – did not provide artists' names.

32 The suggestion made in the RTS minutes »That the overplus Stock of Coloured pictures of Leisure Hour, and Sunday at Home be used in books for the young, and suitable matter be written to them« (USCL/RTS ECM 23 June 1868) indicates that the plan to offer coloured plates for purchase also with weekly issues (while they were included in monthly parts; cf. USCL/RTS 19 Mar 1862) did not succeed. Cf. on this point also Julia Thomas: »In fact, the whole notion of pictures and texts as seamlessly overlapping was undermined by actual illustrative practice, in which it was common for a publisher or engraving firm to sell off used blocks or steel plates for publication elsewhere. Gift books reproduced illustrations outside their original settings, and these pictures were sometimes accompanied by texts different from those that they were intended to illustrate« (Thomas 2004: 8-9).

the best writers of the Victorian age. We mention these together here as recalling more clearly how great was the change which followed in the large place afterwards given to illustrations. This was in part, but only in part, due to the influence of the American magazines. More and more the engraving encroached upon the pages, till at last it became almost more important than the literature. To what perfection the engraving could be carried was perhaps best seen in Macmillan's *English Illustrated Magazine*. In this general aspiration after higher standards *The Leisure Hour* had part. It would be a deeply interesting chapter if we could add an account of all the magazines that appeared and vanished while *The Leisure Hour* held on its way.« (»Fifty Years« 1902: 188)

Following the concept of fiction-carrying periodicals such as the *London Journal* – and the *Leisure Hour* – Strahan/McLeod and Smith/Thackeray, with *Good Words* and the *Cornhill*, respectively, realised the potential of this format mixing fiction and non-fiction. These two magazines, which were initiated at the same time, ran a fierce competition, with Strahan increasingly modelling his *Good Words* on the success of the *Cornhill*, while at its initiation *Good Words* appeared more indebted to the *Leisure Hour* (see Chapter 4). Turner clearly sees the *Cornhill* as formative for the Sixties magazine:

»*Cornhill* [in the 1860s] essentially defined and opened up a new periodicals market in Britain – the middle-class family market. These readers, together with the circulating library readers (and the two were not necessarily different), formed the bulk of [its] audience.« (Turner 2000: 5)

Especially the *Cornhill* and *Good Words* are repeatedly lauded as prime exemplars for these illustrated magazines of the Sixties. Cooke's first mention of a magazine title in the definition quoted above interestingly is the *Leisure Hour*, but he then goes on to introduce the ›Big Three‹, presenting the *Leisure Hour* as a follower to their conduct. Yet by 1860, the *Leisure Hour* had already been on the market for eight years and undergone several changes. These changes went hand in hand with a shift in editorship, as William Haig Miller, after a three-month sick-leave, passed on the full responsibility to James Macaulay, who had already worked as co-editor for the periodical since December 1858.[33] It is uncertain whether this change in editorial personnel was responsible for the *Leisure Hour*'s changes at the same time; however, a obituary for William Haig Miller in the *Leisure Hour*'s sister publication *Sunday at Home* suggests that Miller, in

---

33 Cf. USCL/RTS CCM (Joint 13 Oct 1858), (10 Nov 1858), (12 Oct 1859), (11 Jan 1860), USCL/RTS ECM (17 Jan 1860) and (24 Jan 1860).

addition to his illness, might have resigned »in face of the advancing claims of the magazines« (Page 1891: 60). The minutes during Haig Miller's absence for the final quarter of 1859 are silent on the initiation of changes; however, the *Leisure Hour* of January 1860 featured a new design and larger format.

Given the development of the periodical market during the late 1850s and the 1860s, a shift in the RTS's rhetoric and *Leisure Hour* design seemed fitting in reaction to the genre's increased acceptability. These changes may arguably have been implemented in reaction to the new competition. At the same time, however, the *Leisure Hour* can be seen as a forerunner to the Sixties magazines, as the RTS's rhetoric may to some extent have paved the way for the respectability of the family periodical format also to a (upper) middle-class audience.

That the RTS had a new audience in mind and adapted to changes in the market is evident in the changes of its appropriation of history, as shown in

Fig. 1: Annual Covers for Leisure Hour *1859 and 1860*

Images published with permission of ProQuest. Further reproduction is prohibited without permission.

Chapter 3 on 1852 and Chapter 4 on 1860. This change is also indicated in the respective cover designs of the periodical's annual volumes, which can be attributed an advertising as well as an ornamental function: As marketing tools, they also provide an idea of what the RTS thought of the *Leisure Hour* and its intended audience. Though both the annual volume cover used from 1852 to 1859 and the new 1860 version (Fig. 1) were designed by John Gilbert, the cover for 1860 had become more elaborate in style: it now not only depicted a paterfamilias reading situation but added other reading situations appealing to or reflecting the *Leisure Hour*'s broader (intended) readership. While a paterfamilias reading situation has been moved to a smaller depiction on the right (spanning generations, with the father reading to his son, needle-working mother and a grandmother), the largest illustration at the centre now also offered a different family reading situation in which the mother read to her intently listening family. Furthermore, a third reading situation depicting four individual readers in a train coach still accounted for a cross-class appeal: two gentlemen, a woman and a worker. The new cover thereby emphasised the increasing diversity of the *Leisure Hour*'s audience in terms of age and class by depicting reading as a means of social mobility and a society-unifying process – an idea which also defined the *Leisure Hour*'s outlook on the past.

3. History for the Working Man: The *Leisure Hour* and the *London Journal*, 1852

In its first issue in January 1852, the *Leisure Hour* had promised readers that they would »learn wisdom from the past«, uniting the »sons of genius and wealth« with »the working man« (see epigraph to Chapter 1). History to some extent played a role in the RTS's marketing campaign for the *Leisure Hour*, as in its advertisements the Society also included the initial series »The Working Man in the Olden Time« and »Shades of the Departed in Old London« (see Chapter 2). The Society foregrounded history for its didactic and entertaining quality and during its initial year used representations of the past specifically to attract a working-class audience in order to compete with periodicals such as the *London Journal*.

In order to understand how the *Leisure Hour* used history to comply with its double audience and counter the secular fiction-carrying periodicals arguably aimed at the working classes, this chapter compares its initial year to the *London Journal*'s use of history in the respective volume. In 1852, both periodicals made vast use of the past in their pages, as is not surprising considering the dominant interest in the past displayed in an elaborate historical culture of the time. Nevertheless, they used the past for quite different ends. Generally speaking, the *Leisure Hour* used historical narratives in order to compensate for its lack of the leading fiction which granted success to the *London Journal*.

History, then, was of a different importance to the *Leisure Hour* than the *London Journal*.[1] This chapter considers the two periodicals' different approach

---

1 Fyfe observes on the RTS's focus on history: »History had been particularly recommended by the *Christian Spectator* as a suitable subject for Christian study, for its illustrations of God's relations with his people, and the high acceptance rate [of authors' proposals for ›Monthly Volumes‹ with historical content, as obvious from the

to the past by first providing an overview which looks at the prominence given to history on their covers as well as their overall use of specific genres, types of history and historical topics. It will then focus on a comparative reading of series on the past presented in the *Leisure Hour* and the *London Journal*. True to their subtitles, the *London Journal; A Weekly Record of Literature, Science, and Art* put its sensational fiction first and also placed entertainment, sensation and romance above education in its historical articles; the *Leisure Hour; A Family Journal of Instruction and Recreation* clearly focused on its didactic and educational aims, using sensation and romance grounded in historical facts as a means to attract new audiences to its moralistic conduct. The *Leisure Hour* obviously did not carry a reference to London in its title – a practice, as Andrew King has shown, common in periodicals at the time, which referred to the ›London Journal‹ as a brand (King 2004: 63-74). The early placement of the series »Shades of the Departed in Old *London*« (my emphasis) within the periodical, however, offered the opportunity to have »London« on the cover as well as refer to it in advertisements (see above) and thereby attract readers from or interested in the metropolis.

OVERVIEW

The reference to the past allowed the Society to present sensational content and cover illustrations as attractive as those of the *London Journal* yet on the basis of historical truth. Considering their cover illustrations, the two periodicals may at first sight not have seemed that different, as John Gilbert (see Chapter 2, Fn 29) served as the main illustrator for both periodicals.[2] Most of the cover illustrations for the *Leisure Hour* presented narrative scenes not unlike the illustrations for

---

RTS minutes] suggests that the committee would have been happy to have more histories than biographies or science works in the series« (Fyfe 2004c: 81).

2   Illustrations in the *London Journal* by Gilbert mainly remained unsigned (cf. also King 2004: 114), while in the *Leisure Hour* they were often signed with Gilbert's initials. In the article »The Battle of Naseby« (1852), which discussed a painting by Gilbert, the *London Journal* did not mention that Gilbert was their main illustrator: »The opening of the British Institution in Pall Mall, enables us to present our readers with an engraving from one of the finest pictures in the whole exhibition. It is from the studio of Mr. J. Gilbert, the popular and well-known artist, and in our opinion is one of that gentleman's happiest efforts in the higher branches of historical and descriptive art« (»Battle of Naseby« 1852: 9).

the *London Journal*'s serialised cover fiction. As the covers presented here show, Gilbert's manner of illustration could make both periodicals look equally didactic (Fig. 2) or sensational (Fig. 3). That the *Leisure Hour* also made use of this famous historical artist clearly shows the Society's awareness of popular demand,[3] as Gilbert's illustrations were probably as important as John Frederick Smith's (1806-1890)[4] sensational historical novels for the increase in circulation of the *London Journal* at this time.

In terms of content, the articles placed on the covers of the *Leisure Hour* in 1852 (see Appendix A, Tab. 3), however, clearly showed a focus on factual approaches. In the *London Journal*, the covers (see Appendix A, Tab. 6) were dominated by two (historical) romances by its star author J.F. Smith; »Minnigrey« ([Smith] 1851-1852) and »The Will and the Way« ([Smith] 1852-1853) were both set during the recent past of the 1810s and 1820s and revolved around family intrigues, foundlings, love interests and romantic scheming. While the *London Journal* thus led with serialised sensational fiction, to which these periodicals arguably owed their success, the *Leisure Hour* often featured factual history on its covers: 29 out of 51 covers during 1852 were dedicated to the past, only 9 of them in the form of fiction, while the others were hybrids of (in decreasing order of genre-attribution) life writing (10), (historiographical) descriptive articles (6) and travel writing (4; with a large number of historical references).[5] The focus of the *Leisure Hour* was thus on person-centred approaches which presented largely male historical actors as role models.[6] The series »Shades of the Departed« ([Stoughton] 1852-1853), for instance, featured five times on the cover and clearly helped set the tone for the periodical's historical programme by presenting male figures – dissenters involved in religious struggles, writers and artists, as well as political and social reformers from the seven-

---

3   On Gilbert's possible resignation in 1856 (USCL/RTS ECM 16 Sept and 28 Oct 1856; USCL/RTS FCM 17 Sept 1856), the Society told him in a letter that »we tremble at the result of your withdrawal from the service. Our periodicals have now reached a large circulation, and this must be owing to their illustrations as much as to their articles. The circulation must soon decline if the illustrations degenerate« (USCL/RTS Corr 23 Sept 1856).

4   On J.F. Smith as novelist for the *London Journal*, see Anderson (1991: 100 and 121), King (2004: esp. Chapter 5) and (2011: 47-51).

5   The other covers were dedicated to travel writing (9; with less historical focus), contemporary fiction (7) and descriptive articles (6).

6   On life writing in the two periodicals, see below, as well as Appendix A, Tab. 5 and 8.

Fig. 2: Covers, Didactic Mode: London Journal *(30 Oct 1852: 113) and* Leisure Hour *(18 Nov 1852: 737)*

Fig. 3: Covers, Sensational Mode: London Journal *(10 Apr 1852: 65) and* Leisure Hour *(23 Sept 1852: 609)*

teenth and eighteenth centuries.[7] Descriptive historiographical topics such as »Gladiatorial Combats« (1852) or »The Boy Crusaders« (1852) appear to have been chosen for their connection to Christian history as well as their potential for implementing adventure and action attractive to a young, male audience. Yet besides its instructive articles on biography, history and science, the *Leisure Hour* also featured fiction on its covers, thus reacting to popular demands of the time.[8] In contrast to the *London Journal*'s sole presentation of long serialised (historical) novels on its covers, the *Leisure Hour* only featured short two-parters in the field of historical fiction during this year (»The Crippled Orphan of the Tyrols« 1852, »Edme Champion« 1852, »Hans the Stranger« 1852), with the exception of the four-parter »Poccahontas [sic]« (1852; see below) in September.

The analysis of both periodicals' covers hence shows that the Religious Tract Society largely used (factual) historical narratives to compete with the *London Journal*'s leading fiction. However, the *London Journal* of course also presented factual content on the past within the body of its pages. In terms of genre, both periodicals showed in their treatment of the past a dominance of person-centred approaches and descriptive reports on past events, cultural artefacts and historical locations. History was in addition often related as historical sightseeing in travel accounts. Though the *London Journal* did not present factual history in cover position, it frequently used illustrations for historical articles presented within the body of the magazine (about two-thirds of them were accompanied by illustrations); by contrast, while factual history with illustrations dominated the covers of the *Leisure Hour*, it only included illustrations for about fifteen percent of the historical articles inside the body of the periodical, and focused there mainly on illustrating travel accounts interspersed with historical references. The main mode of illustration in both periodicals was the presentation of narrative scenes (accompanying the fiction, but also historical non-fiction such as life writing) and – often in connection with travel accounts on historical sights – a

---

7   See Chapter 6 for a close analysis of this series. A similar style of presentation was used for the article »A Start at the Stuart Court« ([Stoughton] 1852b), on a female figure, Margaret Blagge Godolphin. The article »Death in Exile« (1852) focused on a moralising intention by contrasting Napoleon with the philanthropist John Howard. While these biographical accounts more clearly fell onto the non-fiction side, two other articles presented on the cover used a romanticising approach (»Historic Tableaux: The Divorce of Josephine« 1852, »An Incident at the Hotel de Rambouillet« 1852).

8   On the cover of the first issue, we therefore also find fiction as a signifier for the Society's new programme.

reproduction of buildings, landscapes and monuments.[9] In contrast to the *Leisure Hour*, the *London Journal* used a larger breadth of illustration modes for the past in 1852, as its focus on contemporary historical culture (see analysis below) also involved frequently presenting historical objects (especially for its series »Selections from the Exhibition of the Industry of All Nations«, 1851-1852) as well as some statues and portraits.

Overall, both periodicals focused on national history, followed by accounts relating to continental Europe, and there, above all, to France (even more so in the *London Journal*; in both mainly related to Napoleon and the Napoleonic Wars) and Germany (in both mainly related to travel accounts; in the *Leisure Hour* also to life writing), while there was little on the United States and even less on colonial issues; in addition, both frequently featured material on the recent past as well as the late seventeenth century up to the early nineteenth century, and another lower peak could be found for accounts of the Middle Ages, with only few articles on ancient history.

Both periodicals presented large amounts of their historical programme in serialised format, and the remainder of this chapter will focus on a comparative reading of these series as a means of outlining the different approaches to the past taken by the two periodicals. Besides J.F. Smith's serialised novels, the 1852 issues of the *London Journal* contained a variety of series on the past (see Appendix A, Tab. 7) which, similar to the series in the *Leisure Hour* (see Appendix A, Tab. 4), ranged from descriptive accounts over biographical approaches to hybrids between fact and fiction. The teasers provided through the titles given to these series further suggest the differing approaches taken by the two periodicals. Both presented history which appeared focused on national topics (*Leisure Hour*: »Shades of the Departed in Old London«, »Poccahontas: A Story of the First English Emigrants«, descriptive reports on destinations of national historic interest such as Fountains Abbey, Bath, Margate, Clifton, Dover, Hastings, Brighton and the Isle of Wight; *London Journal*: »Forest Tales Comprising Sketches [...] of Our National Forests«, »Lives of the Queens of England«). The *Leisure Hour*, however, showed a tendency to explicitly write a history of or for the working classes (»The Working Man in the Olden Time«, »The Lessons

---

9   R. Mitchell notes that both fiction and non-fiction were accompanied during the nineteenth century by narrative scenes (i.e., »[a type of image] which presents a parallel version of an event or moment within the text«) as well as »supplementary images which claim to be authentic in some way«, such as »photographs of places, events, or people, or copies of portraits, views of sites, or historical artefacts« (R. Mitchell 2000: 24).

of Biography: A Lecture for Working Men«). It took a didactic view on the relevance of the past for the present (»Lecture«, »Shades of the Departed«) and was interested in the authenticity of its historical presentations (»Poccahontas: A Story of the First English Emigrants to North America, Founded on Fact«). The *London Journal*, on the other hand, showed a focus on royalty and prominent personnel (»The Three Napoleons«, »Royal Visits to Remarkable Places«, »Lives of the Queens of England«, »Memoir of the Duke of Wellington«) and a groundedness in contemporary manifestations of (material) historical culture (»Royal Visits«, articles on the »New Palace of Westminster«, »Memoir of the Duke of Wellington«), while suggesting a sketchy approach to history (»Forest Tales: Comprising Sketches of the History, Tradition, and Scenery of Our National Forests«). What is already evident, then, is that the periodicals had different ideas on what kind of history their intended (working-class) audience might – or should – be interested in. Led by different marketing strategies of either commercial or educational success, the *London Journal* appears to have focused on entertainment above instruction, while the *Leisure Hour* used entertainment for the purpose of instruction. This idea can be confirmed by the following detailed analysis of the *Leisure Hour*'s and the *London Journal*'s series on the past in 1852 and their different approach to a fact/fiction boundary in historical narratives.

LEISURE HOUR

For the *Leisure Hour*, three series presented in 1852 will be considered as a means of outlining its initial historical programme: »The Working Man in the Olden Time« (M[erryweather] 1852), »Lessons of Biography« (1852) and »Poccahontas« (1852). They show how the RTS approached the idea of writing a ›history from below‹ in the *Leisure Hour* by also including evangelical principles; furthermore, the Society used the factuality of history – also in fictional accounts – to emphasise didactic and moral notions.

The Religious Tract Society put its programme of including the working men in their treatment of the past (as introduced in »A Word With Our Readers«, H.D. 1852; see epigraph to Chapter 1) into action by positioning the first part of »The Working Man in the Olden Time« prominently in the *Leisure Hour*. The historiographical series commenced in second place in the first issue (on pages 4-7), yet even before the mandatory readers' address introducing the new periodical (on pages 8-10). The series hence both prefigured and exemplified the periodical's historical agenda, presented in »A Word with Our Reader«. The six-part series stretched out over the whole year and it

»purpose[d] [...] to depict [...] the social and moral condition of the working man in the Dark Ages; to peep at him at home; to watch him at his work; and to enter into a contemplation of some of the trials and difficulties with which he was surrounded.« (M[erryweather] 1852: 5-6)

The article was signed with the initials F.S.M., and these initials most probably referred to Frederick Somner Merryweather, the author of the antiquarian-historiographical *Glimmerings in the Dark, or Lights and Shadows of the Olden Time*, published in 1850.[10]

Although the series in the *Leisure Hour* appeared to be based on Merryweather's *Glimmerings*,[11] it was a substantially rewritten version of the book, as it took on a working-man perspective. This was already indicated by the title, which emphasised the focus on a historiography of working men. The series seemed to be interested in constructing historical objectivity, as it made vast use of source material documented in footnotes, and the narrator did not identify himself as being part of any of the groups portrayed. However, the narrator made strong value judgements in presenting the working men as suppressed by both nobility and the Roman church, while he portrayed Christianity as the working men's – so to speak – saviour.

---

10 Merryweather (1827-1900; see also Appendix C) was an antiquary who had worked as a bookseller/publisher in London at mid-century and also edited the *Surrey Comet* and *General Advertiser* (Kingston-upon-Thames) from 1878 on. Other books include *Bibliomania in the Middle Ages* (London, Merryweather, 1849) and *Lives and Anecdotes of Misers* (London, Simpkin Marshall, 1850), the latter of which is also referred to in Chapter 6 of Dickens' *Our Mutual Friend* (1864-1865). The *Leisure Hour* practiced anonymity at this time, yet articles in the very first issue gave the contributors' initials. Hence, the first part of »The Working Man in the Olden Time« was signed »F.S.M.«; Merryweather's name was given in payment listings for the *Leisure Hour* in USCL/RTS CCM (21 Apr 1852) and (17 Nov 1852).

11 The series did not reference Merryweather's *Glimmerings*. For a discussion of periodical series in the *Leisure Hour* and their book counterparts, see Chapter 5, as well as Appendix A, Tab. 18. An earlier, expanded version of the analysis of »The Working Man in the Olden Time« has been published in a different context in Lechner (2013: §§8-14), where more emphasis was given to the comparison with Merryweather's book (see also Chapter 5, Fn 1).

First of all, it is interesting to note that what was referred to in Merryweather's book as »the English people« (see Fn 12 below) was in the magazine version frequently paralleled by or substituted with »working men« or »working classes« – terms which never appeared in the book version at all. By using the term »working men« in this context, the series thus, for instance, seemed to identify the struggles between Saxons, Angles, Danes and Normans as the origin of a class struggle and created a history of progress from the Middle Ages up to the present: While after the Norman Conquest »the condition of the working classes [...] was slightly altered [...] [and they] acquired some few privileges [...][,] the Reformation accomplished the first great step towards the political emancipation of the working classes«. (M[erryweather] 1852: 5-7) Accordingly, the final part of the series concluded that

»[f]rom the Reformation to the present day [the working classes of England] have steadily progressed in social and intellectual comforts, and they now possess privileges and blessings [...] unparalleled in the history of the past. Well may the working man lift up his heart in thankfulness as he ponders upon the records of the olden time, and compares his own free condition, his happy home, his domestic comforts, and his means of education, with the miseries of the toiling bondsmen of former day.« (Ibid.: 726)

Besides focusing on the working men, the series also engaged in a commentary on religion. The topic of the oppression and exploitation of »working men« by the Church during the Middle Ages was thus well chosen as a vehicle for implementing the Christian tone so important for the purpose of the Religious Tract Society. The articles on the one hand pointed out the profits found in Christianity, while on the other they debated contemporary issues of anti-Catholicism on the platform of the past. The article in the first issue, for instance, stated at one point:

»Christianity has always been the friend of the oppressed, and in proportion as her presence has been honoured, so has a nation grown in liberty. Through her influence in the dark ages many a working man, born in servitude, received his freedom, had his children restored, and his home made happy.« (Ibid.: 6)

This was contrasted when the article, for example, accused »monkish chroniclers« of »recording [only] the exploits of kings, the triumphs of chivalry, and the quarrels of churchman«, while

»they have thought it beneath the dignity of their calling to describe the social and moral condition of the *English people*. We read of kings and barons, of knights of the tilt-yard, and of mailed crusaders; we read of monks and nuns, their miracles and works; but find no honourable mention of the *working man*.« (Ibid.: 4; my emphases)

Overall, the series thus stressed the importance of working men for society« and Christianity's involvement in bettering their situation over the course of history, which appears to have been precisely the editors' aim – the equivalent passage in Merryweather's book, for instance, did not feature the sentence referring to the working men, who in the periodical, however, were clearly equivalent to the »English people«.[12] Thus, the series deviated from other popular histories that portrayed the common man during the Middle Ages in that it rewrote such accounts by inscribing the working man into the national historical identity as the »common man«.[13]

The *Leisure Hour* not only tried to make content attractive to its intended working-class audience by including them in such a way in the national historical identity, but it also presented content originally directed at them. Over five

---

12 The corresponding passage in the book reads: »The history of old England has never yet been written; monkish pens have chronicled the deeds of kings and nobles; have extolled the piety of prelates and priests, and related those triumphs of arms, which formed the delight and soul of ancient chivalry; [...] but we have no writer of the middle ages, who thought it consistent with the dignity of his clerkly calling; to tell us of the life and household manners of the English people. We deeply regret this, because we are convinced, by the few scraps of intelligence which are incidentally found in old authors; that if it were possible to describe the hearths and homes of mediaeval life, we should observe a striking contrast between the inconveniencies of that age, and the manifold blessings of the present« (Merryweather 1850: 306-307).

13 This is interestingly the inverse of common Victorian historical narratives as analysed by Stefan Berger: »the narrative construction of ›the people‹ was often used to defuse the disruptive potential of class and to unify the national narrative around issues of constitutionalism, freedom and individualism. Writing national history under the framework of ›the people‹ allowed historians such as Trevelyan to merge class and nation and write an inclusive national narrative« (Berger 2007a: 42). See also R. Mitchell's chapter on Charles Knight's *Popular History of England*: »Liberty and fraternity – if not equality – informed a narrative in which the growth of political and economic freedom and the co-operation of all ranks and classes within the national community guaranteed the progress, peace, and prosperity of the English people« (R. Mitchell 2000: 132).

numbers in July 1852, overlapping both with its series »Shades of the Departed« and »The Working Man in the Olden Time«, the *Leisure Hour* printed »The Lessons of Biography: A Lecture for Working Men«, which, as a footnote stated,

> »was lately delivered at Edinburgh (in connexion with the Educational movement referred to in our journal for March last), by a gentleman admirably qualified, from his position and experience, to be the instructor of others [and which we] [...] recommend to the notice of young working men.« (»Lessons« 1852: 425, Fn)

As such, the lecture can be seen as constituting part of historical culture, and its presentation within the periodical enabled others to also participate.[14] The tone of the lecture, with its direct address to the listeners of the original lecture, appeared even more engaging than the usual conduct in the periodical, as many exclamation marks in instances and the addresses to the listeners led the readers to imagine the situation in the lecture hall. It could in this respect be compared – as a secular alternative – to the sermons reprinted in the *Sunday at Home*. Furthermore, the lecture was full of biographical examples and references to the readers' present-day situation. The overall appeal of the series may thus have lain in the accessible format of the oratory lecture, the possibility to break up reading into even smaller parts with chances to pause after the presentation of an individual biography, as well as the frequent references to the audience's lifeworld. This was achieved through parallels between the subjects' lives and those of the listeners/readers, the relevance of technical innovations to their current (working) situation, or the applicability of the biographies to their own life and progress.

This idea was further emphasised in brief summarising paragraphs after some biographies, and especially in the last part of the series on how readers may change their conduct even if they are no geniuses or are not likely to become famous innovators. In the second to fourth part of the series, the lecturer presented exemplary biographies of what might be termed ›working man success stories‹, that is, biographies of men such as Benjamin Franklin, James Lackington, James Ferguson (all covered in the second article) who from poor or deprived families made their way to financial and intellectual success through ambition, self-improvement through reading and studying, and innovative spirit or

---

14 It appears to have been common for lectures to be printed in tract or collected book form (see also the analysis of Thackeray's »Four Georges« in Chapter 4); however, I have not come across other lectures within the *Leisure Hour*. I was unable to identify who authored »The Lessons of Biography«.

genius. The third part collected the biographies of innovators such as Richard Arkwright, James Watt or George Stephenson to also outline the common Victorian narrative of technical progress and innovation for the advancement of society, while the fourth part, with a reflection on »unwritten biographies« (»Lessons« 1852: 479), led over to the final part's list of lessons to learn from such biographies for the common man in the audience. The personnel assembled here was a selection of what was commonly referred to in »[i]ndustrial biograph[ies] provid[ing] a domestic counterpart to [...] imperial heroes« (Atkinson 2010: 20). Thus, the series was similar to improvement literature such as Smiles's *Self-Help* (1859),[15] which also originated from a lecture course and which had a great appeal.

Both *Leisure Hour* and *London Journal* abounded in 1852 with personalised histories in biographical accounts. In the *Leisure Hour*, however, the historical actors mainly came from a cultural background (see Appendix A, Tab. 5), while the *London Journal* more commonly took the approach of political history (see Appendix A, Tab. 8). Hence, the *Leisure Hour* tended to relate common experiences which readers might identify with in their own lifeworld, while the *London Journal* presented great men or women with a political, military or royal background. The *Leisure Hour* thus tried to inscribe working-class identities into its historical narratives, while the *London Journal* focused more on actors of a higher class.

The inclusion of the series »Lessons of Biography« within the *Leisure Hour*'s first volume is above all interesting with regard to the periodical's approach to history, biography and fiction. The first part stressed the importance of reading, and more specifically the reading of books on biography above history and fiction: »To study biography is in some measure to study history. The biography of a nation is a great part of its history.« (»Lessons« 1852: 426) Thus, the lecturer considered biography »an important supplement to history«, since presenting history without »the actings and character of individual men« would be »like plucking all the plums out of a pudding, and leaving but the paste behind« (ibid.). Biography, on the other hand, »lets us into the secret mechanisms of individual minds« and thereby allows an understanding of

»the motives and principles from which the action in history proceeds; we are admitted to hold converse with the persons of the drama, and to get almost into confidential intercourse with them. For this reason, biography has been called the picture gallery in the halls of history. History, properly, is only the record of the result, on society and the

---

15 On Smiles's approach to biography, see Atkinson (2010: esp. 65-72).

world, of the doings of men. Biography introduces us into the house of the interpreter, and explains the springs by which the operations are carried on and their consequences evolved. Hence, biography is fitted to be more popularly acceptable than either history or any merely didactic discourse.« (Ibid.)

The lecturer thereby laid out the didactic benefit to be gained by identifying with the biographies he then went on to present (see above). This benefit might also be gained through negative examples and included an »encouragement in the journey of life« and the providence of »experience without the sorrowful experience itself« (ibid.: 427).

While the *London Journal* owed its large circulation to its serialised novels, the *Leisure Hour*'s initial compromising approach to fiction was moderate. This is not surprising as the agenda thus introduced in the »Lessons of Biography« held equally true for the *Leisure Hour*'s focus on historical narratives and biographical accounts, as became evident when the lecturer concluded: »[biography] is greatly superior to fiction. Fiction is an imitation; biography is a reality, and cannot legitimately trespass beyond the region of what is actual.« (Ibid.) In retrospect, the *Leisure Hour*'s jubilee number noted of the first volume:

»Fiction, too, occupies a smaller proportion of the space than is usual in our popular magazines of to-day. The long serial story is unknown, a story [i.e. »Poccahontas«] running into four weekly numbers being the longest. It should be noted that the *Penny Magazine*, which preceded, had no fiction whatever.« (»Fifty Years« 1902: 177)[16]

Thus styling the didactic *Penny Magazine* as the *Leisure Hour*'s predecessor, the Society was aware that the little fiction initially presented in its periodical certainly had to be realistic, and they appear to have side-stepped this problem by resorting to historical fiction, such as the four-part cover serial »Poccahontas« [sic] in September 1852.

A look at this longest engagement with fiction during the initial year shows how the *Leisure Hour* was meant to compete with the *London Journal* while compromising its prejudice with respect to fiction. The narrative combined adventure story and romance with a male as well as a female protagonist, and was thus ideally fitting for a family audience, as it presented several characters suitable for identification. As an adventure story of »the First English Emigrants to

---

16 The *Leisure Hour* featured its first serial novel in 1854: »In this volume fiction begins to assume the longer serial form. The principal serial, ›Frank Layton,‹ an Australian story by G.E. Sargent, runs for six months« (»Fifty Years« 1902: 178).

North America« (subtitle) with the excitement of battles between settlers and Indians, the narrative mainly adopted the colonisers' view point via Governor Edward Smith and his men, while the parts focusing on the eponymous heroine Pocahontas related her growing love for Smith. The story started out by portraying Edward Smith's virtuous leadership while founding the first British colony Jamestown in Virginia. This was on the one hand exemplified by his influence on the settlers, as his »urging them to perseverance and industry, and warning them against despondency« as well as his belief in »an equable division of labour« soon led to the successful erection of log houses as well as a balanced settlement life; on the other hand, he was also introduced as focusing on the establishment of »a friendly intercourse with the natives« (»Poccahontas« 1852: 579). The story hence served to introduce a perfect moralistic role model, which was emphasised in its purpose to convince readers, as the subtitle of the story explicitly noted that it was »founded on fact«.

This foundedness on fact appears to have enabled the *Leisure Hour* to present fiction of a melodramatic mode similar to the *London Journal* while using just this means to justify sensation.[17] Descriptions of Pocahontas's feelings for Smith, for instance, were interrupted by a metafictional or metahistorical comment:

»As it was, he [Smith] made it his study to please Poccahontas – little suspecting that in the attentions which he paid her, he was insensibly kindling hopes in the untutored breast of the Indian maid which could never be realized [as he has a wife and children in Britain]. *We are narrating, be it remembered, no fancy story. Poccahontas, we may observe – at the risk of anticipating our narrative – was a real character, and her name is well known to those who are familiar with the early history of America.* Surely some misgiving should have entered Smith's manly heart, some fear lest, in his policy to the Indian, a feeling which he could not extinguish might be kindled in the breast of his daughter.« (Ibid.: 581; my emphases)

At the height of suspense, when Pocahontas came to save the British at one instance, a footnote stated that »[a] marble sculpture in the Capitol at Washington commemorates the services which Poccahontas, on this occasion, rendered to the

---

17 In 1858, Oliphant had criticised the melodramatic tendency in the historical accounts of popular periodicals such as the *London Journal*: »even the little make-weights of history with which some of them ballast their lighter wares, have to be enlivened by an anecdote or a melodramatic scene« ([Oliphant] 1858: 204; see also Chapter 2, Fn 11).

inhabitants of James-town« (ibid.: 596, Fn). In the serial's final part, the transitions from the elaborate narration of the encounter between Smith and Pocahontas over three parts to a summary of Pocahontas's further life was made via a quote from »an American chronicler«[18]. The final summary to the fictional approach hence further drew readers' attention to the fictionalisation of the account by trying to create a distance to the romantic rendering. The ending – like the title – therefore pointed again to the factuality of the story, while in addition concluding with a focus on Christian relevance:

»In our opening chapters we have followed the narrative of a German writer, who quotes, as his authority, the Duke de Werner's [sic] travels in North America. All the events recorded in this [final] chapter are in strict harmony with history; and although, upon comparing the German narrative with the English versions, there are traceable some colouring of a poetic fancy, and some slight variations, yet it is gratifying to know that these differences do not affect the main incidents. That Poccahontas saved the life of Smith by offering to sacrifice her own – that she swam the cold river to give timely intelligence of the destruction of James-town – that she married and died as above related – are real events in her life. Justly, therefore, is her memory regarded with a tender and almost romantic interest. She has been praised in song, sculptured in marble, and embalmed in history. But there is a higher satisfaction even than this. It is pleasing to know that there is good reason to hope that this true heroine was led to a heartfelt acquaintance with the Saviour.« (Ibid.: 627)

The reference was to W.O. Horn's *Poccahontas: Eine wahre Geschichte aus den Zeiten der ersten englischen Niederlassungen in Nordamerika* (1852), in which Horn gave Prince Bernhard of Saxe-Weimar-Eisenach's travel accounts as his source. What was presented in the *Leisure Hour* was hence mainly – apart from the metahistorical interruptions and the validation of the story at the ending – a rather close translation of Horn's story, as the final part also stated: »The account which the German writer has followed differs, we may add, from the English version, chiefly in point of chronological arrangement.« (»Poccahontas«

---

18 The chronicler was not identified in the text, but the quote can be traced to John Howard Hinton's *The History and Topography of the United States* (1830, re-edited 1851). The payment details in the RTS minutes for 1852 indicate that Hinton also contributed to the *Leisure Hour* (USCL/RTS CCM 21 Apr, 18 Aug, 17 Nov 1852), though they do not reveal whether he actually might have contributed to this translation and adaptation of »Poccahontas« (see below).

1852: 627)[19] Given that Horn, in a German biographical account, was denied the sensational qualities of a Eugene Sue or Alexandre Dumas – writers whose fiction had featured in the *London Journal* – while he was asserted to relate genuine sociability and ingenuousness,[20] it is not surprising that the *Leisure Hour* felt confident in resorting to authors from the German Biedermeier, in contrast to the sensation the Society disapproved of in French novels.[21]

The story featured on the four September covers with rather melodramatic illustrations (Fig. 3 and 4). The romantic content of the story's exotic female heroine gave the *Leisure Hour* the possibility of showing rather frivolous images of a lightly dressed aboriginal woman surrounded by her native American tribe and the British colonisers. These illustrations, produced by John Gilbert (see above), presented a past that was similar to or even more exotic than that depicted in Gilbert's work found at the same time on the covers of the *London Journal*.

---

19 Interestingly, the *Pfennig-Magazin* appears to have had the story from the *Leisure Hour* retranslated into German as »Poccahontas: Eine indianische Geschichte« (1855) rather than using Horn's German original as a basis.

20 »Die große Kunst Horn's, die ihn beim Volke so sehr beliebt macht, besteht hauptsächlich darin, – und außer Höfer wüßten wir keinen deutschen Autor, der ihm darin gleich käme – daß er mit den einfachsten, schmucklosesten Mitteln das Gemüth des Lesers zu fesseln und zu rühren versteht. Horn ist weder in seinen Erfindungen und Situationen neu und originell, noch weiß er die Nerven à la Sue und Dumas auf die Folterbank der Erwartung zu spannen, aber seine Kenntniß des menschlichen Herzens, die echte Gemüthlichkeit und Treuherzigkeit, die alle seine Erzählungen durchweht, sein tiefes Gefühl für alles Gute und Schöne, und die einfache, fast naive Weise seiner Form, die er in seltenem Grade beherrscht, machen ihn zu einem Lieblingsschriftsteller des Volks, der überall gelesen wird, wo Gemüth und Treuherzigkeit noch Anklang finden« (Joh. Bapt. Heindl, ed: *Galerie berühmter Pädagogen etc.* 1859, in WBIS World Biographical Reference System 2004).

21 While the *London Journal* used and was inspired by popular French literature, the *Leisure Hour* often turned to popular German narratives; see also Appendix B (Fn 1). Vice versa, the minutes indicate a connection between the *Leisure Hour* and German periodicals, as in 1853, Rev. J. Gossner (presumably Johannes Evangelista Gossner, 1773-1858, who also edited periodicals) »request[ed] to be supplied with the ›Leisure Hour‹, that he may translate portions of it for circulation in Germany«, to which the Society agreed (USCL/RTS ECM 22 Febr 1853).

LONDON JOURNAL

In contrast to the *Leisure Hour*, sensational presentations of history in the *London Journal* were not limited to cover illustrations. As the analysis of three series from the *London Journal* in 1852 – namely, »Lives of the Queens of England« (J.F. Smith 1852-1854), »Forest Tales« (1852) and »Royal Visits to Remarkable Places« ([Hall] 1852b) – shows, the *London Journal* tended to fictionalise its factual presentations of history not to emphasise a didacticism as in the *Leisure Hour* but to foreground romance and entertainment. Furthermore, its historical presentations were more closely intertwined with (material) contemporary practices of historical culture. While not overtly focusing on a ›history from below‹, the *London Journal* also included notions of cultural criticism which could contradict the positive outlook on class history presented in the *Leisure Hour*.

Fig. 4: Cover for Leisure Hour *(30 Sept 1852: 625)*

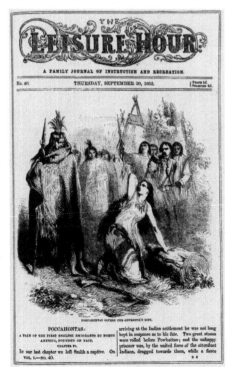

From July 1852 to February 1854, the *London Journal* presented J.F. Smith's[22] »Lives of the Queens of England«, in which Smith took his share in the genre of female royal biographies. Agnes Strickland's *Lives of the Queens of England* (1851-1852 [1840-1848, 12 volumes]) had in this year just been completed in a cheaper re-edition in 8 volumes, and by comparison Smith appeared to lean on her work in many if not all instances. In her preface, Strickland carefully pointed out the need for historical objectivity:

> »›Facts, not opinions,‹ should be the historian's motto; and every person who engages in that difficult and responsible department of literature ought to bear in mind the charge which prefaces the juryman's oath, – ›You shall truly and justly try this cause, you shall present no one from malice, you shall excuse no one from favour,‹ &c. &c.« (Strickland 1851-1852, vol. 1: xi)

Smith, by contrast, in the preliminary observations of his first chapter (i.e., the introduction to the first biography of »Elizabeth Woodville, Queen Consort of Edward IV«, which ran from 24 July to 2 October 1852),[23] marked his series as history but at the same time pointed out his liberty to fictionalise:

> »It has been frequently observed that truth is stranger than fiction. In the sketches of the lives of the Queens of England, which we are about to introduce to our readers, we doubt not but that we shall be able to prove that history is more interesting than romance [...]; the names of many of them are unknown to the general reader, and yet their chequered lives present a page as full of adventure, love, sorrow, and suffering, as any which the imagination of the romancist has created. [...] In painting the literary portraits of these illustrious ladies, we shall adhere with scrupulous fidelity to history. But at the same time we claim the artist's privilege to arrange the material we have found after our own guise, so that the likeness be a faithful one: true taste will never quarrel with the accessories which the painter throws into the picture.« (J.F. Smith 1852b: 313)

In contrast to Strickland, Smith rarely provided sources in his biography of Elizabeth Woodville. Strickland, for instance, was never mentioned, and there was

---

22 In contrast to the *London Journal*'s cover fiction by J.F. Smith, which presented him as the »Author of ›Stanfield Hall,‹ ›Amy Lawrence,‹ etc.« or the »Author of ›The Jesuit,‹ ›Amy Lawrence,‹ etc.«, this factual series was signed with his name. On J.F. Smith, see Fn 4 above.

23 See, by comparison, Strickland's treatment of »Elizabeth Woodville, Queen of Edware IV« (Strickland 1851-52, vol. 2: 315-372).

not a single footnote. Further, where Strickland discussed the inconsistencies between original documents and earlier historians' conclusions, Smith presented a rather straightforward narrative, in which he at instances appeared to either take over Strickland's conclusions from these discussions or to relate traditional findings without acknowledging Strickland's assertions.

This is not to say that Smith's biography contained historical inaccuracies, or rather, the purpose here is not to point to such inaccuracies but to show that Smith's biographies in the *London Journal* followed a different intention as well as regulation through a market logic distinct from Strickland's. While Strickland detailed her evidence in long, explicit footnotes and was hence interested in historical accuracy,[24] Smith's biography fitted into the *London Journal*'s project of sensational entertainment:[25] Smith embellished details on the romance between Elizabeth and Edward and dedicated whole parts of the series to horrific content. These scenes were mainly rendered in imagined dialogues, enhancing readers' emotional involvement in the sensation and adventure. At the outset, Smith still pointed to this imaginative embellishment when relating Elizabeth and Edward's first meeting, though the narrative voice appeared to grow increasingly more convinced in its knowledge of the narrated:

»Tradition has not left us the exact words in which the widowed lady addressed him; and what imagination can supply a mother's eloquence? Perhaps some of his more prudent courtiers whispered in his ear the impolicy of listening to her prayer; but the beauty of the pleader, the romance of the interview, had more power over the amorous heart of Edward than all their prudent suggestions. If for an instant he turned aside – it was but for an instant – the imploring look, the mute entreaty of her tearful eye fascinated him, and the prayer of the petitioner was granted.« (J.F. Smith 1852b: 313)

There was no doubt in the narrator's voice relating the bloodhound chase of Elizabeth's father and brother through the Earl of Warwick and the Duke of Clarence, as this passage focused on presenting the action of the chase in dialogue scene and on describing the terrifying appearance and killing of the dog:

---

24 In the preface to the first edition, Strickland nevertheless stated that »one of my principle objects« was to create »a work of general interest to every class of readers« not chiefly »suited to the researches of the antiquarian than to volumes which [...] may find a place in the popular and domestic libraries of their day« (1840: xi).

25 Tellingly, the US book edition of J.F. Smith's biographies was entitled *Romantic Incidents in the Lives of the Queens of England* (1853). The series was also printed in *The New York Journal: An Illustrated Literary Periodical* from August 1853.

»»Now, John,‹ said Sir Richard Woodville, who saw the approach of the fierce animal with terror; ›now is your time!‹

The sound of the voice caused the dog to raise its head from the ground, to which it had been bent. No sooner did it behold the fugitives than its bloodshot eyes became of a yet deeper red; with a terrific bound it sprang towards them, without taking the slightest notice of Gould. Instinct taught it that he was not the victim he had followed.

Swift as was the motion of the hound, the arm of the woodcutter was yet swifter. With a whizzing sound, something like the hiss of a serpent, the axe flew through the air and buried itself in the skull of the animal, which fell dead, with one deep howl, at the feet of the Woodvilles.«(Ibid.: 326)

Similarly, the account Smith gave of their following execution imagined the scene in close detail and knowledge of the conversation:

»»Do not strike till I pronounce the name of Jesus.‹

›I understand,‹ replied the man.

›Then strike, and strike but once. Thou wilt find withal, in the lining of my doublet, to requite thee.‹

[...] For a few minutes the brother of Elizabeth – who was one of the handsomest men and most accomplished knights in England – remained absorbed in prayer. When he had finished, he twice kissed the block, red with the blood of his father. [...] ›Your prayer is made,‹ he [the ruffian] brutally observed, ›and the axe is ready.‹

With a look of proud defiance, John Woodville laid his head upon the block, and pronounced the sacred name. In an instant the axe fell; and father and son soon slept side by side in the market-place of Northampton.«(Ibid.: 346)

The presentation of the sensational parts of history was here not interrupted anymore by a reflection on historical foundedness but became sensation for its own sake. The *Leisure Hour*'s fictional account on »Poccahontas« inserted metahistorical comments and footnotes to allow for romantic passages, and its biographical series »Shades of the Departed« also, for instance, related the execution of John Russell with much pathos yet in the interest of moralistic, Christian didacticism (see Chapter 6). In contrast to the *Leisure Hour*, where illustrations might have been used to introduce sensation not explicitly found in the texts (though this was rarely used during the first year outside of the illustrations for »Poccahontas«), the *London Journal*'s sensational conduct was further emphasised through the illustrations: While Strickland's book presented a simple por-

Fig. 5: Page from the London Journal's
»Lives of the Queens« (25 Sept 1852: 41)

trait for each queen, each part in the London Journal featured the illustration of
the chapter's prominent narrative scene produced by John Gilbert (Fig. 5).[26]
Smith and Gilbert, who also were responsible for the London Journal's sensational cover fiction, here doubled up to present what was marked as non-

---

26 The illustration entitled »Elizabeth cursing the murderer of her children« corresponded to the following text passage: »»God! [...] the avenger of the widow and the father-
less! Remember the murderer!‹ she added, raising her streaming eyes to heaven, ›and
strike him in his pride; make his heart desolate, as mine is made; a curse – the widow's and the outraged mother's curse – rest on him! Let his name be a bye-rod for
cruelty and treachery throughout the land – scorned and abhorred to future ages!‹«
(J.F. Smith 1852b: 41).

fiction (Gilbert appears not normally to have illustrated the non-fiction for the *London Journal*). The writer/illustrator combination for these biographies here shows a blurring of the boundary between fact and fiction in historical narratives also on the level of production. The blurring of this boundary was also not uncommon to the *Leisure Hour* (as shown with »Poccahontas«), and there, Gilbert produced all cover illustrations for fiction as well as the dominant non-fiction; yet the directions taken by the respective periodicals when crossing this boundary lay at opposites: While the *Leisure Hour* distinctly drew attention to the crossing and used it to support a didactic and Christian tone, the *London Journal* seemed to trespass on the fictional for the enhancement of sensational entertainment.

This agenda of the *London Journal* was also obvious in the five-part »Forest Tales« (1852), which, as their subtitle noted, »compris[e] sketches of the history, traditions, and Scenery of our national forests«. As with many descriptions of historical sights, the genre announced appeared to be non-fictional, but the pattern adopted was a split between non-fiction and fiction: the articles started with a (rather brief) introduction of historical associations and descriptions of the places alluded to, while the articles' main parts were dedicated to love stories with more or (mainly) less historical embedding. Though we may assume that readers were aware that the narratives were spiced up with details of love interests, conversations and emotions which the author probably invented and which might not be ascertained by historical sources, this certainly did not detract from their enjoyment of the tales. And despite this awareness, the historical imagination of past times was presumably still influenced by such invented narratives, as they merged historical facts with fiction with a specific mode of timeless – or rather contemporary – sentiment.

The descriptive lead-ins the *London Journal* used to then present a story most of the time negotiated a national (historical) identity. In the »Forest Tales«, this was achieved by the focus on national forests and their significance for the British, from the Romans, Saxons, Danes and Normans up to the present day. New Forest in Hampshire, for instance, was in the first part described as stable, in contrast to the change of civilisation:

»The landscape of the New Forest, in Hampshire, in the year 1100, was precisely the same hoary fragment of nature as it is in the present day. Man has changed wonderfully since then, but *it* has not altered in the least; and on the 1st of August of that year, a glorious summer's sun shed its splendour over the waving assemblage of oaks and beeches which had sheltered the ancient Britons, the Romans, the Saxons, and the Danes.« (»Forest Tales« 1852: 89)

And in later parts, the forest signified an idyllic, almost utopian space contrasting with the industrial city-space for the English, who »have preserved a passion for forest scenery longer and more fully than any other people« (ibid.: 169). The forest's meaning to the »English« was associated with »the Everlasting«, »Eden« and the »original Paradise« (ibid.), which faced being taken away by modern society:

»From the time of Robin Hood to the present, the process of destruction has proceeded with such relentless severity, that from Nottingham to York, instead of a waving forest, the eye beholds one cheerful and scarcely unbroken expanse of cultivation and industry. Tall chimneys, vomiting smoke to the dense skies above, scattered towns, filled with huge laboratories and squalid dwellings, and old ruins interspersed among halls and hamlets, all speak of the numberless changes which have contributed to the annihilation of the once merry woods of Sherwood. [...] [W]here kings and nobles hunted to the inspiriting strains of the horn, and the welcome baying of the hounds, the shrieking locomotive whirls past towns and villages, cutting up the face of a once smiling landscape into solid tracts, to be regarded in future ages as monuments of the power and splendour of modern civilisation.« (Ibid.)

Forests were defined as »breathing-places«, granting »repose and mediation« to the urban dweller in a rather nostalgic view:

»Apart from its historical associations, which are numerous and exceedingly interesting, its scenery affords to the dwellers amid miles of monotonous bricks and mortar a very lively idea of Nature arrayed in her simplest, unadorned robes. [...] [T]he oaks, hoary and gnarled with age, speak to the eye as well as the mind of things gone by; every magic ring is instinct with revelations of the past, touch them with the wand of thought, and lo! the memories of other ages flash across the mind of the student of history with magic powers.« (Ibid.: 201)

While the purpose of the series appears to have been entertainment through the stories presented in the main parts, the introductions forged an English national identity which was strongly connected to the observation of national forests as witnesses as well as preservers of the past, not only in historical context, but also in an emotional, idyllic or mythically magic image contrary to the changes of modern life.

During this year, the *London Journal* also ran a series on foreign places in Portugal and Normandy and along the German Rhine, which followed the same pattern.[27] The introductions to these articles contained some historical facts on the places, and they commonly presented a connection between the English and what was narrated or negotiated English identity and character with the other nationalities. As with the »Forest Tales«, the main parts of these articles presented romantic stories or legends on love interests obstructed by boundaries of class, origin, pre-dedication or other love interests which were finally, after some fighting, scheming, murder or revolt, resolved into a »happily ever after«. These stories often seemed unconnected to the introductory historical background and would probably have worked without any historical references. They did, however, have a firm place in the *London Journal*'s idea of historical culture: »Forest Tales« and the series on foreign places transported ideas about the (national) past and moulded readers' image of history even with – or perhaps especially because of – their slight rootedness in historical facts and their uncritical use of historical myths. With the non-fictional introductions, the reader was likely to expect that the following would be a narrative of historical truth, and thus, in the *London Journal* even more than in the *Leisure Hour*, it is possible to observe »the blurred and permeable border between historical and fictional texts« (Maitzen 1998: 199; see Chapter 1, Fn 8) at mid-century.

The *London Journal* was most explicitly operating in a factual mode when it brought contemporary historical culture to its readers by commenting on and presenting illustrations of recently erected statues and monuments (especially also in connection with the (re)building of the New Palace of Westminster or in comments on anniversaries for which these monuments were created) or by using other occasions such as exhibitions as triggers for its historical articles;[28] it presented the history of artefacts or innovations in its »Selections from the Exhibition of the Industry of All Nations« (1851-1852), similar to what might have been found in a catalogue of the exhibition; and it repeatedly returned to the ex-

---

27 See on Portugal: »The Convent of Batalha« (1852, 2 parts), »The Foundling Hospital, Lisbon« (1852) and »The Convent of St. Jeronymo« (1852); on Normandy: »The Dead Heart« (1852) and »Mont St. Michel« (1852); on the Rhine: »Marxburg, on the Rhine« (18526), »Bacharach« (1852), »Sternberg and Liebenstein« (1852), »Worms, and its Cathedral« (1852), »Heidelberg« (1852), »Neckar Steinach« (1852) and »Lyons and its Cathedral« (1852).

28 »Sir Robert Peel's Tamworth Statue« (1852), »The Peninsular Veterans' Testimonial to the Duke of Richmond« (1852), »The Nelson Column, Trafalgar Square« (1852), »Memoir of the Duke of Wellington« (1852, 3 parts), »The Duke of Wellington's Tomb – Where Should it Be?« (1852), »The Battle of Naseby« (1852), »Turner« (1852), »Beethoven's Monument« (1852) and »Lord Howe's Victory« (H[all] 1852a).

cavations and findings from Nineveh, not only by describing the same but by including information on other parts of historical culture, such as the exhibition of the Nineveh antiquities at the British Museum as well as Burford's Panorama of Nimrod and Nineveh.[29] These articles connected directly to the present, to parts of material historical culture in the making and accessible to readers in situ; they could walk up to these monuments, could go to the British Museum or the Burford's Panorama at Leicester Square. It is remarkable that this perspective on history appears to have been quite absent from the *Leisure Hour* in 1852, though it had also gained increasing importance in this periodical by the 1860s (see Chapter 4).[30]

Finally, with its series of articles entitled »Royal Visits to Remarkable Places« (H[all] 1852b), the *London Journal* followed a conduct in the presentation of history that stayed strictly within the factual mode. The first three parts, from 19 June to 3 July, were dedicated to »Winchester« and authored by John Parsons Hall (with his signature J.P.H under the third part), who frequently wrote essays for the *London Journal*.[31] These articles on »Winchester« were an exception in

---

29 »Nineveh Antiquities« (1852, 2 parts), »Excavations at Nineveh« (1852) and »Burford's Panorama of Salzburg« (1852). On panoramas, see Hyde (1988); on popular archaeology and the British Museum, see, for instance, Duesterberg (2015) as well as Altick (1978), who also addresses the Burford Panorama as well as the Nineveh exhibition at the British Museum.

30 »A Day in Nineveh« (1852) appears to be a rare exception in the *Leisure Hour* during 1852.

31 See King (2008) on John Parsons Hall as author of these essays. Hall also appears to have authored the essay on »Woman – Her Mission and Destiny« (H[all] 1852c), which was similarly revisionist as it addressed the issue that women had so far not been considered to be »history-worthy« and attempted to present a »history of woman«. Another (unsigned) article in the *London Journal*'s »Essays« series, »Historical Fallacies« (1852), equally reflectively argued that presentations of history needed to be treated with caution. Andrew King notes that these *London Journal* »Essays« were »typical examples of the parergic«, that is, »[t]his split between what is claimed and what is delivered, risible to those with more cultural capital, is exactly where the parergic resides. The style betrays symptoms of inability or *refusal* to ›write well‹. Whether due to resistance, lack of time, money or education, what seems to me to underlie it is resentment at being caught up in and accepting structures of cultural authority while not being in a position to wield that authority. The ›economic literature‹ of which the *London Journal* is an increasingly successful example, does not have high cultural status, yet at the same time it is struggling to validate through the terms

reflectiveness in the journal's approach to the past. While the title suggested a focus on Queen Victoria and descriptions of her travels, this promise was not fulfilled. Rather, the articles on »Winchester« to a great extent displayed a meta-historical account on a redefinition of the Middle Ages, which was, however, triggered by the queen's purpose of introducing the country to her people, as

»[h]er voyages to Ireland, to Scotland, and her visits to the large towns and remarkable places in England, have brought home the history and peculiar features of vast districts of her home empire to the firesides of those who, dwelling at long distances, had only an imperfect conception of them, probably entirely an erroneous one, – and, moreover, gathered as it were several of the extremities of her kingdom together, and by holding them up to general view made the north acquainted with the south, the east with the west, and mighty London itself familiar with the landscape and vital characteristics of some of the remotest concerns in the two islands.« (H[all] 1852b: 232)

Thus, not only the »fruits of inland navigation, stage coaches, and lastly railways«, effected a revolution, which extended to the remotest villages and hamlets«, leading the article to state that »[t]he country is beginning to know itself« while »[u]ntil within the memory of the present generation it was a reproach to the inhabitants of these islands, that their general knowledge of the country was extremely limited«, but the queen was specifically connected with creating this public knowledge by where she travelled, »[t]he ancient city of Winchester this year [being] one of those points of attraction« (ibid.: 232). The first article then provided a brief history of Winchester and a short description of its historical sights, but in the second article, the series turned towards a meta-historical reflection introduced by a meditation on Winchester cathedral and the times during which it was built:

»[W]e unwittingly pay homage to those ages which have been styled dark and barbarous – to those ages which the mere book-men have looked upon as the Great Serbonian bog in which had perished all the knowledge and civilisation of antiquity. The scales of ignorance and prejudice drop from our eyes; and from a clearer reading of the past, we irresistibly arrive at the conclusion that to this period of imputed mental darkness we owe all the discoveries and inventions which have given to the general complexion of modern life so decided a superiority over the vaunted but comfortless civilisation of the ancients.« (Ibid.: 248)

---

of the high what it also and contradictorily imagines as a space for itself independent of the high« (King 2004: 58).

Amongst these important inventions were the »the mariner's compass«, which led not only to geographical but consequently also intellectual expansion, »gunpowder«, which made »warfare less bloody« and secured peace or supremacy and, most importantly, »the invention of printing« (ibid.). Changes were noted to be not only of an intellectual nature but also as having a social dimension, as the Middle Ages were said to have abolished slavery while »creating a middle class of men, unknown to all former times, who, neither masters nor slaves, were to fix their rank in the world by their industry and activity«; as well as promoting emancipation:

»By raising women from the degraded state to which antiquity had sunk them, and from which even Christianity was unable to relieve them, and by making them not the mere instruments of man's pleasures, but the friends and companions of his virtues and his talents, they gave to all the social relations that tone of politeness, sentiment and love, which constitutes the honour and glory of modern civilizations.« (Ibid.: 249)

Finally, education was not restricted by class boundaries, as

»Oxford and Cambridge Universities were not then filled with the sons of gentlemen, seeking to wile [sic] away their times, but with poor men, whose sole chance of preferment lay in their diligence. From the lower classes almost exclusively proceeded the priests, the lawyers, the physicians, and the merchants.« (Ibid.)

While other presentations of the Middle Ages in the *London Journal* tended to foreground the ›dark ages‹ as a time of horror used for sensational entertainment,[32] the articles on Winchester attacked this idea and rather focused on medieval advancements in order to promote a redefinition of the Middle Ages as positive – in contrast to social conditions in contemporary Britain:

»And yet literary compilers will persist in misleading the enquiring, as well as the youthful mind, by the persistent and disgraceful use of the phrase ›dark ages,‹ as applied to those eventful eras in our history. Dark indeed! Why, if the numbers of persons who, in Wykeham's time, were receiving education at the English public schools, be not overrated the proportion of the population which then received instruction, was forty times greater

---

32 Cf. for instance »Lives of the Queens of England« above as well as »Star-Chamber Court in the Palace of Westminster« (1852), »Burford's Panorama of Salzburg« (1852).

than it is now. Our universities were then *open to all classes*, now they are closed against all but the wealthy.« (Ibid.: 249-250)

The »Winchester« articles may therefore have presented an approach to history rather expected from the *Leisure Hour* than the *London Journal*. However, if compared to the progress narrative from the Middle Ages to the present provided in the *Leisure Hour*'s series »The Working Man in the Olden Time« at the beginning of this chapter – demanding the contemporary »working man« to delight in »thankfulness as he ponders upon the records of the olden time, and compares his own free condition, his happy home, his domestic comforts, and his means of education, with the miseries of the toiling bondsmen of former day« – the criticism voiced by Hall towards contemporary society and its regard for the working classes in terms of education following his revision of the Middle Ages was quite different. Hall's comparison to the past accused contemporary society of reserving education for »the wealthy«, while the *Leisure Hour* claimed to include both »the working man« and »the sons of genius or wealth«. The *London Journal*, for commercial reasons, presented to a large extent sensational historical content which its buyers *wanted* to read, hence granting them a sufficient circulation The RTS, following its ideological cross-class double-rhetoric, aimed to appeal to both a working-class audience and their middle-class supporters. In contrast to the *London Journal*, the *Leisure Hour* therefore presented a historical programme based on what the Society – or their evangelical members – thought new readers *ought* to read. The two periodicals' historical programmes were thus defined by a different market logic, which resulted in diverging approaches to sensation, didacticism, fact and fiction in their outlook on the past.

4. Images of History:
The *Leisure Hour, Good Words*
and the *Cornhill Magazine*, 1860

For its initiation in 1852 as a religious alternative to popular but rather secular and sensational periodicals such as the *London Journal*, the *Leisure Hour* had used history as its main tool to circumvent its supporters' criticism while at the same time aiming to make the periodical hopefully attractive to an unconverted working-class audience. By 1860, the *Leisure Hour* had already been on the market for eight years, and the new year brought with it a change in editorship and design (see Chapter 2). The most profound change appeared to be the adaptation to readers' demands for fiction and entertainment. The experience gained from the competition with the *London Journal* probably led to the realisation that fiction was an important feature for drawing in a large cross-class audience. This also resulted in a refocusing of the periodical's historical programme, which now showed an increasing immersion in (material) Victorian heritage culture while toning down religious content even more. With the arrival in 1860 of illustrated family magazines aimed at an (upper-)middle-class audience, such as *Good Words* and *Cornhill*, and with an increased respectability of the genre, the use of illustrations also gained more importance in the *Leisure Hour*'s historical programme during »the great age of history painting« (Strong 2004: 56).[1]

---

1 Roy Strong notes on Victorian history painting: »Roughly speaking, the painters who inhabited the past fall into three groups stretching from the post-Napoleonic period to the close of the century. The first contains the earliest essays of the 1820s and 1830s by artists whose main work lay in other genres. They were succeeded during the period 1840-70 by the generation for whom the past was a major ingredient in their intellectual background and in that of their public. By the close of the century, the tide had ebbed, and activity was confined to an ever-shrinking group of Academy painters who

This chapter hence reads the *Leisure Hour*'s historical representations in 1860 in the context of its new competition, the more strictly religious *Good Words* as well as the up-market *Cornhill*. As with the comparison between the *Leisure Hour* and the *London Journal* in 1852, the chapter starts with an over-view which considers the importance given to history on the periodicals' covers and then briefly compares their overall use of genres and illustrations when ap-proaching the past. Finally, the chapter's main focus will be on the comparison of the varied use of illustrations for person-centred approaches to the past. With the importance of illustrations for the success of the Sixties periodicals, the ana-lysis of the three periodicals' historical programme will devote specific attention to articles on the past accompanied by illustrations in focusing on reading them as »dual texts« (Cooke 2010: 121), that is, it will consider how illustrations in-teracted with textual genres and how texts addressed illustrations.[2] Furthermore, Juliette Atkinson notes that »the nineteenth century was almost as strikingly the Age of Biography« as it »was the Age of the Novel« (Atkinson 2010: 14), though there is a »comparative paucity of studies devoted to Victorian biog-raphy« (ibid.: 10). Roy Strong in addition defines portraits and biographical paintings as an important field in Victorian history painting:

attempted to continue a tradition from which the vitality had already gone. [...] The period 1840-70 was the great age of history painting« (2004: 55-56).

2   This study's approach, like that of Simon Cooke, builds on Gerard Curtis's (2002) as well as Julia Thomas's (2004) ideas on the text/image relation. Curtis notes that »[n]ineteenth-century literary culture in fact drew on a partnership between the textual and visual. Early in the century the line made by the pencil (the visual/ artistic) and that made by the pen (the textual) were united in the Victorian mind« (Curtis 2002: 1). Similarly, Thomas proposes that »[w]hile the majority of critical discussions focus on *how* these genres [Victorian painting and illustration] signify (the artistic mechanisms they employ, their modes of production, and so on), this analysis looks at *what* they signify, and, indeed, the ways in which these two aspects of signification [i.e., text and image] are connected. Meanings are generated, I suggest, in the very interaction be-tween the textual and visual, the points at which they coincide and conflict. These meanings, moreover, are highly political because they are bound up in the cultural events and assumptions that mark the moments of their creation and circulation, from issues of national and international significance (slavery and colonization) to those that are seemingly more domestic (what women should wear and how they are meant to behave)« (Thomas 2004: 15). See Chapter 1 (Fn 45) on Simon Cooke's idea of »dual texts« as well as further literature on this phenomenon. On the necessity to in-clude visual (and material) evidence in historians research, see Jordanova (2012).

»In an age of renewed evangelical piety and religious revival, patterns of the virtuous life needed reinforcing by example, and although Britain as a Protestant country could not turn to the cult of saints, it could make use of its historic mythology. Kings and queens, poets and writers, statesmen and men of action, as they became known through the spread of literacy and the popular reading of national history, took on roles within a pantheon of virtue and vice. The National Portrait Gallery was founded at the close of the 1850s with precisely this in mind. So history was reduced to a parade of heroes and heroines, which of course could all too easily become trivialized.« (Strong 2004: 61)

This chapter will hence focus on the predominant presentation of the past in person-centred approaches in the three periodicals in a comparative reading of their text/image presentations of history.

A look at renderings of the past in text and image in these three periodicals during the year 1860 shows that they used a larger breadth of illustration genres accompanying various text formats, yet with quite different agendas (see also the Periodical Profiles in Appendix A, Tab. 1). The *Leisure Hour* used this combination for the purpose of didactic entertainment, as indicated by its changed masthead. While the subtitle *A Family Journal of* Instruction *and Recreation* (my emphasis) still put education first, a redesign of the masthead now presented the subtitle in one line, thereby not giving prominence to »Instruction and Recreation« as before, and in addition featured the Cowper motto »Behold in these what leisure hours demand, – *amusement* and true knowledge hand in hand« (my emphasis), thus putting entertainment first. *Good Words'* subtitle »A Family Magazine for Leisure Hours and Sundays« clearly placed Strahan's journal in the original, conservative *Leisure Hour* and *Sunday at Home* tradition from the outset (cf. also Turner 2000: 67),[3] which was further emphasised by the use of double-framing of pages reminiscent of the *Leisure Hour*'s design until 1860, in contrast to its now new, modern layout.[4] It also started out as more strictly reli-

---

3 *Good Words* editor Strahan tried during the first years to integrate features from its competitor *Cornhill*, and, as Turner amongst others observes, the »transformation of *Good Words*« away from the religious weekly towards the direction of the secular monthly set by the *Cornhill* would be »complete« by 1864, with its »circulation nearly tripl[ing] that of *Cornhill*« (Turner 2000: 86).

4 From January 1860 on, the *Leisure Hour* featured a more modern design for its weekly covers. The size and paper quality were still the same, but the page design was lightened up through the removal of the double framing of pages, enabling the periodical to present a larger cover illustration as well as increasing the breadth of the double

gious than the *Leisure Hour* in its representations of the past. Yet both *Leisure Hour* and *Good Words* were still printed in double columns (associated with products of a lower standing). The *Cornhill*, by contrast, did not make use of columns; with its clear set-up as a monthly of 128 pages and an article length averaging 10 pages, the *Cornhill* could take a more intellectual approach in its presentations of the past than the other two weeklies.[5]

OVERVIEW

The three periodicals' covers for 1860 already outline a very different approach to the past. In contrast to 1852, all covers of the *Leisure Hour* for 1860 featured fiction (see Appendix A, Tab. 9).[6] Some of these serialised novels, and especially the short two-parters, were still historical – if in some cases, however, only referring to the (very) recent past and using history as a backdrop only for the ra-

---

columns. Also, the masthead did not sit on the top of the cover so heavily anymore as it was more clearly defined through the use of shadow-play for the magazine's title.

5   The *Leisure Hour* had a weekly volume of 16 pages with an average article length of 2 to 3 pages; *Good Words* also amounted to 16 pages per week with an average article length of 1.5 to 2 pages; the *Cornhill* therefore had about twice the volume of the other two periodicals and presented two volumes per year rather than one annual volume.

6   The featured fiction in this volume also indicates the breadth of audience the RTS focused on. The covers for 1860 featured a range of characters as well as a variety of narrative scenes, and the cover illustrations announced the genre of the fiction: domestic novels' illustrations (Walshe's »The Ferrol Family« 1860; Sargent's »Ralph Draper« 1860) switched between the depiction of men or women mainly placed in a domestic setting or, rarely, at gatherings such as in ballrooms; as a domestic novel moving towards the social, the »The Story of the Crooked Sixpence« (1860) also had illustrations that made class and age differences clear by showing »poor« and precarious people of different generations next to representatives of other classes; adventure stories mainly set in the colonies (»The Coast-Guardman's Yarn« 1860, Brooke-Knight's »The Captain's Story« 1859-1860, »A Night in the Bush« 1860) were accompanied by illustrations of scenes set outdoors, depicting people in action in foreign landscapes, on horseback or on the sea. Hence, readers would most probably have been able to judge from the cover illustrations which genre the story belonged to and what the dominant intended audience would be.

ther modern stories.[7] This was in contrast to both of the other periodicals, which in 1860 rarely led with fiction. *Good Words*, very similar to the *Leisure Hour*'s conduct in 1852, dedicated 28 covers to articles or series on the past (see Appendix A, Tab. 12). Of these only three may be classified as fiction – an instalment from Sarah Tytler's historical novel »Lady Somerville's Maidens« (whose other parts were presented further back in the body of the issues),[8] a poem and a fictitious diary entry – while the other 25 covers dedicated to the past featured factual history mainly in the genre of life writing (17), with some travel writing (4) and descriptive historiographical reports or essays (4). In its layout, *Good Words* appeared to set out as a competitor to the *Leisure Hour* in Scotland, with close resemblances to the RTS periodical's design. Its religious conduct was more explicit, and history as Bible history, history of Christianity and missionary history took up a large portion of the content in prominent front positions, emphasised by its presentation in mainly serial formats (see Appendix A, Tab. 13),[9] for in-

---

7 Cleary set in the past were »Father Pedro's Convert« (1860; set in sixteenth-century Malaga) and »Barthel Winkler« (1860; set in mid-eighteenth-century Germany); relating to the more recent past were »The Ferrol Family« ([Walshe] 1860a; set around 1832), »The Captain's Story« ([Brooke-Knight] 1860; set »thirty years ago«) and »A Night in the Bush« (1860; set in 1852); thus, set in contemporary times were only three of the eight cover fictions: »The Coast-Guardman's Yarn« (1860; though [pseudo-]autobiographical fiction), »Ralph Draper« ([Sargent] 1860) and »The Story of the Crooked Sixpence« (1860).

8 The chapter from Tytler's serialised novel on 3 June 1860 was accompanied by an illustration conducted by Keeley Halswelle (1832-1891), a book illustrator and painter living in Edinburgh at the time, whose name was attributed to the illustration in the annual index. While 15 of the novel's 24 parts in *Good Words* were accompanied by illustrations (with two changes in illustrator over the course of its serialisation), this was the only part that featured on the cover. Apart from one frontispiece, Tytler's novel was published unillustrated in book format as *The Diamond Rose* by Strahan in 1867. For a brief discussion of »Lady Somerville's Maidens« in the context of *Good Words*, cf. Srebrnik (1986: 39-40); Srebrnik was not able to establish Tytler's authorship for this anonymously published work and therefore assumed incorrectly that Tytler had first written for the *Cornhill* in 1861 and had afterwards been won over to write for *Good Words* (1986: 46).

9 This table presents all series on the past found in *Good Words* during 1860 (i.e., not only those in cover position). For a comparison (also to the respective table for 1852), see Tab. 10 and Tab. 16 for series on the past in the *Leisure Hour* and the *Cornhill* during 1860.

stance with a series of articles on Scottish saints[10] as well as the biographical series »Missionary Sketches« (1860) and »Pictures from the History and Life of
the Early Church« (1860).[11] As a monthly, the *Cornhill* dedicated six of its 12
covers to history (see Appendix A, Tab. 15). All of them focused on national history, with five approaching this via life writing.

While the *Leisure Hour* led with (historically themed) fiction during this
year, the importance of factual historical representations had decreased in comparison to 1852, for instance through its placement further back in the issue
body. In terms of genre, all three periodicals showed an emphasis on life writing
(as already indicated by the cover presentations of *Good Words* and the *Cornhill*), followed by descriptive and – a special focus of the *Cornhill* – essayist approaches; furthermore, both *Good Words* and the *Leisure Hour* included travel
accounts, though this format was of more importance in the *Leisure Hour*. Like
the *London Journal* and the *Leisure Hour* in 1852, all three periodicals again focused on national history, though in *Good Words* more Scottish and Irish narratives were given a voice. *Good Words* – with a specific focus on missionary narratives already visible in its approach to Ireland – covered colonial issues and
empire history, as did the *Leisure Hour* to a considerable extent, but such an approach appeared largely absent in the *Cornhill*'s representations of the past in
this year. All three included historical perspectives on the continent: *Good
Words* especially focused on Protestant and evangelical narratives from Germany; this could to some extent also be found in the *Leisure Hour*, which showed,
however, a more even distribution by also including Italian as well as Spanish
accounts; the *Cornhill* only rarely covered the continent, and if so then mainly in
references to ancient history. Similar to the *London Journal* and the *Leisure
Hour* in 1852, a general focus lay in recent accounts or accounts from the late
seventeenth to the early nineteenth centuries, though the *Cornhill*, with its series
on »William Hogarth« ([Sala] 1860) as well as »The Four Georges« ([Thacker-
ay] 1860a), presented more on the eighteenth century, and *Good Words*, with its
presentation of early religious history, displayed an unusually large focus on the
Middle Ages and antiquity.

---

10 »The Story of Ninian: Scotland's Earliest Missionary« (12 Feb 1860); »Kentigern«
(26 Feb 1860); and »St Columba« (2 parts, 12-24 June 1860). All of these biographies
of Scottish missionaries from the fourth to the sixth century were presented with narrative cover illustrations.

11 Though the title presents these sketches as »Pictures«, the first part was unillustrated,
while the other two parts featured narrative cover illustrations.

History made up a large portion of the content of these three periodicals, and it often came with illustrations. The illustrations for the cover fiction of the *Leisure Hour* appeared to serve mainly an ornamental or advertising function in that they made stories (more) attractive by signifying the genre to the reader (see Fn 6 above) and introducing sensation or suspense possibly beyond the texts' actual content. The initial illustration for »Father Pedro's Convent« (1860: 241), for instance, placed the story in the genre of historical adventure fiction. The illustration's title »Discovery of Hidden Treasures« indicated the suspense created by the image; it depicted a key scene of the story and attracted the readers' curiosity to find out the secret of the treasure and its discovery story. However, the story itself did not really support this idea of suspense and action but was a rather boring telling of events. The illustration made the story appear more attractive than it was, adding a layer of suspense and refocusing the story's conduct.

The illustrations to factual texts often served additional purposes. Through the selection of illustrations, specific aspects of texts might be highlighted or additional information going beyond the texts' content provided. Not considering the cover fiction, the *Leisure Hour*'s 1860 volume had about three dozen illustrated articles and *Good Words* more than two dozen,[12] while *Cornhill* (as a monthly with a larger page average per article) had about 20 illustrated articles which fell into a broad definition of history. This means that in the *Leisure Hour* we find an average of about three illustrated articles concerned with the past in a monthly number, that is, about two of three weekly numbers contained an illustrated article on the past. *Good Words* presented about two per month (or three per month if we include illustrated historical non-fiction on the covers), and the *Cornhill* had an average of only one factual historical article accompanied by illustrations per month (or two including illustrated non-fiction on the covers).

While fiction was illustrated throughout with narrative scenes, the factual texts on the past also made use of other illustration genres, such as portraits, images of landscapes or material objects like buildings or statues, or they presented sketches of objects or signs as well as maps.[13] This breadth of illustration for the past was mainly used in the *Leisure Hour*, which here seemed to have learned

---

12 This, however, included the 14 illustrated parts of the serialised novel »Lady Somerville's Maidens« ([Tytler] 1860), which were presented in the issue body rather than on the cover. In the *Leisure Hour* for 1860 there was no illustrated historical fiction detached from the issue cover.

13 On different types of illustrations, see Chapter 3 (Fn 9).

from the *London Journal*'s idea of historical culture:[14] Historical representations in the *Leisure Hour* in 1860 often showed a connection to material historical as well as heritage culture, which is evident in the frequent combination of travel writing, life writing and corresponding illustrations of buildings, sceneries and statues. *Good Words* and *Cornhill*, by contrast, focused on narrative scenes. This is not surprising considering their presentation of artistic illustrations, which in the case of *Good Words* were mainly by Scottish artists whose names were also presented in the annual index. In addition, the *Cornhill* – in connection with its series »William Hogarth« – appeared even more to nurture an audience interested in high culture through the inclusion of painting reproductions. *Good Words*, which during this year appeared generally more conservative in text and image, made more use of portraits for its life writings than either of the other two periodicals.

As stated above, all three periodicals included a large amount of person-centred history accompanied by illustrations (see Appendix A, Tab. 11, Tab. 14 and Tab. 17). In his study on serialised fiction in the Sixties magazines, Cooke shows how the illustrations guided or even changed readers' perception of the texts, considering that readers consumed both text and images together – and maybe even with an emphasis on the illustrations (cf. Cooke 2010: Chapter 4). This also holds true for the illustrations to historical non-fiction. Therefore, it is important to consider illustrations not just as an ornamental addition to but also as a semantic interpretation of the written word as well as an intentional constitutive part. The remainder of this chapter will therefore analyse the three periodicals' historical programmes via their life writings by comprehending them as »dual texts«. Unlike the collaborative production of serialised novels in text and image analysed by Cooke, in which authors and illustrators are most of the time known, for the historical non-fiction it is often difficult to establish which kind

---

14 In her study on the use of images in second generation magazines, Anderson in a way also notes this breadth of illustration modes for the *London Journal* when she states that these periodicals »emphasiz[ed] design and its applications over painting and sculpture«, thereby »validat[ing] the prevailing view that there were two kinds of aesthetic experience: for the privileged, the history, theory, and imagery of fine art; and for the people, the principles and exemplars of practical design« (1991: 124). Anderson's conclusion that this stands for the »culturally depleted [...] chorus: work hard; improve yourself; learn design skills; increase English productivity – in short, be civilized according to your station« (ibid.) seems to regard these periodicals under the perspective of cultural pessimism by reinforcing an idea of the superiority of »artworks«, thereby rather devaluing the breadth of their cultural achievement.

of images were specifically produced for original presentation in the periodicals.[15] In some instances it is quite clear that the periodicals appropriated existing graphic material (such as photographs, paintings, engravings, monuments). These reproductions of older picture material therefore reflected the historicity and image conduct appropriate at the originals' time of origin. Yet to actively make the determination of whether the graphic material presented was original or reproductive would presumably not greatly have influenced readers' perception of an image as conservative, innovative or sensational (at least in instances where this was not explicitly addressed in the text).

If we compare the fields, periods or spaces from which the three periodicals selected their historical actors, it is already obvious that they followed quite different agendas in their use of the past. The *Leisure Hour* mainly focused on British persons from the political arena, but also included or combined this with the field of cultural or everyday history (see Appendix A, Tab. 11). Furthermore, the use made of illustrations in these articles and series shows that the *Leisure Hour* had since 1852 moved further towards the *London Journal*'s immersion in contemporary (material) historical culture and connected to Victorian heritage culture. Biographies still supported a didactic function implemented through historical examples – though meta-historical comments and ironic criticism of such practices can also be found, as can some slight notions of a more scientific approach to history.

In its life writings during 1860 (see Appendix A, Tab. 14), *Good Words* took a much more decidedly Christian approach by focusing on missionaries, saints and martyrs, and meta-historical comments were also restricted to a discussion of how (or why) to approach religious history and biographies. Most of the life writings in *Good Words* were accompanied by narrative sketches, while portraits as in the *Leisure Hour* (which, however, showed a broader variety of illustration types for life writing than *Good Words*) only played a minor role.

Both of these religious periodicals took an approach in 1860 that was very different from the rather intellectual, meta-historic presentations provided in the *Cornhill*, which more decidedly appeared to immerse itself in academic ideas of the practice of history. The persons covered in the *Cornhill*'s biographical articles came mostly from the area of the arts and humanities,[16] and meta-

---

15   It can be assumed that most narrative scenes were produced specifically for display in the periodicals; only in the case of *Good Words* was the use of material very obvious, as artists' names were attributed in the table of contents.

16   Exceptions were an article on the explorer John Franklin and Thackeray's 4-parter on »The Four Georges«.

historiographical comments were used to underline a humorous treatment as well as to introduce a justification against more scientific historiography. As can be seen in Appendix A (Tab. 17), only very few of these person-centred depictions of the past in the *Cornhill* came with illustrations.

LEISURE HOUR

The *Leisure Hour*'s volume index for 1860 listed 27 entries under the category »Biography«.[17] This included almost all of the life writing we find in the volume. Jerdan's »Men I Have Known«, which stretched in 45 parts from 1859 to 1865 and had four parts in the 1860 volume, was not listed under this category, but being a longer series was given a separate entry under its title. Although the series presented written portraits of contemporaries whom Jerdan had met in his lifetime, it is remarkable that – in contrast to the book publication – the series in the *Leisure Hour* was entirely unillustrated.

Portraits only played a minor part in the choice of illustration for life writing. Though 12 of the 27 articles indexed in the annual table of contents were illustrated, the table of contents only indicated this for six entries, stating that five were accompanied by a portrait (Fig. 6-7, 11)[18] and one by a cut of a statue (Fig. 8).[19] All of the five persons depicted with portraits in the *Leisure Hour* were public figures of contemporary interest, mainly in the field of politics, who had recently died (Macaulay, Stephenson) or were still alive (Brougham, Grey, Lawrence).

The illustrations accompanying these articles mainly made use of already available photographs or portrait paintings of the respective persons. As such, these illustrations can be attributed, in the first instance, simply to the function of giving a face to the person sketched in the text. Yet the way the persons are de-

---

17 A categorisation of specific rubrics (Biography, Poetry, Tales and Narratives) within the *Leisure Hour*'s alphabetical annual index first occurred in 1859. Other content was given mainly by title in alphabetical order, only singling out series as further specific rubrics.

18 These were the entries for Brougham, Grey, Lawrence, Macaulay and Stephenson. In contrast to the other articles, Brougham's portrait with a reproduction of his signature was presented without accompanying text, an unusual exception for the *Leisure Hour*. Stephenson's portrait also differed from the others, as it was included within a collage of images – and his biography stretched over two parts (see analysis below).

19 This was the entry for Clive (see further analysis below).

picted served as a further means to characterise them as gentlemanly (Fig. 6 and 7), thereby emphasising the texts' intention to present them as role models and hence continuing the *Leisure Hour*'s 1852 agenda towards biography, as outlined in the previous chapter.

When one looks at the interplay between text and image, further functions arise, as the following examples for Macaulay and Lawrence show. The obituary presented on the historian Thomas Babington Macaulay (1800-1859) – which quoted largely from an article in the *Times* as well as a French obituary – presented him as almost larger than life in his achievements as historian as well as politician and poet. For instance, the text stated: »Orator, essayist, poet, and historian – in all these fields of literary activity Macaulay has won for himself the first place« (»Lord Macaulay« 1860: 135); that he »had a more intimate ac-

Fig. 6: »Lord Macauly«, Leisure Hour
(1 Mar 1860: 137)

Fig. 7: »Sir John Lawrence, G.C.B.«,
Leisure Hour *(5 Jan 1860: 9)*

quaintance with English history than any man living, or perhaps any man who ever lived« (ibid.); and that he

»possessed in the highest degree the intellectual and moral qualities of the true historian; he judged men and parties with an elevation of view, and impartiality and a rectitude which give a special authority to his eloquent and solid writings.« (Ibid.)

Where the text interacted with the image, however, the portrait helped to create an almost intimate familiarity between readers and the historian. The biographical sketch included the following passage linking to the portrait (Fig. 6):

»›We have before us,‹ continues M. Peyrat, ›while we write these lines, the portrait of Lord Macaulay, and when our eyes rest on it, we fancy we are again enjoying the rapid moments during which, five years ago, we had the happiness of seeing and hearing him. We are sure that no one who ever knew him, or ever read him, will dispute the justice of the homage we pay to his memory. Such men, whatever country they may belong to, are the glory of the liberal cause; and we believe that it is for the interest and the honour of Liberty to grave their names on the column which commemorates those who have sincerely loved and practically served her.‹« (Ibid.)

Through the accompanying portrait of Macaulay, readers were included in and meant to empathise with the experience related by Peyrat. The portrait was presented as if it were the one Peyrat had been viewing when writing about Macaulay, and the readers were now viewing it together with him. The interplay between text and image clearly strengthened the idea of Macaulay's achievements and commemoration.

On the other hand, as can be seen by the example of the article on the viceroy of India Sir John Lawrence (1811-1879), text and image could also stand in contrast to each other. The gentlemanly portrait of Lawrence (Fig. 7) was called into question by the interplay with the text. The biographical sketch was characterised by a humorous conduct, observing, for instance:

»We, in our gratitude, bind wreaths around [the] brows [of really great men], heap titles on their heads, and fling heavy roles of office round their limbs; but they just shake themselves, and are *men* again.

The subject of our memoir is one of this stamp – emphatically a *man*; and it is with a real hearty satisfaction we bid our readers come with us, and look into his grand, grim countenance. Don't be in a hurry. Look at it well. There's much of the Sphinx in it. Brown, Jones, and Robinson, pic-nic-ing at the foot of the Pyramid, look up from a chick-

en pie, and say (in their slang way) that the Sphinx is ›by no means beautiful.‹ But the ages have seen a mystery and a power in that colossal face, and still come back to peer into
its granite lines, and try to unroll the mummy spirit of the past. And here is a human face
as full of meanings for us living men, embodying, as we think, the better spirit of our day
– the spirit of work and duty. Let us unroll its history, as far as we know and understand
it.« (»Sir John Lawrence, G.C.B.« 1860: 8)

This meta-historical introduction to the biographical sketch contrasted the accompanying prototype gentlemanly portrait cum autograph and thereby criticised
the conduct of role-model portrayal commonly presented in the *Leisure Hour*.
By looking at the practice of hero worship[20] and the creation of role models from
a humorous meta-historical level instead of solely participating in it, the article
managed to ironise and reinforce Victorians' views on eminent persons (and
possibly history *per se*) at the same time: It on the one hand presented a ridicu-
lous everyday scene at the Pyramid and thereby pointed on the other hand to the
humanness of the actors, identifying their eminent portrayal in parts as a reduc-
tive construction.

Similarly, an article on the erection of a statue to Robert Clive (1725-1774),
who had served as army officer in the East India Company, for the centenary of
the Battle of Plassey seemed to pick up on this idea of questioning the heroic
role-model status of eminent men. The text included a long excerpt from Colonel
Herbert Edwardes's speech at the erection ceremony, emphasised in the article
as »a speech worthy of the occasion« (»Lord Clive« 1860: 153). In the excerpt,
Edwardes picked up on arguments which »deprecate such memorials and call
them hero-worship«, while others »are quite willing to pay honour to a hero,
provided that he be perfect, and that Clive was a man of imperfections« (ibid.).
Edwardes concluded with the compromise: »If we, too, are men, let us honour
what is good and great in our fellows, while we sorrow for their faults« (ibid.).

While Lawrence's portrait might have characterised him as a gentlemanly
role model and the image of Clive's statue (Fig. 8) suggested that he was a worthy, honorary national hero, the humorous suggestion of how to view Lawrence's portrait and the serious discussion of the hero concept and statue cult

---

20 Atkinson notes that the »Victorian fascination with ›hero-worship‹« also meant that
   »endless articles and essays devoted to untangling the definition of a ›hero‹ demon-
   strate that the word and what it represented were indeed extremely unstable. This in-
   stability meant that space was created for a whole range of individuals to whom the
   label ›heroic‹ could be applied« (Atkinson 2010: 10). See especially Atkinson's chapter on »Victorian Hero-Worship« (2010: Chapter 2).

questioned these suggested readings of the images only. These critical approaches created through the interplay of text and image clearly referred to a meta-referential and meta-historical level by interrogating and addressing practices of hero worship, and thereby slightly critiqued Victorian historical culture; they appear to have been, however, rather an exception in the *Leisure Hour*'s conduct. Despite their slight criticism, these articles still participated in the construction of role models and aimed at a portrayal of history as progressive in the affirmation of the achievements, innovations and values of contemporary society. Even if Lawrence or Clive showed faults, their biographical sketches (though not whitewashed) still emphasised the benefits gained through their achievements. The *Leisure Hour* overall seemed to follow the idea presented in a brief, meta-historical essay »Past *versus* Present« (1860), in which the author emphasised the benefits of present society against the discomfort of previous times in turning against (cultural) pessimists who longed for the »good old times« – in terms of long history as well as one's youth.

Fig. 8: »Lord Clive«, Leisure Hour *(8 Mar 1860: 153)*

Fig. 9: »Charles James Fox«, Leisure Hour *(19 Jan 1860: 41)*

Images published with permission of ProQuest. Further reproduction is prohibited without permission.

Portraits seem an obvious choice to illustrate life writing, and the *Leisure Hour* used them, as stated above, preferably to depict contemporaries in the fashion of the time. Clive's statue cut (Fig. 8) already introduced another mode of illustration, which with the report on its erection was more firmly grounded in a contribution to and participation in contemporary material historical culture. The distance in time of the person referred to was also obvious from the choice of object depicted as well as the attire he was fashioned in. A further example of this kind is the article on the Whig politician Charles James Fox (1749-1806). The biography, initiated by the recent publication of John Russell's *Life and Times of James Fox* (1859) from which it quoted extensively, started out by stating that »many will read with interest these memorials of the great Whig leader, whose statue now faces that of his illustrious rival in the Statesmen's Gallery of the New Palace at Westminster« (»Charles James Fox« 1860: 40). Accordingly, the accompanying full-page image depicted »The Statesmen's Gallery in the New Houses of Parliament« (ibid.: 41; Fig. 9), showing the interior design of the hall with the various historical statues on its sides as well as contemporary visitors to the hall. In contrast to the Clive article, whose image solely depicted his statue without any surroundings, Fox's statue was not specified, but the image placed him within the chronology of statesmen from England's past to whom statues had been erected in this eminent hall in the nation's seat of parliament. Not only was a successive tradition therefore obvious in the image through the different fashions in which these statesmen were depicted, but the historical aspect becomes further obvious through the contrast between the statues and the visitors to the hall, who were wearing modern dress and thus pointed to an everyday immersion in historical culture.

A different immersion in everyday historical culture can be observed in the article on the portrait painter Abraham Wivell (1786-1875), who in »The Fire Escape« (1860) was introduced as the inventor of the fire escape ladder. While images of portraits and statues served to depict the historical actors themselves, the image for the article classified in the *Leisure Hour*'s annual index as a biography for »Wivell, Abraham« in the respective category, did not present a portrait of Wivell but a narrative scene subtitled »Abraham Wivell's Improved Fire Escape« (ibid.: 601; Fig. 10). The image therefore was in accordance with the article's title, while the text focused on Wivell, for whom it demanded a place in public memory; his invention of the fire escape was defined as a monument to his name. This idea formed the frame of the text, as it started: »Abraham Wivell was a man whose name we should not let die, for there is in London a monument to it of unspeakable value« (ibid: 600); and ended:

Fig. 10: »The Fire Escape«, Leisure Hour
(20 Sept 1860: 601)

Images published with permission of ProQuest. Further
reproduction is prohibited without permission.

»Reader, do you not think with us that his life was a remarkable one – that he has conferred a most providential benefit on his country and fellow-creatures, and that the name
of Abraham Wivell is one which our gratitude ought not easily to let die? All honour to
the inventor of the fire escape, and may its usefulness increase tenfold!« (Ibid.: 602)

The image, which was not directly referenced in the text, showed the ladder in
action during a fire with a crowd in the street.[21] It seems fitting, then, that the
image should present just this commemoration of Wivell in the London city
space – instead of a more conventional portrait – thereby making the fire escape

---

21 The image was quite sensational in its mode and may by readers at first have been associated either with the genre of fiction or a report on the calamities of a real fire.

an everyday object of historic significance to the memory of its inventor, like the statues which commemorate the eminence of their heroes.

This idea of depicting objects as monuments of commemoration also figured in the articles on Robert Stephenson (1803-1859) as well as John Kyrle (1637-1724), as both were accompanied by depictions of these men's architectural achievements – amongst others. These two biographies more clearly showed the *Leisure Hour*'s involvement with Victorian heritage culture: the articles featured a variety of small illustrations of, for instance, buildings and landscapes, which normally indicated the genre of travel writing. The biographical sketch »The Man of Ross« (1860) placed the philanthropic landscape designer John Kyrle within everyday historical culture by presenting a day-trip to Ross on a »glorious summer day«. The article was accompanied by three touristy images depicting »Ross, from the Wye«, »John Kyrle's Summer-House« – both of them with a background featuring »the church spire, rising to the height of more than a hundred and twenty feet [which] was erected according to Kyrle's own designs, under his own superintendence, and not without considerable expense to himself« (»Man of Ross« 1860: 439) – as well as the »Market-Place, Ross«. The article also related a visit to Kyrle's »tomb, which is of pyramidal form, and composed of very beautiful variegated marble, [on which] there is what is supposed to be a portrait of the good man« (ibid.); the tomb or portrait were, however, not presented as an image. Rather, in the fashion of Victorian heritage culture, the article linked the space of the present village with its landscape and historic buildings to Kyrle's past – a blend of present and past frequent in travel writing and historic tours.[22]

In the biographical sketch on the engineer Robert Stephenson, which stretched over two parts, the chronology of the biography and Stephenson's success were mirrored in the progression shown in the illustrations. This was already indicated at the outset of the biography with the depiction of the »Birth-Place of Robert Stephenson, Willington Quay, (Now Pulled Down)« (»Robert Stephenson« 1860: 712, caption to illustration). This illustration was accompanied by a narrative that set in with Stephenson's parents even before his birth but instantly pointed towards his future achievements:

»Joyfully the young husband, with his bride behind him on a pillion, took her on horseback to his home, then at Willington Quay, on the north bank of the Tyre, about six miles

---

22 For a more detailed discussion of such a blending of travel and life writing, see the analysis of Stoughton's narrative pattern for popular history in Chapter 6.

Fig. 11: »Robert Stephenson«, Leisure Hour
(15 Nov 1860: 729)

Images published with permission of ProQuest. Further
reproduction is prohibited without permission.

from Newcastle. Mark another spot, as unpretentious as the preceding. In the second story
of this house, and in the room lighted by the window next to that built up with brickwork,
the wife became a mother, and gave birth to a boy, Robert, worthy his sire's renown, who
lived to send the locomotive whistling through the land of the Pharaohs, span the mighty
St. Lawrence, and leave monuments of his constructive ability upon four continents.«
(Ibid.: 713)

In the following, the contrast in space between the rural home town and Stephenson's international monuments was emphasised through the accompanying
images. The images in the two-parter progressed from his birthplace and other
village dwelling places to »The Engine-House at Killingworth Colliery« (ibid.:
714), and, in the second part, his more eminent mansion – for which the text
clearly pointed out this contrast and progression in Stephenson's life by mention-

ing that it was »a striking contrast to his homely cottage at Killingworth« (ibid.: 727) – to the impressive full-page collage presenting his portrait overlooking his innovations (Fig. 11) – »The Royal Border Bridge over the Tweed«, »The High Level Bridge at Newcastle-on-Tyne«, »The Victoria Bridge across the St. Lawrence at Montreal« and »the Britannia Tubular Bridge across the Menai Straits« (ibid.: 729, illustrations legend). While readers could identify with the everyday buildings of British villages, the other images pointed to Stephenson's achievement of »victory over space and time by quickening locomotion« (ibid.: 711) in foreign countries. The connection of Stephenson's birthplace in a simple house – and hence a regional heritage culture – to the other spaces his innovation managed to surmount was thereby not only given more emphasis. Rather, this imagery used to depict Stephenson's history also called on readers' own ambition and possibility to do something large from small beginnings.

Besides these role-model presentations of life writing, as well as those linked to heritage culture, the *Leisure Hour* also included articles which leaned towards a more scientific approach, such as the entries listed under »Biography« on King Arthur (ca. 6th century) and naval officer George Vancouver (1757-1798). A more academic approach was here underlined by the presentations of images of material objects, historical sights or geographical maps. The article »Arthur and the Round Table« (1860) most clearly bordered on scientific history, as it already started out by debating whether Arthur should be seen as fictitious or real:

»Most certainly we shall hold Arthur the Briton to be a fact in history; for one cannot bring one's self to believe that his name, which was owned for ages as the very talisman of chivalry, and was long acknowledged by the historian in the calm retirement of his laborious cell, is but an imaginative rumour, a wandering echo from the chord of some visionary bard. We are aware that we are *approaching* the ›debatable ground‹ of romance, but will endeavour soberly to keep the beaten track of probability, and not indulge ourselves in a *détour* into the shadowy land of fable, through which the old chroniclers, led by Geoffry of Monmouth, or old minstrels in the following of ›Maister Wace,‹ would be our ready guides.« (»Arthur« 1860: 790)

The article did – unsurprisingly – not provide any real evidence for its assumption. It focused on a retelling of ›facts‹ on Arthur's life, while the images underlined the aim to authenticate Arthur's existence by not presenting fictionalisations but two ›real-world‹ depictions, that is, a material object of Arthurian debate – the »Round Table Presented in Winchester Castle« (ibid.: 792) and a landscape engraving which was supposed to be the »Site and Ruins of King Arthur's Castle, in Cornwall« (ibid.: 793).

Fig. 12: »*Vancouver the Voyager*«, Leisure
Hour *(12 Jan 1860: 32)*

Images published with permission of ProQuest. Further
reproduction is prohibited without permission.

In a similar manner, the article »Vancouver the Voyager« (1860) was more scientific. In an essayist approach to colonial history, it related George Vancouver's
expedition to map the area around Vancouver Island, and in a partly adventurous
style it portrayed the cartographer's contact with native Americans. Obviously
sparked by recent events of the Pig War,[23] the article and its accompanying images not only served to map the area of the present conflict but also clearly
linked geographical names (the mapping of space) to history (the work of earlier
explorers). The final page contained two maps (»Vancouver« 1860: 32; Fig. 12)

---

23 The so-called Pig War was a conflict on the negotiation of the border between the colony of British Columbia and the United States initiated through a farmers' dispute on
the isle of San Juan.

which attributed locations to events, people and actions, thereby also putting history on the map. A larger map presented the »Western Coast of North America, from the Russian Boundary to San Francisco« (ibid.), with its markings for degrees of latitude 40, 50 and 60 clearly related to Vancouver's main activity during his expedition, namely, that he

»addressed himself to the discovery and accurate survey of the coast between California and the Russian settlements, but principally between the forty-seventh and fifty-second or fifty-third degrees of north latitude, where lies the island which now bears his name« (Ibid.: 30).

A second, smaller map focused in on the area of the present conflict, to which it was related through its caption »San Juan Island, with the Boundary Lines as Claimed by the British and Americans Respectively« (ibid.: 32). For the *Leisure Hour*, this appeared to be an uncommonly political article with its direct reference to an ongoing international conflict, though at the outset the article was careful to point out:

»We will shut out politics as much as practicable, though it is impossible to be blind to the scandal of risking so much of human happiness for the sake of outrage in so bad a cause – a cause, too, which could not be advanced towards a just arrangement by the means employed.« (Ibid.: 29)

However, the sparseness of information provided on the present event shows that the *Leisure Hour* expected its readers to already be familiar with the ongoing conflict. Only in the last two paragraphs on the final page (of approx. three pages of text) did the article refer back to the present conflict. What this article thus did was fall back on the past to avoid presenting politics considered unsuitable for a family magazine while still being able to include it. It was unusual to find such a politically charged article in the *Leisure Hour* – even if clad as a biography or narrative of an earlier exploration. Although it appears that contemporary concerns were here presented as a way into the historical narrative, it was the focus on the past which enabled brief discussion of present society and politics.[24]

---

24 As can be seen in the place name »Vancouver«, the preparation of maps, i.e., the process of cartography, is hence in itself a kind of historiography, as the naming of places is most of the time connected to a specific historical occurrence. The findings on the »Vancouver« article can also be confirmed in comparison with other articles accompanied by maps which may be categorised as historiography, such as the »Reference

What is striking in the biographies analysed so far in comparison to 1852 is that an immersion of history in a class narrative or ideas of salvation was very much toned down or absent. A rare exception concerning the implementation of a Christian tone during 1860 was the biographical anecdote on Gustavus Adolphus of Sweden (1594-1632), which indicated this religious embedding already in its title: »The Last Prayer of Gustavus Adolphus« (1860). It related the battle of Lutzen on 6 November 1632 in a narrative account translated from a French biography of Gustavus Adolphus. The article hence approached political history through a religiously coloured anecdote. The topic of the Thirty Years' War between Protestants and Catholics after the Reformation was well-chosen for an approach to this »very ideal of a Christian warrior«, for whom his soldiers, after his death for the Protestant cause at the battle of Lutzen, »mourned [...] as for a father; and all the Protestants of Europe regarded their dearest hopes as buried with him in his tomb« (»Last Prayer« 1860: 234). The article focused on Gustavus Adolphus's Christian conduct in preparing for the battle through prayer. The narrative scene presented in the accompanying image (ibid.: 233; Fig. 13) fitted the narrativised account of the text and highlighted the idea presented at the end of the article, that is, Adolphus »display[ing] throughout the conflict as much the piety of the saint as the heroism of the soldier« (ibid.: 234). Rather than presenting Adolphus in a straightforward portrait or within battle action, the image showed him in preparation for the battle through prayer amongst his soldiers. The image corresponded to the following text sequence:

Map of Sicily« (1860), which stretched over a half page and included a list of »Leading Events in Sicilian History during the Present Century«, as well as the article »Summary of Neapolitan History« (1860), which provided a timeline from the Roman Empire up to the present with a »Reference Map of Southern Italy«. These text and image interplays clearly put history on the map by assigning a geographical location to historical events sparked by recent unrest in Italy. Similar to the »Vancouver« article, »The Dahomians and Ashantees« (1860) was linked to colonial ideas of expansion and expedition and the mapping of unknown territory. While this article also provided insight on historical practices, customs and traditions in Africa and was linked to the past in these terms, the mapping was here also connected to a historisation in terms of civilisation development stages, i.e., mapping history in this sense meant that the Western world – in its manifestation of the British Empire and its cultural, moral and Christian conduct – was considered as the most advanced while other (unmapped) territories and societies were perceived as ›living in the past‹ and therefore in need of modernisation.

Fig. 13: »The Last Prayer of Gustavus Adolphus«,
Leisure Hour *(12 Apr 1860: 233)*

»Towards eleven o'clock the fog dispersed, and the rays of the sun illumined the fields of Lutzen. When the two armies were in sight, Gustavus Adolphus inclined his head, and prayed for the last time mentally and with astonishing fervour. Then raising his eyes to heaven, his hands clasped over the hilt of his sword, he exclaimed, ›Jesus, Jesus, be thou my aid in this day, wherein I strive for the glory of thy holy name.‹ He waved his sword above his head and added, ›Forward now, in the name of the Lord.‹« (Ibid.)

The image presented a pause before the battle action killing the hero took place. It was set up like a melodramatic tableau in which Gustavus Adolphus was assigned a place amongst his soldiers, though their paler representation in the background elevated him and highlighted his religiosity and eminence, thereby creating a sacral space amongst his admiring soldiers. Rather than presenting a monument or portrait of the hero (though Adolphus's pose is almost like an equestrian monument), this presentation of a narrative scene in its historic setting engaged viewers with the story by also pausing on the contemplative moment and thereby further emphasising the elevation of Gustavus Adolphus as »Christian warrior« in their own cause of affirming evangelical values and the choice of dissenting beliefs against Catholicism.

GOOD WORDS

Like the *Leisure Hour* – which placed emphasis on its life writing through the separate category »Biography« in its annual index – *Good Words* foregrounded its biographical articles, mainly published in serial form, by presenting 14 of 17 illustrated stand-alone articles (5) or serial parts (12) prominently on weekly covers (see Appendix A, Tab. 12, 13 and 14). During this year, *Good Words* displayed a decidedly religious conduct in its life writing, which was strictly emphasised through its use of illustrations. Cooke observes on the use of illustrations in *Good Words*:

»They [the publishers] required their artists to provide what, in effect, is a highly programmed response, a visual showing of set iconographies which articulated the magazines' underlying messages and allowed no ambiguities in its relationship with its viewers. In the case of Strahan's *Good Words*, the appeal to the evangelical audience is devoutly upheld, with every image providing a visual reinforcement of the readers' unquestioning faith. Figured as combination of scenes from the Bible [...] and scenes of charity [...], *Good Words* is the visual embodiment of Strahan's belief in the power of illustration as a means of expressing or spreading the Word.« (Cooke 2010: 67)

The early introduction in February 1860 of a series on the Scottish missionary saints Ninian (c.5th-6th cent.), Kentigern (d.612/14) and Columba (c.521-597) on the covers of *Good Words* emphasised the periodical's aim of appealing to a Scottish audience in combination with its evangelical mission. However, though the first part of this series of biographical sketches introduced the Scottish interest in its title, »The Story of Ninian: Scotland's Earliest Missionary« (1860), in the text Ninian was referred to as a »British youth« (»Story of Ninian« 1860: 97) who had built the first church and monastery in Britain. Furthermore, the image presented on the cover did not depict Ninian in Scotland but during a journey to Rome (ibid.; Fig. 14). The text relating to this image noted:

»A strange sight it must have been for that simple British youth, as, fresh from Solway side and Cumberland moors, he gazed from the descent of the Janiculum on the world's capital. True, it had ceased to be that; for the seat of empire ere this had been transferred to the Bosphorus. And, twenty years before Ninian came to Italy, the eastern and western empires had been finally divided; and Rome was no longer the residence even of the Emperor of the West. Still, there lay before the stranger's eyes its temples, palaces, Coliseum, and basilicas, the gathered magnificence of a thousand years, all waiting for Alaric and his destroying Goths. Whatever was pagan and imperial was on the eve of destruction; but the hierarchical and sacerdotal power was still fresh with youth.« (Ibid.)

The image thus presented Ninian at the outset of his mission, as a »simple British youth« probably impressed by the sublimity of Rome's appearance. In itself, this was an image bordering on Biblical allegory, with Saint Ninian depicted like a shepherd overlooking the city. In contrast to the text, which presented Rome as

Fig. 14: »The Story of Ninian«, Good Words *(12 Feb 1860: 97)*

Fig. 15: »Pictures from the History and Life of the Early Church«, Good Words *(11 Nov 1860: 737)*

Images published with permission of ProQuest. Further reproduction is prohibited without permission.

the sublime and Ninian as humble, the image foregrounded him so that he – with the presentation of other figures below him – appeared to be sublime. While the image depicted him at the beginning of his career, it also included the idea of his later work for Britain, thereby building a bridge between Scottish and English readers.

The idea of allegorical images was also taken up in the portrayal of the other two Scottish missionaries Kentigern (who was presented as a young boy being instructed by his tutor St Serf, thereby appealing also to the young members of a family audience) and St Columba (whose »Death of St Columba« related to the saint's softness and religious dedication also to animals). And the same type of allegorical, Christian-themed illustration could be found in the two cover illustrations for the series »Pictures from the History and Life of the Early Church« (1860), which set out to revise a reading of Church history that seemed to the magazine to be »the dullest reading«, as »Church historians [...] have been far from skilful artists«, leading to a situation in which

»[t]he reader does not catch [...] the real features of the life that our Christian ancestors lived [...]. Our aim is not to take up the subject on any such scale as its importance demands, but merely to sketch in reduced popular outline certain characters, events, and scenes, founded, in the main, upon the more elaborate and extended studies of others. We shall be glad, at the same time, if, in this way, our readers shall be able to catch any glimpses of the true life of the Church.« (»Pictures from the History and Life of the Early Church« 1860: 581)

This idea of revising historiography while popularising it was continued in the third part, which dealt with martyr history. While the article noted that »martyrdom in diverse shapes represented so much of the history of Christendom« (ibid.: 738) and hence formed an essential part of early Church history, it nevertheless had to deal with the problem of presentations which were

»half-fact, half-fable. [...] Every student of the early martyrologies of the church must bear in mind this tendency to exaggeration and imaginative embellishment characteristic of such writings. [...] The duty of the historian is neither to accept nor reject on any general principle, but to test all that has descended to him by his own sympathetic feeling, and the most likely and credible standard of the time.« (Ibid.)

Keeping this in mind, the article promised to look at a martyrology »which has been long esteemed by scholars and historians as bearing the most obvious traces of authenticity« and which was »a very interesting document [...] in the simple and touching pictures of Christian heroism which it suggests, as well as in the light which it throws upon the propagation and progress of Christianity« (ibid.). The article in *Good Words* here clearly used a meta-historiographical comment on Church history not only to justify its presentation of martyr history but also to validate the biographies it presented and thereby enhance their didactic intent.

The preamble to the following martyrologies was a rather long one, with about two full pages of text. Another full page on Christians being tried, tortured and »thrown to wild beasts in the amphitheatre« by the Romans (ibid.: 740) followed, before the reader finally reached the text passage relating to the cover image (ibid.: 737; Fig. 15):

> »Attilus seemed at first likely to fare somewhat better. He was a person of reputation, and came forward cheerfully to testify to his faith. He was led round the amphitheatre, and a tablet inscribed in Latin carried before him, ›This is Attalus the Christian.‹« (Ibid.: 740)

While the illustration may have contained an element of sensationalism and also foreshadowed this for the text to keep readers interested throughout the long introduction, the intent was rather to use the kind of voyeurism contradicted in the preamble to reinforce the (decreasing) stability of contemporary Christianity, as the article concluded:

> »[W]hile the [Roman] Empire which he [Marc Aurelius] represented has long since crumbled to pieces, and his religious dreams are only interesting to the curious and the speculative, the cause which they maintained, the religion for which they died, continue imperishably triumphant, ›conquering and to conquer.‹« (Ibid.: 741)

Most series in *Good Words* were accompanied by narrative scenes, and portraits again played a minor role as illustrations for life writing. Only five of the 14 biographical cover illustrations during this year were bust portraits, and these accompanied mainly biographical sketches on German philanthropists with straightforward portrait images which always appeared to underline the serious, disciplined character of the portrayed (Fig. 16 and 17):[25] Because of their limitation to head and shoulders, they appeared more conservative than the fashion-plate-like full-length portraits in the *Leisure Hour*. That these texts aimed at

---

25 These were »John Evangelist Gossner« (1860, 2 parts); »Alexander von Humboldt: By a German Friend« (1860); »A Woman's Work« on Amalie Wilhelmine Sieveking (1860); and »Pastor Harms of Hermannsburg« (1860, 4 parts). The first part of the series »Missionary Sketches« also focused on German missionaries.

transferring strict evangelical values was not only indicated in the selection of persons but directly addressed in the first of these biographies, on the German divine and philanthropist Johannes Evangelista Gossner (1773-1858). The article set out by discussing the importance of the motto »Ora et labora« at a time of changing attitudes towards religion:

»Not many years ago a clever writer suggested that the time was coming when grave, common-sense Englishmen would fall down before the spindle and the steam-engine. And [...] [i]s there not more than ever the disposition to throw over upon praying men, who believe in an invisible power, and skill, and law, and presence, the charge of folly, enthusiasm, fanaticism? Is there not the notion that the world is only what the world sees itself to be, and that if you take other than worldly forces you will come to no result?« (»John Evangelista Gossner« 1860: 177-178).

Fig. 16: »John Evangelist Gossner«,   *Fig. 17: »A Woman's Work«,* Good
Good Words *(18 Mar 1860: 177)*   Words *(5 Aug 1860: 497)*

Images published with permission of ProQuest. Further reproduction is prohibited without permission.

Against these contemporary objections to religion, the article stressed that still »the man who prays best will be the man who works best«, as prayer and work »run into each other [...] as different aspects of the same man« (ibid.: 178). Hence, the article promised to introduce figures

»over whose lives might be written as their clearest exponenta, *ora et labora*. They are men who maintain that God exercises some direct influence in the affairs of the world [...]. Each of them has done something very remarkable in its way, quite independent of the mode of operation. It may be interesting to trace these several works, ascending to the principle asserted by their working. It will be necessary in doing so to dwell at some length upon the character and history of the workers themselves.« (Ibid.)

This approach, then, which was mirrored in the modest cover portrait accompanying the text (Fig. 16), was not only relevant for the two-parter on Gossner; it was also clearly executed in the biographies on geographer, naturalist and explorer Alexander von Humboldt (1769-1859) and German Lutheran pastor Ludwig Harms (1808-1865) – as well as philanthropist and founder of the German Diakonie welfare system Amalie Wilhelmine Sieveking (1794-1859), whose biography with illustration (Fig. 17) also featured on the cover.[26] Sieveking's biography resembled the rare inclusion of a female subject in the three periodicals' life writing during this year, and as the text pointed out, she was, of course, presented specifically for »the earnest-minded of her own sex« (»A Woman's Work« 1860: 498).

These articles in *Good Words* by far exceeded the average length of such biographies in the *Leisure Hour* and therefore had a much higher text/image ratio. *Good Words* here chronologically and in a rather dry way recounted almost every step in the individuals' lives and careers with a focus on their religious achievements. This clearly showed a contrast to the *Leisure Hour*'s historical programme in 1860, as the RTS's periodical tended in its life writings to focus on single events or to present a string of anecdotes which it might have made more attractive and entertaining through dialogue scenes, and which – apart from the biography on Gustavus Adolphus – largely refrained from overt Christian ideas in 1860.

---

26 Though these biographies on *Good Words*' covers throughout 1860 were not strictly presented under a collective serial title, the general introduction given at the beginning of Gossner's biography appeared to be directed at all of them.

CORNHILL MAGAZINE

The *Cornhill*, by contrast, took a rather scholarly and meta-historical as well as cultural approach to the past. This is also evident from the subtitles to Peter Smith's chapter »Of the Past«, in which he analyses the periodical's approach to history during its initial decade: »The Science of History« (P. Smith 1969: 286), »Philogical [sic] Criticism« (ibid.: 301), »The Idea of Progress« (ibid.: 304) or »Classics in Translation« (ibid.: 309). P. Smith concludes on the »function which the *Cornhill* fulfilled worthily in historical matters«:

»On the simplest level it provided ›a little serious thought and information ... which can be dipped into and laid aside.‹ At a different level it did introduce the readers to, and involve them with, some at least of the issues which were exercising men of scholarship.« (Ibid: 347-348)²⁷

This balance between entertainment and ›scientific‹ debate was also obvious in the *Cornhill*'s life writing in 1860, in which meta-historical comments as well as humorous narratives played an important part. Barbara Quinn Schmidt notes that George Smith specifically chose Thackeray as editor in order

»[t]o create the right balance [of information and serialized novels desired by the middle classes] with a mood of fun yet earnestness [...]. Thackeray was bright, humorous, moral, and anxious to improve society. Also he was upper middle class with the right schooling and appealed to the right class of readers.« (B.Q. Schmidt 1980: 76)

The most prominent presentations of illustrated life writing in the *Cornhill*'s two volumes for 1860 were two biographical series: »William Hogarth: Painter, Engraver, and Philosopher. Essays on the Man, the Work, and the Time« ([Sala] 1860) started with five parts in the first volume and stretched into the second

---

27 Turner makes similar observations regarding the *Cornhill*'s non-fiction: »*Cornhill*'s concentration on culture-based articles enforces their overall commitment to non-controversial non-fiction subjects. By avoiding foreign affairs, the American Civil War, political economy and religion and by favouring ›factual‹ science and middle-class culture, the editors attempted to present an apparently uncomplicated version of the real, non-fiction world of its readers. However, these articles are complex and engaged with ideological discourses both inside and outside the magazine. By limiting the range of acceptable topics, the magazine broadens the range of subjects within culture and society available to be discussed« (Turner 2000: 25).

volume with four more articles, thereby overlapping with the four-parter »The Four Georges: Sketches of Manners, Morals, Court and Town Life« ([Thackeray] 1860a).[28] Three of the nine parts on Hogarth remained unillustrated, although this was a series on a visual artist. In the sixth part of the series, which was one of the unillustrated parts, though completely dedicated to Hogarth's painting cycle *The Rake's Progress*, Sala addressed this problem of writing on an artist without presenting illustrations:

»[*W*]*here are the plates?* Can there be anything more meagre and unsatisfactory than the description of a series of pictorial performances without the pictures themselves? and of what avail are these dissertations upon William Hogarth, Painter and Engraver, without some of Hogarth's pictures by way of illustration? [...] I should have wished my bald prose to serve but as a framework to Hogarth's rich, pregnant pictures. [...] Shamefaced, I glance at a few tiny woodcuts which chequer these pages [...]. Only – let this stand on record for all explanation and excuse – were I to give you even the sketchiest copy of every one of Hogarth's pictures to illustrate these Essays on his life and character, you would have to wait until the year 1870 for the delivery of volume the first of my elephant folio. For the writer's life is very short, and the engraver's art is very long.« ([Sala] 1860, vol. II: 97-98)

As it would have been too time-consuming and – as Sala continued to argue – too expensive to have more and better plates, he concluded: »So, for the present, these papers must be performed without plates, and the drama of the RAKE'S PROGRESS must be performed without dresses, scenery, properties, decorations, or even a shovelful of blue fire« (ibid.: 98). As regards the »Hogarth« series, it can hence be noted that the text itself (not only in these unillustrated parts but throughout) constantly conjured up images and paintings by Hogarth without having to print them.

While Sala's explanation suggested commercial reasons for this practice, the *Cornhill* producers also expected that their intended audience be to a considerable extent culturally and intellectually informed. This was obvious from the way the series dealt with the images it presented for Hogarth's biography. These were mainly – as Sala pointed out in the quote above – reproductions of paintings from Hogarth in more or less »tiny woodcuts«. The series was accompanied by eight illustrations, only one of which was a full-page plate. All the smaller

---

28 A brief discussion of these non-fiction series is also included in Delafield (2015: 105-106 and 176-177), who focuses on reading them within the context of the magazine's volume publication.

woodcuts presented works by Hogarth, yet the full-page image was not a repro-duction of a Hogarth painting but a plate produced for the *Cornhill* series by Sala himself.[29] Despite the reproduction of these paintings in the periodical, the text also provided a close description of what could be seen as well as a contextual analysis. Hogarth's *Taste of the Town* was, for instance, accompanied by a full page of detailed text, as the following short extract shows:

»In the centre, Shakespeare and Jonson's works are being carted away for waste paper. To the left you see a huge projecting sign or show-cloth, containing portraits of his sacred Majesty George the Second in the act of presenting the management of the Italian Opera with one thousand pounds; also of the famous Mordaunt Earl of Peterborough and some-time general of the armies in Spain. He kneels, and in the handsomest manner, to Signora Cuzzoni the singer, saying (in a long apothecary's label), ›Please accept eight thousand pounds!‹ but the Cuzzoni spurns at him. Beneath is the entrance to the Opera. Infernal per-sons with very long tails are entering thereto with joyful countenances. The infernal per-sons are unmistakeable reminiscences of Callot's demons in the *Testation de St. Antoine*. There is likewise a placard relating to ›Faux's Long-room,‹ and his ›dexterity of hand.‹« ([Sala] 1860, vol. I: 434)

The text built on the idea of readers' familiarity with a certain knowledge of art and history, which it alluded to without further explanations – such as, in this in-stance, Callot's *Testation*. The *Cornhill*, however, did not appear to use this as a rhetorical device, a practice intrinsic maybe to family magazines directed at a less informed audience to establish a feeling of community and belonging or to create ambition to learn by suggesting that readers really should know this kind of thing.

The *Leisure Hour* rarely presented painting reproductions.[30] Further, the way the »Hogarth« series in the *Cornhill* at the beginning carefully explained its ap-

---

29 Cf. British Museum Number 1875,0508.1409. Illustrations in the series: Part 1: »Mr. Gamble's Apprentice«, full-page illustration conducted by Sala (1860, vol. I: facing page 264); Ellis Gamble's shopcard (ibid.: 277); Part 3: »Burlington Gate, No. I« (ibid.: 433); Part 5: two illustrations from Forrest's journal illustrated by Hogarth and Scott (ibid.: 732 and 733); Part 7: »Laughing Audience« (ibid., vol. II: 281); Part 8: »Taste in High Life« (ibid.: 368); Part 9: »Finis: Or, The Bathos« (ibid.: 461).

30 The biography on »Wilkie and His Pictures« (1860) in the *Leisure Hour* was, for in-stance, presented next to the full-page engraving »Autumn« (1860: 585), yet it is un-clear if this was a reproduction of a painting by Wilkie or if it must simply be seen as an image accompanying the article »Autumn« (1860: 584) on the facing page. Neither

proach in contrast to ›proper‹ historians, that is, the way meta-historical comments were used here in contrast to the *Leisure Hour* and *Good Words*, also underlined its intended appeal to a more educated audience:

»The latitude, therefore, I take through incapactiy for accuracy, saves me from inflicting on you a long prolegomena; saves me from scoring the basement of this page with footnotes, or its margins with references; saves me from denouncing the ›British Dryasdust,‹ from whom I have culled the scanty dates and facts, the mile and year stones in William Hogarth's life. Indeed, he has been very useful to me, this British Draysdust, and I should have made but a sorry figure without him. He or they – Nichols, Stevens, Trusler, Routquet, Ireland, Ducarel, Burn – have but little to tell; but that which they know, they declare in a frank, straightforward manner.« (Ibid.: 179)

This type of meta-historiographical comment justified the *Cornhill*'s popular approach while at the same time acknowledging its indebtedness to academic historians' findings. It also placed the discourse of the past in communication with serious historiography, thereby indicating that the *Cornhill*'s audience possibly would include such intellectuals.

A similar approach was taken in the same year in Thackeray's reprinted lecture on »The Four Georges: Sketches of Manners, Morals, Court and Town Life« (1860a), which overlapped with »William Hogarth« in the second volume. In this four-parter, the *Cornhill* took a decidedly entertaining and humorous approach to the past. In this regard, the analysis of the *Cornhill*'s two biographical series confirms R. Mitchell's perception of »Thackeray and his fellows [...] as the ironic voices of the mid-century crisis of national history, the satirical attackers of the picturesque reconstructions of historical novelists and the didactic ›true stories‹ of the textbooks« (R. Mitchell 2000: 203). Originally designed as a lecture held by Thackeray, the first part of »The Four Georges« again defended its popular approach right at the outset:

---

of the two articles referred to the illustration, although the article on Wilkie may be said to have placed the painting within Wilkie's tradition: »We have said above, that Wilkie stands at the head of a school of followers. [...] All our good artists in this department have accepted and practised the lesson he so modestly taught; and English art at the present day, in this peculiar direction, owes to him what landscape art owes to Turner.« (»Wilkie« 1860: 587) To readers, the placement of the engraving and article next to each other therefore may have suggested that the image represented one of Wilkie's paintings.

»[T]he subject of these lectures has been misunderstood, and I have been taken to task for not having given grave historical treatises, which it never was my intention to attempt. Not about battles, about politics, about statesmen and measures of state, did I ever think to lecture you: but to sketch the manners and life of the old world; to amuse for a few hours with talk about the old society; and, with the result of many a day's and night's pleasant reading, to try and wile away a few winter evenings for my hearers.« ([Thackeray] 1860a: 2)

This »pleasant« idea of using the past to »wile away« time was emphasised again a few pages later when the »distinction« between »history« and »manners and life« was further explained:

»You understand the distinction I would draw between history – of which I do not aspire to be an expounder – and manners and life such as these sketches would describe. The rebellion breaks out in the north; its story is before you in a hundred volumes, in none more fairly than in the excellent narrative of Lord Mahon. [...] [T]hese are matters of history, for which you are referred to the due chroniclers. I read presently of a couple of soldiers almost flogged to death for wearing oakboughs in their hats [...]. It is with these we have to do, rather than with the marches and battles of the armies to which the poor fellows belonged – with statesmen, and how they looked, and how they lived, rather than with measures of State, which belong to history alone. [...] We are with the mob in the crowd, not with the great folks in the procession. We are not the Historic Muse, but her ladyship's attendant, tale-bearer – *valet de chambre* – for whom no man is a hero.« (Ibid.: 16-17)

Similar to Sala's meta-historiographical comments in »William Hogarth«, Thackeray here distanced his popular approach to the past from serious historiography.

The decidedly humorous approach to the past taken in the series, as already indicated in the quotation above, can be seen in two examples of images accompanying the text from the second and third part. The second part, which stated that »[i]n whatever posture one sees this royal George, he is ludicrous somehow« (ibid.: 179), clearly did not present George II (1683-1760) as »a hero« but as a figure to be laughed at. When George II learned that he was Britain's new emperor, the text narrated this in the following way:

»The master was asleep after his dinner; he always slept after his dinner: and woe be to the person who interrupted him! Nevertheless, our stout friend of the jackboots put the affrighted ladies aside, opened the forbidden door of the bedroom, wherein upon the bed lay a little gentleman; and here the eager messenger knelt down in his jack-boots.

He on the bed started up, and with many oaths and a strong German accent asked who was there, and who dared to disturb him?

›I am Sir Robert Walpole,‹ said the messenger. The awakened sleeper hated Sir Robert Walpole. ›I have the honour to announce to your Majesty that your royal father, King George I., died at Osnaburg, on Saturday last, the 10th instant.‹

›*Dat is one big lie!*‹ roared out his sacred Majesty King George II.: but Sir Robert Walpole stated the fact, and from that day until three and thirty years after, George, the second of the name, ruled over England.« (Ibid.: 175)

While the succession to king was a decisive and serious step in the life of the ruler, this important national event was here ridiculed by contrasting the messenger Robert Walpole acting entirely according to decorum with the grumpy yet likable George as a common man who was angry at being disturbed in his sleep

Fig. 18: »The Four Georges«, Cornhill (Aug 1860: facing page 175)

and hence bluntly retorted to the messenger's official announcement. This idea of humour in the everyday presentation of an emperor was further emphasised through the accompanying full-page illustration, humorously entitled »Ave Caesar«, which accordingly depicted George II in his nightgown (Fig. 18).

In the third part on George III (1738-1820), Thackeray repeated his initial project of not attending to political history proper when he objected:

»Wars and revolutions are, however, the politician's province. The great events of this long reign, the statesmen and orators who illustrated it,* I do not pretend to make the subjects of an hour's light talk. Let us return to our humbler duty of court gossip. Yonder sits our little queen, surrounded by many stout sons and fair daughters whom she bore to her faithful George.« (Ibid.: 271)

Fig. 19: »The Four Georges«, Cornhill *(Sept 1860: 271-272)*

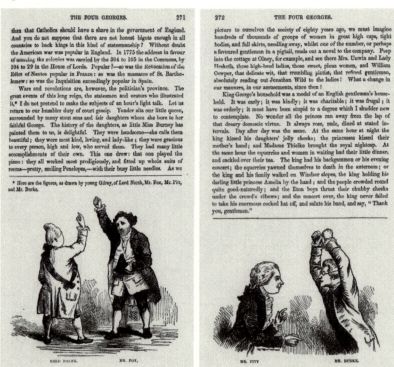

Images published with permission of ProQuest. Further reproduction is prohibited without permission.

This type of history, then, was obviously a female gendered one – which conformed to the *Cornhill*'s idea of writing for a family audience and hence of not involving a female readership in political observations. The asterisk in the quote, however, referred to a footnote which in a humorous way nevertheless introduced these »statesmen and orators«. The text of the footnote read: »Here are the figures, as drawn by young Gilray [sic; i.e., the caricaturist James Gillray], of Lord North, Mr. Fox, Mr. Pitt, and Mr. Burke« (ibid.: 271-272); and in this footnote, set apart from the text by a line, the readers were presented in the lower halves of pages 271 and 272 with the caricatures of these four individuals (Fig. 19). The four-parter otherwise refrained from using footnotes,[31] and the »Hogarth« series had clearly distanced itself from this practice of »scoring the basement of [the] page with foot-notes« (see above). The uncommon practice of presenting illustrations (and specifically caricatures) in a footnote – and especially in one which was meant to give further information on so-called serious aspects of history – therefore added an ironic note to the series' approach to the past, as it might have been understood as a meta-comment on the practice of academic history.

On the other hand, this example nicely reminds one of the original set-up of the series as an orally presented lecture, which was here adapted to the print medium: The text appeared to be an unchanged version of its oral form which frequently acknowledged its original format, as in the »light talk« of the quote above; however, the printed format included illustrations which in the lecture would – if at all – only have been referred to in descriptions. The *Cornhill* thus, in both the »Hogarth« and the »Four Georges« series, not only made use of the print medium's possibility of including illustrations but also showed a playful and self-reflective approach in their implementation, which emphasised the periodical's humorous, popular, yet intellectually challenging approach to the past.

In its humorous meta-historical play with academic history in text and image, the *Cornhill* was therefore quite different to the other periodicals. The *Leisure Hour* at instances contrasted depictions of the past in text and image and hence used meta-history in its heritage culture approach in order to (also ironically) criticise yet at the same time reinforce the function of historical actors as role models. In *Good Words*, serious and conservative historical representations prevailed, which in visual as well as textual form underlined the periodical's Christian, moralistic agenda. Similar to *Good Words*' meta-historical discussion to justify its presentation of martyr history, the *Leisure Hour* had inserted meta-

---

31 There was only one more footnote in the first part, which provided the source of illustrations ([Thackeray] 1860a: 6).

historical interruptions for didactic purposes in »Poccahontas«, analysed in Chapter 3, while the *London Journal* had there taken a meta-historical approach to the past in order to criticise social politics. Readers of family magazine such as the *Leisure Hour*, the *London Journal*, *Good Words* and the *Cornhill* thus came across a vast variety of historical content in text and image which was determined by the periodicals' leanings towards the sacred or the secular as well as questions of class and education.

Part II: Serialising History in the *Leisure Hour*

5. Serialising History into and out of the *Leisure Hour*: The Periodical and Book Transfer

As part of the larger Victorian print market, the popular historical narratives in the *Leisure Hour* corresponded not only to renderings of the past in other family magazines such as the *London Journal*, *Good Words* or *Cornhill* but also to historical non-fiction published in books. The increasing popularity of periodicals coincided with a media transfer between books and periodicals, and this interaction was often linked to a contestation of books and periodicals' status and reputation.[1] An article on the initiation of the *Leisure Hour* in the RTS's *Christian Spectator* concluded:

»The weekly journal is adapted to answer ends which are not attained by books. Materials elsewhere provided are, by this agency, presented in such quantities, and with such a regard to adaptation and variety, that the short and broken intervals of daily toil may be

---

1   This chapter assimilates some passages as well as ideas from my earlier article »Serializing the Past in and out of the *Leisure Hour*: Historical Culture and the Negotiation of Media Boundaries« (Lechner 2013). In this article, I first introduced the approach of analysing the *Leisure Hour*'s historical programme via a media transfer between book and periodical text. These passages, now in slightly changed and recontextualised form, frame this chapter (see also Fn 56 below). In the article, I presented case studies on Merryweather's »Working Man in the Olden Time«, John Stoughton's »Shades of the Departed« and the monthly part on »Windsor Castle«. These case studies may briefly be referenced here, though they are now part of Chapters 3 (see Fn 11) and 6 (see Fn 9 and 30). As my research has progressed since the article's publication, some of the figures regarding periodical series and their book counterparts have been updated here.

turned to profit; and the humblest artisan, though denied access to larger stores of knowledge, may treasure up during his leisure hour abundant facilities of usefulness and pleasure.« (»New Weekly Periodical« 1852: 682)

The RTS here seemed to imply a correspondence between »books« as »[m]aterials elsewhere provided« and »the weekly journal« via »adaptation«, and simultaneously pointed towards the two media's differences in their print as well as textual genres connected to modes of consumption through a reduction in »quantity«. In this, the article similarly indicated the two media's different reputations. Yet many magazine articles on history were collected in book volumes, which, as Beetham noted, »signal[s] the rescue of the text« into a »physically more stable« format as well as into »recognized genre[s]« (Beetham 1989: 97); and books on the past were popularised in periodicals such as the *Leisure Hour* – a publication format disdained by historians for its »popular and sketchy articles« (Mandell Creighton, qtd. in Howsam 2004: 527; see Chapter 1).[2]

This chapter considers serialised historical non-fiction in the *Leisure Hour*, taking the exchange between the periodical and the book format as a specific point of entry.[3] The embedding within a different medium and its materiality often went hand in hand with a change of the text and its negotiation of a (national) historical identity, which means that the past may have been designed differently according to medium and intended audience. The comparison of book and periodical therefore provides insight into the *Leisure Hour*'s historical programme, as changes were implemented in order to fit and highlight the periodical's preferred historical intentions. A look at the travelling of texts and ideas between the two media shows that the RTS not only negotiated media boundaries: The

---

2   See also Neumann and Zierold's observation »that media technologies are never ›neutral‹ but play an active role in the construction of reality« (Neumann/Zierold 2010: 116), as introduced in Chapter 1.

3   The approach follows Aileen Fyfe's (2004b) as well as Laurel Brake's (2001) call for a combination of book history and periodical studies. Other interconnections between books and periodicals worthy of further study are, for instance, advertisements, footnotes, book reviews, book extracts, single articles transferred into book collections and the work of authors and editors for both periodicals and book publications. Brake charts such interconnections (2001: 18), and Fyfe analyses the production of the RTS's Monthly Volumes book series and the *Leisure Hour* as a »joint programme« (2004b: 73) in the RTS's marketing and distribution techniques. For databases charting both books and periodical publications of Victorian fiction, see Troy J. Bassett (2015 [2007]) and Marie Léger-St-Jean (2015 [2010]).

changed reissue of texts in other formats indicates that the Society at the same time operated at the intersection of other categories, such as class and gender. These were linked to the reputation of the different media as well as the modes of representation and approaches to history, as the increasing professionalisation of history at mid-century meant a contestation of popular formats (see Chapters 1 and 2).

The chapter looks at series dealing with the past printed in the *Leisure Hour* which were turned into books or, vice versa, books on the past which informed series in the periodical. In contrast to the periodical's mixture of genres and topics, book publications of these series consisted of a unified text addressed to readers with a specific interest in history. Reissuing texts in another format was, of course, an efficient way to produce new publications. However, this did not simply lead to a presentation of the same historical knowledge to possibly new readerships through a shortening/lengthening of the text or loss/addition of peritexts[4] due to the medium's specific materiality. Semantic changes to appropriate different readerships through the adoption of a specific historical perspective as well as a reproduction of material features from book to periodical may also have occurred to accommodate the periodical's inclusive family readership. Furthermore, the phenomenon shows that the *Leisure Hour*'s series on the past were part of the larger Victorian print market, as they were also disseminated in book form, thereby transgressing the ephemeral character of the periodical.

The chapter falls into two parts which address the transfer that occurred in series on the past between periodical and book on different levels. The first section contextualises the exchange, as it provides an overview of the non-fiction series on the past printed in the *Leisure Hour* during the 1850s and 1860s for

---

4   Konrad Claes (2010) discusses the application of Genette's transtextuality theory in periodical studies, and this study follows his and Genette's understanding of para-, peri- and epitext: »The paratext contains all the information we can gather about the mediation between a text and its public. [...] Genette divides all the elements that come into play into two groups: at the level of the peritext (›around-text‹) we find all aspects of the published text that pertain to its physical appearance [i.e. titles, layout, prefaces, and notes, but also material medium with features such as paper, ink, and bindings], while the epitext (›above-text‹) contains what would commonly be referred to as the context of the publication (author's notebooks, reviews, etc.)« (Claes 2010: 199-200; see also Fn 57 below); on peritext and the periodical form, see also Delafield (2015: 19-20). For the periodical, this distinction is complicated by the question of what is to be considered as the text (i.e., single article, weekly number, monthly part, annual volume, etc.); see Beetham (1989: 96).

which a book counterpart has been identified. This section takes these historical narratives as an example for serialised non-fiction, in contrast to previous scholars' predominant attention to serialised fiction.[5] In contrast to fiction, where periodical series were predominantly collected into books (see Appendix A, Tab. 19 as well as Appendix B: Excursus),[6] the direction for a transfer regarding non-fiction series on the past in the *Leisure Hour* often also went from book to periodical.[7] From the 79 non-fiction series in the *Leisure Hour* identified as dealing with the past (see Appendix A, Tab. 2),[8] at least 30 appear to have had a book counterpart of some sort (see Appendix A, Tab. 18). Of these, 14 series preceded[9] and 16 followed book publication, indicating that historical series often reappropriated »[m]aterial elsewhere provided«. The first section of this chapter points out characteristic changes that might occur when historical texts were disseminated in a different material medium. With this overview in mind, the sec-

---

5   Cf. Chapter 1 (Fn 22).

6   Appendix B: Excursus provides a brief discussion of book transfer regarding historically themed fiction in the *Leisure Hour*.

7   It should, however, be noted that it appears more difficult to establish book counterparts for the non-fiction series than for serialised fiction. Where books could not be identified through the *Leisure Hour*'s biographical entries in its jubilee number (see »Authors« 1902), I searched for historical actors, events or places portrayed in a *Leisure Hour* series or typed in short text passages, references to secondary sources or quotations used in a series and often succeeded in finding a corresponding text (these searches were conducted on *Google books*, *archive.org*, and *hatitrust.org*; see also Leary 2005). The discovery of this dynamic has proved highly beneficiary for the consideration of the periodical's historical programme, as it offers additional information on contributors, intended audience and possibly reception of the series via book reviews (see also Chapter 6). It can be assumed that more book counterparts for non-fiction series exist, as the search for corresponding books is to some extent restricted by the currently possible access to digitalised texts. I have only considered series that were possibly influenced by or correspond to their book counterpart to a larger extent, while excluding merely passing quotes from or marginal references to books.

8   Of the 79 non-fiction series, one had 45 parts (later collected into book form), three had 22 to 24 parts (without a clearly identified book counterpart), eight had 11 to 15 parts (of which four had a book counterpart), seventeen had 6 to 10 parts (of which seven had a book counterpart), and fifty had 3 to 5 parts (of which eighteen had a book counterpart).

9   Some of these were collected into the same book; see Appendix A, Tab. 18.

ond section of the chapter presents case studies of select non-fiction series and discusses the characteristics of the *Leisure Hour*'s popular history in serial form for a family audience, using the idea of the book transfer as well as the comparison between the two media as a means to enhance the analyses. The case studies foreground the exchange between periodical and book in a narrow sense, for instance by considering series on the past that originated from book publications or were collected into book form after their periodical publication. In a broader sense, the correspondence between periodical and book is examined via their material similarity and difference, especially as regards the phenomenon of series printed entirely within one monthly part. The Society used such series to create »special issues« on specific historical topics, similar to books or upmarket monthly periodicals in a thematic as well as material unit. Thus, not only the direct exchange between book and periodical text but also their distinct characteristics as material entities would influence readers' perception of the past.[10]

NON-FICTION SERIES ON THE PAST IN THE *LEISURE HOUR* AND THEIR BOOK COUNTERPARTS

From Periodical to Book

The transfer of non-fictional historical series from periodical into book appears to have been a rather straightforward process. The rescue of the text into book form in these instances mainly went forward with only little semantic changes to the original text, though additions of peritextual features characteristic of book publications were made, turning them rather into reference works on history. This included indices, prefaces or tables of contents, that is, a list of chapters or list of other content, where shorter works were collected together within one volume. On the other hand, the transfer often went hand in hand with a loss, gain or change in illustrations, while authorship might have been reattributed in contrast to the periodical's anonymous publication, possibly adding more prestige through an author who was a known expert on the past. In other words, the transfer signified a shift from the periodical's title-function to the book's author-

---

10 Note in this respect also that monthly parts in contrast to weekly numbers of the *Leisure Hour* tended to include the Society's prerequisite reference to salvation; see Chapter 2 (Fn 23).

function.[11] On the semantic level, the media transfer might result in the deletion of links between single parts characteristic of periodical publication, such as foreshadowing to future instalments and references back to earlier parts in introductory summaries or to information provided in other periodical articles. Furthermore, the structure might be changed, for instance, into a strict chronological order of historical events, or – if the series' text did not make up a full volume – further chapters or other series might have been added to fill the book.[12] The latter might lead to the necessity to rewrite, recontextualise or update the now collectively presented material, thereby also influencing the way in which the past was constructed.

John Scoffern, for instance, noted in his preface to *Stray Leaves of Science and Folk-Lore* (1870), which included the biographical sketches on »Chemists« ([Scoffern] 1857) printed in the *Leisure Hour* together with various other articles he wrote for periodicals,[13] that his previously published material was now

»grouped under appropriate headings, and the scientific points brought up to the cognisance of the times. In this way the attempt has been made to give a continuity and a solidity to the theses, which the exigencies of periodical appearance sometimes do not admit of.« (Scoffern 1870: x)

---

11 James Mussell (2012: 10 and 37-38) contrasts the periodicals' title-function to books' author-function in readers' perception: Though both books and periodicals are collaborative enterprises conducted by a group of people (editors, authors, printers, illustrators, etc.), the (anonymous) author disappears within the periodical's collaborative character, uniting all content under the periodical's title, such as the *Leisure Hour*. Books, by contrast, are rather presented or perceived as the individual author's effort. See Chapter 6 on the authors of historical non-fiction series in the *Leisure Hour* as well as the practice of anonymous periodical publication and reattribution of book authorship as a means of demarcating popular from a more academic historical standing.

12 The biographies of Stoughton's »Shades of the Departed« (1852-1853) were rearranged in chronological order for the book publication, and additional biographies from the *Leisure Hour*'s sister publication the *Sunday at Home* were added (see case study in Chapter 6).

13 Scoffern's preface gave credit above all to the *Leisure Hour* as well as the *Dublin University Magazine, Belgravia, Temple Bar, Tinsleys', St. James's* and *Chambers's Journal* (Scoffern 1870: x).

Similarly, William Jerdan noted in the preface to *Men I Have Known* (1866),[14] which was published a year after the biographical series »Men I Have Known« ([Jerdan] 1859-1865) had concluded in the *Leisure Hour*, that this was an updated version:

»It should be stated that the sketches contained in this volume are reprinted, by permission of the proprietors of the ›Leisure Hour,‹ from the pages of that excellent publication, in which they appeared at intervals during several years. On revising them, however, it was thought that some congenial additional matter, which had since become available, could be advantageously recalled to memory, and this has accordingly been appended under the head of Addenda to the original papers.« (Jerdan 1866: vi)

Adapting a previously published series to book form of course meant fitting it into a larger publishing concept. When the RTS planned to transfer series from the *Leisure Hour* to their own book publishing programme, this at times went hand in hand with the demand that authors rewrite texts to introduce a more Christian tone. Harry Jones, for instance, »declined« the RTS Subcommittee's request to include »more decidedly religious matter« (USCL/RTS CCM 20 Apr 1864) in his »The Regular Swiss Round« ([Jones] 1863) and »Another Swiss Round« ([Jones] 1864), an entertaining travel report interspersed with historical sightseeing in Switzerland. The RTS hence »resolved that it be not published in a separate form« (USCL/RTS CCM 20 Apr 1864).[15] Jones's book was finally published together with a third series by Strahan in Edinburgh in 1865, though the RTS denied Strahan's application »for casts of thirty engravings used in the ›Regular Swiss Round‹« (USCL/RTS CCM 17 May 1865). The book therefore

---

14 The RTS had given »permission [...] to Mr Jerdan to publish in a separate form his papers entitled ›Men I have known‹« though »full liberty being reserved to the Society to publish also, if thought desirable« (USCL/RTS CCM 19 July 1865). The book was consequently published by George Routledge and Sons, while there appears to be no later publication by the RTS itself. As a consequence, the RTS addressed the problem of republication as well as copyright again later that year: »The attention of the Subcommittee was called to the question of reprinting in separate form of articles from the periodicals: when it was directed that the receipt on payments of the same should expressly state that the transference of copyright of MSS. included their issue in separate form by the Society at its discretion« (USCL/RTS CCM 21 Dec 1865).

15 The Subcommittee had a month earlier proposed for »›The Regular Swiss round‹, by Rev. Harry Jones, from Leisure Hour; for the two series, with additional chapters, to be issued as a separate volume« (USCL/RTS CCM 16 Mar 1864).

presented illustrations still similar in depiction yet slightly changed in style and execution. Despite the RTS's neglect to publish Jones's two series in book format or to allow use of the illustrations, his preface still acknowledged the earlier publication in the *Leisure Hour*, as he there »thanked the Proprietors of the ›Leisure Hour‹ for their kind permission to reprint so much of the following volume as appeared in its pages« (Jones 1865b: iv).[16]

In most cases, the transfer from the *Leisure Hour* into book format resulted in a reduction of illustrations, arguably for economic reasons, though this also indicates that periodicals were more prone to a picturesque style of popular history than book publications, which were considered more respectable. Howard Hopley's preface to *Under Egyptian Palms: Or, Three Bachelors' Journeyings on the Nile* (1869) thanked »the Editor of the ›Leisure Hour‹ [...] for the use of the woodcuts which illustrate this work« (Hopley 1869b: v), yet despite the gratitude he expressed towards the RTS, Hopley's book included only one illustration facing page 202 besides the frontispiece on the book's title page. »Shades of the Departed« ([Stoughton] 1852-1853) was accompanied by eight illustrations, as was »Echoes from Westminster Hall« ([Stoughton] 1856). Both series were together collected into *Shades and Echoes from Old London* (Stoughton 1864a), which provided only four illustrations of smaller size due to the book's format. In the case of Cuthbert Bede's *Fotheringhay, and Mary, Queen of Scots* (1886), all illustrations from »Fotheringhay« (Bede 1865) were kept, though this is no surprise, as the series had originated as a three-parter with original illustrations by Bede himself, as he stated in the book's preface (1886: 3).

Bede's preface – like the other book titles mentioned so far – acknowledged the origin with the *Leisure Hour*. Others, however, neglected to make such references to the earlier publication, thereby indicating the lower reputation of the periodical and its popular approach to history. Neither Bitha Fox's *How to See the English Lakes* ([1858]; see case study below) nor Frederick Arnold's *Oxford and Cambridge: Their Colleges, Memories, and Association* (1873) gave credit to the *Leisure Hour*, though both were republished in book form by the RTS itself. Mary Louisa Whately's *Among the Huts in Egypt: Scenes from Real Life*, published by Seeley, Jackson, & Halliday in 1871 and largely similar to her »Life in

---

16 Jones's series »The Idler on the Rhine«, however, which was printed in the *Leisure Hour* in 1865, appears to have remained without a book republication. For an analysis of transcultural perceptions of Germany in »The Idler on the Rhine«, cf. Korte (2015b), who, for instance, also considers the series' description of historical sights via the anonymous author's criticism of the »Rhine's Romantic legacy« portrayed in Baedeker and Murray guidebooks (Korte 2015b: 360).

Egypt«, printed in the *Leisure Hour* in 1865, did not link back to the periodical. And Walter Thornbury's *Haunted London* (1865), published by Hurst and Blackett five years after its serialisation ([Thornbury] 1860), did not reference the *Leisure Hour* either.[17]

The examples outlined here indicate that the transfer from periodical to book resulted in most instances in the addition of peritextual features such as prefaces or introductions, but also tables of contents, indices, authors and publishers names and often a loss of illustrations. As regards illustrations, R. Mitchell sees this transformation in connection with the academisation of history and implicitly links this to different media's reputation and possibly also divergent intended audiences:

»[P]icturesque historical reconstruction was clearly the principle guiding many writers in the first half of the nineteenth century. For many works of this period, illustrations were considered vital [...]. After the middle of the century, although this mode of presentation continued to be important, it was challenged by the development of history as a formal academic discipline. In history books and textbooks, the dramatic narrative texts and metaphorical illustrations of picturesque reconstruction began to give way to a more scientific format and apparently objective metanymic [sic] images. Illustrations became dispensable, and were often considered inappropriate: they ceased to appear in many textbooks, for instance. Illustrations were often being relegated to works intended for a very juvenile audience, or to texts considered inferior as history.« (R. Mitchell 2000: 286)[18]

In reverse, the transformation into book form calls attention to what the *Leisure Hour* ›lacked‹ and which features were possibly lost in the transfer from book into periodical. On the spectrum of a changing historiographical landscape, this hence shifted the representations of the past in the *Leisure Hour* even more towards the popular, while their rendering within book publications with their characteristic peritextual and material features associated them with a more scientific approach as works of reference.

---

17 Thornbury had arranged with the RTS to republish his *Leisure Hour* articles elsewhere (USCL/RTS CCM 14 Dec 1859), though this agreement might not have necessitated a reference to the earlier periodical publication.

18 Cf. also R. Mitchell's chapter on scientific history's influence on »The Evolution of the English History Textbook« (2000: Chapter 3).

From Book to Periodical

Generally, where periodical serialisation followed book publication, textual changes occurred more frequently in order to adapt material to the periodical's historical agenda and popular historical approach. As the case study in Chapter 3 on Merryweather's »Working Man in the Olden Time« has already shown, the RTS appears to have selected popular works that would fit the periodical's historical programme or could easily be changed to conform to its intended readership. This was achieved by adjusting style, expression or terminology as well as reproducing or appropriating only specific chapters or passages, as the serialisation in itself necessitated a significant reduction in text – 14 of these series had three to five parts, one had six parts and the longest one 13 parts, while all of them were linked to longer, monographic works.

The articles often noted at the outset that they were based on and followed the structure of (longer) book publications. At times, they combined this with a hint towards a necessary selection and shortening of text from book to periodical and the resulting cursory look at the past. »Sir Isaac Newton« (1856), for instance, reduced David Brewster's three-volume *Memoirs of the Life, Writings, and Discoveries of Sir Isaac Newton* (1855) to three parts. In addition, the series' initial footnote in the *Leisure Hour*, which gave Brewster's work as its source, stated:

»Exception may, perhaps, be taken to some parts of the arrangement of the materials of this work, and to the almost blinding love of the biographer for his hero; but, as a whole, these volumes form a most valuable contribution to our biographical literature, and entitle the author to our admiring gratitude.« (»Sir Isaac Newton« 1856: 124, Fn)

Similarly, »The Knight of Eskdale« (1857) referenced its source and necessary selectiveness in the appropriation when in its initial article it

»greet[ed] with a hearty welcome the valuable biography of Sir John Malcolm which has recently proceeded from the fertile pen of Mr. J. W. Kaye, whom we might almost designate the Indian historiographer, from the number and excellence of his works in that rich department of historic and biographic literature. From his volumes we purpose gleaning a few of the more noteworthy events and incidents in the active and exciting career of his hero, who, in very many respects, is worthy of the imitation of young men desirous of doing a truly great and good work in the world in their day and generation.« (»The Knight of Eskdale« 1857: 296)

In the same manner, »The Jews of China« (1867), signed »By B. Harris Cowper«, »follow[ed] very much the work of Mr. Finn, who, in ›The Jews in China‹ (London, 1842), has collected, in an interesting form, the chief facts then ascertained« (Cowper 1867: 301).[19]

These three series may be considered historical book review essays in a very broad sense. Other series, however, which displayed similar reductions, merely pointed readers towards another publication without providing clear details such as titles, publishers or year of publication for their book counterparts. In their adaptation of material from other sources,[20] these series leaned even more towards Creighton's idea of ›sketchiness‹ (see above). »The Philadelphia Printer« (1854) and »The Queen of a Literary Coterie« (1855) closely followed the structure of their book counterparts in the passages they selected to present. And although both of them quoted frequently from that one title, they did not clearly present it as the source for their biographical narratives. »The Philadelphia Printer« did not specify from whose edition of Franklin's autobiography it took its narrative and quotes, and »The Queen of a Literary Coterie« on Lady Blessington only referenced quotes as »Dr. Madden very justly remarks« (»Queen« 1855: 360) or as »is pronounced by Dr. Madden« (ibid.: 373), without providing further details on where Dr Madden had said as much.

Another set of series was even more vague about their sources, although they closely followed their book counterparts' structure in presenting the past. A se-

---

19 The second part started again by directly referring to Finn, while the third and last part also presented other sources.

20 This appears similar to what is commonly referred to as scissors-and-paste journalism; see, for instance, Feely (2009) and Nicholson (2012). Nicholson notes the difference to »imitative compilers« (Nicholson 2012: 276), which may rather apply here. Note on this point of copying and appropriating the work of other (though also rather popular) authors also Hesketh's observation of »popularizers« and »interlopers«: »Part of the process of establishing the Rankean approach as the orthodox historical methodology involved emphasizing the *discipline* of history in establishing an appropriate demarcation between good history and bad, between a proper scientific analysis of the past and a mere Romantic narrative of largely imaginary past. Here English historians were also following the lead of their more properly scientific colleagues who were seeking to establish more formal boundaries between the work done by men of science and that done by popularizers and other interlopers who often appropriated the work of others and at times even put forward such findings to suit their own interests while embracing a Romantic form of narration that would appeal to broader audiences« (2011: 5).

ries of articles on »Blind Travellers«, »Blind Mathematicians« and »Blind Me-
chanics« (1856-1857) copied its anecdotes with slight adjustments from James
Wilson's *Biography of the Blind* (1833 [1821]). The only reference to that work
was provided within the series' initial biographical anecdote on the blind Wilson
himself (obviously also amended after the book), who was said to have »committed to memory a vast collection of pieces, which […] assisted him, with much
credit to himself and benefit to others, to compose his ›Biography of the Blind‹«
(»Blind« 1856: 588). »Abraham Lincoln« (1868) commenced by relating that the
illustrator of the series »was employed to illustrate a biography published in the
United States« (103-104). A comparison of text and accompanying illustrations
showed that this must have referred to Joseph Hartwell Barrett's illustrated third
edition of *Life of Abraham Lincoln* (1865), though Barrett's name was never
mentioned. Both the series on the »Blind« and that on »Abraham Lincoln« followed the original text with only slight changes in phrasing or occasional summaries of content. They even used the same quotes in direct speech or quotations
from secondary or primary sources as their book counterparts, yet they never
referenced the books by Wilson or Barrett from which they obviously copied.

Similar vague attributions occurred when series were in parts based on histo-
ry books, while they to some extent also presented original material on the past.
»The Walcheren Expedition« (1855), which was signed »By One Who Survived
It«, closely followed the account given in Archibald Alison's *History of Europe,
Vol. 9* (1849), with some rephrasing. Yet it referred to its book counterpart only
once simply as »says sir Archibald Allison [sic]« (»Walcheren« 1855: 133). And
only in its concluding part did the series obviously include original material by
»One Who Survived It« when the text announced:

»Here ends, then, our history, if we may so call it, of this national disaster; but before
drawing our remarks to a close, a few personal recollections of the expedition may interest
our readers – removed as the event is from the present day by an interval of nearly half a
century.« (Ibid.: 173)

The style of the narrative accordingly changed to the first person, in contrast to
the previous narrative as well as the more objective narrative in the book, a
change to which the periodical text meta-referentially pointed in brackets: »I was
(to drop the indirect form of speech)« (ibid: 173). Similarly, »Periodical Peeps at
Female Costume in England« (1867) appropriated Frederick William Fairholt's
*Costume in England: A History of Dress from the Earliest Period till the Close
of the Eighteenth Century* (1860 [1849]) – though under a feminine perspective
with changes to text and illustrations; only in its final part did the series

acknowledge its indebtedness to Fairholt's book and like »The Walcheren Expedition« then seem to provide original material (see case study below).

Besides »The Jews of China«, it remains unclear who authored the series mentioned so far in which books were transferred to and highly informed the periodical text and historical programme. It can, however, be presumed that the contributors were not the same as the books' authors.[21] This is different in the following examples, in which book as well as periodical text appear to have been authored by the same person. »Sketches of the Crimea« ([Milner] 1855b) closely resembled the text with some simplifications in style, followed the chronology of Thomas Milner's *The Crimea, Its Ancient and Modern History: The Khans, the Sultans, and the Czars* (1855a) in the passages it presented[22] and seems to have been authored for the *Leisure Hour* by Milner himself, as RTS payment listings indicate.[23] The *Leisure Hour* printed »Sketches of the Crimea« unsigned, and Milner was never mentioned in the *Leisure Hour*'s text. Both periodical series and book were published at about the same time,[24] yet neither referred to the other. In commercial terms, the transfer from book to periodical easily created a new text; yet in this instance the exchange surprisingly did not make use of an advertisement of the other publication format. »The Balloon and its Application« (Glaisher 1864) and »Curiosities of [various places in London]« (Timbs 1868-1873), by contrast, were signed by James Glaisher and John Timbs, respectively. Both had conducted research and published on these topics elsewhere in more scientific contexts, yet clear links to earlier book publications were not provided. Similarly, the first part of »The Working Man in the Olden Time« (M[erryweather] 1852) was signed F.S.M. and was an amended version of Merryweather's own *Glimmerings in the Dark, or Lights and Shadows of the Olden Time* (1850; see case study in Chapter 3).

---

21 Though I was not able to identify who authored these series, the RTS minutes do not appear to indicate that payments were made for authors of the respective books identified.

22 While the book was accompanied by three maps, the periodical series included five illustrations of landscape, buildings and a narrative scene.

23 UCLS/RTS CCM (18 Apr 1855) stated that Milner received a payment of £10 for a publication in the *Leisure Hour*.

24 The series ran in the *Leisure Hour* from 15 March until 10 May 1855, and the book was presumably published later, with the preface dating 24 June 1855. However, it can be assumed that the book's text was written and submitted earlier than the periodical text, and I have therefore categorised this as periodical follows book publication.

The series of articles on »Windsor Castle« ([Stoughton] 1859c), presented within the *Leisure Hour*'s monthly part for June 1859, used several books as sources, amongst them Stoughton's *Notices of Windsor in the Olden Time* (1844). The transfer to periodical text, carried out by Stoughton himself, here resulted in a shift not only of material but also of textual genre from historiography to travel guide for historical sightseeing.[25] Similarly, the monthly part for April 1864 on the Shakespeare tercentenary assembled material from a variety of books by well-known authors; yet it also included presumably original material (see Appendix A, Tab. 22 and case study below). Both »Windsor Castle« and the »Shakespeare« series hence made readers aware of more »[m]aterial elsewhere provided« in the books they referenced. A more direct invitation to consult a book for reference was made in »Pictures in Words« (1858), a series of historical puzzles which, with its subsequently printed brief answers, always directed readers to Thomas Milner's *History of England* (1853; see case study below) for further information.

With its link to Milner's *History*, »Pictures in Words« implied a clear distinction between the two media, that is, the periodical's reduced and select depiction versus the book's comprehensive presentation as a work of reference. Though these book publications would arguably still have been considered to be part of the print market for popular history, the fact of being clad in the covers of and furnished with the characteristic features of a book and hence presented within a more reputable format would also affect the reputation of the content. As books, the historical representations did not have the double-column periodical layout, they might have fewer illustrations and, if they had originated from the *Leisure Hour*, they might at times not acknowledge this but would possibly gain more prestige via the attribution of an author's name.

CASE STUDIES (1): FROM BOOK TO PERIODICAL

The different attitudes and expectations towards the medium, as well as the presentation of history embedded within other content in the *Leisure Hour*, meant that the serialised texts on the past most likely reached different audiences than their book counterparts and thereby also conferred a different outlook on a national historical identity in terms of gender and age, but also class. In this re-

---

25 The jubilee number identified Stoughton as having contributed »in 1859 a series on ›Windsor Castle and Neighbourhood‹« (»Authors« 1902: 254); see Chapter 6 for a closer analysis.

spect, the following case studies look more closely at five series and their correspondence to book texts or the idea of the material book. This first set of two case studies (From Book to Periodical) considers books that informed periodical series printed over a longer period of time; a second set of three case studies (Monthly Parts) is dedicated to the phenomenon of series printed entirely within a monthly issue of the *Leisure Hour*. The case studies in both sections analyse how the RTS (re)used popular historical accounts in its attempt to address the *Leisure Hour*'s family audience.

From Book to Periodical (1):
»Periodical Peeps at Female Costume«

With its series »Periodical Peeps at Female Costume« (1867),[26] the *Leisure Hour* reappropriated Fairholt's *Costume in England* under a gendered perspective.[27] Fairholt had written his book specifically for the use of artists, as his preface pointed out:

»A knowledge of costume is in some degree inseparable from a right knowledge of history. We can scarcely read its events without in some measure picturing ›in the mind's eye‹ the appearance of the actors; while correct information on this point has become an acknowledged essential to the historical painter. The reign of imaginary costume has reached its close. A conviction of the necessity and value of ›truth‹ in this particular has been the slow growth of the last half-century. A deaf ear was long turned to the urgency of critical antiquaries by whom it had been studied. Assertions were constantly made of the

---

26 An earlier and shorter (and German) version of this case study conducted by me, which does not, however, address the comparison to Fairholt's book but provides a comparison to popular representations of the past in the German family magazine *Gartenlaube*, can be found in Reusch/Lechner (2013).

27 The RTS minutes list payment entries for Bell & Daldy as well as a T.R. Wright around the time of the series' publication (USCL/RTS CCM 19 Sept 1867). Fairholt's book, as the footnote in the final part of the series referenced, was published with Bell & Daldy, and the footnote also stated that »[s]ome of our illustrations have been copied, by arrangement, from this valuable work« (»Periodical Peeps« 1867: 781, Fn), therefore suggesting that the publisher would have received payment for the engravings. It can, however, at this point not be determined whether »T.R. Wright« might refer to the historian and antiquary Thomas Wright (1810-1877), who used to work with the late artist and antiquary Fairholt (1814/18-1866), and whether Wright might have compiled the series for the *Leisure Hour*.

impossibility of accomplishing their desires, and twice the necessary amount of trouble was taken in inventing a heterogeneous costume that would have been required to procure accuracy.

The great principle that all historic painting *should* be truthful in costume, and *could* be made so, I hope to have proved by the aid of the many woodcuts scattered through the volume. They are unpretending as works of art, and are to be looked on merely as facts; such they undoubtedly are, and they have been got together with no small care and research, and from very varied sources. Ancient delineations and ancient authorities have been solely confided in. [...] As no historian could venture to give wrong dates designedly, so no painter should falsify history by delineating the characters on his canvas in habits not known until many years after their death, or holding implements that were not at the time invented. [...] False costume is now an unnecessary obtrusion, and not worth an excuse.« (Fairholt 1860 [1849]: iii-iv)

Fairholt here at length argued for a correct, truthful depiction of history, for which his work should prepare historical painters of the period.[28] The book seems to have served a similar purpose for the series in the *Leisure Hour*, though its title, »Periodical Peeps at Female Costume«, already indicated, in contrast to the more inclusive *Costume in England*, the changed focus on women as well as a popular history approach. Articles on the past were often marked in their titles as »Rambles«, »Gossip«, »Sketches«, »Curiosities« or »Peeps« (see overview in Appendix A, Tab. 2) and thereby coded as feminine (Maitzen 1998: 50-54; see Chapter 1). Maitzen, however, shifts this possibly deteriorating perception when she states that »the term [gossip] implies easy readability, graceful narrative, colorful details, an anecdotal approach, and a light, rather than serious, attitude towards the material« (Maitzen 1998: 54).

»Periodical Peeps at Female Costume« used just such an approach, and in contrast to Fairholt's preface, the introduction – similar to Thackeray's and Sala's series in the *Cornhill* analysed in Chapter 4 – accordingly appeared to distinguish itself from the practice of academic historiography:

»We are going [...] to indulge in some occasional glances at the costume of the women of England at various periods of our history. Having no intention of compiling anything like a consecutive chronicle of the march of fashion in dress, or of attempting to speculate, as men have speculated before now, upon the connection between costume and character, we shall limit ourselves merely to the selection of what is indicative of a general progress to-

---

28 As such Fairholt's *Costume in England* is discussed together with similar works by Strutt, Plancé and others in Roy Strong's *Painting the Past* (2004: 67-87).

wards good taste on the one hand, and such deviations from it as are manifested by the eccentric, absurd, and grotesque on the other. Being, further, under no obligation binding us to completeness in our casual survey, we shall be as arbitrary as it suits our convenience to be in the choice of matters to be set before the reader.« (»Periodical Peeps« 1867: 519)

The introduction here claimed that it would approach its topic in an unsystematic and selective way with the vague aim of presenting the development of good taste in English society. In reverse to its popular approach, this introduction hence characterised – and maybe criticised – academic historiography as proceeding chronologically with the clear aim of uncovering a specific concept in a comprehensive way.

It may therefore be rather surprising that, contrary to the introduction's claim, the series in its five parts nevertheless presented a quite comprehensive history of costume in chronological order, which followed the typical periodisation of English historical narratives along monarchs' regencies. The series set in with the Roman occupation of Britain, continued with Anglo-Saxon as well as Norman regencies and then chronologically followed monarchies from Richard II onwards. Yet Bonnie G. Smith has pointed out that

»the social history of women also encountered problems of form and narrative. Its practitioners found that this approach to the past did not mesh with traditional political history. [...] Today such subjects are often labeled ›impressionistic‹ [...] [or] ›chatty.‹ But the difficulty in writing about homes and customs was [...] the inappropriateness of conventional chronology [...]. When grand public events appeared on the periphery rather than at the center, historical narratives lacked an accepted (or acceptable) storyline in much the same way as did the antiheroic approach.« (B.G. Smith 1984: 720)

Fairholt's book was arranged in strictly chronological order – presumably for the practical purpose of serving as a reference work for artists:

»Each period is treated distinctly from that which precedes or follows it, and the history of the costume of each period commences with that worn by royalty and nobility; then the dresses of the middle classes are considered, and the commonality in the last place. The civil costume being thus disposed of, that worn by the clergy is next described; and each section closed by a disquisition on the armour and arms of the military classes.« (Fairholt 1860 [1849]: iv-v)

A relapse to conventional chronology in the *Leisure Hour*'s popular account (with the tension with academic historiography implied in its introduction) may therefore on the one hand have been due to the set-up of its source. On the other hand, it was used to inscribe female everyday history into the national narrative, especially as the chronology was here not only used as a structural device in order to attribute dresses to a specific period but at instances described the influence of regents on the public's clothes or discussed the development of fashion in connection to political conditions. Thus, the series noted on Mary Tudor:

»So long as she filled the throne all ranks of her subjects appear to have practised the utmost simplicity in dress; and it may be that they were influenced in so doing by the stringent enactments she passed, seeing that she punished the wearing of silk by any man below the rank of a knight by a fine of ten pounds for each day's offence.« (»Periodical Peeps« 1867: 522-523)

This »simplicity of costume« was then noted to have changed »soon after the accession of Elizabeth«, who,

»though characterised by a certain starched dignity not over attractive, was neither pretty nor graceful; and she was not slow in having recourse to all the arts of dress and personal adornment. Her example was of course speedily followed by the ladies of her court; and from them the love of finery [...] spread through all ranks of society.« (Ibid.: 583-584)

The series' focus on the everyday history of dress may have been perceived as a field gendered as female,[29] but the series also talked about male costume. Yet while women and their clothes were presented predominantly in neutral terms, the grotesque style of costume was mainly attributed to the influence of men. The text, for instance, noted that

»[t]he reign of Richard II, himself a great fop, witnessed more of the freaks of fashion than the most industrious chroniclers were able to record – the man especially indulging in more monstrosities and absurdities of dress than had ever before been witnessed.« (Ibid.: 522)

And on the change of regency from Elizabeth to James, it stated:

---

29 In her study of Victorian historic costume balls, Thrush notes: »Overall, it makes sense that women chose to exercise their interest in history through fashion, as this was one of the few creative avenues open to them« (Thrush 2007: 273).

»It is likely that the reform in dress at which we have hinted as taking place at the close of Elizabeth's reign, was extremely partial and limited in duration; for we find that, not long after the accession of James, the ladies incurred the rebuke of satirists and divines, for the vanity and exorbitancy of their attire, for their painting and blotting, and for the indecent exposure of their necks and breasts. This latter feature in the change of costume, which began with the Stuarts, must be familiar to every one who has paid any attention to the portraits preserved in our public galleries representing the dames of the period.« (Ibid.: 586)

A refocusing on women in contrast to Fairholt's book was above all also evident in the engravings accompanying the text. A footnote in the final part acknowledged that »[s]ome of our illustrations have been copied, by arrangement, from this valuable work« (ibid.: 781, Fn; see Fn 27 above). Only one of the 39 illustrations to the series displayed male figures, and eight of the others were significantly changed for publication in the *Leisure Hour*. »Dame Cicely Page« (ibid.: 534) was portrayed in the *Leisure Hour* as standing, while Fairholt's book presented her in prayer (Fairholt 1860 [1849]: 208), and the other seven amended illustrations erased the male figures which their counterparts in Fairholt's book depicted. »Countess of Somerset« (»Periodical Peeps« 1867: 585), for instance, was presented in the *Leisure Hour* on her own, while Fairholt's book depicted her together with the Earl of Somerset (Fairholt 1860 [1849]: 237). And the »Country Girl and Town Dame« (»Periodical Peeps« 1867: 648) were in Fairholt's original also accompanied by a »gentleman« (Fairholt 1860 [1849]: 287-8).

Articles in the *Leisure Hour* often neglected to reference their sources, and »Periodical Peeps at Female Costume« presented only in its very last part Fairholt as the main source for the previous instalments:

»Hitherto we have been indebted to other authorities – chiefly to Mr. Fairholt's ›Costume in England‹ – for the materials of the rapid and summary survey we have made. From the close of the last century downwards, however, we have no such excellent authority to consult, and are driven to such resources as observation and the reminiscences of the past may avail to supply. It is true we might ransack the old Ladies' Magazines, but then we more than doubt our capacity for making to advantage researches in such a quarter; and therefore we prefer to draw solely on our own experiences, and to set down – necessarily somewhat at random – such changes in the costume of the women of England as may present themselves to our own recollection.« (»Periodical Peeps« 1867: 781)

The reference to Fairholt's book again made clear that the series presented mainly an abridgement of a historiographical (though rather antiquarian) work, which
was in addition accompanied by an extensive glossary »furnish[ing] the reader
with what he requires, as many of the articles there incorporated are in fact illustrated historical essays on various minor articles of costume« (Fairholt 1860
[1849]: v). On the other hand, the contributor here thwarted women's periodicals
as a source.[30] Thus, »Periodical Peeps at Female Costume« took on a middle position between popular and more academic sources represented by the periodical
and book medium when it connected everyday life to public life by discussing
fashion as political and connecting everyday history to political history, thereby
inscribing the common woman into the historical narrative.[31]

From Book to Periodical (2):
»Historical Enigmas« and »Pictures in Words«

While »Periodical Peeps at Female Costume« might have appealed to the female
part of the family audience by focusing on women in national history, acrostics
and riddles such as »Historical Enigmas« (1856-1857) and »Pictures in Words«
(1858) would have been intended especially for young readers. Books of acrostics with puzzles on history and geography were very popular during Victorian
times (cf. Hecimovich 2008, esp. »Introduction«) and had the didactic purpose
of attracting girls and boys to engage with history in a playful manner.

Acrostics could, for instance, in a style very similar to the *Leisure Hour*'s
»Enigmas«, be found in F.M. Ingall's *Historical & Geographical Enigmas*
(1866) as well as Charlotte Eliza Capel's *Victorian Enigmas* (1861), and the
peritexts (title and preface) of these publications may shed some light on the
purpose and intended audience of the *Leisure Hour*'s »Enigmas« as well as the
way in which readers were supposed to engage with history through them. As
the subtitles to Ingall's and Capel's collections suggest, such acrostics were assumed to be attractive »For Her Young Friends« (Ingall) and »Intended in a
Novel Manner to Combine Amusement with Exercise in the Attainment of Gen-

---

30 At other instances, however, the series made use of Joseph Addison and Richard
    Steel's *Spectator* (1711-12/14), a periodical for the upper classes.

31 Similar to Merryweather's »The Working Man in the Olden Time«, the series regret-
    ted the absence of working women in ancient sources: »This was the costume of a
    proud queen; what was that of the average British woman at the same period can only
    be guessed, as no illustrative monuments of the time, if there ever were such monu-
    ments, have come down to us« (»Periodical Peeps« 1867: 519).

eral Knowledge« (Capel). Both Ingall and Capel collected enigmas in their books which they had designed themselves to privately tutor children in history, and in Capel's case they were specifically directed at nurturing »well-educated gentlewom[e]n« (1861: viii). Thus, they used enigmas to increase knowledge of history by inviting readers to »search your histories, [...] fixing firmly in your minds some few facts not known before« (Ingall 1866: v). Capel furthermore recommended »research in many popular works on the various subjects of history, biography, etc.« (1861: viii) in order to solve the enigmas, thereby, as Ingall noted, »gain[ing] instruction while finding amusement in searching perseveringly for every answer that previously-acquired knowledge does not enable you at once to supply« (1866: vi).

The *Leisure Hour* started its series of »Historical Enigmas«[32] on 3 January 1856, and from its fourth instalment in February on this also included »Geographical Enigmas«. The series presented 22 questions and answers in total up until 27 August 1857. The areas covered in the »Historical Enigmas« spanned from antiquity to (modern) British and European history. These puzzles always consisted of a paragraph describing a historical figure (or geographical space) whose name could be found by putting together the initials of answers to a list of riddles on other historical (or geographical) questions, which were provided beneath the longer paragraph of the superordinate enigma. The very first of the »Historical Enigmas« was – in keeping with the *Leisure Hour*'s Christian agenda – dedicated to Martin Luther, with the following superordinate riddle:

»ONE of the most undaunted heroes the world has ever seen: a profound thinker, a conclusive reasoner, he defied, single-handed, his powerful adversaries in many a field of argument, armed only with that ›two-edged sword‹ which he drew from the scabbard in which it had been hid for ages, and which he bequeathed to his countrymen, that with it they might defend the faith for ever.« (»Historical Enigmas« 1856: 16)

After this, the instruction read that »[t]he enigma may be solved by identifying the six subjoined characters, whose initials supply the successive letters of the person's name« and presented the following questions:

1. A luxurious Roman general, to whom Europe is indebted for a luscious fruit.
2. The Alma Mater of a botanist.
3. A famous sculptor of modern times, who was born on the verge of the arctic one.

---

32 The »Enigmas« were published anonymously, and I was unable to determine from the RTS payment listings who might have assembled them.

4. A martyr, whose enemies put him to death by treachery.

5. A brave prince, associated with Marlborough, who fought against his native country.

6. A wily French statesman of the seventeenth century. (Ibid.)

»Answers to the Historical Enigmas« were presented in the next or one of the succeeding numbers. In this case, the solution was given on 10 January 1856 in this manner: »LUTHER. – 1. Lucullus; 2. Upsal; 3. Thorwaldsen; 4. Huss; 5. Eugene; 6. Richelieu« (ibid.: 32).

In contrast to acrostics books, which presented questions and answers within the same or an accompanying volume, »Historical Enigmas« in the *Leisure Hour* used the principle of binding readers through serial publication, as solutions were printed in a different material unit, often even six or seven weekly issues (or one or two monthly issues) away. An easy peak at the answer was hence not possible, neither did earlier representations on the past in the *Leisure Hour* help to find the solutions.[33] Rather, the solvers of these puzzles would have had to consult other sources on history – as suggested in the prefaces to Ingall's and Capel's acrostics.

This implied correspondence to books was directly implemented in the short-lived series »Pictures in Words; or, Scenes from English History«, which ran from May to October 1858 and used a similar set-up. The series presented three riddles, on Prince William, Thomas-à-Becket and Wat Tyler, each of which described historical scenes in a short paragraph – unaccompanied by illustrations, though the title might have indicated them, yet picturesque in style. The first riddle read as follows:

»A NOBLE fleet of vessels is seen leaving a foreign shore. One of them remains behind for some hours, and then sets sail; sounds of revelry are heard from her deck, where a young man and his bride seem to be the principal personages. The wind is gentle and the moon shines brilliantly, and there appears every prospect of a safe and speedy voyage; but suddenly the vessel strikes upon some rocks, fills with water, and goes down. Piercing shrieks of agony are heard from the drowning passengers and crew, and one life alone is spared.« (»Pictures in Words« 1858: 287)

---

33 Electronic searches on the relevant historical actors and terms of the first enigma in the *British Periodical Collection* indicate that the *Leisure Hour* had provided some articles on Luther four years prior in its initial volume, while none of the other characters seem to have been treated in the *Leisure Hour* before this first enigma.

The solution, not provided until 12 weekly numbers (or two monthly parts) later, was »PRINCE WILLIAM, only son of Henry I, coming from France after his marriage« (ibid.: 479). In addition, it was recommended to »[s]ee Milner's ›History of England,‹ p. 181, published by the Religious Tract Society« (ibid.), which presented the following version of the event:

»His daughter Matilda was married in her twelfth year (1114) to Henry V. of Germany, and crowned with great pomp in the cathedral of Mentz, thus becoming an empress; his son William grew up to be cut off in the flower of youth by a fatal casualty; his consort, the ›good queen Maud,‹ was spared the pain which the untimely fate of the heir-apparent would have caused her, dying shortly before a tragical incident which has no parallel in our history. The king and prince were returning from Normandy where the latter had received the hand of a princess of Anjou. They embarked for England in separate vessels at Barfleur, November 25, 1120. Prince William, with his bride, was on board the *Blanche Nef*, or White Ship, and had a number of the juvenile nobility belonging to both countries for his companions, several of whom were of the highest rank. A grandson of the steersman who conducted the Conqueror across the channel was the commander. The king's vessel sailed, with the rest of the fleet, but the prince's was delayed in order to indulge in revelry. It was night when she left her moorings; the wind was gentle and the moon brilliant; but owing probably to the mariners being intoxicated, the *Blanche Nef* struck violently on some rocks at a spot called Catte-raze, now Raz de Catteville, and immediately began to fill. All on board perished, with the sole exception of a burgess of Rouen, who clung to the top of the mast, and was rescued on the following day by some fishermen. The king is said never to have smiled after receiving the tidings of this terrible disaster; but still was active in the pursuit of his selfish and ambitious objects.« (Milner 1853: 181)

The recommendation also directly linked the periodical to the book as a source for the riddles, and the referenced sequence in Milner's book shows by comparison that »Pictures in Words« presented a slightly abridged version of the passage. Thus advertising a work from its own publishing house, the RTS pointed with »Pictures in Words« beyond the boundaries of the *Leisure Hour* and invited readers to further study of the subject in an educational book publication on history, with Milner's *History*, as its subtitle indicated, being specifically intended for »Schools and Families«.

Young readers of the *Leisure Hour* would probably not have been able to find the solutions to the »Pictures« or the »Enigmas« on their own. Both series therefore encouraged an active engagement with history outside the covers of the periodical. Readers would have needed to consult a reference work on history in order to solve the riddles. On the other hand, one could imagine that the »Historical Enigmas« may have served to bring together the family or a circle of friends, who might have solved them in communion, or they might have discussed the historical issues addressed in »Pictures in Words«.[34] Therefore, these series had even more potential to stimulate an active and collective engagement with history across boundaries of gender and age than a possible reading-aloud of the *Leisure Hour*'s historical narratives within the family circle.

CASE STUDIES (2): MONTHLY PARTS

From Monthly Parts to Book: »How to See the English Lakes«

The remaining three case studies which close this chapter all refer to series that were printed entirely within the unit of a monthly part (see Appendix A, Tab. 20).[35] Many of these came in the form of travel writing which crossed over into historical writing by including references to the past through historical sightseeing or the description of historical spaces, such as the series »How to See the English Lakes« ([Fox (Lloyd)] 1857),[36] which was printed in five parts during

---

34 See the (paterfamilias) reading situations on the annual covers of the *Leisure Hour* discussed in Chapter 2 (Fig. 1).

35 Of the *Leisure Hour*'s 79 factual series on the past during the 1850s and 1860s, 34 were presented entirely within a monthly part. Twelve of them were connected to public history in a broader sense, and about 22 (11 of which had book counterparts) referred to the past in a more prominent way. Five monthly parts were descriptive historical reports, while another four descriptive articles referred to some extent – for instance in their introductions – to the past (see Fn 52 below); 10 monthly parts considered historical actors (see Fn 41 below); seven monthly parts were on travel or geographical writing to a large extent, and another 8 referred to the past to a minor extent (see Fn 36 below). Beyond these 34 monthly parts, another two were dedicated to historical fiction (see Appendix A, Tab. 19, Fn 8). Overall, the *Leisure Hour* presented 60 series (fiction as well as non-fiction) of three to five parts within monthly issues during the 1850s and 1860s, only 9 of which could be considered devoid of references to the past.

36 Other examples with a book counterpart were »Windsor Castle« (June 1859; see Chapter 6) and »Fotheringhay (November 1865; see above), and without an identified book counterpart: »A Summer Ramble Through Belgium and Holland« (August 1855), »A Ramble in the Tyrol« (September 1859; see Chapter 6), »The Tale of a West-End Suburb« (May 1862; see Chapter 6) and »The Volcanoes of Auvergne«

July 1857 (see Appendix A, Tab. 21). Through their monthly format, they could serve as take-along travel guides, thereby – like the series on »Historical Enigmas« and »Pictures in Words« – enabling an active engagement with history *in situ* beyond an armchair travel in space and time through reading.

The series described the trip to the Lake District of an »Uncle Charlie« and his two »London nieces« and related in detail their hiking tours through this natural resort, thereby appealing simultaneously to two generations of readers in its narration on a traditional English landscape. Early on in the first article, the series described the geographical space as immersed in ancient national history when it pointed out

»the grand old historic memories which still wander along the side of ›Kentmere High Street‹ and ›Hill Bell.‹ What is that firm line which is drawn along the ridge, looking here and there as if it were partially obliterated, but again standing boldly out from the face of the sod or of the rock? It is the track of the old Roman road, marching in its stern uncompromising way over the hills from Kendal on to Penrith. The deep hollow of Troutbeck was filled with a dense forest in the Roman time; and the Britons are said to have hidden themselves in terror among its dark shades, while their masters were panting one firm footstep after another along the crests of their guardian hills.« ([Fox (Lloyd)] 1857: 426)

The vagueness of Roman traces in the Lake District was again picked up in the final fourth part, which stated that »Egremont has its old Roman memoires and its tales of the Crusaders« (ibid.: 474).

Besides these traces of ancient civilisation, the series of course in large parts linked the Lake District to the more recent past of the »brotherhood of Lake Poets« (ibid.: 439) as well as other prominent figures which were still present in communicative memory (see Chapter 1, Fn 29),[37] thereby transforming the natu-

---

(September 1867), which might have had a book counterpart (see above), and which took rather a topographical or geological approach. Examples with references to the past in terms of historical contextualisation or passing remarks to history were »A Visit to the Staffordshire Potteries« (June 1853), a series of three articles on the Japanese (February 1859), »The South Kensington Museum« (April 1859), »Kew Gardens« (July 1862), »Royal Observatory, Greenwich« (January 1862), »A Trip to North Devon« (May 1862), »Kew Gardens« (July 1862), »West of Killarney« (September 1863) and »A Walk in South Devon« (July 1869).

37 On the phenomenon of the »literary tourist«, see Nicola J. Watson: »Eighteenth-century culture saw the rise of this new phenomenon, and the nineteenth and early twentieth centuries its heyday. [...] This appetite for seeking out the origins of the au-

ral space into a site of national literary and cultural commemoration. This is first evident when the hikers came across a pier at

»Storr's Hall. That well-known causeway still preserves its historic legend of the day, now drifting far back into the past, when Sir Walter Scott, Southey, and Wordsworth kept tryst with Canning upon that narrow pencilled line, while ›Christopher North,‹ as admiral of the fleet, ruled the movements of that famous regatta on Windermere. This was in 1825. They are all gone now; but this is the very land of echoes, and the mountains go on repeating any great name which they have once caught, as if they would never let it drop.« (Ibid.: 426)

Similarly, when the hikers reached Wordsworth's grave they

»drop their voices to a reverential hush, as they approach the remarkable cluster of graves in the Grasmere churchyard. The principal one, with the name of William Wordsworth on it, and nothing more, is as eloquent as it is touchingly simple. They stand long there, but they are all silent; and when they turn away, the eyes of more than one are swimming, as though they were mourning a friend.« (Ibid.: 442)

And the final part stated on Southey's connection to Keswick:

»[T]he unruffled lake and the meditative mountains, the fairy islets and the green and grey shores, the echo-haunted waterfalls and the memory of the one great man which lives so abidingly in the scenes that he loved so well, cannot be turned from without some costly effort.« (Ibid.: 489).

The metaphor of the echo for memory, which throughout the series was projected onto the geographical space, clearly merged nature and past into one and turned the Lake District, as the »very land of echoes«, into an almost sacred reservoir for national history.

---

thor and the locations of the author's writings led by the end of the nineteenth century to the habit of reinventing whole region of the national map as ›Shakespeare country‹, ›Wordsworth's Lake District‹, ›Scott-land‹, ›Brontë country‹, ›Dickens's London‹, ›Hardy's Wessex‹ and so on« (2006: 5). The series »How to See the English Lakes« mentioned figures such as John Wilson, Sir Walter Scott, Robert Southey, William Wordsworth, Charles Lloyd, Elizabeth Smith, Alfred Tennyson, Felicia Hemans, Harriet Martineau, Percy Bysshe Shelley, Samuel Taylor Coleridge, William Wilberforce and Bishop Richard Watson.

Though the text was rather lyrical in its description of the hikers' tours through this culturally immersed landscape, it also provided practical travel advice on board and lodgings, transportation and itineraries for each day. The first part, for instance, concluded with the following footnote:

»We do not think that the inn charges, generally, throughout the lake district, can be called extortionate, even during the season, which may be said to extend from May to November. They rarely exceed, for breakfast, with meat, fish etc., 2*s.*; dinner, 2*s.* 6*d.*; tea, 1*s.* 6*d.* For a private sitting-room you will probably pay 2*s.* 6*d.* per day. You may have a boat for 1*s.* an hour, without an attendant boatman, if you mean to trust to your own strong arms; but you pay 1*s.* 6*d.* per hour if you take the boatman with you. Don't be tempted.« (Ibid.: 426, Fn).

Besides this, the series was accompanied by three full-page and three half-page illustrations of landscapes, as well as a half-page illustration of »The Graves of Wordsworth and his Relatives« (ibid.: 441) and a full-page »Map of the Lake District of England« which »[i]ndicates the general Route described in the papers« (ibid.: 488). As such, the monthly part for July 1857 could have easily served readers as a travel guide through the Lake District.

The series appeared to have been popular, as the Society decided to publish it as a book with almost the same text, and hence historical immersion, only a year later.[38] The book's smaller and bound format might have been more convenient to handle on an actual trip, as with the *Leisure Hour*'s presentation of the series, in the five issues that made up the monthly part, readers would have had a lot of other reading material with them on a trip to the Lake District (see Appendix A, Tab. 21); or they might have cut out the 24 pages on which the series was printed.[39] The book's presentation of the Lake District was thus not interrupted by other articles (such as the *Leisure Hour*'s mix of content) or separated by pauses

---

38 USCL/RTS CCM (13 Jan 1858) noted that »the papers in the Leisure Hour, entitled ›How to see the Lakes‹ by Miss Fox had been recommended for publication as a small book: it was ordered that they be referred to the authoress for her to prepare accordingly.« The note in the RTS minutes half a year after the publication within the *Leisure Hour* appears to indicate that a book publication of the articles was initially not planned; the book was published in July 1858, that is, one year after the original placement within the periodical.

39 The entry on »How to See the English Lakes« (2015) in the *Indiana University Library Catalog* suggests just this, as it reads: »Detached from five numbers of Leisure hour [sic]«.

(such as those induced through the *Leisure Hour*'s weekly publication rhythm). The narrative with its immersion in the past was hence less fragmented, and in addition, the book provided further auxiliary features for travellers, such as a fold-out »Map of the Lake Districts of Cumberland, Westmorlands and Lanca-shire« in its front cover as well as details on the »Route Pursued in this Tour« ([Fox 1858]: 96-98), a five-page index (ibid.: 107-110) and another five pages of a »List of Mountains« with heights, »List of Passes«, »List of Lakes« and »List of Waterfalls« (ibid.: 102-106).

The book could therefore serve better as a work of reference for travellers than the periodical, and as such even more than the series in the *Leisure Hour* might have stimulated active engagement with the Lake District's history be-yond armchair travel. Yet the periodical version of »How to See the English Lakes« was advertised as providing »much useful information« (*Literary Gazette* 1857: 674), just as a review on its book counterpart noted one year later that it »will also be a help to the home traveller« (*Literary Gazette* 1858: 78)[40]. With the small amount of 5*d.* to be invested for the five issues, compared to the book's price of 1*s.* 6*d.*, the periodical version would also have been by far more affordable to less affluent readers. Thus, the periodical medium and the cheaper price meant that different audiences could similarly learn about the Lake Dis-trict's history as a common cultural past and participate in the same national his-torical culture.

From Books to Monthly Parts: »Shakespeare«

Besides travel writing, many series presented within a monthly part approached the past via life writing, at times crossing over into travel or historiographical genres.[41] The monthly part for April 1864 dedicated to Shakespeare (see Appen-dix A, Tab. 22) took such a person-centred approach. »How to See the English Lakes« had commemorated English culture in its focus on the national heritage

---

40 The review was predominantly on Walter White's *A Month in Yorkshire*, with a brief paragraph on *How to See the English Lakes*.

41 Other examples for life writing in monthly parts are »The Lessons of Biography« (Ju-ly 1852; see Chapter 3), »Russia« (October 1854), »The Philadelphia Printer« (De-cember 1854), »The Walcheren Expedition« (March 1855), »The Queen of a Literary Coterie« (June 1855), »The Knight of Eskdale« (May 1857), »School Recollections« (May 1861), »Fenelon« (August 1865) and »Abraham Lincoln« (February 1868), as well as three articles on Wallenstein (January 1857), which were part of the longer se-ries »Studies in History« (1857-1858).

of the Lake District, and the *Leisure Hour*'s Shakespeare monthly part did the same in its dedication to the national bard's tercentenary.[42] Again, the price of 5*d*. for a total of five weekly issues would have made the series affordable to an intended working-class readership, while middle-class readers might rather have bought the entire monthly part at once. Yet this negotiation between classes of readers manifested itself not only in the affordability of the material unit but also in the way the *Leisure Hour* approached the tercentenary, for example by drawing on several book publications to complete its series. Some of the articles were not specifically created for contribution to the *Leisure Hour* but were extracts from books or letters by other literary voices.

In Britain, »the ownership and possession of Shakespeare« at the time was predominantly debated in terms of class (Taylor 2002: 362).[43] The organisation of the tercentenary celebrations meant not only separate involvement of the aristocracy and upper classes versus the trade unions and working classes, but also a contrast between country and metropolis, with commemorations being set up for Stratford-upon-Avon as well as London. Taylor concludes that

»For the aristocratic and theatrical sponsors of the National Shakespeare Committee the occasion [of the Shakespeare tercentenary] was represented as a celebration of ›Englishness‹, and as a homage to the contribution made to world culture by the English stage. [...] In contrast, the Trades Provisional Committee and the Working-Men's Shakespeare Committee, rooted in the trade union and reform circles of the capital, had their own agenda and took the lead in promoting the events as a festival of labour and reform.« (Ibid.: 374-375)

What might have appeared as a democratising, uniting force in a cross-class celebration of the national bard rather showed a division between these groups of

---

42 The *Leisure Hour* was of course not alone in this commemoration of Shakespeare. Habicht notes: »In late April 1864 reports and articles on celebrations of the three-hundredth birthday dominated the front pages of the entire English press for a week. Many papers also had illustrated supplements devoted to Shakespeare's life, career, and influence. Other news, however alarming, was tucked away in marginal columns« (Habicht 2001: 441). On the Shakespeare tercentenary of 1864, see also Foulkes (1984), (1997: Chapter 6), (2002: Chapter 3), Murphy (2008) and Taylor (2002); on Shakespeare in Victorian periodicals, see Prince (2008) and Robinson (1999).

43 See also Habicht (2001: 444-449).

people.[44] Therefore, »the 1864 Tercentenary never managed to bridge the gap between its aristocratic supporters and the working-class committees and associations that were formed to support the commemorations« (ibid.: 374).

This split in the celebrations was also manifest in general uses of Shakespeare. The upper classes focused on Shakespeare's literary genius and links to a rural, English landscape, while neglecting the social implications of Shakespeare's plays. Shakespeare was by this time associated with high culture, so that the upper classes claimed possession of him in his »emerging role as a national bard«, his »centrality to the literary canon« and his inclusion in university curricula, and they associated his figure with ideas of »Englishness, the landscape, and the nation« (ibid.: 361-362). Working class representations, by contrast, focused on a (re-)writing of Shakespeare as a working-class hero and self-made man and highlighted or reinterpreted his work with a focus on social tensions and conflicts. Radicals and the working classes in general uncovered Shakespeare for their own needs, especially as »exposure to the literary canon was important [for them] and allowed them to challenge the pretensions and apparent cultivation of their social betters« (ibid.: 361).

With this charged debate in mind, the *Leisure Hour*'s treatment of Shakespeare in April 1864 seemed to aim at a balance between these positions. The part kicked off with an essay by its regular contributor Reverend John Stoughton (on Stoughton, see Chapter 6), who rather neutrally reflected on the poet's celebration. After a brief introductory recapitulation of a former visit to Stratford,[45]

---

44 While celebrations in Stratford were set up for both an upper-class and local working-class audience, high admission fees excluded the working classes from participation in the official celebrations during the first week. The working classes and local Stratfordians had their own celebrations set up in the following week. In London the celebration, peaking in the planting of an oak tree at Primrose Hill sponsored by the Queen, was similarly marked by radical tensions, including pro-Garibaldi protests by the working classes and trade unions. See Taylor (2002) and Habicht (2001).

45 Stoughton wrote a letter to his wife during a visit to Stratford-upon-Avon on 7 September 1840: »I have been visiting this morning some of the spots hallowed by his memory, his birthplace and his burial-place, the beginning and ending of his earthly history. One feels a thrilling interest in walking over the spot that enshrines his dust, and in inquiring into the present history of his mighty mind, for he still lives, still thinks, still fells – but where? But of all the places I have visited none have pleased me more than the cottage at Shottery inhabited by his wife's father, where he wooed and whence he married his faithful Ann Hathaway, to whom the lines at the commencement were inscribed« (Lewis 1898: 35).

including a description of the main Shakespeare sights (accompanied by illustrations of Ann Hathaway's cottage, Mary Shakespeare's cottage and the church at
Stratford-upon-Avon), Stoughton's article focused on a discussion of the purpose of commemorations in general and the celebration of the Shakespeare tercentenary in particular. The article thereby side-stepped the ongoing controversies by retreating to a meta-historical level:

»Shakespeare needs no commemoration, festival, or statue to make him manifest to England or the world, but he may need something of that sort to make manifest the feeling towards him which exists at the present time in England and the world« (Stoughton
1864b: 219).

This »feeling«, however, appears to have been deliberately designed as an open
space. Although Stoughton's article in the *Leisure Hour* alluded to Shakespeare's genius, his role as a moral teacher and his blemishes, it excluded a discussion of content or biography, focusing on the perception of Shakespeare as
being the national poet. The open space could therefore be filled with whatever
each reader might want to associate with Shakespeare, and the *Leisure Hour*'s
presentation thereby enabled both the upper and the working classes to take possession of Shakespeare.[46]

The five issues of the *Leisure Hour* in April 1864 were made up of 12 articles on Shakespeare (plus a full-page coloured plate and a map)[47] integrated
within 21 items on other topics (see Appendix A, Tab. 22). The articles dedicated to Shakespeare mainly celebrated his heritage in Stratford, which was underlined by the use of illustrations of sites commonly associated with Shakespeare
tourism to Stratford. This heritage character was further explicated by the inclusion of a map of Stratford-upon-Avon, the monthly coloured plate depicting
Stratford-upon-Avon Church, an article on »The Autographs of Shakespeare«
(1864) with reproductions of two such autographs and an article on »Shake-

46 In her study on *Shakespeare in the Victorian Periodicals*, Prince notes: »In contrast to
    erudite articles circulated among learned readers who had already accepted Shake-
    speare's primacy within the canon, popular articles sought to educate a readership
    largely uninvested in Shakespeare's works. [...] Again and again, in magazines for
    children, for women, for the working classes, readers are invited to consider what
    Shakespeare might mean to them on an acutely personal level« (Prince 2008: 9).

47 On the monthly plates, see also Chapter 2 (Fn 30-32).

speare Portraits« (1864).[48] Overall, articles appear to have been selected in order to present the same balance aimed at in the Stoughton article: none of them charged the sites of Shakespeare's life in Stratford with specific symbolic meaning. Further, »Personal History of Shakespeare« (1864) seemed to deconstruct the common (working-class) practice of taking possession of Shakespeare by filling gaps in his biography[49] and instead repeatedly pointed out the lack of authentic facts about Shakespeare's life while simply stating which assessed evidence was available.

Articles reprinted in the *Leisure Hour* from other sources included a passage from Hugh Miller's *First Impressions of England and Its People* (1847), a letter written by Harriet Beecher Stowe on a visit to Stratford taken from *Sunny Memories of Foreign Lands, Vol. I* (1854)[50] and a reproduction of Samuel Johnson's *Preface to His Edition of Shakespear's Plays* (1765). The *Leisure Hour* thereby pointed towards the legacy of Shakespeare as a national poet not only for an English audience but also for the Celtic fringe (by including the Scottish evangelical journalist and geologist Hugh Miller) and the New World (by including the American author Harriet Beecher Stowe). While the *Leisure Hour* at this time still commonly practised anonymity in authorship, these excerpts were, of

---

48 Both of these articles resembled content and images a present-day visitor to Shakespeare's birthplace might commonly encounter on a typical guided tour by the Birthplace Trust.

49 Taylor points out in this context that the »lack of hard knowledge about the personal details of Shakespeare's life [...] helped reformers reconstruct an imaginary Shakespeare, allowing them to project plebeian fantasies on to the sparse details of his biography, and to reclaim him on the slenderest of evidence as a ›son of the soil‹« (Taylor 2002: 362). On Shakespeare in the Victorian working-class press, see Prince (2008: Chapter 1). She notes, for instance, that »Shakespeare was sometimes employed as an instrument of enculturation, but also that dissenting voices used the periodicals to construct alternative ways of understanding Shakespeare and, in so doing, alternative ways of articulating their own place within the hierarchies of their culture. For purposes often acutely contemporary, Shakespeare was rehabilitated into a working-class hero, a Chartist *avant la lettre*, and, contradictorily, an exemplar of the solidly middle-class values to which some magazines hoped working-class readers could be taught to aspire« (Prince 2008: 18).

50 This was sufficiently preceded by an article on the ongoing American Civil War, »The American Blockaded Ports« (see Appendix A, Tab. 22).

course, attributed to their respective authors,[51] thereby emphasising Shakespeare's national and international literary legacy. Readers of a higher standing and education would have been well aware of these authors and would have probably even owned a copy of Johnson's Shakespeare edition. The *Leisure Hour*'s compilation of texts on Shakespeare hence not only celebrated the poet but also served to educate a possibly less literarily informed readership such as the lower-middle and working classes.

Overall, the *Leisure Hour*'s Shakespeare part seems to have leaned more towards the upper-class attitude, since its materiality emphasised the monthly format (and its appeal to a rather middle-class audience) in contrast to the weekly issue (and its appeal to the working classes). The monthly part was furthermore advertised in the official Stratford programme. However, the penny price for each of the five issues that made up the monthly part also enabled less affluent people to participate at least from afar in the commemorations. The *Leisure Hour* thus seems to have focused on Shakespeare's heritage, legacy and canonicity, while nevertheless trying to convey this in class-neutral terms.

Material Correspondence of Monthly Parts and Books: »The Deadly Art of War«

Travel writing such as »How to See the English Lakes« and person-centred approaches to life writing such as the Shakespeare monthly part were the dominant ways in which the *Leisure Hour* included popular history. Plain historiographical approaches were also rare amongst the series in monthly form. An example of such a rendering of the past is »The Deadly Art of War«, which was presented in August 1854 (see Appendix A, Tab. 23).[52] Just like the Shakespeare part, which

---

51 Authorship for articles on Shakespeare was only declared in the first three issues (in titles or footnotes; for Miller the footnote also referenced the source work), including the articles by Stoughton and Henslow, which might have been contributions originally prepared for the *Leisure Hour*. The articles in the fourth and fifth issue, however, remained unsigned. See Appendix A, Tab. 22.

52 Other examples of monthly parts which use a descriptive historiographical approach are »Gossip about the Gipsies« (August 1854), »The Balloon and its Application« (May 1864), »The Jews of China« (May 1867) and »Gossip about Notable Books« (September 1870), which discusses literary history. Other descriptive series referred at least to some extent to the past, that is, in most instances the following monthly parts framed their topic within its historical development at least in their initial part(s):

was sparked by the event of the bard's tercentenary celebrations, »The Deadly Art of War« originated from the topicality of the Crimean War. In the way characteristic of serialised historical non-fiction, the series established a thematic unity across five parts,[53] which was here further supported by the monthly publication unit (i.e., the presentation of the entire series within a monthly part of the *Leisure Hour*). Nevertheless, the thematic unity of the series was threatened by other content within this monthly material unit as well as by thematically related content beyond the monthly covers. »The Deadly Art of War« may therefore serve as a concluding example not of a direct correspondence between book and periodical[54] but of a comparison of the material correspondence as well as similarities and differences between the two media.

The series set in with an article on the »Woolwich Arsenal« (1854), which, besides its military function, according to Simon Werrett also served as »a prominent tourist attraction in late eighteenth- and nineteenth-century London« as it »was a space open to the public« (Werrett 2010: 15). The first part of the series used the report on a visit at the Royal Arsenal to reflect on British society and war:

»We have roamed through acres of cannon, and cannonades, and mortars and mounted artillery, and ordnance of all kinds, the grim ranks of which have stood for long years in storm and sunshine, perhaps regarded by a generation unaccustomed to war as the useless symbols of a forgotten trade. If so, it needed but a breath breathed by a foe of Britain to dissipate such a blissful delusion, and to shed around these deep-mouthed engines of destruction a revived interest [...]. That breath has been breathed by the northern autocrat [...]; and again, and at once, the national mind reverts, like the miser to his concealed hoards, to the national means of defence and of offence – the resources which are at its command for the maintenance of its integrity.

»The Garden« (July 1859), »Leipsic Fair« (April 1863), »Letters Patent« (June 1864), »The Water-Supply of Cities and Towns« (October 1866).

53 The series was made up of an introductory article entitled »Woolwich Arsenal« and four more articles entitled »The Deadly Art of War«.

54 I was unable to clearly identify the author of the series or a book counterpart. It is likely that the series was contributed by John Scoffern, who, judging from the frequent entries in the RTS minutes, was a regular writer for the *Leisure Hour*; Scoffern authored *Projectile Weapons of War, and Explosive Compounds* (1858 [1850]), which similarly related a historiography of weaponry; further, »Dr Scoffern« was listed to have received payment for a contribution to the *Leisure Hour* in USCL/RTS (20 Sept 1854). On Scoffern, see also Chapter 6 and Appendix C.

[…] We could have wished that the cannon cast yesterday had been doomed to grow rusty and honeycombed, like the trophies of Marlborough and of Wellington, and the costly and fanciful weapons of two or three centuries back, which ranged round the Rotunda on Woolwich Common, are available for no other purpose than to show us something of the ›pride, pomp and circumstance‹ of war at different periods of our history.« (»Woolwich Arsenal« 1854: 487)

The article lamented the new need for the Arsenal due to the onset of the Crimean War, since »a generation unaccustomed to war« had grown since the Napoleonic Wars. While the article regretted the »stern necessity [of going to war] not without many sad thoughts, having very little enthusiasm for the so-called ›glories‹ of battle and bloodshed« (ibid.), it nevertheless in this initial as well as the following three parts of the series

»jot[ted] down a few memoranda on the subject, if to serve no better purpose than to assist the reader in forming some idea of the atmosphere of the battle field, and of the material and physical terrors which man lets loose against his fellow-man when he resorts to the *ultima ratio* of brute force as an argument.« (Ibid.)

In this regard, the series proposed a neutral stance towards the political ideas of the war, which it carefully introduced to readers:

»Whatever may be the sentiments of our readers on the question of the war now raging – whether they view it as a painful necessity imposed upon us by a sense of justice – or whether they take the most extreme views as to the preservation of peace, ›at any price‹ – the topic of our paper is one which at the present moment possesses a special interest, and demands an intelligent examination on the part of all.« (Ibid.: 490)

Thus side-stepping political »sentiments«, the *Leisure Hour'*s series relapsed into the past and in this and the four following articles entitled »The Deadly Art of War« related in more or less chronological order (from ancient times over the French Revolution up to Waterloo and after) the development of weaponry (starting with artillery, then cannon, fuses and shells and finally muskets, pistols, rifles and rockets).

This focus on a popular historiography of weaponry created a strong thematic unity in the articles of the series. Buyers of the single issue, however, would have had to wait for the next issue to continue reading. Readers who bought the monthly part would have been able to read the series within one sitting. Yet with the single articles being separated by time as well as other content (see Appendix

A, Tab. 23), they were further linked by direct markers referring to future or earlier instalments. The first article »Woolwich Arsenal« therefore ended: »In some future numbers of our journal we shall resume this subject more fully« (1854: 490), and the second article, which now appeared under the different title of the following series, »The Deadly Art of War«, necessarily referred back to this by again explaining the agenda of the series:

»We lament its [the present war's] existence; we abhor its horrors. If any sacrifice on our part could avert its presence, that sacrifice we would desire to make; but to ignore the existence of this monster evil, to pass it by as though it were not in the world, is a policy of but questionable benefit. That course we shall not adopt, but, following up our introductory article of last number, shall proceed to explain, with as much brevity as is compatible with the subject, the construction and uses of those ingenious but terrible machines which the craft of man has in various ages devised for the destruction of his fellows.« (»Deadly Art« 1854: 503)

At the end, this article briefly made readers aware of a continuation of the series:

»We must now conclude this paper on the more ancient forms of artillery. In our next we shall describe cannon as they are, and the numerous projectiles which at various epochs have been employed in connection with them.« (Ibid.: 508)

Accordingly, the next article started by briefly summing up what had come before: »In our preceding article we described the artillery of the ancients, and, passing on to the discovery of gunpowder and cannons, we showed the difficulties under which our ancestors laboured« (ibid.: 519). Markers like this continued until the end of the series, and from the second part on (or the third if one also counts »Woolwich Arsenal«), the magazine further emphasised a continuation by subtitling articles as »No. II.«, »No. III.« and »Concluding Paper«. The final part was thereby already clearly marked as such, and provided a certain closure to readers through its last paragraph:

»Thus concludes our sketch of the implements employed in the deadly art of war. Engines of destruction as they are, it is painful for a humane mind to contemplate their structure, and to remember the misery which it is their express function to create. We leave, therefore, the description which we have given, to be meditated on by the thoughtful reader. No humane mind can wish the modern Moloch to have his hecatomb of human sacrifices offered up to him, attended by the wails of the widow and the orphan. But, alas, the cure of the evil is difficult to suggest, and he is the best patriot who fervently solicits God to remove the scourge of war from our land.« (»Deadly Art« 1854: 557)

The series thus framed its popular historiography of weaponry by in the end returning to its overall presentist ›pacifist‹ agenda, and it concluded on a Christian tone by drawing on images of sacrifice. The thematic coherence was furthermore emphasised through the repeated direct reader addresses and the appeal to a cross-generational audience, with the prominent inclusive we-narrator referring to earlier generations who still remembered the Napoleonic Wars and the present generation »unaccustomed to war«, culminating in those now affected by the war as »widow« and »orphan«.

Within the five numbers for August, the series hence reinforced the monthly unit through the creation of a strong thematic unity. In contrast to books, however, which clearly confined thematic content within the boundaries of the material unit, the thematic content in the case of the *Leisure Hour* exceeded the boundaries of the monthly part. The topicality of the Crimean War – and the periodical's flexibility in reacting to such current events – resulted in a large variety of content related to the conflict. Given the RTS's – or family magazines' general – agenda of abstaining from politics, the majority of this material related to accounts of history. As regards series on the past, this included »Russia« (a series of biographical articles on former Russian rulers; October 1854), »Golowin's Banishment to Siberia« (fiction; January-February 1855), Milner's »Sketches of the Crimea« (March-May 1855), »The Walcheren Expedition« (March 1855) and »The Englishman in Russia« (fiction; January-July 1856). But there were also many single articles with a historical approach to the topic.[55] Despite the unity

---

55 A search combination for ›Russia‹, ›Crimean War‹ or ›Crimea‹ on the *British Periodicals Collection* produces 46 hits in the *Leisure Hour* for 1854, 44 for 1855 and 58 for 1856. It must, however, be kept in mind that the conflict was also alluded to in other terms. The series on »The Deadly Art of War«, for instance, does not come up with these specific search terms, as they were never directly mentioned in the text. A sample of titles for 1854 and 1855 shows the immersion in past accounts: »A Glance at Sebastopol« (16 February 1854), »The Baltic, and the Russian Towns on its Coasts« (18 May 1854), »An Anecdote of the Russian Police« (18 May 1854), »Russian Campaigns in Turkey in 1828 and 1829« (20 July 1854), »A Russian Aesop« (28 September 1854), »The Mother of the Czar« (21 December 1854), »Prince Michael Woronzoff« (28 December 1854), »Early English Intercourse with Russia« (18 January 1855), »Visit of Peter the Great to the Prussian Court« (8 February 1855), »The Perkin Warbeck of Russian History« (22 March 1855), »A Visit to Sebastopol in the

imposed through the series »The Deadly Art of War«, readers were hence confronted with a fragmented variety of articles and series related to a history of the ongoing conflict. And the thematic and material unit of the monthly part was of course complicated by the original set-up of the *Leisure Hour* in five weekly numbers as well as the intermingling of other material presented at the same time as »The Deadly Art of War« within or exceeding the boundaries of the monthly part towards the annual volume or beyond.[56]

Hughes and Lund's idea that serialisation is intrinsic to an understanding of Victorian historical consciousness, as a »sense of the linearity of time and its forward-moving nature was embodied in the serial form« (see Chapter 1), can also be supported with a focus on specific non-fiction series on the past in the *Leisure Hour*, as they were mostly structured chronologically. The juxtaposition with other articles and series presented at the same time, however, – be it presentations of the same or other historical epochs, contemporary fiction or observations on present-day life – may not only have consoled readers to such a view of historical progression but also led to a more fragmented outlook on the past and its link to the readers' lifeworld. Thus, as Claes points out:

> »Successive articles (not just within one issue, but also throughout the run of the periodical) can transtextually influence each other's signification, making it more problematic for periodicals than for books to achieve some form of textual ›closure‹.« (Claes 2010: 202)

Tables of contents, lists of illustrations and detailed indices transformed texts published in book form to a larger extent into reference works on history or, at instances, on science, geography or travel locations. The indices for annual volumes of the *Leisure Hour*, by contrast, only managed to provide article titles or topics. Also, prefaces and introductions in books might have presented a dedicated discussion of the approach taken to history, which was at times absent in the *Leisure Hour*'s presentation of the original text or lost in the transfer from book to periodical. Editorials or introductory paragraphs might have taken over that function, yet these were soon weeks, months or even years away in an earli-

---

Time of Peace« (31 May 1855), »Russian Literature« (5 July 1855), »Lines Suggested by Reading of John Howard's Death in the Crimea« (poem; 19 July 1855), »The First Ship to St. Petersburg« (19-26 July 1855; fiction, 2 parts), »Recollections of Cronstadt« (9 August 1855), »The Fortress of St. Petersburg« (27 September 1855), »Russia as I Saw It Forty Years Ago« (29 November 1855).

56 See also Lechner (2013: §§27-30) for this idea as well as the concluding paragraphs of this chapter; see Fn 1 above.

er issue of the *Leisure Hour*, and hence separated from the material unit holding a series' newest instalment, which was now in the hands of the reader.[57] Despite the attempt to impose thematic and material unity characteristic of the more reputable book format upon the juxtaposition of content, readers of a specific series on the past in the *Leisure Hour* inevitably came across fragments of other historical presentations. These fragments of the past were held together rather by the *Leisure Hour*'s title (and hence the promise to cater to a broad family audience) than the – often withheld – name of its contributors (see Fn 11 above). This means, however, that instead of the authorial, material and thematic unity of a book text, which addressed readers who were interested solely in a specific historical topic, periodical readers were presented with a fragmented variety of articles and series, which may have informed and complicated their understanding of the past presented within a specific series.

---

57 Claes accordingly notes: »Given that the periodical is such a fragmented body of textual information, the paratextual status of many apparent parallels to book peritexts (preface/editorial? Epilogue/teaser?) can certainly be debated« (2010: 203).

6. Writing History for the Family Audience: Between Popular and Academic

The RTS's historical agenda determined which kinds of series on the past found their way into the *Leisure Hour*. The periodical's title hence stood for a specific historical programme regulated by the RTS's idea of entertainment and instruction with a Christian tone. An idea of unity was supported by the common practice of printing contributions anonymously as well as the frequent use of an editorial ›we‹ also in historical contributions, which disguised multiple authors under the cloak of a presumably single voice (see Chapter 1, Fn 47). Yet still, the *Leisure Hour* was a collaborative enterprise, and its historical representations were created by many different voices.

This chapter looks at the writers of history for the *Leisure Hour*'s family audience and starts with an assessment of its contributors to series on the past during the 1850s and 1860s. The overview below briefly assesses the *Leisure Hour*'s stock of contributors for serialised history in terms of religion, gender and age, as well as academic affiliation or involvement with the Victorian print market. It thereby also looks at the entries provided in the section »Authors« in the *Leisure Hour*'s jubilee number of 1902, which as a kind of »business's history«[1] presumably foregrounded those contributors the RTS deemed most reputable or important while neglecting others. For a brief statistical contextualisation of the periodical's ›historians‹ within the general stock of contributors, the analysis furthermore draws on the payment lists in the RTS minutes.

After this general analysis of historical contributors, the larger part of the chapter focuses on John Stoughton (1807-1897), a continuous and important contributor to the pages of the *Leisure Hour* and as such an exemplary writer on the past for the journal. A close reading of Stoughton's series serves to show

---

1   See Jordanova (2000: 155-161).

how this specific author worked as a producing agent under the regulation of the RTS and accommodated various categories of disparity within a national historical identity in order to cater to a broad audience. At the same time, Stoughton's popular output for the periodical press stood in contrast to his possibly more academic historical ambitions. Stoughton's long-time contribution to the magazine further allows for a diachronic classification of representations of the past within the *Leisure Hour*.

WRITING ON THE PAST FOR THE *LEISURE HOUR*: THE CONTRIBUTORS

In its jubilee number of 1902, the *Leisure Hour* observed in retrospect on its stock of contributors that, as a means of meeting the »popular demand« of providing »information for the people«,

»its writers came from all quarters, and sometimes from strange out-of-the-way places; whoever had anything to tell, had as a rule his hearing. [...] Some of these literary aspirants were virtually beggars, others mere adventurers. The globe-trotter was not then born; the universal tourist, now so prolific a scribe, was still on the horizon; and the runaway lad who had seen the world, or some botanical enthusiast, or hunter of wild animals, had the chance – or thought he had – of telling what he had seen. Sometimes a lady's-maid, relic of the grand touring days, would essay to instruct stay-at-home people. Beside this medley of manuscript, on the same desk fell papers from quiet cultured homes, from the rooms of briefless barristers, from the tables of lone students, from the laboratories of science, or the libraries of scholars.« (»Fifty Years« 1902: 180-181)

A large variety of contributors can be ascertained by looking at the *Leisure Hour*'s jubilee number: Of the 111 entries presented under »Authors« (1902) – which listed prominent contributors to the *Leisure Hour* for the preceding 50 years and might hence be biased – 36 (32%) were women and 75 (68%) men; of the latter, 40 (53% of male contributors) were listed with an academic degree of some kind (including 7 professors, 10 doctors) and 21 (28% of male contributors) were ordained. An assessment of the payment listings provided in the RTS Copyright Committee minutes for 1852, 1860 and 1865 shows that on average 24% of contributors were women; of the male contributors, 25% appear to have been ordained (i.e., listed as »Rev«) and another 5% were recorded as having a doctorate (i.e., listed as »Dr«).[2]

These numbers refer, of course, to the overall content of the *Leisure Hour*, that is, all varieties of factual as well as fictional formats; and the inclusion of the latter may to some extent account for the high average of women writers in the statistics above.[3] Turner, for instance, observes of the gender distribution amongst contributors to the *Cornhill* that »[w]hereas the fiction [in 1862 according to a glance at the *Wellesley Index*] is balanced by having serials, stories, and poems by men and women [...], the non-fiction is almost exclusively dominated by middle-class men« (Turner 2000: 25). And the same male dominance appears to hold true for the *Leisure Hour*, at least when one looks at the 20 contributors who could be identified to have written factual series on the past printed in the periodical during the 1850s and 1860s (see Appendix C).

Accordingly, 57 of the 79 series on the past printed in the *Leisure Hour* during the 1850s and 1870s were unsigned, while another six only attributed authorship by referring to earlier works printed by the same author within the periodical or elsewhere.[4] I was able to determine authorship for 19 of these 63 series, ei-

---

2 Assessing contributors through the payment listings for the *Leisure Hour* provided within the RTS minutes of course depends on the caution of the reporting secretary. Listings mainly provided titles and surnames, enabling to some extent a determination of gender as well as degree; the latter is obviously determined by the possible (in)accuracy of documentation, and these numbers should hence be perceived with a rational degree of circumspection. 1852: 52 contributors, 13 female, 39 male; of the latter, 12 Reverends. 1860: 87 contributors, 21 female, 66 male; of the latter, 14 reverends, 3 doctors. 1865: 78 contributors, 18 female, 60 male; of the latter, 15 reverends, 4 doctors.

3 By comparison in terms of gender distribution, Phegley quotes an evaluation of another family magazine roughly during this period: »Taking the *Cornhill* as an example, Janice Harris claims that women writers contributed about 20 percent of its contents between 1860 and 1900, with women writers rising as high as 60 to 70 percent in certain issues during the 1860s and 1870s – the heyday of the genre (385). Harris compares these figures to Walter Houghton's estimate that only 14 percent of the writers included in the thirty-five journals indexed in his *Wellesley Guide to Victorian Periodicals* were women« (Phegley 2004: 7).

4 These six were: »Two Months in Spain« (1868) by the »Author of ›A Merchant's Holiday‹« (unidentified), »Characteristic Letters« (1868-1869) by the »Author of ›Men I Have Known‹« (William Jerdan), »The Idler on the Rhine« (1865), »Another Swiss Round« (1864) and »A Walk in South Devon« (1869) – all three by the »Au-

ther through identification of a book counterpart or the reattribution of authorship through the biographical entries in the *Leisure Hour*'s jubilee number. Together with the 16 series that provided authors' names, this amounts to 35 series written by 20 different authors.

Fyfe notes that »[t]he RTS writers [for the Monthly Volumes series] were mostly male, and mostly ministers« (Fyfe 2004c: 195), and while »[a]lmost all were part-time writers« (ibid.: 194), she distinguishes between writer-ministers and professional writers.[5] As the overview of biographical information (as well as their contribution to the *Leisure Hour*'s historical programme during the 1850s and 1860s) in Appendix C shows, this distinction can also be observed for the *Leisure Hour*'s ›historians‹. Of the 19 different authors who wrote these series, only three were women (one of them a missionary), and of the 16 male contributors, six were ordained, and at least 11 had an academic degree or affiliation of some kind. At least six of the male writers (Cowper, Heath, Jerdan, Merryweather, Thornbury, Timbs, possibly Pattison) – and possibly two of the female writers (Fox, Walshe) – would qualify as professional writers or journalists. Yet the distinction is, of course, somewhat blurry, as of the writer-ministers at least five (Arnold, Bradley, Jones, Milner, Stoughton; that is, all besides Hopley) had extensive experience as contributors or editors to a multitude of periodicals. Another group amongst the contributors was rather professional scientists (Dunkin, Glaisher, possibly Pattison and Scoffern).

The stock of ›historians‹ in the *Leisure Hour*, with its overlapping mix of journalists and professional writers, writer-ministers, antiquarian amateurs, scientists of various disciplinary affiliation and female writers, hence mirrored the variety of ›historical‹ writers at a time when history was not yet fully established as an academic discipline in Britain.[6] In the face of the ongoing negotiation of a

---

thor of ›The Regular Swiss Round‹« (Harry Jones); »The Walcheren Expedition« (1855) by »One Who Survived It« (unidentified).

5   Cf. Fyfe (2004c: Chapter V: The Ministry of the Press) for her assessment of RTS writers during the publication of the Monthly Series 1845-1855.

6   Philippa Levine distinguished between antiquarians, historians, archaeologists and ›record employees‹ during this time of professionalisation (cf. Levine 1986: Chapter 2), yet notes the overlap within these categories as well as the common interest of members of a specific group also in other fields. Further, a close connection between theology and history can be observed in the establishment of chairs in ecclesiastical history as well as the appointment of churchmen as professors in history. Hesketh, for example, notes: »The appointment of William Stubbs as Regius Professor of Modern and Medieval History at Oxford in 1866 has been viewed as a watershed in the devel-

distinction between history proper, other sciences or popular renderings, this mix of contributors' expertise also determined the various genres and differing historical depth of the accounts on the past written by these ›historians‹ in the periodical.[7] The female writers appear to have drawn on their personal experiences when writing for the *Leisure Hour*, and their accounts of the past pertain to everyday as well as cultural history with strong embedding in contemporary observations. Bitha Fox (Lloyd) and Elizabeth Hely Walshe – about both of whom little is known so far beyond their activity for the periodical press – contributed travel pieces interspersed with historical sightseeing within the British national space (beyond these factual accounts, Walshe also mainly contributed [historical] fiction). Mary Louisa Whately had travelled farther and contributed a series on her »Life in Egypt« (1865), which was an autobiographical, topographical and ethnographical account from her experiences as a missionary twenty years earlier.[8]

Similarly, most of the minister-writers as well as the professional writers drew on their experiences in geographical as well as biographical terms to gain some extra income. Reverend Frederick Arnold contributed series on the places of his academic education Oxford and Cambridge, which described their colleges' histories and could serve as historical tourist guides. Reverend Howard Hopley and Prebendary Harry Jones provided multiple accounts of their travels along the Nile and on the continent (Switzerland, Rhine), respectively, which were interspersed with historical sightseeing. Domestic history could be found in the contributions by Reverend Edward Bradley (alias Cuthbert Bede) and Richard

---

opment of history as a professional discipline of study in Britain« (Hesketh 2011: 45); yet besides this, Stubbs had a career as an ordained churchman. Cf. also Levine's chapter on »The Contribution of the Universities« for this connection between churchmen and the academisation of history (Levine 1986: Chapter 6). On the professionalisation of history and the phenomenon of boundary work, see also Chapter 1 (Fn 6).

7 Howsam notes: »The new scholarly standards affected the credibility of journalists and travel writers, and delimited the authority of historical novelists, but popular and narrative histories, traditional, revised and newly-written, continued to abound« (Howsam 2004: 527).

8 Previous to this, Whately appears to have already made a name for herself by publishing various books on her missionary work in Egypt. In contrast to the other two women writers, her series were therefore printed signed with her name, possibly with an intended advertising function. Writing – as well as missionary work in Whately's instance – were accepted female occupations for financial means (cf. Fyfe 2004c: 208).

Heath, as well as Walter Thornbury and John Timbs, the latter two writing in a more entertaining antiquarian fashion with specific focus on London. And William Jerdan drew on his personal recollections of encounters with prominent Victorian men in his biographical series.

In terms of historical research, the accounts on the past provided by these contributors might be considered the most amateur immersions included in the *Leisure Hour*. A more objective historiographical approach, including references to and discussion of sources, was displayed in antiquarian Frederick Somner Merryweather's social history series »The Working Man in the Olden Time« (see Chapter 3) as well as Reverend Thomas Milner's history of the Crimea (see Chapter 5). The contributions by scientists, who here ›popularised‹ accounts from their own research and academic fields, furthermore indicates the closeness of historical writing at the time to the natural sciences: Edwin Dunkin and James Glaisher, both astronomers, together provided a series on their place of research, the »Royal Observatory, Greenwich« (1862). The first article of this series, as well as that of Glaisher's »The Balloon and its Application« (1864), outlined in a history-of-science fashion earlier developments in the respective fields and the institution of the observatory. Dr John Scoffern, a professor of chemistry, contributed biographical sketches of famous chemists, and Samuel Rowles Pattison wrote on his geological and archaeological findings.

With six series on the past in the *Leisure Hour* identified during the 1850s and 1860s, the most prolific writer of historical series appears to have been Reverend John Stoughton. Like the *Leisure Hour*'s most amateur history writers, Stoughton provided travel accounts on domestic as well as foreign localities, yet he at times combined this with a more objective approach similar to Merryweather or Milner. Besides his clerical career, his appointment as Chair of Historical Theology and Homilectics in New College London in 1872 also places him amongst the academic-scientists popularising their own research. In the stock of the periodical's historical writers, Stoughton – a male writer-minister who contributed to as well as edited periodicals but also held academic credentials in history – can hence be considered exemplary for a mean position on the predominantly amateur to academic spectrum outlined above.

JOHN STOUGHTON: BETWEEN POPULAR AND ACADEMIC HISTORY[9]

Stoughton constantly operated on the boundary of historical demarcation (see Fn 6 above). As a Congregationalist, Nonconformist minister[10] with a strong interest in historical issues, Stoughton fitted well into the RTS agenda of writing in a Christian spirit. He published not only frequently within the pages of the *Leisure Hour* but also for other religious magazines, and he furthermore had a tremendous literary output of books for the Religious Tract Society as well as other publishers.[11] His overall literary work ranged from popular articles and series for periodicals to more academic texts, such as his five-volume *Ecclesiastical History of England* (1864-1874).

Stoughton contributed several series on historical topics to the *Leisure Hour* from its very beginnings in 1852 up until 1887. In fact, the cover of the magazine's second number – which was the first cover to feature history – introduced Stoughton's series »Shades of the Departed in Old London« (1852-1853), which ran over a duration of 17 months. As this series can therefore be considered to have largely contributed to setting the tone for historical representation in the

---

9 An earlier version of the case study on John Stoughton has been published in a different context in Lechner (2013). Some of the passages provided in this section as well as changed extracts from the two following sections on »Shades of the Departed in Old London« and its book publication, and also from the case study on »Windsor Castle«, were in included in that publication, albeit in changed and much shorter form. Overall, the case study is here presented in a much more expanded form. See also Fn 17, 26 and 30 below.

10 See Fyfe, who defines Nonconformity as »those denominations (such as Congregationalism or Baptism) whose members refused to conform to the doctrines, practices of worship, and« method of governance of the established Church« (2004c: 24). Fyfe furthermore notes that amongst her sample of RTS writers, »[n]onconformists outnumbered Church members by two to one. Among the subgroup of ordained writers, nonconformity again outnumbered Church membership by two to one, but in this case there were relatively fewer Baptists and more Congregationalists« (Fyfe 2004c: 195).

11 Stoughton also wrote for the *Leisure Hour*'s sister publication *Sunday at Home*; searches in the *British Periodicals Collection* and *UKPC* show that he also contributed articles to the RTS's *Boy's Own Paper* as well as the British and Foreign Bible Society's *Gleanings for the Young*, the *Quiver* and the *Wesleyan-Methodist Magazine*. Besides his contribution to various periodicals, Stoughton also was editor of the *Evangelical Magazine* »for several years« (J.H. 1876: 201).

Leisure Hour, a thorough analysis of Stoughton's first series will be given below.

As the overview of series which can be attributed to Stoughton in Appendix A (Tab. 24) shows, many of his texts were published anonymously. A helpful resource for attributing authorship to some anonymous *Leisure Hour* articles and series is the biographical entries in the jubilee number (also included in Appendix C where applicable), in which almost all of Stoughton's contributions to the *Leisure Hour* appear to be listed. It nevertheless remains problematic to identify other series or articles by Stoughton which might have been published without attribution in the magazine and the jubilee number. The biographical entry for Stoughton in the jubilee number (»Authors« 1902: 254; see also Appendix C) allows identification for the following series: »Shades of the Departed in Old London« (1852-1853), »The Banks of the Thames« (1853), »Echoes of Westminster Hall« (1856), »Windsor Castle and Neighbourhood« (1859), »A Ramble in the Tyrol« (1859) (all of which were published anonymously), »The Royal Commission on Historical MSS« (1877),[12] »The Black Forest« (1879), »Neglected Books« (1885) and »Glimpses of Queen Anne's Days« (1887). Of these, hence, only the ones after 1877 were identified by the author's name within the periodical; but in 1862 the *Leisure Hour* also published the series »The Tale of a West-End Suburb« under Stoughton's name, which was, however, not listed in the jubilee number's biographical entry. It is therefore uncertain whether the overview provided in Appendix A (Tab. 24) includes all of Stoughton's serial output for the *Leisure Hour*, but it can be assumed that this table lists those series which the RTS perceived to be his most important contributions.

---

12 This was a series of articles in which Stoughton celebrated the newly accessible manuscript archives: »[B]eyond all sources of information relative to our own country are the manuscripts which have been found *hidden* in public offices, in ecclesiastical libraries, and in all sorts of neglected rooms, forgotten closets, and worm-eaten trunks. [...] What valuable documents have they [the Record Office] collected and arranged, calendared and described, and brought within the reach of authors, who, by these helps, have enriched our popular literature with new histories and biographies.« (Stoughton 1877: 245) While the series (together with »Neglected Books« 1885) was a rare exception or deviation from Stoughton's pattern of contributions outlined below, as it focused rather on the ›scientific‹ practice of history, he nevertheless chose an emotional approach and pointed towards the use of these sources for the »popular« author. On the role of the Historical Manuscripts Commission as well as the Record Office in the professionalisation of history, see Levine (1986: Chapter 5).

As Stoughton recalled in his memoirs, *Recollections of a Long Life* (1894),[13] his lifelong interest in history was sparked at an early age:

»my culture in chief resulted from looking on what was ancient. When other boys were at play, I like [sic] to get by myself and read; biography and history having for me pre-eminent charms. [...] From a child I took an interest in historical tales, and felt delight in listening to my mother's memories of early days. She recollected the American war, and spoke of a family dispute amongst her elders, which lasted just as long – ten years. Excitement in William Pitt's day she brought vividly before me; and she told how Thelwall, the orator, delivered revolutionary harangues, and being attacked by a mob, he was glad to escape by clambering over the roofs of houses.« (Stoughton 1894: 4-5)

Stoughton's initiation into history, then, was brought about by his mother's ability to tell exciting stories about the past. Family history or the immersion into a communicative memory (see Chapter 1, Fn 29) influenced Stoughton's historical consciousness from an early age, not only through his mother but through other relatives and acquaintances.

Besides this early immersion in (family) storytelling of the past, historical objects in his birth-town Norwich

»excited [Stoughton's] archaeological tastes. The Norman keep, Herbert de Lozinga's Cathedral, Erpingham Gate, the Grammar School, the Bishop's palace, with ruins in the garden, dilapidated towers on the edge of the river, Guild Hall, St. Andrew's Hall, and the Old Men's Hospital – these had for me a mighty charm, creating fancies by day and dreams by night.« (Ibid.: 5-6)

The vivid perception of the past inscribed into objects and buildings as depicted here by Stoughton constituted a direct link to the observer's lifeworld. This al-

---

13 The *Recollections* was a memoir which was structured strictly chronologically, presenting Stoughton's education, professional affiliations and, above all – and sometimes in connection with this –, his travels in Great Britain as well as the whole world, and retells many conversations and meetings he has had with (important, prominent) persons, scholars and religious authorities. Stoughton put much emphasis on the latter two points, i.e., the travels (abroad) and the people he was acquainted with, as he set out to present »incidents of religious history and aspects of personal character more interesting than any confined to my own experience. It presents associations during a long period spent in various work, in distant journeys, and in friendly intercourse with many distinguished persons« (Stoughton 1894: vii-viii).

most sensuous childhood experience of the past in his birth-town shone through Stoughton's depictions of history – often connected to his places of residence – in the *Leisure Hour*. The local connection to history was further mirrored in his consumption of biographies, and it even appears that Stoughton's immersion in history was due to religious magazines, such as the ones he later chose to write for and edit himself (see Fn 11 above):

»I loved to read the lives of eminent people, and devoured a good many memoirs of men and women in religious magazines. Norwich was at that time distinguished for literary, artistic, and benevolent celebrities, and I felt proud as a boy to think of them as pertaining to my own birthplace.« (Ibid.: 7)

Hence, in an article printed in the RTS's *Sunday at Home* on Stoughton's retirement from his ministry at Kensington, J.H. concluded that

»to Norwich Cathedral and other antiquities of the city, which inspired him with archaeological tastes, we may attribute his partiality for historical study and research, destined in after years to yield valuable fruit in the field of English ecclesiastical literature.« (J.H. 1876: 199)

Certainly, the way in which Stoughton recollected his childhood interest in history as connected to oral history and anecdotes was significant for his own style of writing history in the *Leisure Hour*, as was the imagination sparked by the sight of old historical buildings and the interest in biographies – all mainly connected to his hometown.[14]

It is not surprising that Stoughton, who was meant to follow in his father's footsteps by starting out as a lawyer's apprentice, was less interested in »real and personal property, the rights of persons and the rights of things, the law of descent and the law of entail«, but rather more in »the history of English legislation and the principles of English government, and he formed a taste for inquiries into the foundation and progress of our political constitution in Church and State« (Lewis 1898: 11). Realising his vocation for the Church, Stoughton turned away from law. He trained for the ministry at Highbury College from 1828 onwards

---

14 See also Howsam's »life-cycle approach« to the history of historiography, which »helps us to recognize a tendency in historical writing to narrative replication. Writers of history often find themselves charged with retelling an account of events already well known – to themselves, to their imagined reader, as well as to their publisher« (Howsam 2009b: 3-5).

and started his career as a Congregational minister with stints at Windsor and Kensington. He tended to his historical interests in presenting lectures and writing periodical articles and books, and from 1872 he held a chair as historical theology professor at New College for twelve years.

With his profession as a minister and his interest in history, Stoughton perfectly fitted the RTS's agenda of combining instruction and entertainment in a Christian spirit. His attitude towards novel reading and theatre going strictly conformed to the RTS's moral conduct: He evidently read novels only as recreation during summer holidays while in his youth. As his daughter stated in an article on her father in the RTS's *Sunday at Home*, »as an aid to self-control, he would sometimes put down a novel in the most exciting part, turn to work, and determine not to open the page of fiction again for a week« (Lewis 1897: 185). Furthermore, while encouraged by his grandmother to go to the theatre, his daughter carefully pointed out that he did not immerse himself in the »immoralities of the playhouse [...], his tastes being only for such representations as were connected with history« (Lewis 1898: 12-13). In the same vein, J.H. stated:

»With Dr. Stoughton's unprejudiced habit of mind, we do not wonder that he has found good in men and institutions where others of views more one-sided have discerned only evil. As we have seen, it has been his endeavour in the field of history, while adhering steadfastly to his own ecclesiastical views, to bring that good into light, and obtain for it adequate recognition. Another phase of the same characteristic is his desire for union between Christians of different creeds and denominations – a union based on the sympathy of a common love and obedience to the Saviour; and because so based, in perfect harmony with diversity of individual conviction and Church organization.« (J.H. 1876: 203)

Stoughton had a large network, as his *Recollections* show (see Fn 13 above). With personal connections, as Fyfe points out, being a strong point in the RTS's recruitment of contributors and authors, there certainly were many opportunities for Stoughton to make his way into the RTS group of authors through »mutual involvement in pan-evangelical organisations« (Fyfe 2004c: 196).[15] James Macaulay, editor of the *Leisure Hour* from 1858 until 1895, briefly addressed Stoughton's involvement with the RTS in his review of Stoughton's *Recollections*, printed in the *Sunday at Home*:

---

15 Regarding Stoughton, Fyfe specifically points out his acquaintance with RTS committee member Thomas Coombs and RTS writer John Kennedy (Fyfe 2004c: 197); Fyfe references Stoughton's *Recollections*, where Stoughton mentions Coombs's involvement with the RTS (Stoughton 1894: 81).

»Among many other services we have special reason to mention his being one of the two honorary secretaries of the Religious Tract Society, the other being Canon Fleming.

Dr. Stoughton's love for the Tract Society, and the services rendered to it, are well known. He has written many a volume, some of which are still most popular, and he has been one of the most frequent and welcome contributors to its periodicals.« (J. Macaulay 1894: 475)

Thus, Stoughton was honoured with a longer biographical entry in the *Leisure Hour*'s jubilee number as a »regular and much-valued contributor to the early volumes and for nearly forty years« (»Authors« 1902: 254; see Appendix C).

While some contributors to periodicals, such as James Macaulay, acknowledged Stoughton's work for the periodical press, Stoughton himself never appears to have openly credited himself with the many articles and series he wrote. In his memoir, he did not reference his periodical output or his work as an editor for the *Evangelical Magazine*, but rather gave credit to his more established book publications, such as his five-volume *Ecclesiastical History of England*. It is also interesting to note that the entry in the jubilee number did not refer to the fact that many of Stoughton's series were turned into book publications after (or before) their appearance within the periodical – and also that Stoughton published for the *Leisure Hour*'s sister publication *Sunday at Home*, while it did so for other contributors (see Appendix C). Furthermore, the entry neglected Stoughton's authorship of (more academic) ecclesiastical history work. Vice versa, Stoughton mentioned only briefly in one instance the publication of his *Stars of the East* by the RTS in his memoir (1894: 247) but did not acknowledge any further involvement with the RTS, like his honorary secretaryship.

Although Stoughton's periodical articles must have reached a by far larger public than his books – whether collections of his periodical series or more academic texts – the practice by both sides of not explicitly mentioning his other work may hint at his awareness and possible creation of a division between academic and more popular presentations and audiences, as he thereby seemed to distance himself from his most popular work.[16] Fyfe makes similar observations in her study on the RTS's Monthly Volumes:

---

16 Secord notes that »[a]nonymity was especially rare in history, biography, and science. The chief point of publication in science was to secure authorship of the facts of nature, so that anonymous scientific writings tended to be periodical essays and run-of-the mill textbook surveys. The implication was that unsigned works were unoriginal, part of the emerging genre of ›popular science‹ that aimed to diffuse known truths to the mass audience in useful knowledge tracts and newspapers« (2000: 19-20).

»Popular works, such as the Monthly Volumes and their equivalents, were at least more likely to make money, since they were by definition expected to reach a wide audience. However, the routine omission of these works from the published memoirs of ordained writers, including Stoughton, [...] suggests that they did less for reputation than tracts and sermons. Ministers sought reputations not merely as writers but as theological scholars. A successful Monthly Volume might commend its writer to a publisher seeking a ›popular‹ volume, but it was not equal commendation to the learned.« (Fyfe 2004c: 202)

Periodical work was, after all, also discredited by some as being contract work conducted to gain a living, which was another reason why Stoughton might have tried to distance himself from this popular work.

Following common conduct for periodicals, most series by Stoughton were printed anonymously in the *Leisure Hour*, thereby blurring his authorship and helping him to establish a boundary towards his most popular writings, which suggests that the latter were a necessary and welcome activity for financial ends. Contemporaries might later reattribute the authorship to Stoughton, if series were rescued into book form and acknowledged his authorship (and in parts also referred back to the earlier publication within the periodical). Acknowledgement of Stoughton's work for periodicals can hence only sparsely be found in articles about him within periodicals. Other biographical entries firmly excluded his work for magazines such as the *Leisure Hour*, while they, to a changing degree, might or might not include his more popular book publications. Most of the time they – like periodical articles about him – focused on his most established academic work, *The Ecclesiastical History*.

Lewis, for instance, focused much more on Stoughton's written output in her biography of her father than Stoughton did in his own memoirs. She gave more emphasis to his publications and development as a writer as well as a college man; and she paid more attention to his interest in the study of history. Similarly, J.H. addressed Stoughton's *Ecclesiastical History* and historical approach:

»His purpose has been, as a historian, carefully to ascertain facts by original research, and honestly to state the truth in reference both to events and individuals. Dr. Stoughton's volumes, in consequence, are marked by an entire fairness and impartiality. He has endeavoured to keep himself wholly out of the atmosphere of partizanship – an endeavour easy, perhaps, to a man of his truth-loving catholicity and reverential feelings; and he has certainly given no conscious prominence to any single ecclesiastical party to the disadvantage of others.« (J.H. 1876: 202)

WRITING HISTORY FOR THE FAMILY AUDIENCE: »SHADES OF THE DEPARTED IN OLD LONDON«[17]

In »Shades of the Departed in Old London« (1852-1853), Stoughton established what would become his common pattern for narrating history in the *Leisure Hour*: It used descriptions of present-day objects and manifestations of the past like buildings and landscapes as a starting point to connect to past events and historical actors. The focus on London as metropolis, well-known to many readers, not only placed the *Leisure Hour* at an early date in correspondence to its opponent the *London Journal* (see Chapter 3), but also meant a direct connection to the readers' lifeworld. The attractiveness of the pattern may therefore also have stemmed from the readers' opportunity to actually do the walks suggested by the *Leisure Hour* and relive history *in situ*.

Each part of »Shades of the Departed«, as the overview in Appendix A (Tab. 25) shows, was dedicated to the biography of one or two persons who would have been well known to a Victorian audience. The series overall followed a chronological set-up and roughly covered the 17th and 18th centuries. It can be split up into three sections presenting different types of actors: Dissenters involved in religious struggles, writers and artists, and political and social reformers. Thus, the first four parts on Baxter, Milton, Walton, Marvell and Russell were concerned with and linked through their preoccupation with a time of religious unrest, and the selected persons were presented as role models for integrity, religious faith and strife for the acceptance of Dissenters. These parts on the 17th century reached from the Civil War and the Restoration to the Glorious Revolution, with a clear focus on a religious development towards tolerance of nonconformity. During the 18th century, the focus of the series shifted from actors directly involved in religious struggles to a narration of the cultural achievements of Enlightenment writers, artists and scientists like Addison, Newton, Goldsmith, Reynolds and Johnson. Although they were portrayed with their literary and artistic output in mind, their lives were still always evaluated under the aspect of their religious involvement and beliefs. With the final two parts, the series returned to more political issues by evaluating Howard's and Burke's beneficial influences as a prison reformer and as a statesman, political orator and au-

---

17 The case study on »Shades of the Departed in Old London« found in Lechner (2013: §§16-23) included the first two paragraphs also introducing the series here in slightly changed form; see also Fn 9 above. The case study presented in this section, however, includes a detailed discussion of Stoughton's narrative pattern, use of illustrations and perspective structure of the series, which has not been published before.

thor, respectively, under the idea of Christian duty. It is striking, however, that no political figures, such as Cromwell, Charles II, James II, William III, George I or the first two female monarchs Mary and Anne, were chosen as protagonists. Though these were, of course, at times mentioned within the biographies, the selection of figures made by Stoughton and the focus on them in the respective biographies enabled him to write in a sense a history of religious controversy on Unitarianism from a Protestant, nonconformist perspective, and he thereby appropriated the past to address his contemporary interests in nonconformity (see Fn 10 above).

Stoughton did not present these individuals in simple biographical sketches, however, but framed the historical narratives with town walks through London. The pattern hence deviated from such straightforward biographical sketches, which mainly focus on a historical actor without adding another level of narration or parallel plot line. The combined pattern Stoughton made use of was one which could often be found in descriptive historical articles which mixed travel writing and historiography in a historical-sightseeing approach and hence allowed for a close connection of the readers' lifeworld with the past.

The set-up of »Shades of the Departed« as town walks meant a selection of biographical detail limited to occurrences in London.[18] The two levels of the town walk and the historical action were linked through their plot lines. Thus, the town walks followed historic sites according to the chronological order of the respective historical actor's biography from (pre-)birth or childhood through adulthood and old age onto death, funeral, and occasionally a consideration the person's posthumous influence. At the same time, the town walks in themselves presented a closed narrative: The walks often ended full circle at their starting point, like in the part on Milton, which concluded: »[N]ow, not far from the spot whence we commenced our rambles, we would bid farewell to that illustrious shade« ([Stoughton] 1852a: 117). At other times, their stretch over a day's duration gave closure to the narrative, as in the part on Walton:

»We come back to Temple-bar, and pass under its dark shadow at the midnight hour. [...] The busy, noisy, bustling crowds have disappeared and melted away in silence. So, in a few years, writer and reader will disappear, and sleep the long sleep in the land of silence,

---

18 The narrator, for instance, pointed out that only a short section of the part on Marvell and Russell would be dedicated to Marvell, as »the scanty records of his life furnish us with no other incidents that can be connected here by any local tie« ([Stoughton] 1852a: 365).

where Walton, and Donne, and Ashmole, and all the rest of that generation, have been for nearly two centuries.« (Ibid.: 261)

The concept therefore also allowed for final reflection on one's own transitoriness and often led to considerations of Christianity and salvation according to the subtle Christian tone the RTS called for.

Narrative Technique of Historical Worldmaking in »Shades of the Departed in Old London«

Through the interconnection of the two plot lines, the biography clearly informed the route of the town walk. Constant switches between the two levels linked stages of biographical development to specific sites which made events of the past more memorable to readers by inscribing them into present-day objects.[19] Linking the two levels of town walk and historical action meant using a metaleptic narrative technique which blended the several levels of narration into each other.[20] The model for the series' narrative situation in Fig. 20[21] shows that the *level of the town walk* framed the temporally distinct *level of historical action*, that is, the biography. As will be closely analysed below, Stoughton's we-

---

19 Note at this instance also Berger and Lorenz's observation on »Halbwachs', Nora's and Hartog's thinking [about historical time] [as] a *spatial* conception [...]. According to this view, the past and present exist simultaneously *next to* each other: ›Places of memory inspire creative thinking about history. In that sense, memory makes the past live again‹« (Berger/Lorenz 2008a: 16).

20 John Pier defines this narrative phenomenon of metalepsis as follows: »The embedding of narratives normally respects the separation between the level of narration and that of the narrated events, but metalepsis produces a ›short-circuiting‹ of levels, calling this distinction into question [...]. Such transgressions of narrative level constitute ›narrative metalepsis‹: intrusion into the storyworld by the extradiegetic narrator or by the narratee (or into deeper embedded levels), or the reverse«; through such metalepses, »narrative levels« may become »nearly convergent, the time of the narration and that of the story [may] coincide [...], and the narrator/narratee axis is implicitly doubled by the author/reader axis, demonstrating in a nutshell the potential of metalepsis to undermine heuristic distinctions relating to time, level, and adresser/addressee in narrative« (Pier 2010 [2005]: 303).

21 Amended after Manfred Jahn's general model of narrative communication (2005: N2.3.1).

Fig. 20: Narrative Model for »Shades of the Departed«

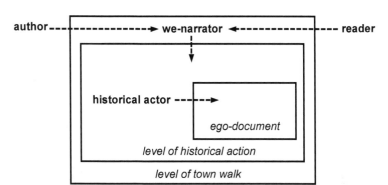

narrator constantly transgressed the narrative – and at the same time temporal – boundary between present and past of the contemporary world towards the embedded world of the historical actors; further, the use of *ego-documents* within the narrative added a third level, in which historical actors transitioned into first-person narrators. This blurring of narrative boundaries effected high degrees of immediacy, suspense and authenticity of the historical, which enabled a connection of present and past by building one lifeworld onto the other.

A close engagement with the past through the blurring of temporal levels was hence guided by the use of a we-narrator. The use of ›we‹ common in periodicals here, however, served not only – or not predominantly – to disguise authorship (see Chapter 1, Fn 47; the series was also not attributed to Stoughton's authorship but printed anonymously), but also to enable further immediacy: it linked narrator and readers as participants in the city tour and allowed them to more easily immerse themselves in the historical world as onlookers, when the narratorial ›we‹ transgressed from the present to the past world.[22]

Thus, the level of historical action, that is, the past world of Baxter, Milton, Johnson and others, was framed by a prominent level of mediation, which was the present world of narrator, author and readers. On this level, the narrator started out with (fictional) walks through contemporary London and thereby connected to the present-day lifeworld of the readers. Using contemporary sites and buildings in London as a starting point, the narrator blended the two levels of

---

22   As the narrative situation is the means which allows readers entrance into the narrative world, the choice of narrator guides – if not determines – readers' perception of the narrated. The perspective adopted by and reflected through the narrator is hence central to an analysis of a text's intentions.

·present and past into each other by describing an imagined transformation of contemporary London into its earlier appearance and simultaneously transgressing the boundary between the two narrative levels by placing both narrator and reader into the past as onlookers to the historical action. He accomplished this technique of »[i]maginative historical reconstruction« (R. Mitchell 2000: 110)[23] by rebuilding and re-peopling the contemporary world as known to the readers in an effect similar to time travel, resulting in the narrator's and readers' finding themselves suddenly present within the historical world.

This can, for instance, be observed in the first transition from present to past introduced in the article on Baxter:

»One day [...] we went down to Whitehall – the stately-looking Whitehall – the palace of so many English kings – with that fine relic of Inigo Jones' architecture, the banqueting house, still standing, with the memory of something far different from revelry connected with it. *The edifice spread out, and other buildings rose around it; the street changed*, and there stood Holbein's gateway, with its eight medallions; and people were going in and coming out, some of them with doublets of silk and collars of pointed lace, wide boots ruffled with lawn, and a short mantle thrown over one shoulder, all crowned with a broadleafed Spanish beaver; and there were men in armour with leather jackets, and people of a very staid appearance with Genevan cloak and lofty wide-brimmed hats. *One of them we saw* with a youth, about eighteen years of age, rather sickly looking, with a wonderfully intelligent face, a forehead which bespoke thought, eyes which flashed with earnestness, and a quick step which showed he was not, and never meant to be, an idler.« ([Stoughton] 1852a: 18; my emphases)

From the present-day appearance of Whitehall as his point of departure, the narrator described how the street architecture actively changed into its past appearance (»spread out«, »other buildings rose around it«, »the street changed«) and former buildings, such as the Holbein gateway, which was demolished in 1759, reappeared. Similarly, the clothing of people changed and Baxter as a young man was soon singled out as the centre of the article's attention, with the narra-

---

23 R. Mitchell, in her analysis of fictional texts, i.e., William Harrison Ainsworth's historical novels (2000: Chapter 4), notes this to be »a technique derived from the novels of Scott and a prominent characteristic of the picturesque history text« (ibid.: 85). She similarly observes an »emphasis on the inclusion of authentic details to create a sense of historical immediacy and presence« as »[i]n these novels, ancient architectural remains and their imagined occupants were composed into tableaux vivants, detailed historical reconstructions replete with authentic details both textual and visual« (ibid.).

tor/readers now situated within the same time frame as Baxter (»One of them we saw«). Within a few sentences, Stoughton thereby managed to transition from contemporary London to the seventeenth century and enabled readers to re-imagine this past by closely connecting it to their present lifeworld.

The transitions were often used to point out a specific time reference, for instance when St Paul's Cathedral was introduced as

»appear[ing] to us as it was *in the year 1660*; not the St. Paul's with a dome, but the St. Paul's with a spire; not with its Italian arcades and decorations, but with its Gothic aisles and choir and medieval adornments [...] *at the time of the Restoration*« (Ibid.: 18; my emphases).

While this first part of the series was written in the past tense and therefore still retained some distance to the historical world, the other parts allowed for even more immediacy in re-imagining the historical world through the use of indicatives as well as exclamations (»Step into the studio.«, ibid.: 696; »Why there he is!«, ibid.: 741), and the presentation of both town walk and historical world mainly in the present tense.[24] This is obvious in the probably longest stretch of past action (in the original, the passage takes up 2 1/2 columns), presented in the part on Russell's execution:

»To place before us this remarkable man [Lord Russell], and the affecting circumstance under which his name will for ever remain associated with Lincoln's-inn-fields, we will transport ourselves into the seventeenth century, and fancy ourselves standing at the end of Queen-street, on the morning of 21st July, 1683. [...] From the windows of the surrounding houses multitudes are looking on the broad area, where a scaffold stands in death-like loneliness. [...] Lord Russell has been accused of treason [for assumed involvement in the Rye-house plot], tried at the Old Bailey, and condemned to die, and is *now* on his way from Newgate hither, along Holborn-hill. [...] The last moment approaches. [...] The sufferer unfastens the upper part of his dress, takes off his outer garment, lays bare his neck, and then places it on the block without change of countenance. [...] The executioner touches him with the axe to take sure aim, but he does not shrink. Faces, like the leaves of forest trees, are all around, looking on with trembling emotion. *But his friends at this moment turn aside their eyes. We do so.* –It is all over. [...] How grateful is it, after picturing the sad scene which Lincoln's-inn-fields exhibited in 1683, to look upon the

---

24 Rosemary Jann briefly makes similar observations concerning a shift to the present tense and identification with the we-narrator in her analysis of Thomas Babington Macaulay's *History of England* (cf. Jann 1985: 94).

quiet, pleasant, open square *now*, with its garden of trees and shrubs and flowers, covering the space set apart for the tragedy of Lord Russell's execution. As we rejoice in our present freedom, we feel as if the drops of the patriot's blood had been as precious seeds from which have grown up those liberties that now ›blossom as the rose.‹« (Ibid.: 365-366; my emphases)

Narrator and readers experienced Russell's execution as if part of his circle of friends, united with them through the action of looking away in the use of historical present (»turn aside their eyes«) and present tense (»We do so«), thereby clearly guiding readers' perception. The blurring of time levels here linked the sensation and spectacle of the execution – which the *Leisure Hour* was able to present on the basis of historical truth, while the RTS eschewed sensational and gruesome depictions in other periodicals such as the *London Journal* (see the analysis of J.F. Smith's »Lives of the Queens« in Chapter 3) – to the evaluation of »our present freedom« as a consequence of Russell's martyrdom. The passage hence bore didactic potential as it combined entertainment and instruction through the immediacy created in the presentation of the historical action as present (note the use of »now«, first for Russell's time, and then also for the reader's time).

As a means of enhancing didacticism by presenting truthful stories, the factuality of the presented historical world was, for instance, pointed out in the following transition in the part on Newton:

»[I]n following the shades of the departed about the streets of London, we pause opposite the place now devoted to business connected with our national revenue, and easily transform it, by a *touch with the wand of fancy*, under the guidance of *archaeological research*, into an old quadrilateral range of buildings, a story high, with attics above, enclosing an open square, refreshed by rows of trees.« ([Stoughton] 1852a: 635; my emphases)

The narrator here described the process of transformation as magic (»touch with the wand of fancy«); he was nevertheless careful to point towards a scientific approach in the use of sources enabling the reconstruction of the past (»archaeological research«).

In the part on Milton, the narrator likened the imaginative act of literary transformation to the palimpsest encountered in the scholarship of manuscript reconstruction:

»Wherever we meet with the memory of Milton in old London, we find the place so changed that we have to bring back the shades of departed scenes, as well as of the departed man, to give anything like vivid reality to our image of him. Manuscripts in the middle ages were defaced and written over again, but antiquaries have deciphered in some cases the under and original writing, and thus restored the book to what it was of old. A like process fancy performs in reference to London streets and houses, in these literary perambulations. Ancient scenes, defaced and covered with modern architecture, we endeavour by a little imaginative power to reproduce.« (Ibid.: 114)

In this instance, an interview with a »present inhabitant« served to authenticate the poet's former residence, and furthermore »[a] neighbour assured us he had gone over the rooms, many years ago, when they preserved unmistakable traces of the 17th century. They are altered now.« (Ibid.) The narrator thereby clearly stayed within the trope of the town walk to affirm his facts to the reader.

Besides the focus on the imaginative city-scape transformation, which the set-up as a town walk brought with it, illustrations such as prints or portraits also served to introduce the transition process, albeit adding a layer of distance in that they might have served to introduce readers to the work of historical research. In the part on Walton, the narrator used a print of Walton's residence in order to reconstruct the past:

»There lies before us an old print of part of Fleet-street, showing the end of Chancery-lane – a representation which we give at the beginning of this paper. It reminds us more of a street in old Paris, or Frankfort, or some Flemish city, than of anything to be found in the vicinity now. There is a tall narrow house of five stories at the corner, with bay windows carved and adorned in front, the edges of the stories supported by odd-looking corbels like caryatides, and the old dwelling crowned with a thatch roof. The second, a narrower strip of building, is a little modern; then comes the third, lower and broader than the first, with windows along the whole front. Here lived Isaak Walton.« (Ibid.: 258)

The narrator here clearly described what readers could also see in the accompanying cover illustration (Fig. 21); however, the text did not make a direct reference to the illustration reproduced for the reader but imagined the narratorial ›we‹ studying the print (see also the discussion of the Macaulay portrait in Chapter 4). This use of text and image, then, was a further blurring of boundaries: The narrator/author revealed his method of re-imagining Walton's place of residence from the print and simultaneously allowed for a parallel ›re-enactment‹ of this process in a possibly communal consumption of the text alongside the presented illustration. This hence allowed readers/listeners in a sense to experience the workings of historical reconstruction described at other instances.

This depiction of objects, such as the buildings in the print of Walton's street-scape, was, however, an exception for the series. Besides another small illustration showing a statue of Howard, »Shades of the Departed« was illustrated with narrative scenes, and these were connected to the text through the respective anecdotes. Four of the six cover illustrations made by John Gilbert presented the iconic figures Baxter, Milton, Johnson and Burke in such a way that they would probably easily have been recognised by Victorian readers from portraits circulating as prints or exhibited in public places.

Samuel Johnson's appearance (Fig. 22), for instance, would have been well-known at least to the *Leisure Hour*'s middle-class readership through Reynold's portrait, which besides Boswell's popular biography accompanied many other biographies of the literary critic and lexicographer. Further, the cover illustration apparently cited Edward Matthew Ward's paintings of historical anecdotes concerning Johnson, which gained high popularity during the 1840s not only

Fig. 21: Cover for »Shades of the Departed«, Leisure Hour *(22 Apr 1852: 257)*

Fig. 22: Cover for »Shades of the Departed«, Leisure Hour *(18 Nov 1852: 737)*

Images published with permission of ProQuest. Further reproduction is prohibited without permission.

through public exhibitions but also through further distribution as collectible prints.[25] However, the illustration in the *Leisure Hour* did not provide a public setting but rather presented »A Domestic Scene at Dr. Johnson's« ([Stoughton] 1852a: 737), as the illustration was subtitled. The caption directed readers to »p. 740« of the magazine, where the historical anecdote connected to the image was narrated:

»Under the date 1766, Boswell informs us: ‹I returned to London in February, and found Dr. Johnson in a good house in Johnson's-court, Fleet-street, in which he had accommo-dated Mrs. Williams with an apartment on the ground floor, while Mr. Levett occupied his post in the garret; his faithful Francis was still attending him.‹ These were three persons well known to the readers of Johnson's life, indeed essential features in his domestic pic-ture. Mrs. Williams was a blind Welsh lady, an admirer of the critic [...]. Robert Levett was a very humble practitioner in the medical profession, to whom Johnson took a great fancy [...]. Francis was a negro who waited on the doctor with great fidelity [...].« (Ibid.: 740)

While the article reported not only on the people presented in the illustration but also on Johnson's intellectual career, the illustration clearly directed the readers' focus on the perception of the domestic sphere. Hence, the open composition of the illustration figuratively invited readers to join Mrs Williams, Dr Levett and Boswell at Johnson's table, granting them access to a space of which the text claims: »The penetralia of Johnson's domestic retirement few were permitted to enter« (ibid.).

The illustration can in this regard also be read as a metaphor for the *Leisure Hour*'s agenda, which, as I have shown in Chapter 3, tried especially in its initial years to reach out to the working classes: Similar to the opening up of Johnson's domestic sphere to the reader, the consumption of the magazine allowed access to the historical culture practices of the middle classes, as the article cited Ward's popular paintings and offered insight into Boswell's biography through the many quotations inserted within the article.

---

25 Edward Matthew Ward's *Doctor Johnson in the Ante-Room of the Lord Chesterfield Waiting for an Audience, 1748* (1845) was presented to the National Gallery by Rob-ert Vernon in 1847 and exhibited in 1848; his *Dr Samuel Johnson Reading the Manu-script of Oliver Goldsmith's ›The Vicar of Wakefield‹, Whilst a Baliff Waits with the Landlady* (1843-1845) was, for instance, distributed as a mezzotint engraving by S. Bellin in 1845.

The frequent use of ego-documents – such as quotations from Boswell's biography in the part on Johnson – added a third level of narration to the articles, aiming for further immediacy and authenticity. Historical sources used by Stoughton included mainly letters, diaries and (auto)biographies written by contemporaries. Though these sources were normally credited their authorship, this referencing and embedding did not follow objective historical practice – the whole series worked almost entirely without footnotes, and sources were (rarely) evaluated in their own subjective status but rather served as eye-witness accounts.

Of a similar category were re-enactments of scenes in direct speech. These resembled adaptations following historical documents; or they might have been rather second-hand accounts rewritten after works from other historians or biographers. The passage on Baxter's trial is likely to have had its origin in Thomas Babington Macaulay's *History of England* (1849: 63-64). In the *Leisure Hour*, the trial was presented as follows:

»We hear the miserable mockery of the Puritans from one who ought to have held even-handed the balance of justice, squeaking and snorting in pretended imitation of their tone and manner; and we catch the smart reply of Pollexfen, Baxter's counsel: ›Why, my lord, some will think it hard measure to stop these men's mouths, and not let them speak through their noses.‹ Then comes a torrent of abuse: ›Come, what do you say for yourself, you old knave. What doth he say? I'm not afraid of you for all the snivelling calves you have got about you‹ – looking at the people in tears. ›Does your lordship think any jury will pretend to pass a verdict upon me upon such a trial?‹ asks Baxter. ›I'll warrant you, Mr. Baxter,‹ say the man in the red robe; ›don't you trouble yourself about that.‹ No story more arouses our indignation than this of the doings at Westminster in 1685.« ([Stoughton] 1852a: 20)

The re-enactment in direct speech created intimacy with the historical world by almost cutting out the mediating narrative voice and instead presenting the dialogue as it may have occurred between the historical actors. R. Mitchell notes that »intent on a visualization of the appearance of the past and its events, the picturesque historian generally preferred dramatic reconstructive narrative to critical use of sources« (2000: 16). Historical documents and sources were hence not used primarily as historical evidence but for dramatic and authenticating effect. In this regard, the frequent insertion of dialogue scenes in »Shades of the Departed« also supported an engaged reading-aloud of the series within the family circle together with a communal viewing of its illustrations.

The Perspective Structure of »Shades of the Departed in Old London«

The articles' perspective structure (see Chapter 1) further supported the inclusion of a family audience, yet it was dominated by the perception of the overt we-narrator as well as the central historical actors. Most importantly for guiding the readers in their perception of the texts' intentions, the psychology of including readers within the narratorial ›we‹ made it harder to disagree with the moral judgements of this overt, subjective voice. This is most obvious when the narratorial ›we‹, as in the following example, bluntly expressed his attitude towards the text's actors and left no room for interpretation or disagreement:

»But much as we admire [Walton's] ›Angler,‹ we admire, in some respects, his ›Lives‹ still more, for though there are sentiments expressed and opinions indicated, with which we do not agree, we have brought before us portraitures of piety, especially in the characters of Hooker, Donne, and Herbert, which may well awaken our Christian sympathies, and stimulate us to holy imitation.« ([Stoughton] 1852a: 260-261)

The we-narrator's perspective could clearly be identified as male and middle-class with a strong tendency to judge non-Christian behaviour or to positively evaluate nonconformist attitudes, which was further supported by the selection and presentation of male protagonists.

While the historical actors were chosen for their quality as role models, Stoughton' series did not present a simplified, one-sided view but also included negative character traits. These especially reflected contemporary evangelical attitudes towards temperance, observation of the Sabbath and work ethic, in connection with the need for salvation. The part on Addison, for instance, pointed out:

»Though it is not known that he was ever decidedly intoxicated, he often transgressed the bounds of moderation – a fact we dare not conceal, but which we record with deep sorrow, furnishing as it does one of a large collection of examples to the effect that the most refined intellectual taste is no sufficient check against temptations to the excessive indulgence of the animal appetites. Whatever might appear to the contrary in his writings, there must have been in Addison a weakness of moral and religious principle as applied to the deportment of his life; but we hope that in his last days, after religion had more than ever occupied his pen, its influence more powerfully touched his heart, producing contrition for the past and reformation for the future.« (Ibid.: 452)

Similarly, the narrator disapproved of Reynolds' motto »[t]he man will never make a painter who looks for the Sunday with pleasure as an idle day« (ibid.: 697) and his neglect to preserve the Christian Sabbath:

»Examples of the past and present show that Reynolds was mistaken about the need of painting *every* day. Religion – deep earnest religion – that which takes in the whole gospel, and which penetrates the depths of the soul – that which transforms the man and brings him into fellowship with the infinite and glorious mind of Christ – that which makes the sabbath a delight, and gives sacredness to every portion of time, by exhibiting it as a talent from the Giver of all good, to be devoted to his glory – is not only in harmony with the profession of the artist, and with all the diversified employments of social life, but it improves, exalts, and dignifies them.« (Ibid.)

The narrator especially found fault with Goldsmith's vanity, religious faith and inconsiderate philanthropy. Thus, that Goldsmith »delighted in velvet and gold lace« showed that »Vanity and good-nature lay obviously enough on the surface of his character; the latter, in spite of the former, ever saving him from contempt, but seldom from derision« (ibid.: 665). Furthermore,

»of religious *faith*, which is another thing [than religious feeling] – by which we mean the realization of Divine truths, especially those revealed in the gospel – we have, alas! no evidence in his works or memoirs. We can admire his delicate genius, and appreciate his generous acts; but we feel it our duty, and we discharge it with pain, to point out and reprobate his moral and religious deficiencies. [...] He was one of the companions of our childhood, fondly cherished, and as an author we love him still; though matured understanding and reflection lead us to speak discriminatingly of his character as a man.« (Ibid.)

The faults the we-narrator found in the historical actors were moral misgivings as regards evangelical understanding, such as intemperance, lack of Christian faith, and disobedience of evangelical morals. The biographies were used to transport these moralistic, Christian tropes by way of examples adequate also to young readers. This was supported by the positive portrayal of the historical actors as role models on the macro-level of their life, while descriptions of moral deficiencies as shown above were limited to a private, domestic level. Overall, the portrayal of their development from childhood onwards and the inclusion of domestic, everyday scenes connected the past lifeworld to readers' experiences by making the historical actors more human and less idealised. The narrator, for instance, directly pointed this out when observing a gathering of Addison, Garth, and Swift:

»[S]ome may think there must have been rare discourse between such a trio – wonderful scintillations, brisk repartees, keen satire, shrewd remarks; only experience teaches that such men in private are often common-place like other people – that the learned do not always appear so very learned, or wits so very witty.« (Ibid.: 451-452)

The introduction to a domestic setting has already been observed above with the cover illustration on Johnson, of which the narrator further explained:

»We are accustomed to think of Johnson only in connection with literature: it is very beautiful, in addition, to recognise him in the character of a philanthropist, bringing upon him the blessing of them that were ready to perish, and making the widow's heart to sing for joy. The healing of wounded hearts, and the assuagement of smarting sorrows, attract less attention than the prizes won in the stadium of scholarship, or than the bays which adorn the brows of genius; and yet we all know there are records kept of the former (when performed from right motives) in that world where the latter distinctions are overlooked as things of nought. Johnson's intellectual efforts defy imitation, but his quiet benevolence is within the reach of every one.« (Ibid.: 740)

The comparison »of every one« to these historical actors and their acceptance as role models for amending one's own faults was thus enhanced.

While the perspective structure was guided by the we-narrator and the prominent male historical actors, the different stages of their biography allowed for the inclusion of a personnel important to attract a diverse family readership. As the quotation from Boswell in the Johnson part introduced above shows, other perspectives were presented, but female and working-class perspectives nevertheless remained marginalised or simply served as foils for the protagonists – in this instance, the blind widow Mrs Williams and the negro-servant Francis underlined Johnson's philanthropy.

Women were mainly shown in their domestic function as good wives, mothers or housemaids, which served vice versa to point out the exemplary matrimonial life led by the protagonists. This can be observed in the following examples: the »tender[] attach[ment]« of Milton to his second wife (ibid.: 115) and his daughter(s), who read to or took notes for the blind Milton (ibid.: 116); the »devotion and heroism« Russell's wife displayed during his trial (ibid.: 367); Walton's »poor wife«, who »died, in 1640, after giving birth to an infant daughter« (ibid.: 259); or Reynolds' sister Fanny, who served as his housekeeper (ibid.: 696). In the part on Goldsmith, poor women were introduced as anonymous persons whom Goldsmith helped financially, and thereby they served the narrator's purpose of outlining Goldsmith's inconsiderate philanthropy (ibid.: 665). An ar-

ticle on Margaret Godolphin ([Stoughton] 1852b: 225-228), which was published in the *Leisure Hour* in between the issues containing the articles on Milton
and Walton, and which also prominently appeared with a cover illustration,
forms part of the book publication of Stoughton's *Shades and Echoes of Old
London* (1864a; see analysis below). In the *Leisure Hour*, however, the article
was published as a stand-alone biography and not as part of the series, which
would have broken the focus on male protagonists as well as women's inferior
role in the series.

The set-up of the biographies alluded to the Victorian ideal of the working
and middle classes as self-made men, as the parts often depicted the protagonists' efforts towards their education and success from youth on. Thus, Milton
even as a »boy was studious, and when only twelve years of age, many a time
did he sit up till midnight, conning his books, thus not only laying the foundation
of his marvellous scholarship« ([Stoughton] 1852a: 114); Addison's »future career« was seen »in connexion with his genial boyhood« (ibid.: 450). Furthermore, the part on Newton compared the work of a shoemaker to Newton's
achievement when visiting his former observatory, which had by then been
turned into a shoemaker's shop:

»We were permitted to ascend into that spot [i.e., the observatory], to see it profaned by its
present use, for there we found a shoemaker busy at his work. Yet, on second thoughts, a
shoemaker's humble employment is no profanation of an astronomer's study, for shoe-
makers have a mission in this world as well as astronomers. They are fellow-workers in
the great hive of human industry. Mutual helpers are they too. For if the star-gazer in-
structs the shoemaker, the shoemaker makes shoes for the star-gazer. We thought, as we
stood in that little airy nest, looking at our humble friend, and thinking of the great philosopher, how Providence binds all ranks together by ties of inter-dependence, and how
wrong it is for the hand to say to the foot, ›I have no need of thee.‹« (Ibid.: 636)

This shows that the series, with its overt we-narrator, favoured a male, middle-
class perspective. By always beginning its biographical narratives with the protagonists' youth, it seemed to address predominantly male, adolescent readers in
its presentation of Christian role models and self-made men, which allowed
identification for intended working-class readers, and at instances also for wom-
en. In this regard, the series hence strictly followed the RTS's agenda of introducing a periodical »to be specially adapted for the Working classes and particularly the Younger members of their families« (USCL/RTS CCM 16 July 1851;
see Chapter 1).

»Shades of the Departed in Old London« and its Book Publication[26]

The reissue of »Shades of the Departed in Old London« in book form indicates that the RTS must have considered the series a success, as they published it together with Stoughton's series »Echoes of Westminster Hall« ([Stoughton] 1856) as *Shades and Echoes of Old London* under the imprint of »the Leisure Hour Office« in 1864, and republished the book again in 1889.[27] While the articles themselves appeared mainly unchanged in the book publication, the introduction to »Shades of the Departed« was expanded and hence gave more information on the intended use of the articles than did the original publication in the *Leisure Hour*.

The book's preface reproduced the first two paragraphs of the series, but then added another eight pages on the history of London mixed with meta-historical references. Thus, the preface added a more academic character to the book, as it could be considered a stand-alone essay on the use of history. It clearly outlined the didactic quality of history:

»Buildings, dingy and dilapidated, or tastelessly modernized, in which great geniuses were born, or lived, or died, are, in connexion with such events, transformed into poetic bowers [...]. Tales of valour and suffering, of heroism and patience, of virtue and piety, of the patriot's life and the martyr's death, crowd thickly on the memory. Nor do opposite reminiscences [...] of vice and crime, of evil passions and false principles, fail to arise, fraught with salutary warnings and cautions.« (Stoughton 1864a: 9-10)

In the book, Stoughton also more explicitly pointed towards London's significance as Britain's metropolis and its importance for the whole nation (ibid.: 10). The introduction identified specific groups of historical actors important to this history, namely »great kings«, »great poets« and finally »reformers«. At the

---

26 An earlier version of this section can be found in Lechner (2013: §§18-23); see also Fn 9 above.

27 The RTS had agreed to Stoughton's proposal of publishing »Shades of the Departed« and »Echoes of Westminster Hall« in volume format in 1859 (USCL/RTS CCM 8 June 1859). The book did not get published until 1864. Since Stoughton did not revise much from the periodical articles to the book publication, it is noteworthy that the publication took so long, given that the RTS normally put its plans into action quite quickly.

same time, Stoughton further explicated his metaphor of »shades« as signifying the lasting importance of these actors for the present (ibid.: 11-12 and 15).

While Stoughton included commercial and political history and their relevant historical actors in the introduction to the book publication, the series in the *Leisure Hour* – as has been shown above – did not prominently feature these aspects. Yet after this expanded introduction, Stoughton again failed to qualify his choice of historical actors and the time-frame for the following chapters. Having written for almost seven pages about the history of London from Roman times up to the Reformation and Shakespeare (the year of publication being Shakespeare's tercentenary), Stoughton only offered a brief one-sentence transition before presenting his first chapter on Milton: »But we must conclude these general recollections, and proceed to notice certain illustrious names of later times, which have left their imprint very distinctly in London localities with which everybody is familiar.« (Ibid.: 16)

Besides a few changes in the chronology of chapters, two more entries were included in the book under the category of the »Shades of the Departed«, namely the article on Margaret Godolphin ([Stoughton] 1852b) printed during the run of »Shades of the Departed« in the *Leisure Hour* (see above) and a chapter on Isaac Watts. While both were biographical sketches, they were not written as town walks and did not feature the respective transformation of present to past; and Stoughton did not amend them to conform to this pattern for the volume publication. Furthermore, the chapter on Watts – which was originally published in 1859 as three parts of the series »Memorial Chapters« ([Stoughton] 1859a) in the more obviously religious *Sunday at Home*, a source not credited in the volume publication – featured a tone different to the *Leisure Hour* articles, which was also due to the chosen topic of the chaplain, preacher and writer Isaac Watts. The inclusion of articles ›foreign‹ to the »Shades of the Departed« series and the combination of two series within the book publication, that is, »Shades of the Departed« plus the 1856 series »Echoes of Westminster Hall«, suggest that Stoughton and the RTS used the book publication as an easy means to gain further profit from their earlier work without having to invest too much additional time. Since the marketing of the *Shilling Books for Leisure Hours* series, in which the book was published, promised a length of 288 pages, the two chapters were probably simply included to make up the mandatory space; and the book itself hints at a neglect of editing with a note that »[t]hese Papers are reprinted from the ›Leisure Hour‹ of 1852 [...], which will account for several references not applicable at the present time« (Stoughton 1864a: 284).

While the text as presented in the *Leisure Hour* (directed at a family audience) did not appear to be intended for an exclusively young readership, advertisements as well as book reviews allow for a further determination of reception and readership. They assessed the book as especially suitable for Sunday schools and children or adolescents. Reviews considered the book to be a »healthy and readable book [...] blend[ing], with no unartistic hand, pleasure and information« (»*Shades and Echoes of Old London*« 1864: 479), and identified it as »exactly fitted for the Sunday School library« (»VII. Our Book Club« 1864: 661), »for the young« ([Doran] 1864: 527),[28] but also as reading matter which »boys and girls will value as long as they live« (»*Shades and Echoes of Old London*« 1889: 473). The *Shilling Books for Leisure Hours* series arose from RTS members' suggestions to turn articles from the *Leisure Hour* and the *Sunday at Home* into books for railway reading.[29] The book series was finally advertised as »interesting reading, especially for the young« with »the higher purpose of« presenting »lessons of Christian faith and duty« (»*Shilling Books for Leisure Hours*« 1863: 830). The *Christian Witness* remarked in its review of the *Shilling Series* that it »consists of a multitude of deeply interesting facts and narratives, which have all the charms of romance, with the striking advantage that they are true« (»Literature« 1863: 830). The adoption of »Shades of the Departed« for the *Shilling* series therefore suggests that in the *Leisure Hour* it served the purpose not only of catering to a broad family readership, but of entertaining while instructing with a Christian tone, thereby thwarting secular papers presenting sensational fiction.

CONTINUATION, VARIATION AND NEGATION OF STOUGHTON'S NARRATIVE PATTERN

In »Shades of the Departed«, Stoughton established a pattern which he also used in most of his other series for the *Leisure Hour* (see Appendix A, Tab. 24). While there was a clear focus on the biographical narrative in »Shades of the Departed«, other series were more loosely structured around a focus on historic sites. They hence foregrounded the genre of travel writing. These other series also made use of a prominent we-narrator to forge allegiance between the narrator

---

28 This review, written by John Doran (1807-1878), complained about the »careless editing and strange blundering« ([Doran] 1864: 527) of the book, as well as Stoughton's neglect to provide sources for some quotations, and thereby indicated a carelessness of Stoughton towards popular publications.

29 See USCL/RTS CCM (9 June 1858), (18 June 1862), (16 July 1862) and USCL/RTS ECM (23 Sept 1862).

(as travel guide) and readers; and they commonly linked present and past by dissolving one into the other to create immediacy and authentication through the insertion of ego-documents and by re-enacting dialogues and historical scenes when presenting anecdotes related to these sites. In none of these series (besides »Queen Anne«, 1887) was the set-up as chronologically determined by a unifying historical/biographical narrative as »Shades of the Departed«. Rather, the inclusion of anecdotes jumped between different times and historical actors and was structured along the route taken on the level of the stroll in the spatial set-up of sites or buildings. As in »Shades of the Departed«, Stoughton also wrote mainly about local national history (London, Westminster, Windsor, Queen Anne) in his other series, but also included some foreign travel series (Tyrol, Black Forest), which displayed a slightly different approach to history.

Local National History: »Banks of the Thames« and »Windsor Castle«

»Banks of the Thames« (1853), »Windsor Castle« (1859) and »The Tale of a West-End Suburb« (1862) on Kensington all focused on localities of personal interest to Stoughton as (former) places of residence. They also all link back to London or were in close proximity to it, and they combined local history with walks. A different approach via localities rather than biographies was, for instance, indicated through the subtitles to »The Banks of the Thames«, which consisted of buildings or areas visited in the articles, such as Fulham Palace, Chiswick or Hampton Court. The series started out by personifying the Thames (male) and by presenting it as an image of England's prosperity and international commerce. Thus, the Thames was presented as

»the king of English rivers, the sovereign of that fair commonwealth of streams which wind and wander, silver-clad, among our green meadows and wooded hills, through our busy towns and by our quiet villages. [...] No river in any clime can boast such wealth of shipping, such a prodigious amount of stores and merchandise [...] and nowhere can such an impression be derived of England's pre-eminent commercial resources, her traffic with other nations, and her own abundance and prosperity.« ([Stoughton] 1853: 504)

The series thereby initially stressed the importance of the eponymous Thames in commercial and global terms. Yet it was less concerned with the presentation of eminent historic sites along the London part of the Thames:

»The Tower, and Somerset House, and Lambeth Palace, and many other object architecturally imposing and full of historic interest, are very tempting; but we have to tear ourselves unwillingly away from them, for we are bent, under the influence of these bright blue skies and yonder magnetic green fields, upon confining ourselves to rustic haunts.« (Ibid.: 505)

Instead, with its prominent we-narrator the series »purpose[d] during the summer weeks to take some strolls along the river-side [...] inviting the friendly companionship of our reader – for we like to feel ourselves in company – and, under that impression, to think aloud« (ibid.: 504-505). Thus, frequent use of present tense and infinitives show that the we-narrator ›spoke‹ as if the stroll were actually taken together with the reader as a guided tour: »Before we cross the moat, and pass through the gates, do just turn and look at the fine avenue of lime-trees, running up besides the moat, as far as the Fulham road.« (Ibid.: 506) This mode of narration continued when the scenery was pictured in its past appearance and peopled with historical figures:

»We soon reach the principal entrance [to Fulham Palace], under a large brick gateway, built by Fitzjames in the reign of Henry VII. [...] Here in loneliness and quietude, as the hot sun disposes the imagination to indulge in dreamy pictures of the past, one thinks of antique processions which have swept through that old gateway [...]. In addition to dim visions of what *might* have been in earlier times, there comes very distinctly before us reminiscences of what *has* been. The high and mighty sovereign Elizabeth enters with all her courtiers and attendants on a visit to bishop Bancroft, whom we see with lowly reverence advancing to meet his royal mistress. And then there comes king [sic] James, just before his coronation, to enjoy the hospitalities of the same bishop. [...] [H]aving amused one's self with these facts of the past, it is time to enter into the palace, where, however, but few vestiges of its former character remain, the building being for the most part modernized, and presenting now the aspect of an abode commodious, handsome, and tasteful, rather than magnificent and imposing.« (Ibid.: 505)

In this manner, narrator and reader followed the course of the Thames and took various manifestations of the past on the way as triggers to transition into historical ›re-enactments‹.

The idea of a guided trip was also programmatic for the articles on »Windsor Castle«. The series, presented entirely within the monthly part for June 1859, consisted of three parts entitled »Windsor Castle« and two further articles in the succeeding issues, namely »The Neighbourhood of Windsor« about Eton and »A Summer's Day at Windsor«, and could be considered a kind of »travel guide for historical sightseeing«.[30] The series was one of the rare occasions in which an earlier book publication of Stoughton formed the basis for the periodical articles, yet he also used other books as sources. A footnote in the first article stated that »[i]n this and the following papers we have made considerable use of the recently published ›Annals of Windsor‹, by R. R. Tighe and J. E. Davis, but still more of ›Windsor in the Olden Time‹, by the Rev. J. Stoughton« ([Stoughton] 1859c: 343). It thereby referenced sources which were of a historical – though rather antiquarian than academic – interest. By comparison, Stoughton's *Notices of Windsor in the Olden Time* (1844) was much more concise and antiquarian in layout than Tighe and Davis's *Annals of Windsor* (1858). Stoughton's *Notices* had a basic one-page table of contents (listing chapter titles only) and presented its historical narrative on 236 pages without an index. Tighe and Davis's two-volume reference work, by contrast, presented very detailed chapter outlines in the table of contents and gave a total of 1367 pages of text followed by a 90-page index. In their preface they provided a review of literature, which laudably referenced Stoughton's *Notices*, though also regretting its popular approach:

>»The work that has the strongest claim to be regarded in the light of a History of Windsor, is Mr Stoughton's ›Notices of Windsor in the Olden Time,‹ published in 1844. In this unpretending but interesting little volume there is, undoubtedly, more matter connected with Windsor than had been put together by any previous writer; but still it does not possess the character of a Local History. The substance of it formed a series of lectures delivered at the Mechanics' Institute at Windsor, and the author's principal sources of information were the previous works already noticed, aided by an occasional reference to other authorities, and a few extracts from second-hand notes of local documents. [...] Not only have the national records of the country remained unsearched, but the printed works of the chroniclers and historians of England have been neglected.« (Tighe/Davis 1858, vol. 2: ix-x)[31]

---

30 The case study on »Windsor Castle« presented here is a much changed expansion of Lechner (2013: §§26-27), where I focus on the series' presentation as a monthly part and the transfer from book to periodical, which »resulted in a transition of the textual genre from historiography to travel guide for historical sightseeing« (ibid.: §26); see also Fn 9 above. In addition, I here present a closer reading of the series' source texts, which has not been published before. On monthly parts in the *Leisure Hour* and book transfer, see also Chapter 5.

31 While Tighe and Davis criticised Stoughton's neglect to consider »the national records«, in 1877 Stoughton also contributed a series on »The Royal Commission on Historical Manuscripts« to the *Leisure Hour*; see Fn 12 above.

Stoughton appears to have acknowledged Tighe and Davis's criticism in his new edition of the book as *Windsor: A History and Description of the Castle and the Town*, published in 1862, where he displayed remorse about his popular approach.[32] That he referenced Tighe and Davis in the *Leisure Hour* clearly shows that he engaged with their work, even in this popular rendering.

The initial article promised that »we are not going to repeat what all the guide-books say about Windsor« ([Stoughton] 1859c: 343) and continued to announce that

»[t]hings of the past, not so unfamiliar to the many, will be noticed in the visit we now propose to pay to the royal castle on the hill, though we shall be on the look-out for what commonly does not occur to local cicerones, or may not be found recorded in the guide-books.« (Ibid.: 345)

The set-up of the *Leisure Hour*'s part on Windsor basically followed the division of Stoughton's book into historical and descriptive sections and used the narrative pattern combining walk with transitions from present to the past in anecdotes modified after Tighe and Davis's as well as Stoughton's book.

Yet since the series portrayed a location outside of London, it also provided practical travel information. Especially the last article, »A Summer's Day at Windsor«, gave specific instructions and recommendations on how to conduct a visit to Windsor from London:

»In previous articles we have given descriptive and historical notices of the chief points of interest in Windsor and its neighbourhood. To examine in detail the many objects of antiquarian or architectural interest would require a long sojourn and frequent study; but for the benefit of those who have only leisure for a hasty visit, a few practical hints may be acceptable, as to how to make the most of a summer's day at Windsor.« (Ibid.: 406)

Furthermore, for a long quotation on St George's Chapel this article referenced »Brown's useful ›Windsor Guide,‹ Castle Hill, Windsor«, but with the derogato-

---

32 The preface to this 1862 edition stated that *Notices* (Stoughton 1844) had been »very favourably received, and especially by those best acquainted with the Castle and neighbourhood [...], and though repeatedly requested to republish it, sensible of its imperfection, [the author] has always refused to do so. At length, however, having collected materials to render the book more complete, and more generally acceptable as a guide to the Castle, he has recast the whole, and now presents to the public a substantially new work« (Stoughton 1862b: »Preface«, n. pag.).

ry comment that »[o]ne of the guide-books describes this portion of the edifice, in the style characteristic of that class of publications« (ibid.: 407). Thus, while Stoughton attempted to distance himself from »guide-books«, the series presented within the monthly part for June 1859 rather pertained to this genre itself. This was also due to the inclusion of many illustrations (overall, the five articles were accompanied by 13 smaller, two half- and two full-page engravings) as well as of a »bird's eye view of the Castle« (ibid.: 360) in the second article and a »Map of Windsor and Its Environs« (ibid.: 408) in the concluding part.[33] Furthermore, the monthly part was advertised as »A Summer's Day at Windsor [...] Contain[ing] a Series of Five descriptive Papers on Windsor and its Neighbourhood. With 18 Beautiful Engravings and Map« (*Leader* 1859: 852). It therefore appears that the *Leisure Hour* was very interested in serving a ›tourist‹ audience, and Stoughton had to follow this agenda in his contribution to the periodical.

Foreign Accounts: »A Ramble in the Tyrol« and »The Black Forest«

Stoughton also wrote for the *Leisure Hour* for financial reasons, and accordingly his daughter noted: »Almost all his journeys on the continent were paid for out of the articles and books he wrote on the subject as he travelled« (Lewis 1897: 185). In two of his series for the *Leisure Hour*, Stoughton appears to have made use of such material from his foreign travels, namely »A Ramble in the Tyrol« (1859) and »The Black Forest« (1879). In contrast to his series on British topics, they more closely narrated how each day of the travel was spent and thereby included useful advice for travellers as well as information on historical sightseeing. Stoughton's common style of blurring present and past, was here, however, accomplished with less smooth transitions between present and past. Rather, the two levels were kept separate, and the accounts on the past created less immediacy through a different use of the we-narrator – who here referred to an actual tourist (or group of tourists) writing a travel account – as well as its abrupt inclusion of sources.

In »A Ramble in the Tyrol«, a visit to the castle at Salzburg was described in the following way:

»Climbing up the steep road to the castle, you find there are now barracks in what was once the palace and fortress of the bishops of Saltzburg [sic], princes, petty kings of yore. It is horrible to look into the prisons, to see the remains of racks and tortures; pleasant to

---

33 Stoughton's book had been unillustrated.

survey some of the state apartments, now restored, brilliantly painted and gilded, according to medieval fashion and taste, so that one can repeople it with the bishop prince and his court, his chaplain, priests, and guards.« ([Stoughton] 1859b: 558)

The past was here not re-imagined, but the narrator/guide rather gave a description of what the traveller might actually find at the historic site and only hinted at the possibility of a ›re-peopling‹. Furthermore, the use of »you« created a distance between the we-narrator and readers, and hence also to the immersion in the past world. After all, this was a foreign past, not the communal British past.

While Stoughton's series usually used historical documents to smoothly blur present and past, there were no such careful transitions here. »Rambles in the Tyrol« presented two long quotations of historical content, which were simply introduced as »[h]ere we pass the Martinsward, a huge rock connected with the following legend« (ibid.: 564) or »[b]efore we leave the Finstermunz, we must refer to a scene in the Tyrolese war« (ibid.). Both of these instances were followed by almost an entire column of past narrative in quotations marks. A source, also for further quotations of less historical content, was not referenced beyond »[a]nother traveller observes« (ibid.: 586), yet all of these passages appear to have been directly copied from Murray's *A Handbook for Travellers in Southern Germany* (1857). These narratives were rendered in third person, and the narrator did not further comment on them but continued his voyage. Present of travel and historical account thus remained separate from each other.

An even stronger way of distancing appeared in the five-part series »The Black Forest« (Stoughton 1879), whose first two articles were dedicated to »Its History«. It should, however, be noted that this series was published more than twenty years later in 1879, which may account for a change in Stoughton's style. The narrator in »The Black Forest« seldom referred to readers directly as companions but rather talked about »the tourist« or »the visitor« in the third person and past tense, observing manifestations of the past:

»And as the tourist ascends to the top of the remaining towers, and beholds with delight villages, spires, and water-mills, he is reminded by the force of contrast how different was the aspect of the country when in the middle ages the ladies of the family in hours of peace leaned over those battlements. [...] [T]he present castle [...] enables an intelligent visitor to picture to himself what it has been, and to surround the court, and enliven the apartments, with the scenes and associations of other days.« (Stoughton 1879: 330)

Although this passage again suggests a historical re-enactment, no such re-imagining, historical anecdote or re-peopling of the scenery as in other articles followed. The experience of the past in »The Black Forest« was therefore less immediate, as readers were not invited to immerse themselves in the past of this ›foreign‹ narrative as in »Shades of the Departed«.

Furthermore, »The Black Forest« applied a second level of narrative distance, as information was often provided not as direct knowledge of the narrator, but as second-hand information from an unidentified and vague external source:

> »We saw also the passage containing a well or pit under the floor [...] down which, *you are told*, the condemned were thrown after being led up to a figure of the Virgin, which they were directed to kiss. Moreover, we had a glimpse of the pit itself [...] once containing a machine consisting of lancet-studded wheels, which tore to pieces the wretched victims thrown against their sharp sides. This mystery of iniquity was discovered, *as the story goes*, in the attempt to recover a little dog that had fallen into the mist of the cruel machinery.« (Ibid.; my emphases)

The tone in »The Black Forest« was hence more remote. Longer tales, legends or anecdotes, which had still been included in »A Ramble in the Tyrol«, were rare, while the series was rather dry in its historical presentation:

> »A FEW large towns arose on the edges of the Great Forest in mediæval times. Freiburg is the principal, founded by the Duke of Zähringen in 1118, then handed over to the Counts of Urach, and next transferred to the house of Hapsburg. In 1386 it became a free town – hence its present name. In 1490 it was constituted an imperial city, and here a celebrated Diet was held in 1499, after which the Treaty of Basle was signed, recognising the independence of Switzerland. Its ancient cathedral is a magnificent structure, and its archbishop is the ecclesiastical superior of the Hohenzollern principality together with the Grand Duchy of Baden. No other place of equal importance belongs to the Black Forest district.« (Ibid.: 396)

The series here stuck to a listing of historical facts, underlined by the many year dates included, in a rather objective way.

Stoughton's Historical Legacy: »Glimpses of Queen Anne's Days«

In his presumably last contribution to the *Leisure Hour*, »Glimpses of Queen Anne's Days«, which was published in 1887, Stoughton returned to common territory, as the series was geographically structured into sections on Windsor, Kensington and London, as well as the provinces. The title might suggest that this short two-parter would focus on a female historical actor – and a sovereign as well – and thus promised a deviation from Stoughton's otherwise rather male focus on and down-to-earth approach to the past. However, the title also indicated that Queen Anne served mainly as a chronological marker, and in the end, Stoughton appears to have used this short two-parter mainly to effect a meta-historical conclusion on the use of the past.

»Glimpses of Queen Anne's Days« was unillustrated, yet in its introductory paragraph proposed a picturesque style:

»The Germans have a proverb, ›You can't see the wood for the trees,‹ and never was that proverb more applicable than in reference to the topic before us, comprising such a num-ber of facts of all sorts, that it is difficult to generalise them, next to impossible to bring them into close connection and unity. We must endeavour to clear an open space as we proceed through this forest of objects; and passing from point to point notice *illustrations* clustering round them. We shall place ourselves in different localities, and *sketch* hastily *scenes* and circumstances relating to the days of Queen Anne.« (Stoughton 1887: 680; my emphases)

Accordingly, the articles for each geographical section described the difference between past and present through the depiction of buildings and scenery before turning to anecdote:

»The appearance of the palace there [at Kensington] is little altered. William III made it what it is, and the red-brick building is a good specimen of a palatial structure at the end of the seventeenth and the beginning of the eighteenth centuries. The Gardens then did not contain a scientific arboretum, but they comprised a lake and its present park-like avenues.

Anne seems to have spent her autumns at Kensington, and there she lived in much state, surrounded by courtiers, spending a good deal of time, by day and night, at her favourite game of basset.« (Ibid.: 680-681)

Half of the first article, in its sections on Windsor and Kensington, gave anec-dotes about Queen Anne – such as hearing about the victory at the battle of Blenheim (ibid.: 680), enjoying »her favourite game of basset«, »indulg[ing] in her favourite afternoon beverage«, tea (ibid.: 681), or having »contemptible squabbles« with the Duchess of Marlborough (ibid.) – and hence focused on a portrayal of her vanity in domestic settings. Yet the two-parter was not one of those royal biographies fashionable at the time, and in the remaining text, Queen Anne served merely as a chronological marker when the series described literary and scientific developments and talked about the history of travelling, architecture, social caste, church service, the lower classes and industry, as well as the religious questions and ecclesiastical controversies between high and low church. The two articles hence covered a variety of topics in a brief, anecdotal yet distanced style, but in the end the chosen era seemed to have been presented to show its despicable contrast to the present:

»In conclusion we are struck with the fact that in the period reviewed there was little or no feeling of responsibility on the part of one class towards another. [...] [N]o idea then prevailed to the effect that property has its *duties* as well as its *rights;* and it was forgotten that genius and talent had debts to pay to society as well as honour to receive. The moralities of commerce, of art, of literature, were little if at all understood: and in this respect the age of Victoria has the advantage over the times of Anne.« (Ibid.: 780)

Stoughton here emphasised the contrast between »Queen Anne's Days« and »the age of Victoria« through the progression of British society in terms of cross-class responsibility. While he appeared to laud contemporary advancements, this was followed by a concluding half-column of reflection on the purpose and importance of history:

»[W]e are persuaded that all will be united in the important conviction that there is a real and operative connection between past and present and between present and future. Whatever our generation is, former generations have contributed to fashion it. Whatever we are, the influence of it will flow down over those who come after us. We have inherited both evil and good. While we lament the former we are to be grateful for the latter; and diminishing the evil as far as possible through our own conduct, we are bound to hand down the good in augmented measure.

And as we are, in one sense, debtors to the past, so we are, in another sense, debtors to the future. [...] What we do in this century will tell upon the next. There is ignorance to be dispelled, knowledge to be circulated, vices to be rooted up, and virtues to be sown; and all that will benefit posterity when we are gone.« (Ibid.: 780)

In »Shades of the Departed« (1852-1853), the forty-nine-year-old Stoughton had introduced his narrative pattern of merging past and present to the readership of the *Leisure Hour*, which directly appealed to and involved the entire family through his didactic implementation of history by example of role models. In his final series, Stoughton explained his historical agenda of learning from the past in retrospect at the age of almost eighty. The image of generations he thereby used for the »connection between past [... ,] present and future« referred not only to the abstract layers of historical time but also to family generations, turning the more distanced public aspects of political and cultural history portrayed in »Glimpses of Queen Anne's Days« into a private, familial responsibility of historical inheritance to »diminish[] the evil« and »hand down the good«.

With this idea of responsibility to past and future generations, Stoughton realised, from the *Leisure Hour*'s initial year up to his final contribution, the family magazine's originally proclaimed agenda of »learning wisdom from the past« across boundaries, introduced at the very beginning of this study. As a Congregational, Nonconformist minister with an almost academic interest in the past, Stoughton was exemplary within the *Leisure Hour*'s stock of authors for historical contributions. The constant presence of his articles and series in the *Leisure Hour*'s pages from its beginning up until the late 1880s in a way superseded the ephemeral character of the periodical, and continuously realised and possibly also determined the *Leisure Hour*'s historical programme. Stoughton's longstanding work for the *Leisure Hour* therefore made his approach to the past a trademark for the family magazine.

7. Conclusion

Histories for the Many has analysed the *Leisure Hour*'s historical programme during the 1850s and 1860s, and hence at a stage of transition. As such, the representations of the past in the RTS's *Leisure Hour* during this period were regulated by three discourses intersecting in terms of class, gender, age and religion: the decreasing dominance of evangelicalism, the increasing reputation of the family magazine genre, and the academisation of history. Following a research perspective of historical culture informed by the cultural studies model of the circuit of culture as well as the narratological approach of perspective structure, I have read the *Leisure Hour*'s (serialised) articles on the past within the development of the Victorian periodical marketplace, with respect to a transfer between series and book, considering the *Leisure Hour*'s stock of ›historians‹ and – intersecting with these three areas – regarding the family magazine's (intended) readership.

The RTS used history in its periodical to reach both an intended working-class audience and the Society's middle-class supporters. At the same time, historical narratives served to consolidate RTS members for the publication within a still disrespected genre. As such, with its implementation of history the *Leisure Hour* bridged the gap between earlier secular periodicals such as the *London Journal*, with their sales-granting sensational fiction, and the more reputable illustrated monthlies of the 1860s such as *Good Words* and *Cornhill*. In its representations of the past in text and image, the *Leisure Hour* had by this time moved towards the *London Journal*'s immersion in heritage culture and was even less religious than at its outset. It thus took on a middle position between the religious *Good Words* and the (more intellectual) secular *Cornhill* in its historical programme.

The analysis of the four periodicals' historical programmes was thus not only connected to their orientation towards different intended audiences but also to the idea that the past was designed differently depending on the medium through which it was disseminated. Where historical narratives travelled between book and periodical, semantic changes showed that the *Leisure Hour* negotiated historical identities along media boundaries by inscribing, for instance, a specifically working-class or female perspective into the national narrative of the past. The transfer of history between the different media also indicated the respectability attributed to them and their content. While it might be expected that academic history tried to demarcate itself from popular renderings, the periodicals' popular accounts at this rather early stage of the professionalisation of history already also defined their approach as distinct from ›scientific‹ history. In addition, the comparison of the unified book text to the mixed periodical content also indicated that family magazines' presentation of the past might have resulted in a more fragmented idea of Victorian historical consciousness. The intermediary position of the *Leisure Hour*'s historical programme between popular and academic was most evident with regard to the periodical's spectrum of contributors on the past. These and their presentations of the past ranged from amateur to professional, and writer-minister John Stoughton in particular operated on the boundary between popular and academic history.

In conclusion, it can thus be said that the *Leisure Hour*'s historical programme in text, image and serial form was determined by the periodical's design as an intermediary: between secular and religious; working and middle class; male and female; young and old; popular and academic. Such an intermediary position was, of course, also due to the *Leisure Hour*'s requirement to cater to a broad family audience. Family magazines were a particularly popular genre through which history reached broad audiences of all classes, genders and ages. The contemporary periodical press not only reported on the various approaches and elements that constituted Victorian historical culture, such as heritage sites, celebratory events and cultural products, material manifestations or recent developments of various kinds in the field of popular, public or academic history; through its many historically-toned articles and series, it was also in itself an important actor in disseminating ideas of a (national) historical identity.

Even if we allow for the fact that periodical readers may not have consumed every article presented, the distribution of the past via the magazines arguably had a farther reach than the books to which a middle-class readership was accustomed. Thus, Wynne notes that family magazines at mid-century also changed the way literature was consumed:

»The emergence of numerous fiction-carrying magazines during the 1860s changed the reading practices of the middle classes by offering supplementary texts alongside instalment novel, all intended to arouse excitement. [...] [T]he ›sobriety‹ which critics from the weighty reviews associated with reading novels in book form was collapsing before a tendency among middle-class readers to ›dance‹, ›skip‹, and ›hurry‹ through the lively pages of new magazines with their stimulating instalments of sensation novels, popular journalism, and short stories.« (Wynne 2001: 13-14)

Similar to novel reading, volumes on history would previously have been sought out by an audience with a specific interest in the past and certain historical topics, actors or epochs. Yet readers who might not have sought out history books were inevitably confronted with the past in the family magazines. They were presented with a variety of historical topics, actors and epochs predetermined through the ideological choices made by editors, authors and illustrators. As the comparative reading of the four periodicals' historical programmes has shown, producers' decisions were determined not only by their ideological agenda but also by the mechanisms of the market, so that, like the *Leisure Hour*, a periodical might tone down religious content in order to reach a broader readership. The periodicals' construction of the past was hence determined not only by the producers' ideological stance but also by the medium's material constraints as well as the specific market logic of both the family magazine and history as commercial products. Readers of course had the choice to consume a periodical that fitted their own identity and expectations towards a treatment of the past in terms of religion, class, instruction or entertainment. Yet it stands without question that these successful periodicals were important agents of Victorian historical culture. With their dissemination of histories to the many, they suggested how history was to be perceived and engaged with, and they hence asserted an important influence on Victorian society's outlook on the past.

Appendix

Appendix A: Tables

Tab. 1: Periodical Profiles.[1]

Leisure Hour: A Family Journal of Instruction and Recreation	*London Journal and Weekly Record of Literature, Science and Art*	*Good Words: A Family Magazine for Leisure Hours and Sundays*	*Cornhill Magazine*
Duration			
1852-1905	1845-1928	1860-1911	1860-1975
Price / Frequency (size)			
1d / weekly 5d / monthly (1852-1881; 16pp. weekly, two columns)	1d / weekly (16pp.; three columns)	1 ½d weekly (1860-1861; 16pp., two columns)	1s / monthly (128pp.)
6d / monthly (1881-1905)		6d / monthly (64pp.)	
annual volume	bi-annual volume	annual volume	bi-annual volume

---

1   Sources: *Waterloo Directory* (North 2003) as well as the *Dictionary of Nineteenth Century Journalism DNCJ* (2009); for further literature on the periodicals, see also Chapter 1 (Fn 25, 33, 34, 35).

Circulation			
80,000-100,000	100,000-450,000	80,000-130,000	80,000-110,000 (during first two years)
Editorship			
William Haig Miller (1852-1858), James Macaulay (1858-1895)	G.W.M. Reynolds (1845-1847), John Wilson Ross, Mark Lemon (1857-1860), Pierce Egan (1860-1880)	Norman Macleod (1860-1872)	William Makepeace Thackeray (1860-1862); Frederick Greenwood (1862-1868?); George Smith (1862-1871); George Henry Lewes (1860s); Leslie Stephen (1871-1882)
Publishers / Issuers			
Religious Tract Society	George Stiff (1845-1857; 1859-1862)	Alexander Strahan	George Smith
Important Contributors			
Frances Browne, G.E. Sargent, John Stoughton, Margaret Oliphant, Ellen Wood, John Keast Lord	M.E. Braddon, John Parsons Hall, Percy B. St John, Charles Reade, John Wilson Ross, J.F. Smith, E.D.E.N. Southworth	J.A. Froude, George Eliot, William Gladstone, Dora Greenwell, Thomas Hardy, Margaret Oliphant, Alfred Tennyson, Anthony Trollope	Matthew Arnold, Charlotte Brontë, Wilkie Collins, George Eliot, Elizabeth Gaskell, Harriet Martineau, Margaret Oliphant, Charles Reade, George August Sala, Anthony Trollope

Tab. 2: Leisure Hour *(1852-1870): Non-Fiction Series on the Past.*[2]

Duration	Title	Author	Genre Focus
1 Jan-11 Nov 1852 6 parts	»The Working Man in the Olden Time«	F.S.M. [Frederick Somner Merryweather]	descriptive / report
8 Jan 1852-12 May 1853 11 parts	»Shades of the Departed in Old London«	unsigned [John Stoughton]	life writing
1-29 July 1852[3] 5 parts	»The Lessons of Biography«	unsigned	life writing
2-30 June 1853 4 parts	»A Visit to the Staffordshire Potteries«	unsigned	travel / topographical
4 Aug-22 Sept 1853 8 parts	»The Banks of the Thames«	unsigned [John Stoughton]	travel / topographical
10-31 Aug 1854 4 parts	»The Deadly Art of War«	unsigned	descriptive / report
17 Aug 1854-26 Apr 1855 3 parts	»Incidents of Irish Railway Scenery«	unsigned	travel / topographical
5-26 Oct 1854 4 parts	»Russia«	unsigned	life writing
7-21 Dec 1854 3 parts	»The Philadelphia Printer«	unsigned	life writing
1-15 Mar 1855 3 parts	»The Walcheren Expedition«	By One Who Survived It	life writing

2 This study focuses on series with three and more parts only; see Chapter 1.
3 Bold duration dates indicate that these series were presented entirely within one month; see also Tab. 20.

15 Mar-10 May 1855 5 parts	»Sketches of the Crimea«	unsigned [Thomas Milner]	travel / topographical
7-21 June 1855 3 parts	»The Queen of a Literary Coterie«	unsigned	life writing
9-30 Aug 1855 4 parts	»A Summer Ramble Through Belgium and Holland«	unsigned	travel / topographical
3 Jan 1856-27 Aug 1857 22 parts	»Historical Enigmas«	unsigned	descriptive / report
31 Jan-21 Aug 1856 4 parts	»Macaulay«	unsigned	life writing
2 Feb-6 Mar 1856 3 parts	»Sir Isaac Newton«	unsigned	life writing
17 Apr-19 June 1856 8 parts	»Echoes of Westminster Hall«	unsigned [John Stoughton]	descriptive / report
21 Aug-4 Sept 1856 3 parts	»Some Remarkable Old French Chateaux«	unsigned	travel / topographical
11 Sept 1856-26 Feb 1857 5 parts	»Blind«	unsigned	life writing
15 Jan 1857-17 June 1858 9 parts	»Studies in History«	unsigned	life writing
7-28 May 1857 4 parts	»The Knight of Eskdale«	unsigned	life writing

25 June-15 Oct 1857 3 parts	»Chemists«	unsigned [John Scoffern]	life writing
2-30 July 1857 5 parts	»How to See the English Lakes«	unsigned [Bitha Fox (Lloyd)]	travel / topographical
30 July-3 Sept 1857 6 parts	»The Art Palace at Manchester [Manchester Palace of Art / Manchester Art Treasures]«	unsigned	travel / topographical
5 Nov-31 Dec 1857 9 parts	»The Overland Route to India«	unsigned	travel / topographical
19 Nov-10 Dec 1857 3 parts	»London a Century Ago«	unsigned	travel / topographical
6 May-21 Oct 1858 4 parts	»Pictures in Words«	unsigned	descriptive / report
3-24 Feb 1859 3 parts	»Japanese«	unsigned	travel / topographical
7-28 Apr 1859 4 parts	»The South Kensington Museum«	unsigned	travel / topographical
2-30 June 1859 5 parts	»Windsor Castle«	unsigned [John Stoughton]	travel / topographical
7-28 July 1859 4 parts	»The Garden«	unsigned	descriptive / report
1-15 Sept 1859 3 parts	»A Ramble in the Tyrol«	unsigned [John Stoughton]	travel / topographical

20 Oct 1859-28 Oct 1865 45 parts	»Men I Have Known«	unsigned [William Jerdan]	life writing
2 Feb-20 Dec 1860 6 parts	»Haunted London«	unsigned [Walter Thornbury]	travel / topographical
19 July-11 Oct 1860 13 parts	»The Tourist in Scotland«	unsigned [Elizabeth Hely Walshe]	travel / topographical
2-30 May 1861 5 parts	»School Recollections«	unsigned	life writing
4-16 July 1861 3 parts	»Gossip about the Gipsies«	unsigned	descriptive / report
2-23 Jan 1862 4 parts	»Royal Observatory, Greenwich«	James Glaisher (part 1) Edwin Dunkin (part 2-4)	travel / topographical
13 Feb-5 July 1862 6 parts	»Representative Characters of the Renaissance«	unsigned	life writing
3-31 May 1862 5 parts	»A Trip to North Devon«	unsigned	travel / topographical
10-31 May 1862 4 parts	»The Tale of a West-End Suburb«	John Stoughton	travel / topographical
5-26 July 1862 4 parts	»Kew Gardens«	unsigned	travel / topographical
6 Sept-11 Oct 1862 6 parts	»The Tourist in Ireland«	unsigned [Elizabeth Hely Walshe]	travel / topographical
4-25 Apr 1863 4 parts	»Leipsic Fair«	unsigned	descriptive / report

2 May-25 July 1863 13 parts	»The Regular Swiss Round«	unsigned [Harry Jones]	travel / topographical
15 Aug-28 Nov 1863 4 parts	»The Revival of Science«	unsigned	life writing
5-26 Sept 1863 4 parts	»West of Killarney«	Edwin Dunkin	travel / topographical
2-30 Apr 1864 5 parts	»Shakespeare«	several (see Tab. 22)	life writing
7-28 May 1864 4 parts	»The Balloon and its Application«	James Glaisher	descriptive / report
4-25 June 1864 4 parts	»Letters Patent«	unsigned	descriptive / report
2 July-27 Aug 1864 9 parts	»Another Swiss Round«	The Author of ›The Regular Swiss Round‹ [Harry Jones]	travel / topographical
7 Jan-23 Dec 1865 22 parts	»Hints on Legal Topics«	unsigned	descriptive / report
14 Jan-12 Aug 1865 7 parts	»Life in Egypt«	M[ary] L[ouisa] Whately	travel / topographical
17 June-12 Aug 1865 9 parts	»The Idler on the Rhine«	Author of ›The Regular Swiss Round‹ [Harry Jones]	travel / topographical
5-19 Aug 1865 3 parts	»Fenelon«	unsigned	life writing
9 Sept-14 Oct 1865 7 parts	»Russ Pictures«	unsigned	travel / topographical

11-25 Nov 1865 3 parts	»Fotheringhay«	Cuthbert Bede [Edward Bradley]	travel / topographical
3 Feb-29 Dec 1866 9 parts	»Illustrations of Jewish Customs«	unsigned	descriptive / report
14 Apr-22 Nov 1866 3 parts	»Celts«	S[amuel] R[owles] Pattison	descriptive / report
5 May-15 Dec 1866 7 parts	»Oxford and its Colleges«	F.A. [Frederick Arnold]	travel / topographical
6-27 Oct 1866 4 parts	»The Water-Supply of Cities and Towns«	unsigned	descriptive / report
17 Nov-8 Dec 1866 4 parts	»A Summer Tour in Northern Europe«	unsigned	travel / topographical
23 Feb-20 July 1867 16 parts	»On the Nile«	Howard Hopley	travel / topographical
9 Mar-4 May 1867 3 parts	»Signboards«	unsigned	descriptive / report
11-25 May 1867 4 parts	»The Jews of China«	B[enjamin] Harris Cowper	descriptive / report
17 Aug-7 Dec 1867 5 parts	»Periodical Peeps at Female Costume in England«	unsigned	descriptive / report
14-28 Sept 1867 3 parts	»The Volcanoes of Auvergne«	S[amuel] R[owles] Pattison	travel / topographical

1 Feb 1868-1 Nov 1873 13 parts	»Curiosities of [London]«	John Timbs	travel / topographical
15-29 Feb 1868 3 parts	»Abraham Lincoln«	unsigned	life writing
29 Feb 1868-18 Dec 1869 24 parts	»Characteristic Letters«	Author of ›Men I Have Known‹ [William Jerdan]	life writing
16 May-25 July 1868 8 parts	»Two Months in Spain«	Author of ›A Merchant's Holiday‹	travel / topographical
12 Sept-21 Nov 1868 13 parts	»A Lady's Journey Through Spain«	unsigned	travel / topographical
6 Feb-3 July 1869 15 parts	»From Nubia Down the Nile«	Howard Hopley	travel / topographical
3-31 July 1869 5 parts	»A Walk in South Devon«	Author of ›The Regular Swiss Round‹ [Harry Jones]	travel / topographical
29 Jan-3 Dec 1870 14 parts	»The Natural History of Dress«	unsigned	descriptive / report
5 Mar-31 Dec 1870 10 parts	»Cambridge and its Colleges«	F[rederick] Arnold	travel / topographical
28 May-17 Dec 1870 3 parts	»The Man in the Iron Mask«	unsigned	descriptive / report
6 Aug-10 Dec 1870 5 parts	»The Cottage Homes of England«	unsigned [Richard Heath]	descriptive / report
10-24 Sept 1870 3 parts	»Gossip about Notable Books«	John Timbs	descriptive / report

Tab. 3: Leisure Hour *(1852): Covers Relating to the Past.*

Date	Title	Genre Focus
8 Jan	»Shades of the Departed«	life writing
29 Jan	»Gladiatorial Combats«	descriptive / report
5 Feb	»The Capitol at Washington«	travel / topographical
19 Feb	»Shades of the Departed«	life writing (series)
11 March	»Visit to the Haunts of Luther«	travel / topographical
8 April	»A Star at the Stuart Court«	life writing
15 April	»Death in Exile«	life writing
22 April	»Shades of the Departed«	life writing
29 April	»The First British Steam-Boat«	descriptive / report
13 May	»The Boy Crusaders«	descriptive / report
27 May	»Historic Tableaux: The Divorce of Josephine«	life writing
3 June	»A Ramble to Fountains Abbey«	travel / topographical
10 June	»An Incident at the Hotel de Rambouillet«	life writing
1 July	»Covent Garden Market, As It Was and Is«	descriptive / report
8 July	»The Two Scholars of Westminster«	historical fiction
15 July	»Shades of the Departed«	life writing
22 July	»Bath Revisited«	travel / topographical
29 July	»Margate and Its Environs«	travel / topographical
9-30 Sept	»Poccahontas«	historical fiction

28 Oct & 4 Nov	»Edme Champion«	historical fiction
18 Nov	»Shades of the Departed«	life writing
25 Nov	»The Funeral of Lord Nelson«	life writing
16 & 23 Dec	»Hans the Stranger«	historical fiction

Tab. 4: Leisure Hour *(1852): Series Relating to the Past.*

Duration	Title	Genre Focus
1 Jan-11 Nov 6 parts	»The Working Man in the Olden Time«	descriptive / report
2 Jan 1852-12 May 1853 11 parts (9 in 1852)	»Shades of the Departed in Old London«	life writing
1-29 July 5 parts	»The Lessons of Biography: A Lecture for Working Men«	life writing (lecture)
9-30 Sept 4 parts	»Poccahontas: A Story of the First English Emigrants to North America, Founded on Fact«	historical fiction
3 June-30 Sept 11 parts	Series on short trips to British locations: »A Ramble to Fountains Abbey«; »Bath Revisited«; »Margate and its Environs«; »A Glance at Clifton«; »A Day or Two at Ramsgate«; »A Few Days at Dover«; »A Day or Two at Hastings«; »A Day or Two at Brighton«; »Our Second Day at Brighton«; »Rambles in the Isle of Wight« (2 parts)	travel / topographical

Tab. 5: Leisure Hour *(1852): Life Writing and Person-Centred Writing.*

Date	Title	Biographical Information
1 Jan	»Hartley Coleridge«	(David) Hartley Coleridge (1796-1849), writer
8 Jan-12 May 1853 **9 parts** in 1852 (of 11 parts) **illustrated** (5 of 9)	»Shades of the Departed in Old London«	Richard Baxter (1615-1691), ejected minister and religious writer John Milton (1608-1674), poet and polemicist Izaak Walton (1593-1683), author and biographer Andrew Marvell (1621-1678), poet and politician William Russell, Lord Russell [called the Patriot, the Martyr] (1639-1683), politician and conspirator Joseph Addison (1672-1719), writer and politician Isaac Newton (1642-1727), natural philosopher and mathematician Oliver Goldsmith (1728?-1774), author Joshua Reynolds (1723-1792), portrait and history painter and art theorist Samuel Johnson (1709-1784), author and lexicographer
29 Jan	»The Lady Traveller«	Ida Laura Pfeiffer (1797-1858), Austrian traveller and travel book author
29 Jan	»Felicia Hemans«	Felicia Dorothea Hemans [née Browne] (1793-1835), poet
5 Feb	»The Lyonese Weaver«	Joseph Marie Jacquard (1752-1834), French weaver and merchant

19 Feb	»France and Its Rulers«	Napoleon Bonaparte (1769-1812), French military and political leader various kings
11 Mar **illustrated**	»Visit to the Haunts of Luther«	Martin Luther (1483-1546), German monk, Catholic priest, professor of theology
11 Mar	»Anecdotes of Eminent Men«	Isaac D'Israeli (1766-1848), writer Samuel Taylor Coleridge (1772-1834), poet, critic and philosopher Georges Cuvier, Jean Léopold Nicolas Frédéric Cuvier (1769-1832), French naturalist and zoologist Edward Prince, duke of Kent and Strathearn (1767-1820) Millard Fillmore (1800-1874); 13th President of the United States
18 Mar **illustrated**	»Bonapartiana«	Napoleon Bonaparte (1769-1812), French military and political leader
1 Apr	»Niebuhr and His ›Milly‹«	Carsten Niebuhr (1733-1815), German mathematician, cartographer and explorer
8 Apr **illustrated**	»A Star at the Stuart Court«	Margaret Blagge Godolphin [née Blagge] (1652-1678), courtier
8 Apr	»Roger Payne, the Bookbinder«	Roger Payne (bap. 1738, d. 1797), bookbinder
15 Apr **illustrated**	»Death in Exile«	Napoleon Bonaparte (1769-1812), French military and political leader John Howard (1726?-1790), philanthropist

15 Apr	»The Cold-Water Doctor«	Vincent Priessnitz (1799-1851), Austrian Silesian peasant farmer
13 May	»William Caxton«	William Caxton (1415x24-1492), printer, merchant and diplomat
27 May **illustrated**	»Historic Tableaux«	Joséphine de Beauharnais (1763-1814), first wife of Napoleon Napoleon Bonaparte (1769-1812), French military and political leader
27 May	»Lord George Bentinck«	Lord (William) George Frederic Cavendish-Scott-Bentinck [known as Lord George Bentinck] (1802-1848), politician and sportsman
10 June	»A Passage in the Life of General Victoria«	Guadalupe Victoria, José Miguel Ramón Adaucto Fernández y Félix (1786-1843), Mexican politician and military officer
17 June	»Conspiracy of the Clocks«	Pope Sixtus V (1520-1590)
17 June	»Go to Work!«	Giotto Italian (1267-1337), painter and architect Antonio Canova (1757-1822), Italian sculptor James Ferguson (1710-1776), lecturer on natural philosophy and inventor of scientific instruments Sir Richard Arkwright (1732-1792), inventor of cotton-spinning machinery and cotton manufacturer George Stephenson (1781-1848), colliery and railway engineer
24 June	»Eau de Cologne and John Maria Farina«	Giovanni Maria Farina (1685-1766), Italian perfume designer and maker

8-31 July 5 parts	»The Lessons of Biography«	Benjamin Franklin (1706-1790), American natural philosopher, writer and revolutionary politician James Lackington (1746-1815), bookseller and publisher John Leyden (1775-1811), linguist and poet Alexander Murray (1775-1813), linguist Richard Arkwright (1732-1792), inventor of cotton-spinning machinery and cotton manufacturer James Watt (1736-1819), engineer and scientist Thomas Telford (1757-1834), civil engineer George Stephenson (1781-1848), colliery and railway engineer Josiah Wedgwood (1730-1795), master potter Thomas Bewick (1753-1828), wood-engraver Alexander Paterson (1766-1831), Roman Catholic bishop and vicar apostolic of the eastern district of Scotland
22 July	»The ›Marseillaise‹ and Its Author«	Claude Joseph Rouget de Lisle (1760-1836), French army officer
19 Aug	»The Two Duellists«	Robert Haldane (1764-1842), theological writer and evangelical patron James Alexander Haldane (1768-1851), Baptist minister and author

19 Aug-23 Dec **2 parts**	»Remarkable Boys«	Truman Henry Safford (1836-1901), American calculating prodigy Blaise Pascal (1623-1662), French mathematician, physicist, inventor, writer and Christian philosopher
2 Sept	»The Singer of Eisenach«	Ursula Cotta (1483-1546), benefactress to Martin Luther Martin Luther (1483-1546) German monk, Catholic priest and professor of theology
9-30 Sept **4 parts** **illustrated**	»Poccahontas: A Story of the First English Emigrants to North America, Founded on Fact«	Pocahontas [Matoaka, Amonute; married name Rebecca Rolfe] (c.1596-1617), Algonquian Indian princess
9-16 Sept **2 parts**	»The Peasant-Nobles; Or, the Bethune Brothers«	John Bethune (1812-1839), poet Alexander Bethune (1804-1843), poet
23 Sept	»The Late William Lennie, of Edinburgh«	William Lennie (1779-1852), grammarian and educational benefactor
7 Oct	»The Adventures of Johann Gottfried Seume«	Johann Gottfried Seume (1736-1810), German author
28 Oct-4 Nov **2 parts** **illustrated**	»Edme Champion«	Edme Champion (1766-1852), French jeweller
4 Nov	»The Duke of Wellington«	Wellesley [formerly Wesley], Arthur, first duke of Wellington (1769-1852), army officer and prime minister

11 Nov	»An Artist in Earth«	Bernard Palissy (1510-c.1589), French Huguenot potter, hydraulics engineer and craftsman
25 Nov **illustrated**	»The Funeral of Lord Nelson«	Horatio Nelson, Viscount Nelson (1758-1805), naval officer
25 Nov	»A Page in the Chronicles of Versailles«	Louis XIV of France (1638-1715)
25 Nov	»An Anecdote from Australia«	Thomas Braidwood Wilson (1792-1843), Australian surgeon and explorer
9 Dec	»The Duke's Funeral«	Wellesley [formerly Wesley], Arthur, first duke of Wellington (1769-1852), army officer and prime minister
16 Dec	»The Life of a Remarkable Man«	Pierre Loustaunau (dates unknown; WBIS years cited: 1793-1808), French merchant

Tab. 6: London Journal *(1852): Covers Relating to the Past.*

Date	Title	Genre Focus
3 Jan-2 Oct	»Minnigrey«	historically themed fiction
9 Oct-25 Dec	»The Will and the Way«	historically themed fiction

Tab. 7: London Journal *(1852): Series Relating to the Past.*

Duration	Title	Genre Focus
11 Oct 1851-2 Oct 1852 52 parts (40 in 1852)	»Minnigrey«	historically themed fiction
9 Oct 1852-3 Sept 1853 48 parts (12 in 1852)	»The Will and the Way«	historically themed fiction
17 Apr-10 July 5 parts	»Forest Tales: Comprising Sketches of the History, Tradition, and Scenery of Our National Forests«	descriptive / report
24 July-4 Feb 1854 76 parts (23 in 1852)	»Lives of the Queens of England«	life writing
12 June-2 Oct 6 parts	Series on New Palace of Westminster: »Hampden's Statue in the Palace of Westminster«; »Lord Falkland's Statue in the Palace of Westminster«; »Lord Clarendon's Statue in the Palace of Westminster«; »Star-Chamber Court in the Palace at Westminster«; »St. Stephen's Hall, in the New Palace of Westminster«; »The Commons' Lobby in the Palace of Westminster«	descriptive / report
20 Nov-4 Dec 3 parts	»Memoir of the Duke of Wellington«	life writing

19 July-6 Nov 8 parts	»Royal Visits to Remarkable Places«	descriptive / report
13 Mar-3 Apr 3 parts	»The Three Napoleons«	fiction

Tab. 8: London Journal *(1852): Life Writing and Person-Centred Writing.*

Date	Title	Biographical Information
15 Feb 1851-6 Nov 1852 38 parts in 1852 (of 81 parts) **6 parts** in 1852 relating biographies	»How to Speak the French Language«	Voltaire (1694-1778), French writer, historian and philosopher Claude Prosper Jolyot de Crebillon (1707-1777), French novelist Marie Joseph Chénier (1764-1811), French poet, dramatist and politician Jean-Francois Regnard (1655-1709), French playwright Philippe Néricault Destouches (1680-1754), French playwright Alain-René Lesage (1668-1747), French playwright
13 Mar-3 Apr **4 parts illustrated** (1 of 4)	»The Three Napoleons«	Napoleon Bonaparte (1769-1812), French military and political leader
27 March **illustrated**	»Turner«	Joseph Mallord William Turner (1775-1851), landscape and history painter
3 Apr **illustrated**	»Mr. Joshua Silsbee«	Joshua S. Silsbee (1813-1855), American actor
10 Apr **illustrated**	»Mr. Alfred C. Hobbs«	Alfred Hobbs (1812-1891), American locksmith

17 Apr **illustrated**	»Thomas Moore«	Thomas Moore (1779-1852), poet
12-26 June **3 parts** **illustrated**	Series on statues in the palace of Westminster: »Hampden's Statue in the Palace of Westminster«; »Lord Falkland's Statue in the Palace of Westminster«; »Lord Clarendon's Statue in the Palace of Westminster«	John Hampden (1596-1643), politician Lucius Cary, second Viscount Falkland (1609/10-1643), politician and author Edward Hyde, first earl of Clarendon (1609-1674), politician and historian
24 July-4 Feb 1854 **23 parts** in 1852 (of 76 parts until 1854) **illustrated**	»Lives of the Queens of England«	Elizabeth [née Elizabeth Woodville] (c.1437-1492), queen of England, consort of Edward IV Eleanor [Eleanor of Aquitaine], suo jure duchess of Aquitaine (c.1122-1204), queen of France, consort of Louis VII, and queen of England, consort of Henry II Matilda [Matilda of Flanders] (d. 1083), queen of England, consort of William I
11 Sept	»The Dream of Columbus«	Christopher Columbus (1451-1506), Italian explorer, navigator and coloniser
20 Nov-4 Dec **3 parts** **illustrated**	»Memoir of the Duke of Wellington«[4]	Arthur Wellesley, first duke of Wellington (1769-1852), army officer and prime minister

---

4   The commemoration of Wellington's death started on 13 November with Martin F. Tupper's poem »A Dirge for the Duke of Wellington« (1852); the first part of the »Memoir of the Duke of Wellington« was followed by Charles Mackay's poem »Mourn for the Mighty Dead« (1852); and the series was followed by an article on the

Tab. 9: Leisure Hour *(1860): Covers Relating to the Past.*

Date	Title	Genre Focus
5 Jan-29 Mar 1860	»The Ferrol Family; Or, Keeping up the Appearance«	historically-toned fiction (series)
19-26 Apr	»Father Pedro's Convert«	historical fiction (2-parter)
3 May-12 July	»The Captain's Story: Or, Adventures in Jamaica Thirty Years Ago«	historically-toned fiction (series)
20-27 Dec	»Barthel Winkler; A Tale of Hesse-Darmstadt«	historical fiction (two-parter)

Tab. 10: Leisure Hour *(1860): Series Relating to the Past.*

Duration	Title	Genre Focus
2 Feb-20 Dec 6 parts unillustrated	»Haunted London«	travel / topographical
20 Oct 1859-21 Oct 1865 45 parts (4 in 1860) unillustrated	»Men I Have Known«	life writing
19 July-11 Oct 13 parts[5] 7 illustrated	»The Tourist in Scotland«	travel / topographical

---

question of »The Duke of Wellington's Tomb – Where Should it Be?« in December (1852).

5   This includes the initial part published under the deviating title »Over the Boarder«.

Tab. 11: Leisure Hour *(1860): Life Writing and Person-Centred Writing.*[6]

Date	Title	Biographical Information
5 Jan **illustrated**	»Sir John Lawrence, G.C.B.«	John Lawrence (1811-1879), viceroy of India
12 Jan **illustrated**	»Vancouver the Voyager«	George Vancouver (1757-1798), naval officer and hydrographer
19 Jan **illustrated**	»Charles James Fox«	Charles James Fox (1749-1806), politician
26 Jan	»Prince Metternich«	Klemens von Metternich (1773-1859)
9 Feb	»A Self-Taught Linguist«	Alexander Murray (1775-1813), linguist
16 Feb	»Duncan Forbes of Culloden, the Scottish Patriot«	Duncan Forbes (1685-1747), politician and judge
1 Mar **illustrated**	»Lord Macaulay«	Thomas Babington Macaulay (1800-1859), historian, essayist and poet
8 Mar **illustrated**	»Lord Clive«	Robert Clive (1725-1774), army officer in the East India Company and administrator in India
12 Apr **illustrated**	»The Last Prayer of Gustavus Adolphus«	Gustavus Adolphus of Sweden (1594-1632)
18 Apr	»Lord Dundonald«	Thomas Cochrane, tenth earl of Dundonald (1775-1860), naval officer

---

6 All of these were listed under category »Biography« in the annual index; the table here hence excludes Jerdan's series »Men I Have Known«.

3 Mar	»Governor Sir George Grey«	George Grey (1812-1898), colonial governor and premier of New Zealand
24 May	»Lord Chancellor Clarendon«	Edward Hyde, first earl of Clarendon (1609-1674), politician and historian
31 May	»Sir Henry Havelock«	Henry Havelock (1795-1857), army officer
7 June	»Haller the Physician«	Albrecht von Haller (1708-1777), anatomist, physiologist, naturalist and poet
28 June	»Dr. Van der Kemp«	John Theodore van der Kemp (d.1811), Dutch missionary
12 July **illustrated**	»The Man of Ross«	John Kyrle (1637-1724), philanthropist and landscape designer
19 July	»Authentic Anecdote of Frederic William IV of Prussia«	Frederick William IV (1795-1861), king of Prussia
9-16 August **2 parts**	»The Fisherman of Naples«	Masaniello (1622-1647)
6 Sept	»Bianconi and His Cars«	Charles Bianconi (1786-1875)
13 Sept	»The Death of Martin Luther«	Martin Luther (1483-1546)
13 Sept	»Wilkie and His Pictures«	David Wilkie (1785-1841), painter of genre, historical subjects and portraits
20 Sept **illustrated**	»The Fire Escape«	Abraham Wivell (1786-1849), portrait painter
20 Sept	»Juan Diaz«	unknown

18 Oct portrait	»The President of the Social Science Conference«	Henry Peter Brougham, first Baron Brougham and Vaux (1778-1868), lord chancellor
8-15 Nov **2 parts illustrated**	»Robert Stephenson«	Robert Stephenson (1803-1859), railway and civil engineer
29 Nov	»The Presidential Election in America: Good Old Abe«	Abraham Lincoln (1809-1865), 16th President of the United States of America
13 Dec **illustrated**	»Arthur and the Round Table«	Arthur (supp. fl. in or before 6th cent.), legendary warrior and supposed king of Britain

Tab. 12: Good Words *(1860): Covers Relating to the Past.*

Date	Title	Genre Focus
22 Jan[7] & 5 Feb	»A Journey by Sinai to Syria«	travel / topographical
12 Feb	»The Story of Ninian«	life writing
19 Feb	»The Fate of Franklin«	life writing
26 Feb	»Kentigern«	life writing
18 Mar	»John Evangelist Gossner«	life writing
25 Mar	»Missionary Sketches«	life writing
1 Apr	»Alexander von Humboldt«	life writing
15 Apr	»A Journey by Sinai to Syria«	travel / topographical
22 Apr	»Constance De V-------.«	poem
29 Apr	»Our Scandinavian Ancestors«	descriptive / report

---

7   Covers were unillustrated during the first month of publication.

13 May	»A Journey by Sinai to Syria«	travel / topographical
3 June	»Lady Somerville's Maidens«	historical fiction
10 June	»The Happy Warrior«	life writing
17 & 24 June	»St Columba«	life writing
8 July	»The Song of Antioch«	descriptive / report
15 & 29 July	»Dr Wichern and the Rauhes Haus«	life writing
5 Aug	»A Woman's Work«	life writing
12 Aug	»God's Glory in the Heavens«	descriptive / report
2 Sept & 14 Oct	»Dr Wichern and the Rauhes Haus«	life writing
21 Oct	»Pastor Harms of Hermannsburg«	life writing
11 & 18 Nov	»Pictures from the History and Life of the Early Church«	life writing
2 Dec	»David Chart's Memoranda«	life writing
9 Dec	»Christmas Memories«	descriptive / report

Tab. 13: Good Words *(1860): Series Relating to the Past.*

Duration	Title	Genre Focus
22 Jan-29 Dec 7 parts 5 illustrated (4 on cover)	»A Journey by Sinai to Syria«	travel / topographical
5 Feb-14 Oct 24 parts 15 illustrated (1 on cover)	»Lady Somerville's Maidens«	historical fiction

19 Feb-4 Mar 3 parts 2 illustrated (1 on cover)	»The Fate of Franklin«	life writing
25 Mar-21 Oct 6 parts 2 illustrated (1 on cover)	»Missionary Sketches«	life writing
10 June-14 Oct 5 parts, 5 illustrated (4 on cover)	»Dr Wichern and the Rauhes Haus«	life writing
12 Feb-24 June 4 parts 4 illustrated (4 on cover)	Series on Scottish Saints: »The Story of Ninian«, »Kentigern«, St Columba«	life writing
5-19 Aug 3 parts unillustrated	»The Gold[en] Thread«	historical fiction
9 Sept-18 Nov 3 parts 2 illustrated (2 on cover)	»Pictures from the History and Life of the Early Church«	life writing
21 Oct-2 Dec 4 parts 1 illustrated (1 on cover)	»Pastor Harms of Hermannsburg«	life writing

Tab. 14: Good Words (1860): Life Writing and Person-Centred Writing.

Date	Title	Biographical Information
8 Jan	»In Memoriam«	George Wilson (1818-1859), chemist and museum director
12 Feb-24 June **4 parts illustrated**	Scottish Saints: »The Story of Ninian«, »Kentigern«, »St Columba [2 parts]«	Ninian (supp. fl. 5th-6th cent.), missionary and bishop Kentigern (d. 612x14), patron of the diocese (later archdiocese) of Glasgow Columba (c.521-597), monastic founder
19 Feb-4 Mar **3 parts illustrated** (2 of 3)	»The Fate of Franklin«	John Franklin (1786-1847), naval officer and Arctic explorer
11 Mar-13 May **2 parts**	»Latimer at the Pulpit«	Hugh Latimer (c.1485-1555), bishop of Worcester, preacher and Protestant martyr
18 Mar-29 April **2 parts illustrated** (1 of 2)	»John Evangelist Gossner«	Johannes Evangelista Gossner (1773-1858), German divine and philanthropist
25 Mar-21 Oct **6 parts illustrated** (2 of 6)	»Missionary Sketches«	Heinrich Plütschau (1676-1752) and Bartholomäus Ziegenbalg (1683-1719), Protestant missionaries to India »Duff« (missionary ship) Serampore Missionaries: William Carey (1761-1834), orientalist and missionary Joshua Marshman (1768-1837), orientalist and missionary William Ward (1769-1823), missionary in India and journalist

1 Apr illustrated	»Alexander von Humboldt«	Alexander von Humboldt (1769-1859)
22 Apr illustrated	»Constance De V------« [poem]	Charles Maurice de Talleyrand-Périgord (1754-1838)
22 Apr illustrated	»Recollection of Professor Wilson«	John Wilson [pseud. Christopher North] (1785-1854), author and journalist
10 June illustrated	»The Happy Warrior«	Henry Havelock (1795-1857), army officer
5 Aug illustrated	»A Woman's Work«	Amalie Wilhelmine Sieveking (1794-1859)
9 Sept-18 Nov 3 parts illustrated (2 of 3)	»Pictures from the History and Life of the Early Church«	Plycarp of Smyrna (69-155), bishop Justin Martyr (103-165), apologist
30 Sept	»John Woolman«	John Woolman (1720-1772), Quaker minister and anti-slavery campaigner
21 Oct-2 Dec 4 parts illustrated (1 of 4)	»Pastor Harms of Hermannsburg«	Ludwig Harms (1808-1865), German Lutheran pastor

Tab. 15: Cornhill *(1860): Covers Relating to the Past.*

Date	Title	Genre Focus
Feb	»Nil Nisi Bonum«	life writing
March	»A Few Words on Junius and Macaulay«	life writing
Jun	»London the Stronghold of England«	descriptive / report
Jul, Sept Oct	»The Four Georges: Sketches of Manners, Morals, Court and Town Life«	life writing

Tab. 16: Cornhill *(1860): Series Relating to the Past.*

Duration	Title	Genre Focus
Jan 1860-Feb 1863 28 parts (9 parts in 1860)	»Roundabout Papers«	descriptive / report (essay, nostalgia)
Feb-Oct 9 parts illustrated	»William Hogarth: Painter, Engraver, and Philosopher. Essays on the Man, the Work, and the Time«	life writing
Jul-Oct 4 parts illustrated	»The Four Georges: Sketches of Manners, Morals, Court and Town Life«	life writing

Tab. 17: Cornhill *(1860): Life Writing and Person-Centred Writing.*

Date	Title	Biographical Information
Jan	»A Man of Letters of the Last Generation«	Leigh Hunt (1784-1859), poet, journalist, literary critic
Jan **illustrated**	»The Search for Sir John Franklin«	John Franklin (1786-1847), naval officer and Arctic explorer
Feb	»Nil Nisi Bonum«	Washington Irving (1783-1859), American author, essayist and historian Thomas Babington Macaulay (1800-1859), historian, essayist and poet
Feb-Oct **9 parts illustrated** (6 of 9)	»William Hogarth: Painter, Engraver, and Philosopher. Essays on the Man, the Work, and the Time«	William Hogarth (1697-1764), painter and engraver
Mar	»A Few Words on Junius and Macaulay«	Philip Francis (alias Junius?; 1740-1818), politician and political writer Thomas Babington Macaulay (1800-1859), historian, essayist and poet
Mar	»Sir Joshua and Holbein«	Joshua Reynolds (1723-1792), portrait and history painter and art theorist Hans Holbein (c.1497-1543), German artist
Apr **illustrated**	»Dante« [poem]	Dante Alighieri (c.1265-1321), Italian poet

Apr	»The Last Sketch«	Charles Robert Leslie (1794-1859), literary genre painter and author Charlotte Brontë (1816-1855), novelist
July-Oct **4 parts** **illustrated**	»The Four Georges: Sketches of Manners, Morals, Court and Town Life«	George I (1660-1727) George II (1683-1760) George III (1738-1820) George IV (1762-1830)
Dec **illustrated**	»Ariadne at Naxos« [poem]	Ariadne, Greek mythology

Tab. 18: Leisure Hour *(1852-1870): Non-Fiction Series and their Book Counterparts.*

Duration	Title	Author	Book Publication
8 Jan 1852-12 May 1853 11 parts	»Shades of the Departed in Old London«	unsigned [John Stoughton]	John Stoughton (1864): *Shades and Echoes of Old London*
1 Jan-11 Nov 1852 6 parts	»The Working Man in the Olden Time«	F[rederick] S[omner] M[erryweather]	Frederick Somner Merryweather (1850): *Glimmerings in the Dark: Or Lights and Shadows of the Olden Time*
7-12 Dec 1854 3 parts	»The Philadelphia Printer«	unsigned	unknown which biography of Franklin was used

15 Mar-10 May 1855 5 parts	»Sketches of the Crimea«	unsigned [Thomas Milner]	Thomas Milner (1855): *The Crimea, Its Ancient and Modern History: The Khans, the Sultans, and the Czars, with Notices of Its Scenery and Population*
7-21 June 1855 3 parts	»The Queen of a Literary Coterie«	unsigned	Richard Robert Madden (1855): *Literary Life of the Countess of Blessington* (1855)
1-15 Mar 1855 3 parts	»The Walcheren Expedition«	By One Who Survived It	Archibald Alison (1849): *History of Europe, Vol 9*
11 Sept 1856-26 Feb 1857 5 parts	»Blind«	unsigned	James Wilson (1833 [1821]): *Biography of the Blind*
17 Apr-19 June 1856 8 parts	»Echoes of Westminster Hall«	unsigned [John Stoughton]	John Stoughton (1864): *Shades and Echoes of Old London*
2 Feb-6 Mar 1856 3 parts	»Sir Isaac Newton«	unsigned	David Brewster (1855): *Memoirs of the Life, Writings, and Discoveries of Sir Isaac Newton*
25 June-15 Oct 1857 3 parts	»Chemists«	unsigned [John Scoffern]	John Scoffern (1870): *Stray Leaves of Science and Folk-Lore*
2-30 July 1857 5 parts	»How to See the English Lakes«	unsigned [Bitha Fox (Lloyd)]	[Bitha Fox (Lloyd)] ([1858]): *How to See the English Lakes*

7-28 May 1857 4 parts	»The Knight of Eskdale«	unsigned	John William Kaye (1856): *The Life and Correspondence of Major-General Sir John Malcolm, G. C. B.*
6 May-21 Oct 1858 4 parts	»Pictures in Words; Or, Scenes from English Histo- ry«	unsigned	Thomas Milner (1853): *History of England*
20 Oct 1859-28 Oct 1865 45 parts	»Men I Have Known«	unsigned	William Jerdan (1866): *Men I Have Known*
2-30 June 1859 5 parts	»Windsor Cast- le«	unsigned [John Stoughton]	John Stoughton (1844): *Notices of Windsor in the Olden Time*; and other titles
2 Feb-20 Dec 1860 6 parts	»Haunted Lon- don«	unsigned [Wal- ter Thornbury]	Walter Thornbury (1865): *Haunted Lon- don*
2 May-25 July 1863 13 parts	»The Regular Swiss Round«	unsigned [Harry Jones]	Harry Jones (1865): *The Regular Swiss Round*
2-30 Apr 1864 5 parts	Shakespeare (see Tab. 22)	several	Samuel Johnson (1765): *Mr. Johnson's Preface to His Edition of Shakespear's Plays* Hugh Miller (1847): *First Impressions of England and Its Peo- ple* Harriet Beecher Stowe (1854): *Sunny Memo- ries of Foreign Lands*

2 July-27 Aug 1864 9 parts	»Another Swiss Round«	Author of ›The Regular Swiss Round‹ [Harry Jones]	Harry Jones (1865): *The Regular Swiss Round*
7-28 May 1864 4 parts	»The Balloon and its Application«	James Glaisher	several publications by James Glaisher, e.g.: *Travels in the Air* (1871); *Scientific Experiments in Balloons etc* (1863)
11-25 Nov 1865 3 parts	»Fotheringhay«	Cuthbert Bede [Edward Bradley]	Cuthbert Bede (1886): *Fotheringay and Mary Queen of Scots*
14 Jan-12 Aug 1865 7 parts	»Life in Egypt«	M[ary] L[ouisa] Whately	Mary Louisa Whately (1871): *Among the Huts in Egypt: Scenes from Real Life*
5 May-15 Dec 1866 7 parts	»Oxford and its Colleges«	F.A. [Frederick Arnold]	Frederick Arnold (1873): *Oxford and Cambridge: Their Colleges, Memories and Associations*
23 Feb-20 July 1867 16 parts	»On the Nile«	Howard Hopley	Howard Hopley (1869): *Under Egyptian Palms: Or, Three Bachelors' Journeyings on the Nile*
17 Aug-7 Dec 1867 5 parts	»Periodical Peeps at Female Costume in England«	unsigned	Frederick William Fairholt (1860 [1849]): *Costume in England: A History of Dress from the Earliest Period till the Close of the Eighteenth Century*

11-25 May 1867 4 parts	»The Jews of China«	B[enjamin] Harris Cowper	James Finn (1843): *The Jews in China: Their Synagogue, Their Scriptures, Their History. &c*
15-29 Feb 1868 3 parts	»Abraham Lincoln«	unsigned	Joseph Hartwell Barrett (1865): *Life of Abraham Lincoln*
1 Feb 1868-1 Nov 1873 13 parts	»Curiosities of [London]«	John Timbs	John Timbs (1855): *Curiosities of London*
5 Mar-31 Dec 1870 10 parts	»Cambridge and its Colleges«	F[rederick] Arnold	Frederick Arnold (1873): *Oxford and Cambridge: Their Colleges, Memories and Associations*
6 Aug-10 Dec 1870 5 parts	»The Cottage Homes of England«	unsigned	Richard Heath (1893): *The English Peasant: Studies: Historical, Local, and Biographic*

Tab. 19: Leisure Hour *(1852-1870): Historically Themed Fiction and Book Counterparts.*[8]

Duration	Title	Author	Book Publication
9-30 Sept 1852 4 parts	»Poccahontas; A Story of the First English Emigrants to North America, Founded on Fact«	unsigned	W.O. Horn (1852): *Poccahontas: Eine* *wahre Geschichte aus* *den Zeiten der ersten* *englischen Niederlas-* *sungen in Nordameri-* *ka*
1 Jan-17 Feb 1853 8 parts	»The Refugees of the Black Forest«	unsigned	unknown
4 Jan-22 Feb 1855 8 parts	»Golowin's Banishment to Siberia«	unsigned	Philipp Körber (1851): *Feodor Golowin's* *Verbannung nach Si-* *birien*
3 Jan-3 July 1856 27 parts	»The English- man in Russia; A Tale of the Time of Cathe- rine II«	unsigned	unknown

---

8   As with the non-fiction series on the past, only series of three and more parts are in-
    cluded here (see Chapter 1). Nine of the twenty-one fiction series on the past had 24 to
    28 parts, three had 11 to 18 parts, and eight had ten parts or less. Of the latter, only
    three had a book counterpart, and only for two of these – »Poccahontas« (1852) and
    »The Angel's Oak« (1858) – were all instalments presented entirely within one
    monthly part of the *Leisure Hour*. See Appendix B for a brief discussion of this histor-
    ically themed fiction.

3 July-4 Sept 1856 10 parts	»The Weaver of Naumburg; Or, the Triumphs of Meekness«	unsigned	Carl Gustav Nieritz (1853): *Die Hussiten von Naumburg*; Carl Gustav Nieritz ([1874]): *The Weaver of Naumburg; Or, a City Saved by Children*
16 July-13 Aug 1857 5 parts	»Tales Illustrative of Chinese Life and Manners«	unsigned	unknown
7 Jan-8 July 1858 27 parts	»The Indian Nabob; Or, A Hundred Years Ago«	Author of ›Frank Layton‹ etc. [George Eliel Sargent]	unknown
15-29 July 1858 3 parts	»The Angel's Oak; A Story of New England«	unsigned	unknown
30 Sept-23 Dec 1858 12 parts	»The Schoolmaster and His Son; A Memoir of the Thirty Years' War«	unsigned	K.H. Caspari (1851): *Der Schulmeister und sein Sohn*; (1864): *The Schoolmaster and his Son. A Story of the Thirty Years' War, etc.*
6 Jan-5 May 1859 18 parts	»Golden Hills; Or, Single Influence: A Tale of Ribandism and the Irish Famine«	unsigned	[Elizabeth Hely Walshe] ([1865]): *Golden Hills, a Tale of the Irish Famine*

1 Sept 1859-12 July 1860 24 parts	»The Captain's Story; Or, Adventures in Jamaica Thirty Years Ago«	unsigned	Captain Brooke-Knight (1883): *The Captain's Story; or, Jamaica Sixty Years Since*
3 Jan-27 June 1863 26 parts	»The Franklins; or, the Story of a Convict«	unsigned	George Eliel Sargent (1882): *The Franklins, or the Story of a Convict*
5 Sept-24 Oct 1863 8 parts	»The Doones of Exmoor«	unsigned	unknown
2 Jan-25 June 1864 26 parts	»The Foster-Brothers of Doon; A Tale of the Irish Rebellion«	unsigned	[Elizabeth Hely Walshe] (1866): *The Foster-Brothers of Doon, a Tale of the Irish Rebellion of 1798*
4 July 1865-24 Oct 1868 17 parts	»James Braithwaite the Supercargo«	unsigned	William Henry Giles Kingston (1882): *James Braithwaite, the Supercargo*
6 Jan-30 June 1866 26 parts	»The Great Van Broek Property«	unsigned	James Alexander Maitland (1867): *Captain Jack: or, The Great Van Broek Property. A Story*
7 July-29 Dec 1866 26 parts	»George Burley; His History, Experiences, and Observations«	G.E. Sargent	George Eliel Sargent (1869): *George Burley*

5 Oct-14 Dec 1867 11 parts	»The Exile's Trust; A Tale of the French Revolution«	unsigned	Frances Browne ([1869]): *The Exile's Trust, a Tale of the French Revolution and other Stories*
4 Jan-11 July 1868 28 parts	»The Mortons of Morton Hall«	Author of »The Great Van Broek Proper-ty«	unknown (Maitland)
24 Oct-26 Dec 1868 10 parts	»The Exiles of Salzburg«	unsigned	Carl Gustav Nieritz (1843): *Die protestantischen Salzburger und deren Vertreibung durch den Fürst-Erzbischof von Firmi-an*; Carl Gustav Nie-ritz (1880): *The Exiles of Salzburg and other Stories*
1 Jan-11 June 1870 24 parts	»The House of de Valdez«	Frances Browne	unknown

Tab. 20: Leisure Hour *(1852-1870): Monthly Parts on the Past.*

Monthly Parts	Title	Author
Genre Focus: travel / topographical		
June 1853	»A Visit to the Staffordshire Pot-teries«, 4 parts	unsigned
Aug 1855	»A Summer Ramble Through Belgium and Holland«, 4 parts	unsigned
July 1857	»How to See the English Lakes«, 5 parts	unsigned [Bitha Fox (Lloyd)]
Feb 1859	»Japanese«, 3 parts	unsigned
Apr 1859	»The South Kensington Muse-um«, 4 parts	unsigned
Sept 1859	»A Ramble in the Tyrol«, 3 parts	unsigned [John Stoughton]
June 1859	»Windsor Castle«, 5 parts	unsigned [John Stoughton]
Jan 1862	»Royal Observatory, Greenwich«, 4 parts	James Glaisher (part 1) Edwin Dunkin (part 2-4)
May 1862	»A Trip to North Devon«, 5 parts	unsigned
May 1862	»The Tale of a West-End Sub-urb«, 4 parts	John Stoughton
July 1862	»Kew Gardens«, 4 parts	unsigned
Sept 1863	»West of Killarney«, 4 parts	Edwin Dunkin
Nov 1865 3 parts	»Fotheringhay«, 4 parts	Cuthbert Bede [Edward Bradley]
Sept 1867	»The Volcanoes of Auvergne«, 3 parts	S[amuel R[owles] Pat-tison

July 1869	»A Walk in South Devon«, 5 parts	Author of ›The Regular Swiss Round‹ [Harry Jones]
Genre Focus: life writing		
July 1852	»The Lessons of Biography«, 5 parts	unsigned
Oct 1854	»Russia«, 4 parts	unsigned
Dec 1854	»The Philadelphia Printer«, 3 parts	unsigned
Mar 1855	»The Walcheren Expedition«, 3 parts	By One Who Survived It
June 1855	»The Queen of a Literary Cote-rie«, 3 parts	unsigned
May 1857	»The Knight of Eskdale«, 4 parts	unsigned
May 1861	»School Recollections«, 5 parts	unsigned
Apr 1864	»Shakespeare«, 5 parts	several, see Tab. 22 be-low
Aug 1865	»Fenelon«, 3 parts	unsigned
Feb 1868	»Abraham Lincoln«, 3 parts	unsigned
Genre Focus: descriptive / report		
Aug 1854	»The Deadly Art of War«, 4 parts	unsigned [John Scoffern?]
July 1859	»The Garden«, 4 parts	unsigned
July 1861	»Gossip about the Gipsies«, 3 parts	unsigned
Apr 1863	»Leipsic Fair«, 4 parts	unsigned

May 1864	»The Balloon and its Application«, 4 parts	James Glaisher
June 1864	»Letters Patent«, 4 parts	unsigned
Oct 1866	»The Water-Supply of Cities and Towns«, 4 parts	unsigned
May 1867	»The Jews of China«, 4 parts	B[enjamin] Harris Cowper
Sept 1870	»Gossip about Notable Books«, 3 parts	John Timbs

Tab. 21: Leisure Hour, *Monthly Parts: »How to See the English Lakes«* *(July 1857).*

Date	Title	Author
2 July 1857	»A Tale of the Last Mudborough Election: Chapter I«	unsigned
	»The Months in London: July«	unsigned
	»How to See the English Lakes: First Paper«	**unsigned**
	»The Phenomena of Criminal Life: Part IV«	unsigned
	»The Last Embassy to China«	unsigned
	»Echoes of a Mother's Voice«	unsigned
	»The Three Physicians«	unsigned
	»Lizzie«	Josephine [poem]
	»Untitled«	unsigned
	»Varieties«	Unsigned

9 July 1857	»A Tale of the Last Mudborough Election: Chapter II«	unsigned
	»The Last Embassy to China: Part II«	unsigned
	»How to See the English Lakes: Second Paper«	**unsigned**
	»Some Curious Fishes«	unsigned
	»The Transatlantic Telegraph«	unsigned
	»A Glimpse of Some Remarkable London Interiors«	An American
	»The Spirit of Adoption«	Joseph Milner
	»Hints on Profitable Reading«	Dr. Haves
16 July 1857	»Tales Illustrative of Chinese Life and Manners: Chapter I«	A Chinese Migrant
	»The Phenomena of Criminal Life: Part V, The Autobiography of a Thief«	unsigned
	»How to See the English Lakes: Third Paper«	**unsigned**
	»Electric Animals«	unsigned
	»A Landsman's Periods by Sea: Chapter I«	unsigned
	»Science and Religion«	Dr. James Hamilton
	»Calico Patterns in Rocks«	unsigned
	»Happiness«	unsigned
	»Varieties«	Unsigned
23 July 1857	»Tales Illustrative of Chinese Life and Manners: Chapter II«	The Chinese Migrant

	»Studies in History: Napoleon's Confidential Correspondence«	unsigned
	»How to See the English Lakes: Fourth Paper«	**unsigned**
	»Persian Fables«	unsigned
	»A Naturalist's Ramble to Eltham«	unsigned
	»A Landsman's Perils by Sea: Chapter III«	unsigned
	»Advice to Servants«	Dr. James Hamilton
30 July 1857	»Tales Illustrative of Chinese Life and Manners: The Merchant and His Lost Child«	unsigned
	»The Art Palace at Manchester: First Paper«	unsigned
	»How to See the English Lakes: Fifth Paper«	**unsigned**
	»A Landsman's Perils by Sea: Chapter IV«	unsigned
	»The Voice-Telegraphs of Montenegro«	unsigned
	»Varieties«	unsigned

Tab. 22: Leisure Hour, *Monthly Parts: Shakespeare (April 1864).*

Date	Title	Author
2 April 1864	»The Foster-Brothers of Doon: A Tale of the Irish Rebellion [of 1798], Chapter XXVII«	unsigned [Elizabeth Hely Walshe]
	»Servants and ›Characters‹«	unsigned
	»Shakespeare«	**Rev. John Stoughton**
	»A Paper on Alligators«	unsigned

	»Recent African Explorations: Chapter V«	unsigned
	»Varieties«	unsigned
9 April 1864	»The Foster-Brothers of Doon: A Tale of the Irish Rebellion [of 1798], Chapter XXIX«	unsigned [Elizabeth Hely Walshe]
	»The Wild Flowers of Shakespeare«	Rev. G. Henslow
	»Hugh Miller's Visit to Stratford-on-Avon«	Hugh Miller
	»Stratford-on-Avon Church«	unsigned [Full-page coloured plate]
	»The Holocaust at Santiago«	unsigned
	»The Patriarchs of Constantinople«	unsigned
	»Varieties«	unsigned
16 April 1864	»The Foster-Brothers of Doon: A Tale of the Irish Rebellion [of 1798], Chapter XXXI«	unsigned [Elizabeth Hely Walshe]
	»The American Blockaded Ports«	British Settler in Texas
	»Mrs. Stowe's Visit to Shakespeare's House and Tomb«	[Harriet Beecher] Stowe
	»Want and Woe in London«	unsigned
	»A Night Adventure in Persia«	unsigned
	»Dr. Johnson's Preface to Shakespeare«	Dr. [Samuel] Johnson
	»Map of Stratford-on-Avon and Surrounding Country«	unsigned [Map]

23 April 1864	The Foster-Brothers of Doon: A Tale of the Irish Rebellion [of 1798], Chapter XXXIII«	unsigned [Elizabeth Hely Walshe]
	»A Narrow Escape in Eastern Waters«	unsigned
	»Personal History of Shakespeare: *Stat magni nominis umbra!*«	**unsigned**
	»The Autographs of Shakespeare«	**unsigned**
	»Shakespeare Portraits«	**unsigned**
	»Contemporary Notices of Shakespeare«	**unsigned**
	»The Last Days of Dr. Johnson«	unsigned
	»Stags of the New World«	unsigned
30 April 1864	»The Foster-Brothers of Doon: A Tale of the Irish Rebellion [of 1798], Chap. XXXV«	unsigned [Elizabeth Hely Walshe]
	»The Two Great Centres of Our Home Population«	unsigned
	»The Shakespeare Property at Stratford«	**unsigned**
	»The Guildhall, Guild Chapel, and Grammar-School at Stratford«	**unsigned**
	»Shakespeare as a Moral Teacher«	**unsigned**
	»Paul Flemming, and His Embassy from Holstein to the Shah of Persia«	unsigned
	»Varieties«	unsigned

Tab. 23: Leisure Hour, *Monthly Parts:* »*The Deadly Art of War*« *(August 1854).*

Date	Title	Author
3 Aug 1854	»Three Visits to the Hotel Des Invalides, 1705, 1806, 1840«	unsigned [From the French]
	»A Chapter on Ashes«	unsigned
	»Woolwich Arsenal«	**unsigned**
	»The Military Key of Asiatic Turkey«	unsigned
	»A True Story, Though a Fairy Tale	unsigned
	»A Question for the Day«	Mr. [Nicholas] Baines
	»The Religion for a Dying Hour«	unsigned
	»Varieties«	unsigned
10 Aug 1854	»An Old Soldier's Story«	unsigned
	»A Naturalist's Glance at the Zoological Society's Fish House: No. I«	unsigned
	»The Deadly Art of War«	**unsigned**
	»Moving House«	unsigned
	»The Eagle's Rock«	unsigned [poem]
	»Inundation of St. Petersburg«	unsigned
	»The Vacant Hour«	[Henry Augustus] Boardman
	»The Source of True Satisfaction«	[William] Jay
17 Aug 1854	»David the Scholar: A Tale of the Scottish Reformation«	unsigned

	»Incidents of Irish Railway Scenery: The Poet Spenser«	unsigned
	»The Deadly Art of War: No. II«	**unsigned**
	»A Naturalist's Glance at the Zoological Society's Fish House: Second Paper«	unsigned
	»A Brick Field in London«	unsigned
	»Last Hours of the Haldanes«	[William Burns] Landell[s?]
24 Aug 1854	»David the Scholar: A Tale of the Scottish Reformation, Part II«	unsigned
	»A Naturalist's Glance at the Zoological Society's Fish House: Third Paper«	unsigned
	»The Deadly Art of War: No. III«	**unsigned**
	»My Fellow Passenger«	unsigned
	»The English Borough of Calais«	unsigned
	»The Benefits of Punctuality«	unsigned
31 Aug 1854	»Pierre, The Parisian Shoeblack«	unsigned
	»A Naturalist's Glance at the Zoological Society's Fish House: Fourth Paper«	unsigned
	»The Deadly Art of War: Concluding Paper«	**unsigned**
	»Sea-Side Phenomena«	unsigned
	»Things to Be Remembered«	unsigned
	»Varieties«	unsigned

Tab. 24: Leisure Hour *(1852-1887): Overview of Series by John Stoughton.*

Duration	Title	Identification
8 Jan 1852-12 May 1853 **11 parts** **8 illustrations** (6 on cover)	»Shades of the Departed in Old London«	unsigned Jubilee Number
4 Aug 1853-22 Sep 1853 **8 parts** **4 illustrations**	»The Banks of the Thames«	unsigned Jubilee Number
17 Apr 1856-19 June 1856 **8 parts** **8 illustrations** (2 full-page)	»Echoes of Westminster Hall«	unsigned Jubilee Number
2 June 1859-30 June 1859 **5 parts** **19 illustrations** (2 full-page)	»Windsor Castle«	unsigned Jubilee Number
1 Sept 1859-15 Sept 1859 **3 parts** **unillustrated**	»A Ramble in the Tyrol«	unsigned Jubilee Number
10 May 1862-31 May 1892 **4 parts** **3 illustrations**	»West-End Suburb«	unsigned Jubilee Number
21 Apr 1877-6 Oct 1877 **5 parts, unillustrated**	»The Royal Commission on Historical Manuscripts«	John Stoughton, D.D. second part published unsigned
24 May 1879-13 Sept 1879 **5 parts** **6 illustrations**	»The Black Forest«	John Stoughton, D.D. Jubilee Number
Oct 1885-Nov 1885 **2 parts, unillustrated**	»Neglected Books«	John Stoughton, D.D. Jubilee Number
Oct 1887-Nov 1887 **2 parts, unillustrated**	»Glimpses of Queen Anne's Days«	John Stoughton, D.D. Jubilee Number

Tab. 25: John Stoughton's »Shades of the Departed in Old London«,
Leisure Hour *1852-53.*

Date	Title	Historical Actors
8 Jan 1852	»Shades of the Departed in Old London: Baxter«	Richard Baxter (1615-1691), ejected minister and religious writer
19 Feb 1852	»Shades of the Departed in Old London: Milton«	John Milton (1608-1674), poet and polemicist
22 Apr 1852	»Shades of the Departed in Old London: Isaak Walton«	Izaak Walton (1593-1683), author and biographer
3 June 1852	»Shades of the Departed: Andrew Marvell and Lord W.M. Russell«	Andrew Marvell (1621-1678), poet and politician William Russell, Lord Russell [called the Patriot, the Martyr] (1639-1683), politician and conspirator
15 July 1852	»Shades of the Departed: Joseph Addison«	Joseph Addison (1672-1719), writer and politician
30 Sept 1852	»Shades of the Departed: Sir Isaac Newton«	Isaac Newton (1642-1727), natural philosopher and mathematician
14 Oct 1852	»Shades of the Departed: Oliver Goldsmith«	Oliver Goldsmith (1728?-1774), author
28 Oct 1852	»Shades of the Departed: Sir Joshua Reynolds«	Joshua Reynolds (1723-1792), portrait and history painter and art theorist

18 Nov 1852	»Shades of the Departed: Dr. Samuel Johnson«	Samuel Johnson (1709-1784), author and lexicographer
27 Jan 1853	»Shades of the Departed: John Howard«	John Howard (1728-1790), prison reformer
12 May 1853	»Shades of the Departed: Edmund Burke«	Edmund Burke (1729-1797), Politician, philosophical writer

Appendix B: Excursus – Fictional Series on the Past and Their Book Counterparts

During the 1850s and 1860s, the *Leisure Hour* increasingly turned to presenting fiction, frequently in prominent position on its covers (see Chapter 4, Fn 6). This also included historically themed fiction, that is, historical fiction or fiction within a historical setting. In contrast to the non-fiction series on the past, I could in the *Leisure Hour* only identify a book transfer for these fictional renderings in the direction from periodical to book (see Appendix A, Tab. 19). Twelve of the 21 historically themed fictional series were collected into book form after their appearance in the *Leisure Hour*,[1] and like the non-fiction transfer from periodical to book, this appears to have been a rather straightforward process in which the texts also took on peritextual features characteristic of book publications. Some brief examples indicate similarities to the non-fiction transfer from periodical to book outlined in Chapter 5.

Frances Browne's eleven-parter »The Exile's Trust« (1867) was, for instance, collected into the volume *The Exile's Trust: A Tale of the French Revolu-*

---

1 Four series were translations from German book titles, which – such as the »Poccahontas« (1852) series analysed in Chapter 3 – would have been classified as children's literature. Because of their earlier German book publication, they might not be considered a strict periodical to book transferral; yet in the *Leisure Hour* the RTS appears to have been the first to present an English translation of these German books, while afterwards at least two of the four series were also collected into English book publications (I was unable to establish an English book publication for »Golowin's Banishment to Siberia« or »Poccahontas«). And the books might even have appeared in German periodicals previous to their German book form. On the translation of German titles for the English children book market, cf. Blamires (2009), who includes a brief discussion of Nieritz's *Exiles of Salzburg*.

tion, and Other Stories ([1869]) together with six other (and less historical) narratives as well as poems. Furthermore, »The Exile's Trust« was accompanied in
the book publication by only four of the periodical's eleven cover illustrations.
The book named Frances Browne as the author of the work, and while it was
published at the RTS's alter ego imprint »Leisure Hour Office«, the earlier
presentation of »The Exile's Trust« within the *Leisure Hour* went unacknowl-
edged.[2]

Similarly, Elizabeth Hely Walshe's *Golden Hills: A Tale of the Irish Famine*
([1865])[3] did not acknowledge its origin in the *Leisure Hour*, though the book
was published six years later with the RTS itself and was accompanied by illustrations similar to those in the periodical serialisation. Walshe's authorship was
not attributed by name, but she was referred to as »the author of ›Cedar
Creek‹«.[4] *Golden Hills* provided a preface which commemorated the incident of
the Irish Famine twenty years earlier, noted that the author's knowledge
stemmed from oral history reports and lauded the progress of Ireland since that
time ([Walshe 1865]: v-vi). This additional peritext therefore placed the literary

2   The volume only noted that Browne's poems printed here had been taken from the
    Leisure Hour and the *Sunday at Home* (Browne [1869]: 277). Browne appears in 1870
    to have applied to the RTS for a transfer of her serialised historical novel »The House
    of de Valdez« (1870) into book form, a request which »was declined; and permission
    given to its author, Miss Browne, to publish it on her own responsibility« (USCL/RTS
    CCM 16 June 1870).

3   The »memorandum of Editorial Prospects for 1862« given in USCL/RTS CCM (13
    Nov 1861) falsely presented »Golden Hills« as having been authored by Sargent.
    However, Sargent finished writing the novel *Within Sea Walls, or: How the Dutch
    Kept the Faith*, published by the RTS without date, which bears both Sargent and
    Walshe's names as authors. In its preface, Sargent stated: »A portion of the story was
    written by a lady, whose health failed during its progress, and the Editor of the *Sunday
    at Home*, in which magazine the story originally appeared, asked me to examine the
    chapters already prepared, and a few notes as to the conduct of the after part of the
    story, with a view to completing it« (Walshe/Sargent [1880]: v). Walshe died in 1869
    and »Within Sea Walls« was printed in the *Sunday at Home* during 1870; it is hence
    unlikely that Walshe and Sargent may also have worked together on *Golden Hills*, es-
    pecially when one considers the author's preface to that work referenced in the text
    above.

4   This was an emigration novel also published anonymously by the RTS as *Cedar
    Creek; From the Shanty to the Settlement: A Tale of Canadian Life* (probably in
    1863/4) and in the *Leisure Hour* (26 parts, 3 January 1861-27 June 1861).

content more clearly within a historical narrative of progress than the serialisation of the novel in the *Leisure Hour* would have been able to.

In the same way, Walshe's *The Foster-Brothers of Doon: A Tale of the Irish Rebellion of 1798*, published by the RTS in book form in 1866, was presented as »By the Author of ›Golden Hills, a Tale of the Irish Famine‹, ›Cedar Creek‹, Etc.«. The RTS Subcommittee had recommended for »The Foster-Brothers of Doon« (1864) to be published in book form »with the introduction of more specific religious teaching« (USCL/RTS CCM 21 Dec 1865), and RTS minutes later reported that »the author was preparing an additional chapter« (USCL/RTS CCM 22 Feb 1866). Furthermore, the book provided a preface which focused on the historical authenticity of the narrative:

»Though the following pages are in the form of fiction, no pains have been spared to preserve minute accuracy in all that concerns the history of that terrible outbreak, known as the Irish Rebellion of 1798. The various volumes, written on both sides of the question, have been carefully studied, and innumerable contemporary documents – pamphlets, newspapers, broadsheets, and ballads – have been collected and examined. The sole desire of the writer has been to discover and present the truth. [...] It may be stated, in conclusion, that *The Foster-Brothers of Doon* appeared in the ›Leisure Hour‹ previously to the outbreak of the present Fenian agitation. The writer need scarcely say that the descriptions given refer exclusively to a by-gone era in the history of the country. They cannot, without the grossest violation of truth and good faith, be pleaded as justifying the incendiary projects which are now once more disturbing the peace of Ireland.« ([Walshe] 1866: 5-6)

The preface hence acknowledged the narrative's original place of publication within the *Leisure Hour*. In contrast to the periodical publication, it outlined the fictional approach of the narrative to factual history and in a way argued against a presentist reading of the story. Such a reading, however, might have been suggested to the original readers of the ›uncontextualised‹ narrative published in the *Leisure Hour* in 1864, that is, during the ongoing conflict between Protestants and Catholics in Ireland.

This brief excursus shows that the transfer from periodical to book led to a more reputable placement of the historical content even regarding fiction. Prefaces and introductions might also have discussed historical topics or approaches here, and both fiction and non-fiction on the past underwent similar dynamics in terms of authorship attribution or acknowledgement of earlier periodical publication, the addition of peritexts, change of illustrations and revision to fit into a publisher's programme.

Appendix C: Contributors on the Past in the *Leisure Hour* (1852-1870)

This alphabetical overview on the contributors of series on the past in the *Leisure Hour*, 1852-1870, lists series for which authorship has been identified.[1] Authorship for series is stated as signed in the *Leisure Hour*. Sources for the biographical entries are:

- DNCJ: *Dictionary of Nineteenth-Century Journalism in Great Britain and Ireland*
- ODNB: *Oxford Dictionary of National Biography Online*
- WBIS: *World Bibliographical Information System Online*
- Fyfe: »Appendix A: *Biographical Sketches of RTS Writers and Staff*« (in Fyfe 2004c).[2]

Occupations are listed as presented in these sources. The entry from »Authors« (1902) given in the *Leisure Hour*'s jubilee number is provided where applicable.

---

1   It may be assumed that most authors contributed further series and also single articles to the periodical. The RTS minutes, for instance, frequently list payments for *Leisure Hour* contributions by Merryweather, Scoffern and Stoughton, amongst others.

2   There is significantly little overlap with Fyfe's appendix on RTS writers and staff during the publication of the Monthly Volumes series, i.e., only Milner and Stoughton are presented here as well as in Fyfe's overview.

REV. FREDERICK ARNOLD (1832-1891)

Series in *Leisure Hour*
- F.A.: »Oxford and its Colleges« (1866)
- F. Arnold: »Cambridge and its Colleges« (1870)

Occupation and biography
chaplain; writer; editor: B.A. 1860 in Classics (Math.), Law and Modern History; studied at Glasgow University, Christ's College Cambridge, Christ Church Oxford; ordained deacon, priest and chaplain; editor of *Literary Gazette*, *Churchman's Family Magazine*; writer for magazines such as *London Society*; various book publications. (WBIS)

REV. EDWARD BRADLEY (PSEUD. CUTHBERT BEDE) (1827-1889)

Series in *Leisure Hour*
- Cuthbert Bede: »Fotheringhay« (1865)

Occupation and Biography
author; humorous writer; Church of England clergyman: theology 1849; studied at University College Durham; ordained, vicar, rector; writer and sketcher for magazines such as *Illustrated London News, Bentley's Miscellany, Punch, The Months, The Man in the Moon, Town and Country Miscellany, Sharpe's London Magazine, All the Year Round, The Field, St. James's, The Gentleman's Magazine, London Review, Once a Week, Leisure Hour, Churchman's Family Magazine, The Quiver, Fores's Sporting Notes and Sketches, The Boy's Own Paper, Notes and Queries*; various book publications, also novels and children's books. (DNCJ, ODNB, WBIS)

BENJAMIN HARRIS COWPER (1853-1878)

Series in *Leisure Hour*
- B. Harris Cowper: »The Jews of China« (1867)

Occupation and Biography
translator; miscellaneous writer: various book publications. (WBIS)

JAMES BRIDGE DAVIDSON, MA (C.1823-1885)

Series in *Leisure Hour*
- unsigned: »Hints on Legal Topics« (1865)

Occupation and Biography
miscellaneous writer: M.A. Trinity College Cambridge; conveyancer and equity draftsman, barrister. (WBIS)

EDWIN DUNKIN FRAS (1821-1898)

Series in *Leisure Hour*
- Edwin Dunkin Esq. F.R.S.: »West of Killarney« (1863)
- Edwin Dunkin, Esq., F.R.S.: »Royal Observatory, Greenwich« (1864, Parts 2-4)

Occupation and Biography
astronomer: Royal Observatory at Greenwich (1838-1884); President of Royal Astronomical Society; writer for various periodicals such as *Leisure Hour*; various book publications. (ODNB, WBIS)

Jubilee Number on Dunkin
»The late Dr. Edwin Dunkin, of the Royal Observatory, Greenwich, was a constant contributor of astronomical papers from 1861 to 1892. His most important articles were those on ›The Midnight Sky,‹ which appeared during the year 1868, and are still published in book form, beautifully illustrated, by the Religious Tract Society. It was this book which made Carlyle exclaim, ›O why did not somebody teach me the stars!‹« (»Authors« 1902: 247)

BITHA FOX (LLOYD) (1811-1894)

Series in *Leisure Hour*
- unsigned: »How to See the English Lakes« (1857)

Occupation and Biography
miscellaneous writer: wife to William Reynolds Lloyd; writer for periodicals such as *Leisure Hour*, *Sunday at Home*; various book publications. (WBIS)

JAMES GLAISHER FRS (1809-1903)

Series in *Leisure Hour*

* James Glaisher: »The Balloon and its Application« (1864)
* James Glaisher, Esq., F.R.S.: »Royal Observatory, Greenwich« (1864, Part 1)

Occupation and Biography

astronomer, meteorologist: Ordnance Survey Ireland; Cambridge University Observatory; Royal Observatory Greenwich; Royal Astronomical Society; co-founder, President and Secretary of British Meteorological Society; writer for periodicals such as *Illustrated London News*, *Daily News* (weather reports), various book publications. (ODNB, WBIS)

Jubilee Number on Glaisher

»Mr. James Glaisher, F.R.S., founder of the Royal Meteorological Society, and for more than forty years connected with Greenwich Observatory, was for some years a frequent contributor. Among his articles were a series (in 1864) on ›The Balloon and its Application.‹ No more interesting papers ever appeared in our pages. In the third of the series he described his famous ascent (Sept. 5th, 1863), in which he attained the greatest height ever reached – nearly seven miles. He was insensible for more than ten minutes, and was only brought back to consciousness through the prompt action of his companion, Mr. Coxwell, who seized the valve-cord with his teeth. In 1872 he wrote a paper on ›Snow-Crystals.‹« (»Authors« 1902: 247)

RICHARD HEATH (UNKNOWN)

Series in *Leisure Hour*

* unsigned: »The Cottage Homes of England« (1870)

Occupation and Biography

biographer; historical writer: various book publications; according to »Preface« in *English Peasant*, the book was collected from articles in periodicals such as *Contemporary Review, Leisure Hour, Golden Hours*. (WBIS)

Jubilee Number on Heath

»Mr. Richard Heath has written on various subjects, chiefly historical or biographical, with a social bearing. He wrote ›Jean F. Millet‹ (1882); ›Mediaeval Shoes,‹ ›Blenheim‹ (1884); a series on ›Story-Telling in all Ages‹ (1885); ›Victor Hugo‹ (1886); ›Woman's

Influence‹ (1887); ›Count Leo Tolstoi,‹ ›The Taking of the Bastille‹ and other papers on France (1889); ›The Continental Tourist‹ (1890); ›Electioneering in Former Time‹ (1892).« (»Authors« 1902: 248)

REV. HOWARD HOPLEY (UNKNOWN)

Series in *Leisure Hour*
* Howard Hopley: »On the Nile« (1867)
* Howard Hopley: »From Nubia Down the Nile« (1869)

Occupation and Biography
vicar, travel writer: ordained 1871; rector and vicar; book and periodical publications. (WBIS)

Jubilee Number on Hopley
»Mr. (afterwards the Rev.) Howard Hopley described his travels ›On the Nile,‹ afterwards published as a book (1866). He has also written on ›The Catacombs‹ (1865); ›From Nubia down the Nile‹ (1869); ›Virgil's Tomb‹ (1877), and other travel papers.« (»Authors« 1902: 249)

WILLIAM JERDAN, ESQ., MRSL, FSA (PSEUD. BUSHEY HEATH) (1782-1869)

Series in *Leisure Hour*
* unsigned: »Men I Have Known« (1859-1865)
* Author of »Men I Have Known«: »Characteristic Letters« (1868-1869)

Occupation and Biography
journalist, editor, man of letters, critic, miscellaneous writer, antiquary: merchant clerk; meant to study law at Edinburgh University; foreign correspondent during Napoleonic Wars; book editor (e.g. for John Murray); editor for *Aurora, Satirist, The Sun, Literary Gazette, Sheffield Mercury, Foreign Literary Gazette*; Royal Society of Literature; Zoological Society; Royal Geographical Society; Garrick Club; Camden Society; Royal Society of Antiquaries; writer for periodicals such as *Aurora, The Pilot, Morning Post, British Press, North Staffordshire Pottery Gazette, Chelmsford Chronicle, Edinburgh Review, Quarterly Review, Bentley's*

Fraser's Magazine, Gentleman's Magazine, Notes and Queries, various book publications. (DNCJ, ODNB, WBIS)

Jubilee Number on Jerdan

»One of the most regular contributors to the early volumes of this magazine was Mr. William Jerdan, editor of the *Literary Gazette*. A native of Kelso, where he was born in 1772 [sic], he was educated for the Scottish bar, but came to London when still a young man to push his way in literature. He became sole editor of the *Literary Gazette*, soon after it was started in 1817, and filled the editorial chair for nearly thirty-five years. For most of that time the *Gazette* was the only journal devoted to literature and art. Mr. Jerdan retired from the editorship in 1850.

It was he who, in the lobby of the old House of Commons, seized Bellingham, the assassin of Mr. Perceval.

The principal papers contributed by Mr. Jerdan to *The Leisure Hour* bore the general title of ›Men I Have Known,‹ published in 1867 as a volume dedicated to the then Chief Baron (Sir Frederick) Pollock. In 1868, the year before his death, he contributed to our pages a series of ›Characteristic Letters,‹ consisting of letters written to himself by Faraday, Hans Christian Andersen, Sir Walter Scott, Sir David Brewster, Wordsworth, James Hogg, Allan Cunningham, J.G. Lockhart, John Murray, William Blackwood, Samuel Lover, and others.« (»Authors« 1902: 249)

PREB. HARRY JONES, MA (1823/4-1900)

Series in *Leisure Hour*

- unsigned: »The Regular Swiss Round« (1863)
- Author of »The Regular Swiss Round«: »Another Swiss Round« (1864)
- Author of »The Regular Swiss Round«: »The Idler on the Rhine« (1865)
- Author of »The Regular Swiss Round«: »A Walk in South Devon« (1869)

Occupation and Biography

rector, miscellaneous writer: M.A. St. John's College Cambridge; ordained deacon, priest, chaplain, rector, vicar, prebendary, minister, honorary chaplain to the queen; S.P.C.K.; editor of *People's Magazine*; writer for periodicals such as *Leisure Hour*, various book publications. (WBIS)

Jubilee Number on Jones

»The late Prebendary Harry Jones, who died in 1900, was for nearly forty years a regular contributor to this magazine. his most notable papers were a series of vivacious articles on

›The Regular Swiss Round‹ (1863); ›Another Swiss Round‹ (1864); ›The Idler on the Rhine‹ (1865); ›Practical Social Sciences,‹ a series of nine articles (1877); seven papers entitled ›Bible Lessons for Everyday Life‹ (1880); ›Past and Present in the East‹ (1881), a series of descriptive papers on Egypt, Sinai, and Palestine, which are still so fresh and interesting as to repay perusal.« (»Authors« 1902: 249)

FREDERICK SOMNER MERRYWEATHER (1827-1900)

Series in *Leisure Hour*
• F.S.M.: »The Working Man in the Olden Time« (1852)

Occupation and Biography
miscellaneous writer, bookseller, newspaper editor: editor of *The Surrey Comet*; various book publications. (WBIS)

REV. THOMAS MILNER, MA, FRGS (1808-1882/3)

Series in *Leisure Hour*
• unsigned: »Sketches of the Crimea« (1855)

Occupation and Biography
Congregational minister, clergyman; miscellaneous writer: M.A. at Glasgow University; minister; Royal Geographical Society; various book publications. (Fyfe, WBIS)

SAMUEL ROWLES PATTISON, FGS (1809-c.1901)

Series in *Leisure Hour*
• S.R. Pattison: »Celts« (1866)
• S.R. Pattison: »The Volcanoes of Auvergne« (1867)

Occupation and Biography
solicitor, miscellaneous writer: various book publications. (WBIS)

DR. JOHN SCOFFERN (1814-1882)

Series in *Leisure Hour*
• unsigned: »Chemists« (1857)

Occupation and Biography
chemistry professor, writer: Professor of Chemistry and Medical Jurisprudence at Aldergate School of Medicine; special correspondent of morning paper at commencement of Franco-Prussian War in 1870; Iron Cross of Prussia; various book publications. (WBIS)

REV. JOHN STOUGHTON, D.D. (1807-1897)

Series in *Leisure Hour*
• unsigned: »Shades of the Departed in Old London« (1852-1853)
• unsigned: »The Banks of the Thames« (1853)
• unsigned: »Echoes of Westminster Hall« (1856)
• unsigned: »A Ramble in the Tyrol« (1859)
• unsigned: »Windsor Castle« (1859)
• John Stoughton: »The Tale of a West-End Suburb« (1862)

Occupation and Biography
Congregational minister, Independent Divine, Church of England clergyman: worked at office of Roman Catholic lawyer; educated at Highbury College Islington, New College, University College London; ordained, co-pastor, pastor, minister; Chair of Historical Theology and Homiletics in New College London; honorary D.D. Edinburgh University; Chairman of Congregational Union; Athenaeum Club; London Missionary Society; Evangelical Alliance; British and Foreign Bible Society; Young Men's Christian Association; editor of *The Evangelical Magazine*. (Fyfe, ODNB, WBIS)

Jubilee Number on Stoughton
»The late Rev. John Stoughton, D.D., was a regular and much-valued contributor to the early volumes and for nearly forty years. He wrote for the first number a paper on ›The Old Year's Last Hour,‹ and in the same and following years he wrote a series of papers on ›Shades of the Departed in Old London,‹ being an account of old London's famous men. In 1853 he contributed a series on ›The Banks of the Thames‹; in 1856 a series on ›Echoes of Westminster Hall‹; in 1859 a series on ›Windsor Castle and Neighbourhood‹ and ›A

Ramble in the Tyrol‹; in 1864 on ›Shakespeare‹; in 1873 ›The Royal Borough‹; in 1877 ›The Royal Commission on Historical MSS.‹; in 1878 a series on ›the Black Forest‹; in 1883 ›A Scotch Story: As True As It Is Strange‹; in 1886 ›Neglected Books‹; and in 1888 ›Glimpses of Queen Anne's Days.‹ He died in 1897.« (»Authors« 1902: 254)

(GEORGE) WALTER THORNBURY (1828-1876)

Series in *Leisure Hour*
• unsigned: »Haunted London« (1860)

Occupation and Biography
author, art critic, poet, novelist, miscellaneous writer: meant to enter church but wanted to be artist; trained at academy of James Mathews Leigh; translator; writer for periodicals such as *Bristol Journal, Bentley's Miscellany, Ainsworth's, Welcome Guest, Once a Week, Chambers's Journal, Household Words, All the Year Round, The Athenaeum, Art Journal, New Monthly Magazine, Dublin University Magazine, Eclectic, Notes and Queries*; various book publications, also novels and poetry. (ODNB, WBIS)

JOHN TIMBS, FSA (PSEUD. HORACE WELBY, HAROLD FOOTE) (1801-1875)

Series in *Leisure Hour*
• John Timbs: »Curiosities« (1868)
• John Timbs: »Gossip about Notable Books« (1870)

Occupation and Biography
author, writer and compiler, miscellaneous writer: printer and druggist apprentice; amanuensis to R. Phillips, publisher of *Monthly Magazine*; Society of Antiquaries; editor of *Mirror of Literature, Arena of Science, Literary World, Illustrated London News* (sub-editor), *Year Book of Science and Art* (founder); writer for periodicals such as *Monthly Magazine, Mirror of Literature, The Harlequin, Literary World, Illustrated London News*; various book publications. (DNCJ, ODNB, WBIS)

Jubilee Number on Timbs

»John Timbs was for a lifetime associated with the London press, and the author of many useful and entertaining books, largely compiled from his immense collection of newspaper gleanings, or from his miscellaneous readings. He contributed many ›Recollections‹.« (»Authors« 1902: 254)

ELIZABETH HELY WALSH(E) (C.1835-1869)

Series in *Leisure Hour*

*   unsigned: »The Tourist in Scotland« (1860); unsigned: »The Tourist in Ireland« (1862)

Occupation and Biography

miscellaneous writer: various book publications. (WBIS)

Jubilee Number on Walsh(e)

»The late Miss Elizabeth H. Walsh, of Limerick, was for many years a regular contributor. In 1859 appeared her serial story, ›Golden Hills‹; in 1860 a series entitled ›The Tourist in Scotland‹, in 1861 ›Cedar Creek,‹ a popular serial story, afterwards published in book form; in 1862 a series on ›The Tourist in Ireland‹; in 1864 the serial story ›The Foster Brothers of Doon‹; in 1865 ›The Main Chance,‹ a serial story; besides numerous short papers and sketches. She died early, and lies buried at Bonchurch.« (»Authors« 1902: 255)

MARY LOUISA WHATELY (1824-1889)

Series in *Leisure Hour*

*   M.L. Whately: »Life in Egypt« (1865)

Occupation and Biography

educationist, missionary: left Ireland for warmer climate because of bad health; missionary work in England and Egypt; established school in Cairo; various book publications. (ODNB, WBIS)

Jubilee Number on Whately

»The late Miss E. J. Whately, daughter of the late Archbishop of Dublin, was a constant contributor for several years. In 1864 she wrote ›Ten Days in Biscay and Navarre‹; in 1865 a series of papers on Egypt; in 1871 on ›Charles Dickens‹; in 1878 on ›Charles Kingsley‹; and in 1891 ›A Story of Three Russian Ladies.‹« (»Authors« 1902: 255)

References

»Abraham Lincoln.« 1868. *Leisure Hour* 15-29 February (3 parts).

Adams, Edward. 2014. »Historiography.« In *A New Companion to Victorian Literature and Culture*, edited by Herbert F. Tucker, 414-29. John Wiley & Sons.

Adams, Thomas, and Barker. 1993. »A New Model for the Study of the Book.« In *A Potencie of Life: Books in Society*, edited by Nicolas Barker, 5-43. London: British Library.

»The Adventures of Johann Gottfried Seume.« 1852. *Leisure Hour* 7 October: 650-55.

»Advertisement.« 1852. *Hampshire Telegraph and Sussex Chronicle* 10 January: 2.

»Alexander von Humboldt.« 1860. *Good Words* 1 April: 209-15.

Alison, Archibald. 1849. *History of Europe: The Commencement of the French Revolution to the Restoration of the Bourbons in MDCCCXV*. Vol. 9. Edinburgh: William Blackwood and Sons.

Altholz, Josef L. 1989. *The Religious Press in Britain, 1760-1900*. New York: Greenwood Press.

Altick, Richard D. 1978. *The Shows of London*. Cambridge: Belknap.

Altick, Richard D. 1989. »English Publishing and the Mass Audience in 1852.« In *Writers, Readers and Occasions: Selected Essays on Victorian Literature and Life*, 141-58. Columbus: Ohio State University Press.

Altick, Richard D. 1998 [1957]. *The English Common Reader: A Social History of the Mass Reading Public, 1800-1900*. Columbus: Ohio State University Press.

Anderson, Benedict. 2009. *Imagined Communities: Reflections on the Origin and Spread of Nationalism*. London: Verso.

Anderson, Patricia J. 1991. *The Printed Image and the Transformation of Popular Culture: 1790-1860*. Oxford: Clarendon.

Anderson, Patricia J. 1992. »»Factory Girl, Apprentice and Clerk«: The Readership of Mass-Market Magazines, 1830-60.« *Victorian Periodicals Review* 25 (2): 64-72.

»An Anecdote from Australia.« 1852. *Leisure Hour* 25 November: 767-68.

»An Anecdote of the Russian Police.« 1854. *Leisure Hour* 18 May: 318.

»Anecdotes of Eminent Men.« 1852. *Leisure Hour* 11 March: 176.

»The Angel's Oak; A Story of New England.« 1858. *Leisure Hour* 15-29 July (3 parts).

»Ariadne at Naxos.« 1860. *Cornhill Magazine* II, December: 674-78.

A[rnold], F[rederick]. 1866. »Oxford and Its Colleges.« *Leisure Hour* 5 May-15 December (7 parts).

Arnold, F[rederick]. 1870. »Cambridge and Its Colleges.« *Leisure Hour* 5 March-31 December (10 parts).

Arnold, Frederick. 1873. *Oxford and Cambridge: Their Colleges, Memories and Associations.* London: Religious Tract Society.

»Arthur and the Round Table.« 1860. *Leisure Hour* 13 December: 790-94.

»An Artist in Earth.« 1852. *Leisure Hour* 11 November: 729-33.

»Artists.« 1902. *Leisure Hour* Jubilee Number, January: 256-57.

»The Art Palace at Manchester [Manchester Palace of Art / Manchester Art Treasures].« 1857. *Leisure Hour* 30 July-3 September (6 parts).

Assmann, Aleida. 2007. *Geschichte im Gedächtnis: Von der individuellen Erfahrung zur öffentlichen Inszenierung.* Munich: Beck.

Assmann, Jan. 1995. »Collective Memory and Cultural Identity.« *New German Critique* 65: 125-33.

Assmann, Jan. 2007. *Das kulturelle Gedächtnis: Schrift, Erinnerung und politische Identität in frühen Hochkulturen.* Munich: Beck.

Atkinson, Juliette. 2010. *Victorian Biography Reconsidered: A Study of Nineteenth-Century »Hidden« Lives.* Oxford: Oxford University Press.

»Authentic Anecdote of Frederic William IV of Prussia.« 1860. *Leisure Hour* 19 July: 457-58.

»Authors.« 1902. *Leisure Hour* Jubilee Number, January: 244-56.

»The Autographs of Shakespeare.« 1864. *Leisure Hour* 23 April: 263-64.

»Autumn.« 1860. *Leisure Hour* 13 September: 584-85.

»Bacharach.« 1852. *London Journal* 10 April: 73-74.

»The Baltic, and the Russian Towns on Its Coasts.« 1854. *Leisure Hour* 18 May: 311-14.

Bann, Stephen. 1984. *The Clothing of Clio: A Study of the Representation of History in Nineteenth-Century Britain and France.* Cambridge: Cambridge University Press.

Barrett, Joseph H. 1865. *Life of Abraham Lincoln.* Cincinnati: Moore, Wilstach & Baldwin.

»Barthel Winkler; A Tale of Hesse-Darmstadt.« 1860. *Leisure Hour* 20-27 December (2 parts).

Bassett, Troy J. 2015 [2007]. *At the Circulating Library.* http://www. victorianresearch.org/atcl/ (accessed 18 August 2015). Victorian Research Web.

»Bath Revisited.« 1852. *Leisure Hour* 22 July: 465-66.

»The Battle of Naseby.« 1852. *London Journal* 13 March: 9-10.

Bede, Cuthbert [Edward Bradley]. 1865. »Fotheringhay.« *Leisure Hour* 11-25 November (3 parts).

Bede, Cuthbert [Edward Bradley]. 1886. *Fotheringhay, and Mary, Queen of Scots: Being an Account, Historical and Descriptive, of Fotheringhay Castle, the Last Prison of Mary, Queen of Scots, and the Scene of Her Trial and Execution.* London: Simpkin, Marshall, & Co.

Beetham, Margaret. 1989. »Open and Closed: The Periodical as a Publishing Genre.« Edited by Laurel Brake and Anne Humpherys. *Victorian Periodicals Review* Special Issue: Theory, 22 (3): 96-100.

Beetham, Margaret. 2009. »Magazines.« In *Dictionary of Nineteenth Century Journalism in Great Britain and Ireland*, edited by Laurel Brake and Marysa Demoor, 391-92. Ghent: Academia Press.

»Beethoven's Monument.« 1852. *London Journal* 7 February: 361.

Bennett, Scott. 1982. »Revolutions in Thought: Serial Publication and the Mass Market for Reading.« In *The Victorian Periodical Press: Samplings and Soundings*, edited by Joanne Shattock and Michael Wolff, 225-57. Leicester: Leicester University Press.

Bentley, Michael. 2011. »Shape and Pattern in British Historical Writing, 1815-1945.« In *The Oxford History of Historical Writing*, edited by Stuart Macintyre, Juan Maiguashca, and Attila Pók, 4: 1800 – 1945: 204-24. Oxford: Oxford University Press.

Berger, Stefan. 2007a. »The Power of National Pasts: Writing National History in Nineteenth- and Twentieth-Century Europe.« In *Writing the Nation: A Global Perspective*, edited by Stefan Berger, 30-62. Houndmills: Palgrave Macmillan.

Berger, Stefan, ed. 2007b. *Writing the Nation: A Global Perspective.* Houndmills: Palgrave Macmillan.

Berger, Stefan. 2011. »The Invention of European National Traditions in European Romanticism.« In *The Oxford History of Historical Writing*, edited by

Stuart Macintyre, Juan Maiguashca, and Attila Pók, 4: 1800 – 1945: 19-40. Oxford: Oxford University Press.

Berger, Stefan, Linas Eriksonas, and Andrew Mycock, eds. 2008. *Narrating the Nation: Representations in History, Media and the Arts*. Oxford: Berghahn.

Berger, Stefan, Heiko Feldner, and Kevin Passmore, eds. 2003. *Writing History: Theory & Practice*. London: Arnold.

Berger, Stefan, and Chris Lorenz, eds. 2008a. *The Contested Nation: Ethnicity, Class, Religion and Gender in National Histories*. Basingstoke: Palgrave Macmillan.

Berger, Stefan, and Chris Lorenz. 2008b. »Introduction: National History Writing in Europe in a Global Age.« In *The Contested Nation: Ethnicity, Class, Religion and Gender in National Histories*, edited by Stefan Berger and Chris Lorenz, 1-23. Basingstoke: Palgrave Macmillan.

Berger, Stefan, Chris Lorenz, and Billie Melman, eds. 2012. *Popularizing National Pasts*. New York: Routledge.

Berridge, Virginia. 1986. »Content Analysis and Historical Research on Newspapers.« In *The Press in English Society from the Seventeenth to Nineteenth Centuries*, edited by Michael Harris and Alan Lee, 201-18. Rutherford: Fairleigh Dickinson University Press.

»Bianconi and His Cars.« 1860. *Leisure Hour* 6 September: 565-66.

Bills, Mark. 2011. »»A Distinctive Character to the Illustration of News«: Sir John Gilbert and the Pictorial Press.« In *Sir John Gilbert: Art and Imagination in the Victorian Age*, edited by Spike Bucklow and Sally Woodcock, 96-117. London: Lund Humphries Publishers.

Black, Barbara J. 2000. *On Exhibit: Victorians and Their Museums*. Charlottesville: University Press of Virginia.

Blamires, David. 2009. *Telling Tales: The Impact of Germany on English Children's Books 1780-1918*. Cambridge: Open Book Publishers.

»Blind.« 1856-57. *Leisure Hour* 11 September 1856-26 February 1857 (5 parts).

»Bonapartiana.« 1852. *Leisure Hour* 18 March: 198-200.

Bösch, Frank. 2005. »Zwischen Populärkultur und Politik: Britische und deutsche Printmedien im 19. Jahrhundert.« *Archiv für Sozialgeschichte* 45: 549-84.

Bowler, Peter J. 1989. *The Invention of Progress: The Victorians and the Past*. Oxford: Blackwell.

»The Boy Crusaders.« 1852. *Leisure Hour* 13 May: 305-7.

Boyd, Kelly. 2003. *Manliness and the Boy's Story Paper in Britain: A Cultural History, 1855 – 1940*. Basingstoke: Macmillan.

Brake, Laurel. 1994. *Subjugated Knowledges: Gender, Journalism and Literature in the Nineteenth Century*. Basingstoke: Macmillan.

Brake, Laurel. 2001. *Print in Transition, 1850-1910: Studies in Media and Book History*. Basingstoke: Palgrave.

Brake, Laurel. 2011. »The Advantage of Fiction: The Novel and the ›Success‹ of the Victorian Periodical.« In *A Return to the Common Reader: Print Culture and the Novel, 1850-1900*, edited by Beth Palmer and Adelene Buckland, 9-21. Farnham: Ashgate.

Brake, Laurel, Bill Bell, and David Finkelstein, eds. 2000. *Nineteenth-Century Media and the Construction of Identities*. Basingstoke: Palgrave.

Brake, Laurel, and Marysa Demoor, eds. 2009. *The Lure of Illustration in the Nineteenth Century: Picture and Press*. Basingstoke: Palgrave.

Brake, Laurel, and Anne Humpherys. 1989a. »Critical Theory and Periodical Research.« Edited by Laurel Brake and Anne Humpherys. *Victorian Periodicals Review* Special Issue: Theory, 22 (3): 94-95.

Brake, Laurel, and Anne Humpherys, eds. 1989b. *Victorian Periodicals Review* Special Issue: Theory, 22 (3).

Brake, Laurel, Ed King, Roger Luckhurt, and James Mussell, eds. 2012. *W. T. Stead: Newspaper Revolutionary*. London: British Library.

Brewster, David. 1855. *Memoirs of the Life, Writings, and Discoveries of Sir Isaac Newton*. 2 vols. Edinburgh: Thomas Constable and Co.

British Periodicals Collection. 2015. http://search.proquest.com/britishperiodicals (accessed 18 August 2015). ProQuest.

[Brooke-Knight, Captain]. 1859-60. »The Captain's Story; Or, Adventures in Jamaica Thirty Years Ago.« *Leisure Hour* 1 September 1859-12 July 1860 (24 parts).

Brooke Knight, Captain. 1883. *The Captain's Story; Or, Jamaica Sixty Years Since, Etc.* London: Religious Tract Society.

Brosch, Renate. 2008. *Victorian Visual Culture*. Heidelberg: Universitätsverlag Winter.

Brougham, Henry. 1858. *Addresses on Popular Literature, and on the Monument to Sir Isaac Newton: Delivered at Liverpool and Grantham*. London: Edward Law.

[Browne, Frances]. 1867. »The Exile's Trust; A Tale of the French Revolution.« *Leisure Hour* 5 October-14 December (11 parts).

Browne, Frances. [1869]. *The Exile's Trust, a Tale of the French Revolution and Other Stories*. London: Leisure Hour Office.

Browne, Frances. 1870. »The House of de Valdez.« *Leisure Hour* 1 January-11 June (24 parts).

Brundage, Anthony. 1994. *The People's Historian: John Richard Green and the Writing of History in Victorian England.* Westport: Greenwood Press.

Bryman, Alan. 2004. *Social Research Methods.* Oxford: Oxford University Press.

Bucklow, Spike, and Sally Woodcock, eds. 2011. *Sir John Gilbert: Art and Imagination in the Victorian Age.* London: Lund Humphries Publishers.

»Burford's Panorama of Salzburg.« 1852. *London Journal* 12 June: 217-18.

Burke, Peter. 2011. »Lay History: Official and Unofficial Representations, 1800-1914.« In *The Oxford History of Historical Writing*, edited by Stuart Macintyre, Juan Maiguashca, and Attila Pók, 4: 1800 – 1945: 115-32. Oxford: Oxford University Press.

Burstein, Miriam Elizabeth. 1999. »From Good Looks to Good Thoughts: Popular Women's History and the Invention of Modernity, Ca. 1830-1870.« *Modern Philology* 97 (1): 46-75.

Burstein, Miriam Elizabeth. 2004. *Narrating Women's History in Britain, 1770-1902.* Burlington: Ashgate.

Butts, Dennis. 2006. »Introduction.« In *From the Dairyman's Daughter to Worrals of the WAAF: The Religious Tract Society, Lutterworth Press and Children's Literature*, edited by Dennis Butts and Pat Garrett, 7-12. Lutterworth.

Butts, Dennis, and Pat Garrett, eds. 2006. *From the Dairyman's Daughter to Worrals of the WAAF: The Religious Tract Society, Lutterworth Press and Children's Literature.* Lutterworth.

Buurma, Rachel Sagner. 2007. »Anonymity, Corporate Authority, and the Archive: The Production of Authorship in Late-Victorian England.« *Anonymity, Corporate Authority, and the Archive: The Production of Authorship in Late-Victorian England.* 50 (1): 15-42.

Cannadine, David. 2006. *Trafalgar in History: A Battle and Its Afterlife.* Basingstoke: Palgrave Macmillan.

Cantor, Geoffrey, Gowan Dawson, Graeme Gooday, Richard Noakes, Sally Shuttleworth, and Jonathan R. Topham, eds. 2004. *Science in the Nineteenth-Century Periodical: Reading the Magazine of Nature.* Cambridge: Cambridge University Press.

Cantor, Geoffrey, and Sally Shuttleworth, eds. 2004. *Science Serialized: Representations of the Sciences in Nineteenth-Century Periodicals.* Cambridge: MIT.

Capel, Charlotte Eliza. 1861. *Victorian Enigmas; Or, Windsor Fireside Researches.* London: Lockwood and Co.

»The Capitol at Washington.« 1852. *Leisure Hour* 5 February: 81-83.

Carr, David. 2006. »The Reality of History.« In *Meaning and Representation in History*, edited by Jörn Rüsen, 7: 123-36. Making Sense of History. New York: Berghahn Books.

Caspari, Karl Heinrich. 1851. *Der Schulmeister und sein Sohn: eine Erzählung aus dem dreißigjährigen Krieg für das christliche Volk in Stadt und Land.* Stuttgart: Steinkopf.

[Caspari, K.H.]. 1858. »The Schoolmaster and His Son; A Memoir of the Thirty Years' War.« *Leisure Hour* 30 September-23 December (12 parts).

Caspari, K. H. 1864. *The Schoolmaster and His Son. A Story of the Thirty Years' War, Etc.* London: John Morgan.

Chapman, Raymond. 1986. *The Sense of the Past in Victorian Literature.* London: Croom Helm.

»Charles James Fox.« 1860. *Leisure Hour* 19 January: 40-43.

Chen, Shih-Wen. 2013. *Representations of China in British Children's Fiction, 1851–1911.* Farnham: Ashgate.

»Christmas Memories.« 1860. *Good Words* 9 December: 785-89.

Claes, Koenraad. 2010. »Supplements and Paratext: The Rhetoric of Space.« *Victorian Periodicals Review* 43 (2): 196-210.

»The Coast-Guardman's Yarn.« 1860. *Leisure Hour* 5-12 April (2 parts).

Colby, Robert A. 1999. »»Into the Blue Water«: The First Year of *Cornhill Magazine* under Thackeray.« *Victorian Periodicals Review* 32 (3): 209-22.

»The Cold-Water Doctor.« 1852. *Leisure Hour* 15 April: 246-47.

Collins, K. K. 2006. *Identifying the Remains: George Eliot's Death in the London Religious Press.* Victoria: ELS Editions.

[Collins, Wilkie]. 1858. »The Unknown Public.« *Household Words* 18 (439): 217-22.

»The Commons' Lobby in the Palace of Westminster.« 1852. *London Journal* 2 October: 61-62.

»Conspiracy of the Clocks.« 1852. *Leisure Hour* 17 June: 390-91.

»Contemporary Notices of Shakespeare.« 1864. *Leisure Hour* 23 April: 267-68.

»The Convent of Batalha.« 1852. *London Journal* 3-24 January (2 parts).

»The Convent of St. Jeronymo.« 1852. *London Journal* 17 January: 313-15.

Cooke, Simon. 2010. *Illustrated Periodicals of the 1860s: Contexts & Collaborations.* London: British Library.

Corbin, Juliet M., and Anselm L. Strauss. 2008. *Basics of Qualitative Research.* Los Angeles: Sage.

»Covent Garden Market, As It Was and Is.« 1852. *Leisure Hour* 1 July: 417-22.

Cowper, B[enjamin] Harris. 1867. »The Jews of China.« *Leisure Hour* 11-25 May (4 parts).

Creighton, M[andell]. 1885-91. »The Story of Some English Shires.« *Leisure Hour* April 1885-April 1891 (22 parts).

»The Crippled Orphan of the Tyrol.« 1852. *Leisure Hour* 5-12 February (2 parts).

Culler, Arthur Dwight. 1985. *The Victorian Mirror of History*. New Haven: Yale University Press.

Curtis, Gerard. 2002. *Visual Words: Art and the Material Book in Victorian England*. Aldershot: Ashgate.

»The Dahomians and Ashantees.« 1860. *Leisure Hour* 18 October: 670-72.

[Dallas, E.S.]. 1859a. »Popular Literature. The Periodical Press (No. I).« *Blackwood's Edinburgh Magazine* 85 (January): 96-112.

[Dallas, E.S.]. 1859b. »Popular Literature. The Periodical Press (No. II).« *Blackwood's Edinburgh Magazine* 85 (February): 180-95.

»Dante.« 1860. *Cornhill Magazine* I, April: 483-84.

Darnton, Robert. 1982. »What Is the History of Books?« *Daedalus* 111 (3): 65-83.

»David Chart's Memoranda.« 1860. *Good Words* 25 November-2 December (2 parts).

»A Day in Nineveh.« 1852. *Leisure Hour* 13 May: 307-11.

»A Day or Two at Brighton.« 1852. *Leisure Hour* 2 September: 568-71.

»A Day or Two at Hastings.« 1852. *Leisure Hour* 26 August: 535-40.

»A Day or Two at Ramsgate.« 1852. *Leisure Hour* 12 August: 520-25.

»The Dead Heart.« 1852. *London Journal* 31 January: 341-43.

»The Deadly Art of War.« 1854. *Leisure Hour* 10-31 August (4 parts).

»Death in Exile.« 1852. *Leisure Hour* 15 April: 241-43.

»The Death of Martin Luther.« 1860. *Leisure Hour* 13 September: 583-84.

Degele, Nina, and Gabriele Winker. 2007. »Intersektionalität als Mehrebenen-analyse.« *Portal Intersektionalität*. portal-intersektionalitaet.de/uploads/media/Degele_Winker_01.pdf (accessed 18 August 2015).

De Groot, Jerome. 2010. *The Historical Novel*. London: Routledge.

Delafield, Catherine. 2015. *Serialization and the Novel in Mid-Victorian Magazines*. Farnham: Ashgate.

Dellheim, Charles. 1982. *The Face of the Past: The Preservation of the Medieval Inheritance in Victorian England*. Cambridge: Cambridge University Press.

DiCenzo, Maria, Lucy Delap, and Leila Ryan. 2011. *Feminist Media History: Suffrage, Periodicals and the Public Sphere*. Houndmills: Palgrave Macmillan.

Dickens, Charles. 1864-65. *Our Mutual Friend*. London: Chapman and Hall.

Dictionary of Nineteenth Century Journalism in Great Britain and Ireland DNCJ. 2009. Edited by Laurel Brake and Marysa Demoor. Ghent: Academia Press.

[Dixon, J. Hepworth]. 1847a. »The Literature of the Lower Orders. Batch the First.« *Daily News* 26 October: 3.

[Dixon, J. Hepworth]. 1847b. »The Literature of the Lower Orders. Batch the Third.« *Daily News* 9 November: 2-3.

»The Doones of Exmoor.« 1863. *Leisure Hour* 5 September-24 October (8 parts).

[Doran, John]. 1864. »Our Library Table.« *The Athenaeum* 22 October: 527-28.

»The Dream of Columbus.« 1852. *London Journal* 11 September: 4-6.

»Dr. Van der Kemp.« 1860. *Leisure Hour* 28 June: 406-7.

»Dr Wichern and the Rauhes Haus.« 1860. *Good Words* 10 June-14 October (5 parts).

Duesterberg, Susanne. 2015. *Popular Receptions of Archaeology: Fictional and Factual Texts in 19th and Early 20th Century Britain*. Bielefeld: Transcript.

Du Gay, Paul, Stuart Hall, Keith Negus, Hugh Mackay, and Linda Janes. 1997. *Doing Cultural Studies: The Story of the Sony Walkman*. London: Sage.

»The Duke of Wellington.« 1852. *Leisure Hour* 4 November: 713-18.

»The Duke of Wellington's Tomb – Where Should It Be?.« 1852. *London Journal* 11 December: 217-18.

»The Duke's Funeral.« 1852. *Leisure Hour* 9 December: 788-90.

»Duncan Forbes of Culloden, the Scottish Patriot.« 1860. *Leisure Hour* 16 February: 105-7.

Dunkin, Edwin. 1863. »West of Killarney.« *Leisure Hour* 5-26 September (4 parts).

»Early English Intercourse with Russia.« 1855. *Leisure Hour* 18 January: 45-46.

Easley, Alexis. 2004. *First-Person Anonymous: Women Writers and Victorian Print Media, 1830-70*. Aldershot: Ashgate.

Easley, Alexis. 2011. *Literary Celebrity, Gender, and Victorian Authorship, 1850-1914*. Newark: University of Delaware Press.

»Eau de Cologne and John Maria Farina.« 1852. *Leisure Hour* 24 June: 413-15.

Eder, Franz X., ed. 2006. *Historische Diskursanalysen: Genealogie, Theorie, Anwendungen*. Wiesbaden: VS.

»Edme Champion.« 1852. *Leisure Hour* 28 October-4 November (2 parts).

Ehnes, Caley. 2012. »Religion, Readership, and the Periodical Press: The Place of Poetry in *Good Words*.« *Victorian Periodicals Review* 45 (4): 466-87.

Eliot, Simon. 1993. *Some Patterns and Trends in British Publishing, 1800-1919*. London: Bibliographical Society.

Eliot, Simon. 2007. »From Few and Expensive to Many and Cheap: The British Book Market 1800-1890.« In *A Companion to the History of the Book*, edited by Simon Eliot and Jonathan Rose, 291-302. Chichester: Wiley-Blackwell.

»The Englishman in Russia; A Tale of the Time of Catherine II.« 1856. *Leisure Hour* 3 January-3 July (27 parts).

Epple, Angelika. 2003. *Empfindsame Geschichtsschreibung: Eine Geschlechtergeschichte der Historiographie zwischen Aufklärung und Historismus*. Cologne: Böhlau.

Epple, Angelika, and Angelika Schaser, eds. 2009. *Gendering Historiography: Beyond National Canons*. Frankfurt/Main: Campus.

Erll, Astrid. 2005. *Kollektives Gedächtnis und Erinnerungskulturen: Eine Einführung*. Stuttgart: Metzler.

Erll, Astrid, and Ansgar Nünning, eds. 2004. *Medien des kollektiven Gedächtnisses: Konstruktivität – Historizität – Kulturspezifität*. Berlin: de Gruyter.

Erll, Astrid, and Ansgar Nünning, eds. 2005. *Gedächtniskonzepte der Literaturwissenschaft: Theoretische Grundlegung und Anwendungsperspektiven*. Berlin: De Gruyter.

Erll, Astrid, and Ansgar Nünning, eds. 2008. *Cultural Memory Studies: An International and Interdisciplinary Handbook*. Berlin: Walter de Gruyter.

»Excavations at Nineveh.« 1852. *London Journal* 22 May: 172-73.

Fairholt, Frederick William. 1860 [1849]. *Costume in England: A History of Dress from the Earliest Period until the Close of the Eighteenth Century*. London: Chapman and Hall.

»The Fate of Franklin.« 1860. *Good Words* 19 February-4 March (3 parts).

»Father Pedro's Convert.« 1860. *Leisure Hour* 19-26 April (2 parts).

Feather, John. 1988. *A History of British Publishing*. London: Routledge.

Feely, Catherine. 2009. »Scissors-and-Paste Journalism.« In *Dictionary of Nineteenth Century Journalism in Great Britain and Ireland*, edited by Laurel Brake and Marysa Demoor, 561. Ghent: Academia Press.

Felber, Lynette, ed. 2007. *Clio's Daughters: British Women Making History, 1790-1899*. Associated University Press.

»Felicia Hemans.« 1852. *Leisure Hour* 29 January: 72-76.

»Fenelon.« 1865. *Leisure Hour* 5-19 August (3 parts).

»A Few Days at Dover.« 1852. *Leisure Hour* 19 August: 535-40.

»A Few Words on Junius and Macaulay.« 1860. *Cornhill Magazine* I, March: 257-63.

»Fifty Years of *The Leisure Hour*.« 1902. *Leisure Hour* Jubilee Number, January: 177-92.

Finkelstein, David, ed. 2006. *Print Culture and the Blackwood Tradition 1805-1930.* Toronto: Toronto University Press.

Finn, James. 1843. *The Jews in China: Their Synagogue, Their Scriptures, Their History, &c.* London: B. Wertheim.

»The Fire Escape.« 1860. *Leisure Hour* 20 September: 600-602.

»The First British Steam-Boat.« 1852. *Leisure Hour* 29 April: 273-76.

»The First Ship to St. Petersburg.« 1855. *Leisure Hour* 19-26 July (2 parts).

»The Fisherman of Naples.« 1860. *Leisure Hour* 9-16 August (2 parts).

»Forest Tales: Comprising Sketches of the History, Tradition, and Scenery of Our National Forests.« 1852. *London Journal* 17 April-10 July (5 parts).

»The Fortress of St. Petersburg.« 1855. *Leisure Hour* 27 September: 616-18.

»Forum: Teaching and Learning in the Digital Humanities Classroom.« 2012. *Victorian Periodicals Review* 45 (2): 200-209.

Foulkes, Richard. 1984. *The Shakespeare Tercentenary of 1864.* London: Society for Theatre Research.

Foulkes, Richard. 1997. *Church and Stage in Victorian England.* Cambridge: Cambridge University Press.

Foulkes, Richard. 2002. *Performing Shakespeare in the Age of Empire.* Cambridge: Cambridge University Press.

»The Foundling Hospital, Lisbon.« 1852. *London Journal* 10 January: 297-99.

[Fox (Lloyd), Bitha]. 1857. »How to See the English Lakes.« *Leisure Hour* 2-30 July (5 parts).

[Fox (Lloyd), Bitha]. [1858]. *How to See the English Lakes. With Illustrations.* Religious Tract Society: London.

»France and Its Rulers.« 1852. *Leisure Hour* 19 February: 139-40.

Fraser, Hilary, Stephanie Green, and Judith Johnston. 2003. *Gender and the Victorian Periodical.* Cambridge: Cambridge University Press.

F.R.H. 1860. »Constance De V-------.« *Good Words* 22 April: 257-60.

Fuchs, Eckhardt. 2011. »Contemporary Alternatives to German Historicism in the Nineteenth Century.« In *The Oxford History of Historical Writing*, edited by Stuart Macintyre, Juan Maiguashca, and Attila Pók, 4: 1800 – 1945: 59-77. Oxford: Oxford University Press.

»The Funeral of Lord Nelson.« 1852. *Leisure Hour* 25 November: 753-57.

Füßmann, Klaus. 1994. »Historische Formungen: Dimensionen der Geschichtsdarstellung.« In *Historische Faszination: Geschichtskultur heute*, edited by Klaus Füßmann, Heinrich Theodor Grütter, and Jörn Rüsen, 27-44. Cologne: Böhlau.

Füßmann, Klaus, Heinrich Theodor Grütter, and Jörn Rüsen, eds. 1994. *Historische Faszination: Geschichtskultur heute.* Cologne: Böhlau.

Fyfe, Aileen. 2004a. »Commerce and Philanthropy: The Religious Tract Society and the Business of Publishing.« *Journal of Victorian Culture* 9 (2): 164-88.

Fyfe, Aileen. 2004b. »Periodicals and Book Series: Complementary Aspects of a Publisher's Mission.« In *Culture and Science in the Nineteenth-Century Media*, edited by Louise Henson, Geoffrey Cantor, Gowan Dawson, Richard Noakes, Sally Shuttleworth, and Jonathan R. Topham, 71-82. Aldershot: Ashgate.

Fyfe, Aileen. 2004c. *Science and Salvation: Evangelical Popular Science Publishing in Victorian Britain.* University of Chicago Press.

Fyfe, Aileen. 2005. »Societies as Publishers: The Religious Tract Society in the Mid-Nineteenth Century.« *Publishing History* 58: 5-42.

Fyfe, Aileen. 2006. »A Short History of the Religious Tract Society.« In *From the Dairyman's Daughter to Worrals of the WAAF: The Religious Tract Society, Lutterworth Press and Children's Literature*, edited by Dennis Butts and Pat Garrett, 13-35. Lutterworth.

Fyfe, Aileen. 2012. *Steam-Powered Knowledge: William Chambers and the Business of Publishing, 1820-1860.* Chicago: University of Chicago Press.

Gabriele, Alberto. 2009. *Reading Popular Culture in Victorian Print: Belgravia and Sensationalism.* New York: Palgrave Macmillan.

Garcia-Fernandez, Erin. 2012. »»Delicious Plural‹: The Editorial ›We‹ in Nineteenth-Century Fiction and Periodicals.« Ph.D. dissertation, Vanderbilt University.

»The Garden.« 1859. *Leisure Hour* 7-28 July (4 parts).

Giesenfeld, Günter. 1994. *Endlose Geschichten: Serialität in den Medien: ein Sammelband.* Hildesheim: Olms.

»Gladiatorial Combats.« 1852. *Leisure Hour* 29 January: 65-68.

Glaisher, James. 1863. *Scientific Experiments in Balloons: A Lecture.* London: J. Nisbet.

Glaisher, James. 1864. »The Balloon and Its Application.« *Leisure Hour* 7-28 May (4 parts).

Glaisher, James. 1871. *Travels in the Air.* London: R. Bentley.

Glaisher, James, and Edwin Dunkin. 1862. »Royal Observatory, Greenwich.« *Leisure Hour* 2-23 January (4 parts).

»A Glance at Clifton.« 1852. *Leisure Hour* 5 August: 504-9.

»A Glance at Sebastopol.« 1854. *Leisure Hour* 16 February: 104-6.

»God's Glory in the Heavens.« 1860. *Good Words* 12 August: 513-17.

Golby, J.M., and A.W. Purdue. 1984. *The Civilisation of the Crowd: Popular Culture in England 1750-1900.* London: Batsford Academic and Educational.

Goldman, Paul. 1996. *Victorian Illustration: The Pre-Raphaelites, the Idyllic School and the High Victorians.* Aldershot: Scolar Press.

Goldman, Paul. 2005. *Beyond Decoration: The Illustrations of John Everett Millais.* London: British Library.

Goldstein, Doris S. 1986. »The Role of Historical Journals in the Professionalization of History in England, 1886-1923.« *Tijdschrift Voor Geschiedenis* 99: 591-605.

»Gossip about the Gipsies.« 1861. *Leisure Hour* 4-16 July (3 parts).

»Go to Work!« 1852. *Leisure Hour* 17 June: 398-400.

»Governor Sir George Grey.« 1860. *Leisure Hour* 3 March: 280-83.

Gray, Elizabeth, ed. 2012. *Women in Journalism at the Fin de Siècle: Making a Name for Herself.* New York: Palgrave Macmillan.

Green, Samuel G. 1899. *The Story of the Religious Tract Society: For One Hundred Years.* Religious Tract Society.

Grever, Maria. 2008. »The Twofold Character of Time.« *Culturahistorica.es.* http://www.culturahistorica.es/grever/twofold_character_of_time.pdf (accessed 18 August 2015).

Grever, Maria. 2009. »Fear of Plurality: Historical Culture and Historiographical Canonization in Western Europe.« In *Gendering Historiography: Beyond National Canons,* edited by Angelika Epple and Angelika Schaser, 45-62. Chicago: University of Chicago Press.

»The Guildhall, Guild Chapel, and Grammar-School at Stratford.« 1864. *Leisure Hour* 30 April: 280-81.

Habicht, Werner. 2001. »Shakespeare Celebrations in Times of War.« *Shakespeare Quarterly* 52 (4): 441-55.

Halbwachs, Maurice. 1985. *Das kollektive Gedächtnis.* Frankfurt/Main: Suhrkamp.

»Haller the Physician.« 1860. *Leisure Hour* 7 June: 366-67.

H[all], J[ohn] P[arsons]. 1852a. »Lord Howe's Victory.« *London Journal* 14 August: 357-58.

H[all], J[ohn] P[arsons]. 1852b. »Royal Visits to Remarkable Places.« *London Journal* 19 July-6 November (8 parts).

H[all], J[ohn] P[arsons]. 1852c. »Woman – Her Mission and Destiny.« *London Journal* 28 February: 413-14.

Hall, N. John. 1980. *Trollope and His Illustrators.* London: Macmillan.

»Hampden's Statue in the Palace of Westminster.« 1852. *London Journal* 12 June: 220-21.

A Handbook for Travellers in Southern Germany. 1857. London: John Murray.

»Hans the Stranger.« 1852. *Leisure Hour* 16-23 December (2 parts).

»The Happy Warrior.« 1860. *Good Words* 10 June: 369-73.

Harris, Janice H. 1986. »Not Suffering and Not Still: Women Writers at the *Cornhill Magazine*, 1860-1900.« *Modern Language Quarterly* 47 (4): 382-92.

»Hartley Coleridge.« 1852. *Leisure Hour* 1 January: 14-15.

Harvey, John R. 1970. *Victorian Novelists and Their Illustrators*. London: Sidwick & Jackson.

Haskell, Francis. 1993. *History and Its Images: Art and Interpretation of the Past*. New Haven: Yale University Press.

Haskins, Katherine. 2012. *The Art-Journal and Fine Art Publishing in Victorian England, 1850–1880*. Farnham: Ashgate.

Haslinger, Peter. 2006. »Diskurse, Sprache, Zeit, Identität: Plädoyer für eine erweiterte Diskursgeschichte.« In *Historische Diskursanalysen: Genealogie, Theorie, Anwendungen*, edited by Franz X. Eder, 27-50. Wiesbaden: VS.

Hayward, Jennifer. 2008. *Consuming Pleasures: Active Audiences and Serial Fictions from Dickens to Soap Opera*. Lexington: University Press of Kentucky.

Haywood, Ian. 2004. *The Revolution in Popular Literature: Print, Politics and the People 1790-1860*. Cambridge: Cambridge University Press.

H.D. 1852. »A Word with Our Readers.« *Leisure Hour* 1 January: 8-10.

[Heath, Richard]. 1870. »The Cottage Homes of England.« *Leisure Hour* 6 August-10 December (5 parts).

Heath, Richard. 1893. *The English Peasant: Studies Historical, Local, and Biographic*. London: T.F. Unwin.

Hecimovich, Gregg. 2008. *Puzzling the Reader: Riddles in Nineteenth-Century British Literature*. New York: Peter Lang.

»Heidelberg.« 1852. *London Journal* 15 May: 153-54.

Henslow, G. 1864. »The Wild Flowers of Shakespeare.« *Leisure Hour* 9 April: 229-31.

Henson, Louise, Geoffrey Cantor, Gowan Dawson, Richard Noakes, Sally Shuttleworth, and Jonathan R. Topham, eds. 2004. *Culture and Science in the Nineteenth-Century Media*. Aldershot: Ashgate.

Hesketh, Ian. 2008. »Diagnosing Froude's Disease: Boundary Work and the Discipline of History in Late-Victorian Britain.« *History and Theory* 47 (3): 373-95.

Hesketh, Ian. 2011. *The Science of History in Victorian Britain: Making the Past Speak*. London: Pickering & Chatto.

Hewitt, Gordon. 1949. *Let the People Read: A Short History of the United Society for Christian Literature: Religious Tract Society 1799, Christian Litera-*

ture Society for India and Africa 1858, Christian Literature Society for China (British Support) 1887. London: Lutterworth Press.

Hewitt, Martin. 2014. *The Dawn of the Cheap Press in Victorian Britain: The End of the »Taxes on Knowledge«, 1849-1869*. London: Bloomsbury.

Hinton, John Howard. 1851. *The History and Topography of the United States of North America*. Boston: Samuel Walker.

»Hints on Legal Topics.« 1865. *Leisure Hour* 7 January-23 December (22 parts).

»Historical Enigmas.« 1856-57. *Leisure Hour* 27 January 1856-27 August 1857 (22 parts).

»Historical Fallacies.« 1852. *London Journal* 22 May: 173-74.

»Historic Tableaux: The Divorce of Josephine.« 1852. *Leisure Hour* 27 May: 337-40.

Hopley, Howard. 1867. »On the Nile.« *Leisure Hour* 23 February-20 July (16 parts).

Hopley, Howard. 1869a. »From Nubia Down the Nile.« *Leisure Hour* 6 February-3 July (15 parts).

Hopley, Howard. 1869b. *Under Egyptian Palms; Or, Three Bachelors' Journeyings on the Nile*. London: Chapman and Hall.

Hopwood, Nick, Simon Schaffer, and Jim Secord. 2010. »Seriality and Scientific Objects in the Nineteenth Century.« *History of Science* 48 (3-4): 251-85.

Horn, W. O. 1852. *Poccahontas: eine wahre Geschichte aus den Zeiten der ersten englischen Niederlassungen in Nordamerika*. Frankfurt/Main: Sauerländer.

Howsam, Leslie. 2004. »Academic Discipline or Literary Genre? The Establishment of Boundaries in Historical Writing.« *Victorian Literature and Culture* 32 (2): 525-45.

Howsam, Leslie. 2006. *Old Books and New Histories: An Orientation to Studies in Book and Print Culture*. Toronto: University of Toronto Press.

Howsam, Leslie. 2007. »Searching for History in (Digitized) Victorian Periodicals (Or, You Have 1066 Hits).« presented at the ProQuest Lecture in Modern Book History, University of Oxford, November.

Howsam, Leslie. 2008. »What Is the Historiography of Books? Recent Studies in Authorship, Publishing, and Reading in Modern Britain and North America.« *The Historical Journal* 51 (4): 1089-1101.

Howsam, Leslie. 2009a. »History and Journalism.« In *Dictionary of Nineteenth Century Journalism in Great Britain and Ireland*, edited by Laurel Brake and Marysa Demoor, 282-83. Ghent: Academia Press.

Howsam, Leslie. 2009b. *Past into Print: The Publishing of History in Britain, 1850-1950*. London: The British Library.

Howsam, Leslie. 2012. »Growing Up with History in the Victorian Periodical Press.« In *Popular History Now and Then: International Perspectives.*, edited by Barbara Korte and Sylvia Paletschek, 55-71. Bielefeld: transcript.

Howsam, Leslie. 2014a. »*History in the Periodical Press Online*: A Revised Informal Introduction to *HiPPo*.« *History Publications*. http://scholar.uwindsor.ca/historypub/14 (accessed 18 August 2015).

Howsam, Leslie. 2014b [2012]. *History in the Victorian Periodical Press Online: HiPPo.* http://www1.uwindsor.ca/historybook/6/history-in-the-victorian-periodical-press-online-hippo (accessed 18 August 2015). Historybooks – University of Windsor.

»How to See the English Lakes.« 2015. *IUCAT Indiana University Library Catalog*. http://iucat.iu.edu/catalog/10343689 (accessed 18 August 2015).

»How to Speak the French Language.« 1851-52. *London Journal* 15 February 1851-6 November 1852 (81 parts).

Huett, Lorna. 2005. »Among the Unknown Public: *Household Words, All the Year Round* and the Mass-Market Weekly Periodical in the Mid-Nineteenth Century.« *Victorian Periodicals Review* 38 (1): 61-82.

Hughes, Linda K. 2015. »On New Monthly Magazines, 1859-60.« *BRANCH: Britain, Representation and Nineteenth-Century History.* http://www.branchcollective.org/?ps_articles=on-new-monthly-magazines-1859-60 (accessed 18 August 2015).

Hughes, Linda K., and Michael Lund. 1991. *The Victorian Serial.* Charlottesville: University of Virginia Press.

Humpherys, Anne, and Louis James, eds. 2008. *G. W. M. Reynolds*. Aldershot: Ashgate.

Husserl, Edmund. 1970. »The Life-Worlds and the World of Science.« In *The Crisis of European Sciences and Transcendental Phenomenology: An Introduction to Phenomenological Philosophy*, translated by David Carr, 379-84. Evanston: Northwestern University Press.

Hyde, Ralph. 1988. *Panoramania! The Art and Entertainment of the »All-Embracing« View*. London: Trefoil.

Iggers, Georg G. 2011. »The Intellectual Foundations of Nineteenth-Century ›Scientific‹ History: The German Model.« In *The Oxford History of Historical Writing*, edited by Stuart Macintyre, Juan Maiguashca, and Attila Pók, 4: 1800 – 1945: 41-58. Oxford: Oxford University Press.

»Illustrations of Jewish Customs.« 1866. *Leisure Hour* 3 February-29 December (9 parts).

»An Incident at the Hotel de Rambouillet.« 1852. *Leisure Hour* 10 June: 369-73.

»Incidents of Irish Railway Scenery.« 1854. *Leisure Hour* 17 August 1854-26 April 1855 (3 parts).

Ingall, F. M. 1866. *Historical and Geographical Enigmas, Consisting of Interesting Exercises on Ancient and Modern History and Geography*. London: Suter, Alexander, & Co.

»In Memoriam.« 1860. *Good Words* 8 January: 19-23.

Ives, Keith A. 2011. *Voice of Nonconformity: William Robertson Nicoll and the British Weekly*. Cambridge: Lutterworth Press.

Jahn, Manfred. 2005. *Narratology: A Guide to the Theory of Narrative.* http://www.uni-koeln.de/~ame02/pppn.htm#N2.3 (accessed 18 August 2015). English Department, University of Cologne.

James, Louis. 1982. »›The Trouble with Betsy‹: Periodicals and the Common Reader in Mid-Nineteenth-Century England.« In *The Victorian Periodical Press: Samplings and Soundings*, edited by Joanne Shattock and Michael Wolff, 349-66. Leicester: Leicester University Press.

Jann, Rosemary. 1985. *The Art and Science of Victorian History*. Columbus: Ohio State University Press.

»Japanese.« 1859. *Leisure Hour* 3-24 February (3 parts).

[Jerdan, William]. 1859-65. »Men I Have Known.« *Leisure Hour* 20 October 1859-28 October 1865 (45 parts).

Jerdan, William. 1866. *Men I Have Known*. London: George Routledge and Sons.

[Jerdan, William]. 1868-69. »Characteristic Letters.« *Leisure Hour* 29 February 1868-18 December 1869 (24 parts).

J.H. 1876. »The Rev. John Stoughton, D.D.« *Sunday at Home* 25 March: 199-203.

»John Evangelist Gossner.« 1860. *Good Words* 18 March-29 April (2 parts).

Johnson, Samuel. 1765. *Mr. Johnson's Preface to His Edition of Shakespear's Plays*. London.

Johnson, Samuel. 1864. »Dr. Johnson's Preface to Shakespeare.« *Leisure Hour* 16 April: 255-56.

Johnson-Woods, Toni. 2000. »The Virtual Reading Communities of the London Journal, the New York Ledger, and the Australian Journal.« In *Nineteenth-Century Media and the Construction of Identities*, edited by Laurel Brake, Bill Bell, and David Finkelstein, 350-61. Basingstoke: Macmillan.

»John Woolman.« 1860. *Good Words* 30 September-4 November (2 parts).

[Jones, Harry]. 1863. »The Regular Swiss Round.« *Leisure Hour* 2 May-25 July (13 parts).

[Jones, Harry]. 1864. »Another Swiss Round.« *Leisure Hour* 2 July-27 August (9 parts).

[Jones, Harry]. 1865a. »The Idler on the Rhine.« *Leisure Hour* 17 June-12 August (9 parts).

Jones, Harry. 1865b. *The Regular Swiss Round in Three Trips*. London: Alexander Strahan.

[Jones, Harry]. 1869. »A Walk in South Devon.« *Leisure Hour* 3-31 July (5 parts).

Jones, Jason B. 2006. *Lost Causes: Historical Consciousness in Victorian Literature*. Columbus: Ohio State University Press.

Jones, William. 1850. *The Jubilee Memorial of the Religious Tract Society: Containing a Record of Its Origin, Proceedings, and Results. A.D. 1799 to A.D. 1849*. London: Religious Tract Society.

Jordan, John O., and Robert L. Platten, eds. 1995. *Literature in the Marketplace: Nineteenth-Century British Publishing and Reading Practices*. Cambridge: Cambridge University Press.

Jordanova, Ludmilla. 2000. *History in Practice*. London: Arnold.

Jordanova, Ludmilla. 2012. *The Look of the Past: Visual and Material Evidence in Historical Practice*. Cambridge: Cambridge University Press.

»A Journey by Sinai to Syria.« 1860. *Good Words* 22 January-29 December (7 parts).

»Juan Diaz.« 1860. *Leisure Hour* 20 September: 602-5.

»Jubilee Number: Completion of Fiftieth Year of ›The Leisure Hour.‹« 1902. *Leisure Hour* January.

Kaye, John William. 1856. *The Life and Correspondence of Major-General Sir John Malcolm, G.C.B., Late Envoy to Persia, and Governor of Bombay; from Unpublished Letters and Journals*. 2 vols. London: Smith, Elder, and Co.

Keller, Reiner. 2008. *Wissenssoziologische Diskursanalyse: Grundlegung eines Forschungsprogramms*. Wiesbaden: VS Verlag für Sozialwissenschaften.

Kelleter, Frank, ed. 2012. *Populäre Serialität: Narration – Evolution – Distinktion*. Bielefeld: Transcript.

»Kentigern.« 1860. *Good Words* 26 February: 129-32.

»Kew Gardens.« 1862. *Leisure Hour* 5-26 July (4 parts).

King, Andrew. 2000. »A Paradigm of Reading the Victorian Penny Weekly: Education of the Gaze and *The London Journal*.« In *Nineteenth-Century Media and the Construction of Identities*, edited by Bill Bell, Laurel Brake, and David Finkelstein, 77-92. Basingstoke: Palgrave.

King, Andrew. 2002. »Sympathy as Subversion? Reading *Lady Audley's Secret* in the Kitchen.« *Journal of Victorian Culture* 7 (1): 60-85.

King, Andrew. 2004. *The* London Journal, *1845-83: Periodicals, Production and Gender*. Aldershot: Ashgate.

King, Andrew. 2008. »The *London Journal*, 1845-1883.« *Victorian Fiction Research Guides*. http://www.victoriansecrets.co.uk/victorian-fiction-research-guides/ (accessed 18 August 2015).

King, Andrew. 2009. »*London Journal; and Weekly Record of Literature, Science and Art* (1845-1928).« In *Dictionary of Nineteenth Century Journalism in Great Britain and Ireland*, edited by Laurel Brake and Marysa Demoor, 374-75. Ghent: Academia Press.

King, Andrew. 2011. »›Literature of the Kitchen‹: Cheap Serial Fiction of the 1840s and 1850s.« In *A Companion to Sensation Fiction*, edited by Pamela K. Gilbert, 38-53. Chichester: Blackwell.

King, Andrew, and John Plunkett, eds. 2004. *Popular Print Media, 1820-1900*. Vol. 1. 3 vols. London: Routledge.

[Kingston, William Henry Giles]. 1865-68. »James Braithwaite the Supercargo.« *Leisure Hour* 4 July 1865-24 October 1868 (17 parts).

Kingston, William Henry Giles. 1882. *James Braithwaite, the Supercargo: The Story of His Adventures, etc.* London: Hodder & Stoughton.

Kirkpatrick, Robert J. 2013. *From the Penny Dreadful to the Ha'Penny Dreadfuller: A Bibliographic History of the Boys' Periodical in Britain, 1762 – 1950*. London: British Library.

»The Knight of Eskdale.« 1857. *Leisure Hour* 7-28 May (4 parts).

Kooistra, Lorraine Janzen. 2014. »›Making Poetry‹ in *Good Words*: Why Illustration Matters to Periodical Poetry Studies.« *Victorian Poetry* 52 (1): 111-39.

Körber, Philipp. 1851. *Feodor Golowin's Verbannung nach Sibirien: unterhaltende und belehrende Erzählungen für die Jugend*. Nürnberg: J.L. Lotzbeck.

[Körber, Philipp]. 1855. »Golowin's Banishment to Siberia.« *Leisure Hour* 4 January-22 February (8 parts).

Korte, Barbara. 2015a. »Between Fashion and Feminism: History in Mid-Victorian Women's Magazines.« *English Studies* 96 (4): 424-43.

Korte, Barbara. 2015b. »From Picturesque to Political: Transcultural Perspectives on Germany in Victorian Popular Periodicals, 1850 to 1875.« *German Life and Letters* 68 (3): 356-69.

Korte, Barbara, and Doris Lechner. 2014. *Popular History in Victorian Magazines Database (PHVM)*. http://phvm.ub.uni-freiburg.de/ (accessed 18 August 2015). University Library at University of Freiburg.

Korte, Barbara, and Sylvia Paletschek. 2009. »Geschichte in populären Medien und Genres: Vom Historischen Roman zum Computerspiel.« In *History Goes Pop: Zur Repräsentation von Geschichte in populären Medien und Genres*, edited by Barbara Korte and Sylvia Paletschek, 9-60. Bielefeld: transcript.

Korte, Barbara, and Sylvia Paletschek. 2012. »Nineteenth-Century Magazines and Historical Cultures in Britain and Germany: Exploratory Notes on a Comparative Approach.« In *Popular History Now and Then: International Perspectives.*, edited by Barbara Korte and Sylvia Paletschek, 73-103. Bielefeld: transcript.

Korte, Barbara, and Sylvia Paletschek. 2013. »Blick zurück nach vorn: (Frauen-) Geschichte in feministischen Zeitschriften des 19. Jahrhunderts in Großbritannien und Deutschland.« In *Geschlecht und Geschichte in populären Medien*, edited by Elisabeth Cheauré, Sylvia Paletschek, and Nina Reusch, 105-36. Bielefeld: transcript.

Korte, Barbara, and Eva Ulrike Pirker. 2011. *Black History – White History: Britain's Historical Programme between Windrush and Wilberforce*. Bielefeld: transcript.

Kreisel, Deanna. 2012. *Economic Woman: Demand, Gender, and Narrative Closure in Eliot and Hardy*. Toronto: University of Toronto Press.

»A Lady's Journey Through Spain.« 1868. *Leisure Hour* 12 September-21 November (13 parts).

»The Lady Traveller.« 1852. *Leisure Hour* 29 January: 69-72.

»The Last Prayer of Gustavus Adolphus.« 1860. *Leisure Hour* 12 April: 232-34.

Latané, David E. 2013. *William Maginn and the British Press: A Critical Biography*. Farnham: Ashgate.

»The Late William Lennie, of Edinburgh.« 1852. *Leisure Hour* 23 September: 619-21.

»Latimer at the Pulpit.« 1860. *Good Words* 11 March-13 May (2 parts).

Law, Graham. 2000. *Serializing Fiction in the Victorian Press*. Basingstoke: Palgrave.

Law, Graham. 2009a. »Anonymity and Signature.« In *Dictionary of Nineteenth Century Journalism in Great Britain and Ireland*, edited by Laurel Brake and Marysa Demoor, 18-19. Ghent: Academia Press.

Law, Graham. 2009b. »Family Paper.« In *Dictionary of Nineteenth Century Journalism in Great Britain and Ireland*, edited by Laurel Brake and Marysa Demoor, 214-15. Ghent: Academia Press.

Leader. 1859. 16 July: 852.

Leary, Patrick. 2005. »Googling the Victorians.« *Journal of Victorian Culture* 10 (1): 72-86.

Leary, Patrick. 2010. *The* Punch *Brotherhood: Table Talk and Print Culture in Mid-Victorian London.* London: The British Library.

Lechner, Doris. 2013. »Serializing the Past in and out of the *Leisure Hour*: Historical Culture and the Negotiation of Media Boundaries.« *Mémoires Du Livre / Studies in Book Culture* 4 (2): http://id.erudit.org/iderudit/1016740ar (accessed 18 August 2015).

Ledbetter, Kathryn. 2009. *British Victorian Women's Periodicals: Beauty, Civilization, and Poetry.* Basingstoke: Palgrave.

Léger-St-Jean, Marie. 2015 [2010]. *Price One Penny: A Database of Cheap Literature, 1837-1860.* http://www.priceonepenny.info/ (accessed 18 August 2015). Faculty of English, Cambridge.

»Leipsic Fair.« 1863. *Leisure Hour* 4-25 April (4 parts).

»The Lessons of Biography.« 1852. *Leisure Hour* 1-29 July (5 parts).

»Letters Patent.« 1864. *Leisure Hour* 4-25 June (4 parts).

Levine, Philippa. 1986. *The Amateur and the Professional: Antiquarians, Historians and Archaeologists in Victorian England; 1838-1886.* Cambridge: Cambridge University Press.

Lewis, Georgina. 1897. »John Stoughton, D.D.: Personal Reminiscences by His Daughter.« *Sunday at Home* 145: 184-86.

Lewis, Georgina. 1898. *John Stoughton, D.D.: A Short Record of a Long Life.* London: Hodder & Stoughton.

Liddle, Dallas. 2009. *The Dynamics of Genre: Journalism and the Practice of Literature in Mid-Victorian Britain.* Charlottesville: University of Virginia Press.

»The Life of a Remarkable Man.« 1852. *Leisure Hour* 16 December: 814-16.

»Lines Suggested by Reading of John Howard's Death in the Crimea.« 1855. *Leisure Hour* 19 July: 463.

Lingelbach, Gabriele. 2011. »The Institutionalization and Professionalization of History in Europe and the United States.« In *The Oxford History of Historical Writing*, edited by Stuart Macintyre, Juan Maiguashca, and Attila Pók, 4: 1800 – 1945: 78-96. Oxford: Oxford University Press.

Literary Gazette. 1857. 18 July: 674.

Literary Gazette. 1858. 17 July: 77-78.

»Literature.« 1863. *Christian Witness* 10: 140.

»Literature of the People.« 1859. *London Review* 13 (25): 1-31.

Lloyd, Amy. 2009. »*Good Words* (1860-1911).« In *Dictionary of Nineteenth Century Journalism in Great Britain and Ireland*, edited by Laurel Brake and Marysa Demoor, 254. Ghent: Academia Press.

Lloyd, Amy, and Graham Law. 2009. »*Leisure Hour* (1852-1905).« In *Dictionary of Nineteenth Century Journalism in Great Britain and Ireland*, edited by Laurel Brake and Marysa Demoor, 356-57. Ghent: Academia Press.

Logan, Deborah A., ed. 2012. *Harriet Martineau and the Irish Question: Condition of Post-Famine Ireland*. Bethlehem: Lehigh University Press.

»London a Century Ago.« 1857. *Leisure Hour* 19 November-10 December (3 parts).

»London the Stronghold of England.« 1860. *Cornhill Magazine* I, June: 641-51.

»Lord Chancellor Clarendon.« 1860. *Leisure Hour* 24 May: 326-27.

»Lord Clarendon's Statue in the Palace of Westminster.« 1852. *London Journal* 26 June: 245-46.

»Lord Clive.« 1860. *Leisure Hour* 8 March: 153-54.

»Lord Dundonald.« 1860. *Leisure Hour* 19 April: 250-53.

»Lord Falkland's Statue in the Palace of Westminster.« 1852. *London Journal* 19 June: 236-37.

»Lord George Bentinck.« 1852. *Leisure Hour* 27 May: 346-49.

»Lord Macaulay.« 1860. *Leisure Hour* 1 March: 135-38.

»The Lyonese Weaver.« 1852. *Leisure Hour* 5 February: 85-87.

»Lyons and Its Cathedral.« 1852. *London Journal* 17 July: 293-95.

»Macaulay.« 1856. *Leisure Hour* 31 January-21 August (4 parts).

Macaulay, James. 1894. »Dr. Stoughton's *Recollections*.« *Sunday at Home* 26 May: 473-76.

Macaulay, Thomas Babington. 1849. *The History of England: From the Accession of James the Second*. Vol. 2. Leipzig: B. Tauchnitz.

Macintyre, Stuart, Juan Maiguashca, and Attila Pók, eds. 2011. *The Oxford History of Historical Writing*. Vol. 4: 1800–1945. Oxford: Oxford University Press.

Mackay, Charles. 1852. »Mourn for the Mighty Dead.« *London Journal* 20 November: 166.

Mackenzie, Hazel, and Ben Winyard, eds. 2013. *Charles Dickens and the Mid-Victorian Press, 1850–1870*. Buckingham: University of Buckingham Press.

M[a]cL[eod], N[orman]. 1860. »The Gold[en] Thread.« *Good Words* 5-19 August (3 parts).

Madden, Richard Robert. 1855. *The Literary Life and Correspondence of the Countess of Blessington*. 3 vols. London: T.C. Newby.

Maidment, Brian. 2001. *Reading Popular Prints, 1790-1870*. Manchester: Manchester University Press.

Maidment, Brian. 2013. *Comedy, Caricature and the Social Order, 1820–50*. Manchester: Manchester University Press.

Maidment, Brian, and Aled Jones. 2009. »Illustration.« In *A Dictionary of Nineteenth Century Journalism in Great Britain and Ireland*, edited by Laurel Brake and Marysa Demoor, 304-6. Ghent: Academia Press.

[Maitland, James Alexander]. 1866. »The Great Van Broek Property.« *Leisure Hour* 6 January-30 June (26 parts).

Maitland, James Alexander. 1867. *Captain Jack: Or, The Great Van Broek Property: A Story*. London: Tinsley.

[Maitland, James Alexander]. 1868. »The Mortons of Morton Hall.« *Leisure Hour* 4 January-11 July (28 parts).

Maitzen, Rohan Amanda. 1998. *Gender, Genre, and Victorian Historical Writing*. New York: Garland.

Mandler, P. 1997. »»In the Olden Time‹: Romantic History and the English National Identity.« In *A Union of Multiple Identities: The British Isles, c.1750-c.1850*, edited by Laurence W. Brockliss and David Eastwood, 78-92. Manchester and New York: Manchester University Press.

»The Man in the Iron Mask.« 1870. *Leisure Hour* 28 May-17 December (3 parts).

»A Man of Letters of the Last Generation.« 1860. *Cornhill Magazine* I, January: 85-96.

»The Man of Ross.« 1860. *Leisure Hour* 12 July: 438-41.

»Map of Stratford-on-Avon and Surrounding Country.« 1864. *Leisure Hour* 16 April: 256.

»Margate and Its Environs.« 1852. *Leisure Hour* 29 July: 481-85.

»The ›Marseillaise‹ and Its Author.« 1852. *Leisure Hour* 22 July: 472-73.

»Marxburg, on the Rhine.« 1852. *London Journal* 20 March: 25-26.

Mason, Nicholas. 2013. *Literary Advertising and the Shaping of British Romanticism*. Baltimore: Johns Hopkins University Press.

Maunder, Andrew. 1999. »»Discourses of Distinction‹: The Reception of the *Cornhill Magazine*, 1859-60.« *Victorian Periodicals Review* 32 (3): 239-58.

Mayring, Philipp. 2007. *Qualtiative Inhaltsanalyse: Grundlagen und Techniken*. Weinheim: Beltz.

Mayring, Philipp, and Michaela Gläser-Zikuda. 2005. *Die Praxis der Qualitativen Inhaltsanalyse*. Weinheim: Beltz.

Mays, Kelly J. 1995. »The Disease of Reading and Victorian Periodicals.« In *Literature in the Marketplace: Nineteenth-Century British Publishing and*

Reading Practices, edited by John O. Jordan and Robert L. Platten, 165-94. Cambridge: Cambridge University Press.

Meisel, Martin. 1983. *Realizations: Narrative, Pictorial, and Theatrical Arts in Nineteenth-Century England*. Princeton: Princeton University Press.

Melman, Billie. 1993. »Gender, History and Memory: The Invention of Women's Past in the Nineteenth and Early Twentieth Centuries.« *History and Memory* 5 (1): 5-41.

Melman, Billie. 2006. *The Culture of History: English Uses of the Past, 1800-1953*. Oxford: Oxford University Press.

»Memoir of the Duke of Wellington.« 1852. *London Journal* 20 November-4 December (3 parts).

Merryweather, Frederick Somner. 1850. *Glimmerings in the Dark: Or Lights and Shadows of the Olden Time*. London: Simpkin Marshall.

M[erryweather], F[rederick] S[omner]. 1852. »The Working Man in the Olden Time.« *Leisure Hour* 1 January-11 November (6 parts).

Miller, Elizabeth Carolyn. 2013. *Slow Print: Literary Radicalism and Late Victorian Print Culture*. Stanford: Stanford University Press.

Miller, Hugh. 1847. *First Impressions of England and Its People*. London: John Johnstone.

Miller, Hugh. 1864. »Hugh Miller's Visit to Stratford-on-Avon.« *Leisure Hour* 9 April: 231-35.

Milner, Thomas. 1853. *The History of England: From the Invasions of Julius Cæsar to the Year A.D. 1852*. London: Religious Tract Society.

Milner, Thomas. 1855a. *The Crimea, Its Ancient and Modern History: The Khans, the Sultans, and the Czars, with Notices of Its Scenery and Population*. London: Longmans.

[Milner, Thomas]. 1855b. »Sketches of the Crimea.« *Leisure Hour* 15 March-10 May (5 parts).

»Missionary Sketches.« 1860. *Good Words* 25 March-21 October (6 parts).

Mitchell, Rosemary. 2000. *Picturing the Past: English History in Text and Image*. Oxford: Clarendon Press.

Mitchell, Sally. 1989. *The Fallen Angel: Chastity, Class and Women's Reading 1835-1880*. Bowling Green: Bowling Green University Popular Press.

»Mont St. Michel.« 1852. *London Journal* 28 February: 409-10.

Morrison, Robert, and Daniel S. Roberts, eds. 2013. *Romanticism and* Blackwood's Magazine: *»An Unprecedented Phenomenon.«* Houndmills: Palgrave Macmillan.

»The Mother of the Czar.« 1854. *Leisure Hour* 21 December: 811-13.

»Mr. Alfred C. Hobbs.« 1852. *London Journal* 10 April: 77-78.

»Mr. Joshua Silsbee.« 1852. *London Journal* 3 April: 61-61.

Murphy, Andrew. 2008. *Shakespeare for the People*. Cambridge: Cambridge University Press.

Murray, Frank. 2009. »Gilbert, John (1817-1897).« In *Dictionary of Nineteenth Century Journalism in Great Britain and Ireland*, edited by Laurel Brake and Marysa Demoor, 248. Ghent: Academia Press.

Mussell, James. 2007. *Science, Time and Space in the Late Nineteenth-Century Periodical Press: Movable Types*. Aldershot: Ashgate.

Mussell, James. 2009. »New Journalism.« In *Dictionary of Nineteenth Century Journalism in Great Britain and Ireland*, edited by Laurel Brake and Marysa Demoor, 443. Ghent: Academia Press.

Mussell, James. 2012. *The Nineteenth-Century Press in the Digital Age*. Basingstoke: Palgrave.

Myers, Robin, and Michael Harris, eds. 1993. *Serials and Their Readers, 1620-1914*. Winchester: St Paul's Bibliographies.

Nash, Sarah. 2010. »What's in a Name? Signature, Criticism, and Authority in *The Fortnightly Review*.« *Victorian Periodicals Review* 43 (1): 57-82.

»The Natural History of Dress.« 1870. *Leisure Hour* 29 January-3 December (14 parts).

»Neckar Steinach.« 1852. *London Journal* 29 May: 185-86.

»The Nelson Column, Trafalgar Square.« 1852. *London Journal* 23 October: 104.

Neumann, Birgit, and Martin Zierold. 2010. »Media as Ways of Worldmaking: Media-Specific Structures and Intermedial Dynamics.« In *Cultural Ways of Worldmaking: Media and Narratives*, edited by Vera Nünning, Ansgar Nünning, and Birgit Neumann, 103-18. Berlin: De Gruyter.

»New Weekly Periodical: The *Leisure Hour*.« 1852. *Christian Spectator* 21 January: 682.

Nicholson, Bob. 2012. »›You Kick the Bucket; We Do the Rest!‹: Jokes and the Culture of Reprinting in the Transatlantic Press.« *Journal of Victorian Culture* 17 (3): 273-86.

»Niebuhr and His ›Milly.‹« 1852. *Leisure Hour* 1 April: 215-16.

Nieritz, [Carl] Gustav. 1843. *Die protestantischen Salzburger und deren Vertreibung durch den Fürst-Erzbischof von Firmian: als Beispiel christlicher Duldung und Glaubensfestigkeit für evangelische Familienkreise und deren reifere Jugend erzählt*. Leipzig: Wöller.

Nieritz, [Carl] Gustav. 1853. *Die Hussiten vor Naumburg: eine geschichtliche Erzählung aus dem fünfzehnten Jahrhundert*. Berlin: Simion.

[Nieritz, Carl Gustav]. 1856. »The Weaver of Naumburg; Or, the Triumphs of Meekness.« *Leisure Hour* 3 July-4 September (10 parts).

[Nieritz, Carl Gustav]. 1868. »The Exiles of Salzburg.« *Leisure Hour* 24 October-26 December (10 parts).

[Nieritz, Carl Gustav]. [1874]. *The Weaver of Naumburg; Or, a City Saved by Children*. London: RTS.

Nieritz, Carl Gustav. 1880. *The Exiles of Salzburg and Other Stories: Translated from the German by Mrs. L. H. Kerr*. London: Religious Tract Society.

»A Night in the Bush.« 1860. *Leisure Hour* 30 August: 545-48.

»Nil Nisi Bonum.« 1860. *Cornhill Magazine* I, February: 129-34.

»Nineveh Antiquities.« 1852. *London Journal* 6 March-3 April (2 parts).

Nissen, Martin. 2009. *Populäre Geschichtsschreibung*. Cologne: Böhlau.

Nora, Pierre. 1990. *Zwischen Geschichte und Gedächtnis*. Berlin: Wagenbach.

North, John S., ed. 2003. *Waterloo Directory of English Newspapers and Periodicals 1800-1900, Series 2*. 20 vols. Waterloo: North Waterloo Academic Press. Available online: http://www.victorianperiodicals.com/series2 /default.asp (accessed 18 August 2015).

Nünning, Ansgar, and Vera Nünning. 2010. »Ways of Worldmaking as a Model for the Study of Culture: Theoretical Frameworks, Epistemological Underpinnings, New Horizons.« In *Cultural Ways of Worldmaking: Media and Narratives*, edited by Vera Nünning, Ansgar Nünning, and Birgit Neumann, 1-25. Berlin: De Gruyter.

ODNB Oxford Dictionary of National Biography. 2004-2015. http://www. oxforddnb.com (accessed 18 August 2015). Oxford University Press.

O'Hanlon, W. M. 1851. *The Operative Classes of Great Britain: Their Existing State and Its Improvement*. Religious Tract Society.

[Oliphant, Margaret]. 1858. »The Byways of Literature: Reading for the Million.« *Blackwood's Edinburgh Magazine* 84 (August): 200-216.

»Our Scandinavian Ancestors.« 1860. *Good Words* 29 April: 273-77.

»Our Second Day at Brighton.« 1852. *Leisure Hour* 9 September: 582-84.

»The Overland Route to India.« 1857. *Leisure Hour* 5 November-31 December (9 parts).

Page, Jesse. 1891. »The Late William Haig Miller.« *Sunday at Home* 28 November: 58-61.

»A Page in the Chronicles of Versailles.« 1852. *Leisure Hour* 25 November: 761-64.

Paletschek, Sylvia, and Sylvia Schraut, eds. 2008. *The Gender of Memory: Cultures of Remembrance in Nineteenth- and Twentieth-Century Europe*. Frankfurt/Main: Campus.

Palmegiano, E. M. 2009. »The First Common Market: The British Press on Nineteenth-Century European Journalism.« *Media History Monographs* 11 (1): 1-44.

Palmer, Beth. 2009. »Religious Tract Society.« In *Dictionary of Nineteenth Century Journalism in Great Britain and Ireland*, edited by Laurel Brake and Marysa Demoor, 535. Ghent: Academia Press.

Palmer, Beth. 2011. *Women's Authorship and Editorship in Victorian Culture: Sensational Strategies*. Oxford: Oxford University Press.

Palmer, Beth, and Adelene Buckland, eds. 2011. *A Return to the Common Reader: Print Culture and the Novel, 1850-1900*. Farnham: Ashgate.

»A Passage in the Life of General Victoria.« 1852. *Leisure Hour* 10 June: 382-83.

»Pastor Harms of Hermannsburg.« 1860. *Good Words* 21 October-2 December (4 parts).

»Past *versus* Present.« 1860. *Leisure Hour* 19 April: 255-56.

Patten, Robert L. 2012a. *Charles Dickens and »Boz«: The Birth of the Industrial Age Author*. Cambridge: Cambridge University Press.

Patten, Robert L., ed. 2012b. *Dickens and Victorian Print Cultures*. Farnham: Ashgate.

Patterson, Anthony. 2013. *Mrs. Grundy's Enemies: Censorship, Realist Fiction and the Politics of Sexual Representation*. Oxford: Peter Lang.

Pattison, S[amuel] R[owles]. 1866. »Celts.« *Leisure Hour* 14 April-22 November (3 parts).

Pattison, S[amuel] R[owles]. 1867. »The Volcanoes of Auvergne.« *Leisure Hour* 14-28 September (3 parts).

»The Peasant-Nobles; Or, the Bethune Brothers.« 1852. *Leisure Hour* 9-16 September (2 parts).

»The Peninsular Veterans' Testimonial to the Duke of Richmond.« 1852. *London Journal* 7 February: 357.

»Periodical Literature: A New Weekly Magazine.« 1851. *Christian Spectator* 19 November: 663-65.

»Periodical Peeps at Female Costume in England.« 1867. *Leisure Hour* 17 August-7 December (5 parts).

»Periodicals.« 1851. *Christian Spectator* 1 August: 339.

»The Perkin Warbeck of Russian History.« 1855. *Leisure Hour* 22 March: 182-83.

»Personal History of Shakespeare: Stat Magni Nominis Umbra!« 1864. *Leisure Hour* 23 April: 262-63.

Phegley, Jennifer. 2004. *Educating the Proper Woman Reader: Victorian Family Literary Magazine and the Cultural Health of the Nation.* Columbus: Ohio State University Press.

Phegley, Jennifer. 2009. »*Cornhill Magazine* (1860-1975).« In *Dictionary of Nineteenth Century Journalism in Great Britain and Ireland*, edited by Laurel Brake and Marysa Demoor, 145. Ghent: Academia Press.

»The Philadelphia Printer.« 1854. *Leisure Hour* 7-21 December (3 parts).

Phillips, Mark Salber. 2000. *Society and Sentiment: Genres of Historical Writing in Britain, 1740-1820.* Princeton: Princeton University Press.

Pickering, Paul A., and Alex Tyrrell. 2004. *Contested Sites: Commemoration, Memorial and Popular Politics in Nineteenth-Century Britain.* Aldershot: Ashgate.

»Pictures from the History and Life of the Early Church.« 1860. *Good Words* 9 September-18 November (3 parts).

»Pictures in Words; Or, Scenes from English History.« 1858. *Leisure Hour* 6 May-21 October (4 parts).

Pier, John. 2010 [2005]. »Metalepsis.« In *Routledge Encyclopedia of Narrative Theory*, edited by David Herman, Manfred Jahn, and Marie-Laure Ryan, 303-4. London: Routledge.

Pittard, Christopher. 2011. *Purity and Contamination in Late Victorian Detective Fiction.* Farnham: Ashgate.

Plunkett, John. 2003. *Queen Victoria: First Media Monarch.* Oxford: Oxford University Press.

»Poccahontas [sic]: A Story of the First English Emigrants to North America, Founded on Fact.« 1852. *Leisure Hour* 9-30 September (4 parts).

»Poccahontas: Eine Indianische Geschichte.« 1855. *Pfennig-Magazin* 22 November-13 December (4 parts).

»Popular Literature of the Day.« 1840. *British and Foreign Review* 10 (January): 223-46.

Porciani, Ilaria, and Lutz Raphael, eds. 2010. *Atlas of European Historiography: The Making of a Profession 1800-2005.* Basingstoke: Palgrave.

»The Presidential Election in America: Good Old Abe.« 1860. *Leisure Hour* 29 November: 765-66.

»The President of the Social Science Conference.« 1860. *Leisure Hour* 18 October: 665.

Prince, Kathryn. 2008. *Shakespeare in the Victorian Periodicals.* New York: Routledge.

»Prince Metternich.« 1860. *Leisure Hour* 26 January: 59-61.

»Prince Michael Woronzoff.« 1854. *Leisure Hour* 28 December: 820-23.

»Pure Literature.« 1856. *Saturday Review* 2 (27): 16-17.

Pykett, Lyn. 1989. »Reading the Periodical Press: Text and Context.« Edited by Laurel Brake and Anne Humpherys. *Victorian Periodicals Review, Special Issue: Theory* 22 (3): 100-108.

»The Queen of a Literary Coterie.« 1855. *Leisure Hour* 7-21 June (3 parts).

»Rambles in the Isle of Wight.« 1852. *Leisure Hour* 16-30 September (2 parts).

»A Ramble to Fountains Abbey.« 1852. *Leisure Hour* 3 June: 353-56.

Ray, Gordon Norton. 1992. *The Illustrator and the Book in England from 1790 to 1914*. Courier Dover Publications.

»Recollection of Professor Wilson.« 1860. *Good Words* 22 April: 263-67.

»Recollections of Cronstadt.« 1855. *Leisure Hour* 9 August: 508-12.

»Reference Map of Sicily.« 1860. *Leisure Hour* 28 June: 416.

»The Refugees of the Black Forest.« 1853. *Leisure Hour* 1 January-17 February (8 parts).

Reid, Forrest. 1975. *Illustrators of the Eighteen Sixties: An Illustrated Survey of the Work of 58 British Artists*. New York: Dover Publications.

Religious Tract Society. 1851. *The Fifty-Second Annual Report*. Vol. 52. London: RTS.

Religious Tract Society. 1859. *The Sixtieth Annual Report*. Vol. 60. London: RTS.

»Remarkable Boys.« 1852. *Leisure Hour* 19 August-23 December, (2 parts).

Report from the Select Committee on Newspaper Stamps: Together with the Proceedings of the Committee, Minutes of Evidence, Appendix, and Index. 1969 [1851]. Shannon: Irish University Press.

»Representative Characters of the Renaissance.« 1862. *Leisure Hour* 13 February-5 July (6 parts).

Reusch, Nina. 2015. *Populäre Geschichte im Kaiserreich: Familienzeitschriften als Akteure der deutschen Geschichtskultur 1890-1913*. Bielefeld: transcript.

Reusch, Nina, and Doris Lechner. 2013. »Klio in neuen Kleidern: Geschichte in Familienzeitschriften des 19. Jahrhunderts im deutsch-britischen Vergleich.« In *Geschlecht und Geschichte in populären Medien*, edited by Elisabeth Cheauré, Sylvia Paletschek, and Nina Reusch, 83-103. Bielefeld: transcript.

»Robert Stephenson.« 1860. *Leisure Hour* 8-15 November (2 parts).

Robinson, Ainslie. 1999. »Invoking the Bard: The *Cornhill Magazine* and *Revival* in the Victorian Theatre, 1863.« *Victorian Periodicals Review* 32 (3): 259-68.

»Roger Payne, the Bookbinder.« 1852. *Leisure Hour* 8 April: 230-31.

Rüsen, Jörn. 2006. »Introduction: What Does ›Making Sense of History‹ Mean?« In *Meaning and Representation in History*, edited by Jörn Rüsen, 7: 1-5. Making Sense of History. New York: Berghahn Books.

Russell, John. 1859. *The Life and Times of Charles James Fox*. London: Richard Bentley.

»Russia.« 1854. *Leisure Hour* 5-26 October (4 parts).

»Russia as I Saw It Forty Years Ago.« 1855. *Leisure Hour* 29 November: 758-59.

»A Russian Aesop.« 1854. *Leisure Hour* 28 September: 619-20.

»Russian Campaigns in Turkey in 1828 and 1829.« 1854. *Leisure Hour* 20 July: 455-58.

»Russian Literature.« 1855. *Leisure Hour* 5 July: 425-28.

»Russ Pictures.« 1865. *Leisure Hour* 9 September-14 October (7 parts).

[Sala, August]. 1860. »William Hogarth: Painter, Engraver, and Philosopher. Essays on the Man, the Work, and the Time.« *Cornhill Magazine* I-II, February-October (9 parts).

Salmon, Richard. 2013. *The Formation of the Victorian Literary Profession*. Cambridge: Cambridge University Press.

Sánchez Marcos, Fernando. 2009. »Historical Culture.« *Culturahistorica.es*. http://www.culturahistorica.es/sanchez_marcos/historical%20_culture.pdf (accessed 18 August 2015).

[Sargent, George Eliel]. 1858. »The Indian Nabob; Or, A Hundred Years Ago.« *Leisure Hour* 7 January-8 July (27 parts).

[Sargent, George Eliel]. 1860. »Ralph Draper.« *Leisure Hour* 19 July-23 August (6 parts).

[Sargent, George Eliel]. 1863. »The Franklins; Or, the Story of a Convict.« *Leisure Hour* 3 January-27 June (26 parts).

Sargent, G[eorge] E[liel]. 1866. »George Burley; His History, Experiences, and Observations.« *Leisure Hour* 7 July-29 December (26 parts).

Sargent, George Eliel. 1869. *George Burley: His History, Experiences, and Observations*. London: Religious Tract Society.

Sargent, George Eliel. 1882. *The Franklins: Or, The Story of a Convict*. London: The Religious Tract Society.

Schmidt, Barbara Quinn. 1980. »The *Cornhill Magazine*: The Relationship of Editor, Publisher, Chief Novelist and Audience.« Ph.D. dissertation, Missouri: Saint Louis University.

»School Recollections.« 1861. *Leisure Hour* 2-30 May (5 parts).

Schwartz, Vanessa R., and Jeannene M. Przyblyski. 2004. *The Nineteenth-Century Visual Culture Reader*. Routledge.

Science in the Nineteenth-Century Periodical: An Electronic Index, v. 3.0. 2007 [2005]. http://www.sciper.org (accessed 18 August 2015). hriOnline.

[Scoffern, John]. 1857. »Chemists.« *Leisure Hour* 25 June-15 October (3 parts).

Scoffern, J[ohn]. 1858 [1850]. *Projectile Weapons of War, and Explosive Compounds*. London: Longman.

Scoffern, John. 1870. *Stray Leaves of Science and Folk-Lore*. London: Tinsley Brothers.

Scott, Tania. 2010. »*Good Words*: At the Back of the North Wind and the Periodical Press.« *North Wind: Journal of George MacDonald Studies* 29: 40-51.

»Search for Sir John Franklin.« 1860. *Cornhill Magazine* I, January: 96-121.

Secord, James A. 2000. *Victorian Sensation: The Extraordinary Publication, Reception and Secret Authorship of »Vestiges of the Natural History of Creation.«* Chicago: University of Chicago Press.

»Selections from the Exhibition of the Industry of All Nations.« 1851-52. *London Journal* 24 May 1851-15 May 1852 (48 parts).

»A Self-Taught Linguist.« 1860. *Leisure Hour* 9 February: 90-91.

»*Shades and Echoes of Old London*.« 1864. *The Reader* 4 (94): 479-479.

»*Shades and Echoes of Old London*. By John Stoughton, D.D.« 1889. *The Practical Teacher* 9 (10, Dezember): 473.

»Shakespeare as a Moral Teacher.« 1864. *Leisure Hour* 30 April: 281-85.

»Shakespeare Portraits.« 1864. *Leisure Hour* 23 April: 264-67.

»The Shakespeare Property at Stratford.« 1864. *Leisure Hour* 30 April: 279-80.

»*Shilling Books for Leisure Hours*.« 1863. *Leisure Hour* 3 January: 830.

Shuttleworth, Sally, and Geoffrey Cantor. 2004. »Introduction.« In *Science Serialized: Representations of the Sciences in Nineteenth-Century Periodicals*, edited by Geoffrey Cantor and Sally Shuttleworth, 1-16. Cambridge: MIT.

»Signboards.« 1867. *Leisure Hour* 9 March-4 May (3 parts).

»The Singer of Eisenach.« 1852. *Leisure Hour* 2 September: 571-74.

Sinnema, Peter W. 1998. *Dynamics of the Pictured Page: Representing the Nation in the* Illustrated London News. Aldershot: Ashgate.

»Sir Henry Havelock.« 1860. *Leisure Hour* 31 May: 350-52.

»Sir Isaac Newton.« 1856. *Leisure Hour* 2 February-6 March (3 parts).

»Sir John Lawrence, G.C.B.« 1860. *Leisure Hour* 5 January: 8-13.

»Sir Joshua and Holbein.« 1860. *Cornhill Magazine* I, March: 232-328.

»Sir Robert Peel's Tamworth Statue.« 1852. *London Journal* 29 May: 189.

Smiles, Samuel. 1859. *Self-Help: With Illustrations of Character and Conduct*. London: J. Murray.

Smith, Bonnie G. 1984. »The Contribution of Women to Modern Historiography in Great Britain, France, and the United States, 1750-1940.« *American Historical Review* 89 (3): 709-32.

[Smith, J.F.]. 1851-52a. »Minnigrey.« *London Journal* 11 October 1851-2 October 1852 (52 parts).

Smith, J.F. 1852b-54. »Lives of the Queens of England.« *London Journal* 24 July 1852-4 February 1854 (76 parts).

[Smith, J.F.]. 1852c-53. »The Will and the Way.« *London Journal* 9 October 1852-3 September 1853 (48 parts).

Smith, J.F. 1853. *Romantic Incidents in the Lives of the Queens of England.* New York: Garrett.

Smith, Peter. 1969. »The *Cornhill Magazine* 1860-1870: A Consideration of Some of Its Non-Fiction Articles.« Ph.D. dissertation, York: University of York.

Soffer, Reba N. 1996. *Discipline and Power: The University, History, and Making of an English Elite, 1870-1930.* Stanford: Stanford University Press.

»Some Remarkable Old French Chateaux.« 1856. *Leisure Hour* 21 August-4 September (3 parts).

»The Song of Antioch.« 1860. *Good Words* 8 July: 433-38.

»The South Kensington Museum.« 1859. *Leisure Hour* 7-28 April (4 parts).

Srebrnik, Patricia Thomas. 1986. *Alexander Strahan: Victorian Publisher.* Ann Arbor: University of Michigan Press.

»Star-Chamber Court in the Palace at Westminster.« 1852. *London Journal* 10 July: 281.

»St Columba.« 1860. *Good Words* 17-24 June (2 parts).

»Sternberg and Liebenstein.« 1852. *London Journal* 24 April: 105-6.

»The Story of the Crooked Sixpence.« 1860. *Leisure Hour* 6 September-13 December (15 parts).

»The Story of Ninian.« 1860. *Good Words* 12 February: 97-99.

Stoughton, John. 1844. *Notices of Windsor in the Olden Time.* London: D. Bogue.

[Stoughton, John]. 1852a-53. »Shades of the Departed in Old London.« *Leisure Hour* 8 January 1852-12 May 1853 (11 parts).

[Stoughton, John]. 1852b. »A Star at the Stuart Court.« *Leisure Hour* 8 April: 225-28.

[Stoughton, John]. 1853. »The Banks of the Thames.« *Leisure Hour* 4 August-22 September (8 parts).

[Stoughton, John]. 1856. »Echoes of Westminster Hall.« *Leisure Hour* 17 April-19 June (8 parts).

[Stoughton, John]. 1859a. »Memorial Chapters: Isaac Watts.« *Sunday at Home* 4-18 August (2 parts).

[Stoughton, John]. 1859b. »A Ramble in the Tyrol.« *Leisure Hour* 1-15 September (3 parts).

[Stoughton, John]. 1859c. »Windsor Castle;« »The Neighbourhood of Windsor;« »A Summer's Day at Windsor.« *Leisure Hour* 2-30 June (5 parts).

Stoughton, John. 1862a. »The Tale of a West-End Suburb.« *Leisure Hour* 10-31 May (4 parts).

Stoughton, John. 1862b. *Windsor: A History and Description of the Castle and the Town.* London: Ward and Co.

Stoughton, John. 1864a. *Shades and Echoes of Old London.* London: Leisure Hour Office.

Stoughton, John. 1864b. »Shakespeare.« *Leisure Hour* 2 April: 215-20.

Stoughton, John. 1867. *Ecclesiastical History of England.* 5 vols. London: Jackson, Walford, and Hodder.

Stoughton, John. 1877. »The Royal Commission on Historical Manuscripts.« *Leisure Hour* 21 April-6 October (5 parts).

Stoughton, John. 1879. »The Black Forest.« *Leisure Hour* 24 May-13 September (5 parts).

Stoughton, John. 1885. »Neglected Books.« *Leisure Hour* October-November (2 parts).

Stoughton, John. 1887. »Glimpses of Queen Anne's Days.« *Leisure Hour* October-November (2 parts).

Stoughton, John. 1894. *Recollections of a Long Life.* London: Hodder & Stoughton.

Stowe, Harriet Beecher. 1854. *Sunny Memories of Foreign Lands.* 2 vols. Boston: Phillips, Sampson & Co.

Stowe, Harriet Beecher. 1864. »Mrs. Stowe's Visit to Shakespeare's House and Tomb.« *Leisure Hour* 16 April: 247-52.

»Stratford-on-Avon Church.« 1864. *Leisure Hour* 9 April: Facing 233.

Strickland, Agnes. 1840. *Lives of the Queens of England, From the Norman Conquest.* Vol. 1. 12 vols. London: Henry Colburn.

Strickland, Agnes. 1851-52 [1840-48, 12 vols.]. *Lives of the Queens of England: From the Norman Conquest.* 8 vols. London: Colburn & Co.

Strong, Roy. 2004. *Painting the Past: The Victorian Painter and British History.* London: Pimlico.

»St. Stephen's Hall, in the New Palace of Westminster.« 1852. *London Journal* 18 September: 21-22.

»Studies in History.« 1857-58. *Leisure Hour* 15 January 1857-17 June 1858 (9 parts).

Sullivan, Alvin, ed. 1984. *British Literary Magazines: The Victorian and Edwardian Age, 1837-1913*. Vol. 3. 4 vols. London: Greenwood Press.

»Summary of Neapolitan History.« 1860. *Leisure Hour* 1 October: 655-56.

»A Summer Tour in Northern Europe.« 1866. *Leisure Hour* 17 November-8 December (4 parts).

Surkamp, Carola. 2010 [2005]. »Perspective.« In *Routledge Encyclopedia of Narrative Theory*, edited by David Herman, Manfred Jahn, and Marie-Laure Ryan, 423-25. London: Routledge.

»Tales Illustrative of Chinese Life and Manners.« 1857. *Leisure Hour* 16 July-13 August (5 parts).

Taylor, Antony. 2002. »Shakespeare and Radicalism: The Uses and Abuses of Shakespeare in Nineteenth-Century Popular Politics.« *The Historical Journal* 45 (02): 357-79.

Teare, Elizabeth. 2000. »*Cornhill* Culture.« *Victorian Periodicals Review* 33 (2): 117-37.

[Thackeray, William Makepeace]. 1860a. »The Four Georges: Sketches of Manners, Morals, Court and Town Life.« *Cornhill Magazine* II, July-October (4 parts).

T[hackeray], W[illiam] M[akepeace]. 1860b. »The Last Sketch.« *Cornhill Magazine* I, April: 485-87.

[Thackeray, William Makepeace]. 1860c-1863. »Roundabout Papers.« *Cornhill Magazine* I-V, January 1860-February 1863 (28 parts).

Thomas, Julia. 2004. *Pictorial Victorians: The Inscription of Values in Word and Image*. Athens: Ohio University Press.

»Thomas Moore.« 1852. *London Journal* 17 April: 93-94.

Thompson, Nicola Diane. 1996. *Reviewing Sex*. Basingstoke: Macmillan.

[Thornbury, George Walter]. 1860. »Haunted London.« *Leisure Hour* 2 February-20 December (6 parts).

Thornbury, George Walter. 1865. *Haunted London*. London: Hurst and Blackett.

»The Three Napoleons.« 1852. *London Journal* 13 March-3 April (3 parts).

Thrush, Nanette. 2007. »Clio's Dressmakers: Women and the Uses of Historical Costume.« In *Clio's Daughters: British Women Making History, 1790-1899*, edited by Lynette Felber, 258-77. Newark: University of Delaware Press.

Tighe, Robert Richard, and James Edward Davis. 1858. *Annals of Windsor, Being a History of the Castle and Town; With Some Account of Eton and Places Adjacent*. 2 vols. London: Longman, Brown, Green, Longmans, and Roberts.

Timbs, John. 1855. *Curiosities of London: Exhibiting the Most Rare and Re-markable Objects of Interest in the Metropolis*. London: D. Bogue.

Timbs, John. 1868-73. »Curiosities of [London].« *Leisure Hour* 1 Febru-ary 1868-1 November 1873 (13 parts).

Timbs, John. 1870. »Gossip about Notable Books.« *Leisure Hour* 10-24 Sep-tember (3 parts).

»A Trip to North Devon.« 1862. *Leisure Hour* 3-31 May (5 parts).

Tupper, Martin F. 1852. »A Dirge for the Duke of Wellington.« *London Journal* 13 November: 148.

»Turner.« 1852. *London Journal* 27 March: 45-46.

Turner, Mark W. 2000. *Trollope and the Magazines: Gendered Issues in Mid-Victorian Britain*. Basingstoke: Macmillan.

Turner, Mark W. 2005. »›Telling of My Weekly Doings‹: The Material Culture of the Victorian Novel.« In *A Concise Companion to the Victorian Novel*, ed-ited by Francis O'Gorman, 113-33. Oxford: Blackwell.

»The Two Duellists.« 1852. *Leisure Hour* 19 August: 533-35.

»Two Months in Spain: By the Author of ›A Merchant's Holiday‹.« 1868. *Lei-sure Hour* 16 May-25 July (8 parts).

»The Two Scholars of Westminster.« 1852. *Leisure Hour* 8 July: 433-35.

[Tytler, Sarah]. 1860. »Lady Somerville's Maidens.« *Good Words* 5 February-14 October (24 parts).

Tytler, Sarah. 1867. *The Diamond Rose: A Life of Love and Duty*. London: Alexander Strahan.

UKPC 19th Century UK Periodicals. 2013. http://find.galegroup.com/ukpc/ (ac-cessed 18 August 2015). GALE CENGAGE Learning.

USCL/RTS CCM Copyright Committee Minutes. Archives of the United Socie-ty for Christian Literature (Religious Tract Society): School of Oriental and African Studies, London.

USCL/RTS Corr Correspondence. Archives of the United Society for Christian Literature (Religious Tract Society): School of Oriental and African Studies, London.

USCL/RTS ECM Executive Committee Minutes. Archives of the United Society for Christian Literature (Religious Tract Society): School of Oriental and Af-rican Studies, London.

USCL/RTS FCM Finance Committee Minutes. Archives of the United Society for Christian Literature (Religious Tract Society): School of Oriental and Af-rican Studies, London.

»Vancouver the Voyager.« 1860. *Leisure Hour* 12 January: 29-32.

»VII. Our Book Club.« 1864. *Eclectic Review* 7 (December): 660-66.

»Visit of Peter the Great to the Prussian Court.« 1855. *Leisure Hour* 8 February: 93-95.

»A Visit to Sebastopol in the Time of Peace.« 1855. *Leisure Hour* 31 May: 350-51.

»Visit to the Haunts of Luther.« 1852. *Leisure Hour* 11 March: 161-63.

»A Visit to the Staffordshire Potteries.« 1853. *Leisure Hour* 2-30 June (4 parts).

»The Walcheren Expedition: By One Who Survived It.« 1855. *Leisure Hour* 1-15 March (3 parts).

[Walshe, Elizabeth Hely]. 1859. »Golden Hills; Or, Single Influence: A Tale of Ribandism and the Irish Famine.« *Leisure Hour* 6 January-5 May (18 parts).

[Walshe, Elizabeth Hely]. 1860a. »The Ferrol Family; Or, Keeping up the Appearance.« *Leisure Hour* 5 January-29 March (13 parts).

[Walshe, Elizabeth Hely]. 1860b. »The Tourist in Scotland.« *Leisure Hour* 19 July-11 October (13 parts).

[Walshe, Elizabeth Hely]. 1862. »The Tourist in Ireland.« *Leisure Hour* 6 September-11 October (6 parts).

[Walshe, Elizabeth Hely]. 1864. »The Foster-Brothers of Doon; A Tale of the Irish Rebellion.« *Leisure Hour* 2 January-25 June (26 parts).

[Walshe, Elizabeth Hely]. [1865]. *Golden Hills: A Tale of the Irish Famine.* London: The Religious Tract Society.

[Walshe, Elizabeth Hely]. 1866. *The Foster-Brothers of Doon. A Tale of the Irish Rebellion of 1798. By the Author of »Golden Hills, a Tale of the Irish Famine,« Etc.* London: Religious Tract Society.

Walshe, Elizabeth Hely, and George Eliel Sargent. [1880]. *Within Sea Walls; Or, How the Dutch Kept the Faith.* London: Religious Tract Society.

»The Water-Supply of Cities and Towns.« 1866. *Leisure Hour* 6-27 October (4 parts).

Watson, Nicola J. 2007. *The Literary Tourist: Readers and Places in Romantic & Victorian Britain.* Basingstoke: Palgrave Macmillian.

WBIS World Biographical Information System Online. 2004. http://db.saur.de/ WBIS (accessed 18 August 2015). De Gruyter / K.G. Saur.

Weber, Tanja, and Christian Junklewitz. 2008. »Das Gesetz der Serie: Ansätze zur Definition und Analyse.« *MEDIENwissenschaft* 1: 13-31.

»Weekly Penny Literature.« 1858. *Monthly Christian Spectator* November: 678-88.

Werrett, Simon. 2010. »The Arsenal as Spectacle.« *Nineteenth Century Theatre and Film*, Literature Online, 37 (1): 14-22.

Whately, M[ary] L[ouisa]. 1865. »Life in Egypt.« *Leisure Hour* 14 January-12 August (7 parts).

Whately, M[ary] L[ouisa]. 1871. *Among the Huts in Egypt: Scenes from Real Life*. London: Seeley, Jackson, & Halliday.

Wiener, Joel H. 2011. *The Americanization of the British Press, 1830s–1914: Speed in the Age of Transatlantic Journalism*. Houndmills: Palgrave Macmillan.

»Wilkie and His Pictures.« 1860. *Leisure Hour* 13 September: 584-87.

»William Caxton.« 1852. *Leisure Hour* 13 May: 317-19.

Wilson, James. 1833 [1821]. *Biography of the Blind: Including the Lives of All Who Have Distinguished Themselves as Poets, Philosophers, Artists, &c. &c.*. Birmingham: W. Showell.

Winker, Gabriele, and Nina Degele. 2009. *Intersektionalität: Zur Analyse Sozialer Ungleichheiten*. Bielefeld: transcript.

»A Woman's Work.« 1860. *Good Words* 5 August: 497-500.

Woolf, Daniel. 2003. *The Social Circulation of the Past: English Historical Culture 1500-1730*. Oxford: Oxford University Press.

Woolf, D.R. 1997. »A Feminine Past? Gender, Genre, and Historical Knowledge in England, 1500 – 1800.« *The American Historical Review* 102 (3): 645-79.

»Woolwich Arsenal.« 1854. *Leisure Hour* 3 August: 487-90.

»Worms, and Its Cathedral.« 1852. *London Journal* 8 May: 137-38.

Worth, George J. 2003. Macmillan's Magazine, *1859-1907: »No Flippancy or Abuse Allowed.«* Aldershot: Ashgate.

Wynne, Deborah. 2001. *The Sensation Novel and the Victorian Family Magazine*. Basingstoke: Palgrave.

Young, George M. 1977. *Victorian England: Portrait of an Age*. Oxford: Oxford University Press.

Zimmermann, Virginia. 2008. *Excavating Victorians*. Albany: State University of New York Press.

Index

»Abraham Lincoln« 150
acrostics 158-160
Addison, J. 192, 203-204, 206
age 31, 65, 83, 147, 158-162, 163,
    187, 204, 206, 208-209, 218-219
Alison, A. 150
allegorical images: in *Good*
    Words 123-124
amateur 182, 184, 222
Among the Huts in Egypt 146
anecdote 120, 127, 150, 154, 188,
    200-201, 210, 215-218
Annals of Windsor 212-213
anonymity 37, 190n16; in *Leisure*
    Hour 40, 78n10, 143, 170-171,
    179, 181, 186, 191
»Another Swiss Round« 145
antiquarian 78, 153, 158, 182, 184,
    212
Arnold, F. 146, 182, 183
»Arthur and the Round Table« 117
authenticity 76n9, 77, 117, 124, 195,
    196n23, 199, 202, 210. *See also*
    ego-documents, re-enactment
author-function (book) 143-144, 177
authorship. *See* anonymity; historians;
    media transfer; periodicals

»Balloon and its Application,
    The« 151, 184
»Banks of the Thames, The« 186,
    210-211
Barrett, J.H. 150
Baxter, R. 192, 196-197
Bede, C. *See* Bradley, E.
Biography of the Blind 150
»Black Forest, The« 186, 214-215,
    215-216
Blackwoods 67
»Blind« 150
book (as work of reference) 155, 160,
    166, 176, 212
book counterparts. *See* media transfer
book history 33n42, 140n3
book transfer. *See* media transfer
Boswell, J. 200-201, 205
boundary work. *See* historians; *Lei-*
    sure Hour as intermediary
Bradley, E. (Bede, C.) 146, 182, 183
Brewster, D. 148
Burke, E. 192

Chambers's 46, 67
Capel, C.E. 158-159
caricatures (in *Cornhill*) 135

Cassell's 46, 63, 67
categories of disparity 14n1, 29, 34, 141, 152, 179-180, 221, 222; Victorian discourses on 28. *See also* age; class; gender; readership; religion
»Charles James Fox« 113
»Chemists« 144
Child's Companion 46
Christian Spectator 52, 53
Christian tone 52, 53, 55-56, 79, 85, 92, 120, 127, 145, 179, 185, 189, 194, 209
circuit of culture 29, 33, 221. *See also* consumption; identity; production; regulation; representation (historical)
class 14n1, 30, 78-82, 87, 94, 97-98, 167-171, 205-206, 222. *See also* readership
Clive, R. 111
close reading 32, 36. *See also* content analysis
Collins, W. 50-51
Columba 122, 124
communal reading of periodicals 37-38, 70, 161-162, 199, 202. *See also* consumption; lifeworld; readership
communicative memory 27, 163, 187
community, imagined community 15, 27, 34, 38, 55, 130. *See also* identity
consumption 19-20, 24, 27, 29, 32, 33, 41, 50, 53, 61, 64, 106, 140, 188, 199, 201, 222-223
content analysis (quantitative/qualitative) 29-30, 37-39, 41
contested genre. *See* family magazines

Cornhill 28, 66, 67, 68, 99; initial reception 64; intended readership (intellectual) 129-131; writers 181
Costume in England 150-151, 153-158
Cottager 63
Cowper, B.H. 149, 182
Creighton, M. 17, 140, 149
Crimea, Its Ancient and Modern History 151, 184
»Curiosities« 151

Davis, J.E. 212-213
»Deadly Art of War, The« 171-176
Dickens, C. 67
Dixon, J.H. 50
dual texts (text/image), reading of periodicals as 30, 36, 41, 100, 106-107, 199-201, 221. *See also* mixed genre
Dunkin, E. 182, 184

Ecclesiastical History of England 190, 191
»Echoes of Westminster Hall« 146, 186, 207-208
ego-documents 195, 202, 210. *See also* authenticity
English Illustrated Magazine 68
»Englishman in Russia, The« 175
ephemeral character of periodicals, transgression of 20, 141, 219
Evangelical Magazine 190
evangelicalism: decreasing influence 28, 31, 221; influence on reading matter (also Sunday reading) 25-26, 47-48, 54; influence on Victorian society 25, 189, 203-204; objection to fiction 26, 189

everyday (also domestic) 20, 27, 79,
  82, 98, 107, 111, 113, 115, 117,
  134, 156, 158, 183, 201, 204-205,
  183. *See also* lifeworld

Fact/fiction boundary, blurring of 18-
  19; in *Leisure Hour* 92; in *London
  Journal* 92, 94. *See also* history,
  increasing academisation
Fairholt, F.W. 150, 153-158
Family Herald 63
family magazines: 1850s and 1860s as
  stage of transition 24; circulation
  of 46n2; as contested genre 19, 30,
  31, 45, 48-51, 53, 56-57, 62, 63-
  65, 139, 143, 221; as democratising medium 22; historical representations in 20, 22-23; increasing
  popularity and respectability 19-
  20, 99, 221; readership 27-28, 32;
  reputation of 19; and sensational
  fiction 46, 48; stages of development 30, 45, 46-48, 61-70. *See also* penny weeklies; shilling monthlies
family readership 22, 66, 124, 135; of
  Leisure Hour 27-28, 31, 70, 83,
  141, 143, 153, 158, 162, 177, 180,
  202, 203, 205, 209, 218, 222
»Father Pedro's Convent« 105
Finn, J. 149
»Fire Escape, The« 113-115
*First Impressions of England and Its
  People* 170
»Forest Tales« 92-94
Fotheringhay 146
»Fotheringhay« 146
»Four Georges, The« 129, 131-135
Fox (Lloyd), B. 146, 162, 182, 183

Fox, C.J. 113
Franklin, B. 149
Freiburg 216

Gender 31, 65, 83, 127, 135, 150-
  151, 153-158, 180-182, 203, 205-
  206, 217, 222
generations 20, 70, 96, 163, 172-173,
  175, 218-219. *See also* age; family
  readership
Gilbert, J. 66, 70, 72-73, 86, 91-92,
  200
Glaisher, J. 151, 182, 184
Glimmerings in the Dark 78, 151
»Glimpses of Queen Anne's
  Days« 186, 210, 216-218
Godolphin, M. 206, 208
Goldsmith, O. 192, 204, 205
»Golowin's Banishment to Sibe-
  ria« 175
Good Words 28, 66, 67, 68, 99;
  title 101
gossip. *See* historiography
Gossner, J.E. 126
Gustavus Adolphus 120

Hall, J.P. 95
Haunted London 147
»Haunted London« 147
Heath, R. 182, 184
heritage culture (also material historical culture) 16; in *Leisure
  Hour* 99, 106, 107, 113, 115, 135,
  162-166, 166-167, 169-171, 221;
  in *London Journal* 77, 87, 94-95,
  106, 221
hero worship 82, 101, 111n20; in
  Cornhill 132; in *Good Words* 125;

in *Leisure Hour* 82, 111-112, 115, 120-122
historians (writers of popular history): boundary work between popular and academic 17, 31, 185, 190-191, 222; identification of writers of history 181-182; *Leisure Hour* 31, 179-184, 221, 222; professional writers 182-183; women 18, 180, 182-183; writer-ministers 182-183, 184
Historical & Geographical Enigmas 158-159
historical chronology (also chronological markers) 113, 115, 127, 144, 151, 155-156, 173, 176, 192, 193, 208, 210, 217
historical content in *Leisure Hour* (overview) 26-28
historical culture 15-16, 29, 33-34, 221; Victorian 16-18, 71, 222. *See also* heritage culture
historical discourse analysis 34
»Historical Enigmas« 158, 159-160
historical fiction: in *Leisure Hour* 75, 83, 279-281; in *London Journal* 73, 75
historical genres: blending of travel and life writing 115, 193, 194; in *Cornhill* 104; in *Good Words* 103-104; in *Leisure Hour* 73-75, 102-104; in *London Journal* 75
historical periods: in *Cornhill* 104; in *Good Words* 104; in *Leisure Hour* 76, 104, 155; in *London Journal* 76
historical programme 15, 33, 41; *Cornhill* 102, 107-108, 128, 135-136, 221; *Good Words* 101, 107,

127, 135-136, 221; *Leisure Hour* 14, 15, 60, 71-72, 77, 98, 101, 107, 127, 135-136, 148, 179, 185-186, 219, 221-223, change in 69-70, 99; *London Journal* 71-72, 87, 98, 136, 221
historical sightseeing 75, 92, 117, 145-146, 152, 162, 183, 211-212, 214
historical sources and references, use of (objectivity) 17, 78, 85, 88-89, 92, 94, 148-150, 152, 155-156, 157-158, 160, 184, 186n12, 198-199, 202, 212, 215, 216
historiography: *Leisure Hour* 77-78, 171-176; *London Journal* 94, 95-96; popular representations marked as gossip 18, 154; scientific writing 18, 107-108, 117, 147, 198. *See also* fact/fiction boundary; science of history
history: academic approach to h.: *Cornhill* 107, 128, 131-132, 135, *Leisure Hour* 117; approach linked to materiality and reputation of medium 29, 140-141, 177, 221-222 (*see also* family magazines; media transfer); categories and typology 26-28, 30, 38-39; church h. (in *Good Words*) 107, 124-125; as democratising force 15, 18; domestic / everyday h. (*see* lifeworld); foreign h. 214-216, f. h. and narrative distance 216; h. and geographical space: *Cornhill* 104, *Good Words* 104, *Leisure Hour* 76, 104, *London Journal* 76; humorous approach to h.: *Cornhill* 108, 128,

131, 132-135, *Leisure Hour* 110-111; identification of articles and series on h. 39; increasing academisation of h. 17, 141, 147, 182-183, 221; local h. 210-214; picturesque h. 146, 202, 217; popular vs. academic h. 16n3, 17, 29, 154-158, 149, 180, 182-183, 185-191, 212-214, 222; social h. . *See also* popular history
History of England (Macaulay) 202
History of England (Milner) 152, 161
History of Europe 150
history painting (Victorian) 99-101. *See also* illustrations
Hogarth, W. 128
Hopley, H. 146, 182, 183
Horn, W.O. 85-86
How to See the English Lakes 146
»How to See the English Lakes« 162-166
Howard, J. 192

Identity (national historical) 29, 34, 80, 92-93, 122, 140, 152, 180, 206, 207, 215, 222
»Idler on the Rhine, The« 146n16
illustrations (in family magazines) 19, 66; *Cornhill* 105-106, 128-135; *Good Words* 105-106, 122-127; *Leisure Hour* 66, 72-73, 75-76, 86, 90, 99, 105-106, 108-122, 157, 165, 169-170, 199-201, 214; *London Journal* 72-73, 75-76, 90-92. *See also* allegorical images; caricature; dual texts; maps; narrative scenes; objects, depiction of; painting reproductions; portraits; statues, depictions of

Ingall, F.M. 158-159
intersectionality 14n1, 29, 34-35, 41. *See also* categories of disparity

Jerdan, W. 108, 145, 182, 184
Jews in China, The 149
»Jews of China, The« 149
»John Evangelist Gossner« 126-127
Johnson, S. 170, 192, 200-202, 205
Jones, H. 145-146, 182, 183

Kentigern 122, 124
»Knight of Eskdale, The« 148
Kyrle, J. 115

Lake Poets 163-164
»Last Prayer of Gustavus Adolphus, The« 120-122
Lawrence, J. 110
Leisure Hour: circulation 25, 58n17, 61-62, 67; to counter secular periodicals 14, 26, 28, 53, 56, 62-63, 71, 198, 209; design of annual cover 70; double discourse regulating content 30, 45; dual publication format (weekly/monthly) 61-62, 67, 166, 167, 171, 172-176; editor, change of 68-69, 99; as exemplary for family magazine genre 24-25; fiction, use of 48, 53, 99, 102, historical f., approach to 83, 84, history as substitute for f. 26, 48, 53, 71, 75; first issue 14, 59-60, 77-78; free distribution 59-60; German Biedermeier 86; historical content aimed at working classes 30; illustrated magazines of the sixties, adaptation to 62, 67, 68-69, 99; index to annual vol-

umes 176; initiation 13-15, 30, 48, 53, 71, 139; as intermediary 15, 28, 30, 31, 45, 221, 222; issued by Religious Tract Society 13, 25; jubilee number 25n25, 67, 83, 179, 180, 186, 190; marketing strategies 53, 59-60; monthly parts 61-62, 143, 152, 162-176, 211; monthly plates 67, 169; readership: intended middle-class 63, 167, 221, intended working-class 13-15, 26, 29, 30, 59, 70-71, 76-77, 77, 167, 201, 206, 221, negotiation between intended working-class r. and RTS supporters 30, 45, 53, 57-59, 61-62, 71, 168-171, 221; title 58n18, 61n22, 72, 101; *Visitor*, absorption of 52-53;

»Lessons of Biography, The« 81-83

»Life in Egypt« 146-147

Life of Abraham Lincoln 150

life writing 100; in *Cornhill* 128-135; *Good Words* 122-127; *Leisure Hour* 82-83, 90, 108-122, 166-171; *London Journal* 82, 88-89, 90

lifeworld (Lebenswelt) 27, 81-82, 95, 115, 134, 156, 176, 187-188, 192-197; active engagement with history 162, 163, 166, 192; blurring of narrative boundaries to link to 194-196, 211, 214-215, 218. *See also* everyday

Lives of the Queens of England (A. Strickland) 88-89, 90

»Lives of the Queens of England« (J.F. Smith) 88-92, 198

London Journal 28, 46, 48, 49, 51, 52, 53, 54, 62-63, 65, 68, 99; secular

opponent to *Leisure Hour* 30, 192, 198; title 72

»Lord Clive« 111-113

»Lord Macaulay« 109-110

Macaulay, J. 68, 189-190

Macaulay, T.B. 109, 202

Macleod, N. 68

Madden, R.R. 149

»Man of Ross, The« 115

maps (in *Leisure Hour*) 118-119, 165-166, 169, 214

Marvell, A. 192

materiality, material culture. *See* heritage culture; history; media transfer; periodicals

media: as means of production of knowledge 35-36, 140n2; readerships, different intended 152, 166, 208-209, 223; reputation of different m. 152, 177, 190-191, 222. *See also* media transfer; periodicals; book.

media transfer (between book publications and periodicals) 31, 78-80, 88-91, 139-177, 207-209, 212-213, 221; authorship, (re)attribution of 143-144, 151, 152, 171; book to periodical 148-152, 152-162, 166-171, 212-214; identification of book counterparts 142n7; illustrations 146, 151n22, 157; and *Leisure Hour* (overview) 141-142; materiality and publication format 143, 165-166, 172-176, 208-209, 222; as means to gain profits 208; monthly parts and m. t. 162-176; peritext, loss/addition of 141, 143,

147, 158, 176, 207-208, 212; periodical to book 143-147, 162-166, 207-209; semantic changes 143, 144, s. c. to fit historical programme 148; shift of textual genre 152, 213; source text, acknowledgement of 146, 148-151, 161, 191

Memoirs of the Life, Writings, and Discoveries of Sir Isaac Newton 148

»Memorial Chapters« 208

Men I Have Known 145

»Men I Have Known« 108, 145

Merryweather, F.S. 60, 78, 151, 182, 184

meta-history: in *Cornhill* 107, 128, 130-131, 135-136; *Good Words* 125, 135-136; *Leisure Hour* 84-85, 111-112, 135-136, 169, 217; *London Journal* 96, 136

Miller, H. 170

Miller, W.H. 63, 68-69

Milner, T. 151, 152, 161, 175, 182, 184

Milton, J. 192, 193-194, 205-206

»Minnigrey« 73

mixed genre 19, 141, 222; threatening thematic and material unit 172, 175-177

Mr. Johnson's Preface to His Edition of Shakespear's Plays 170

Murray's *A Handbook for Travellers in Southern Germany* 215

museum (also exhibitions)

Narrative pattern (Stoughton) 192-218

narrative scenes: in *Leisure Hour* 113, 120-122, 200; *Good Words* 125

narratology 29, 31, 37, 221. *See also* lifeworld; narrative pattern; perspective structure; worldmaking

»Neglected Books« 186

»New Weekly Periodical« 139-140

Newton, I. 192, 206

Ninian 122

Notices of Windsor in the Olden Time 152, 212

Objects, depiction of: in *Leisure Hour* 115-117, 199-200

O'Hanlon, W.M. 55-56

Oliphant, M. 51

Once a Week 66

Oxford and Cambridge 146

Painting reproductions: in *Cornhill* 129-130; *Leisure Hour* 130

paterfamilias 70

Pattison, S.R. 182, 184

Penny Magazine 46, 83

penny weeklies (first and second generation f.m.) 30, 31, 45-48, 54, 62, 69, 99, 221

periodical archive, abundance of 24, 29, 32

»Periodical Literature« 53-60

»Periodical Peeps at Female Costume in England« 150-151, 153-158

periodicals: agents of Victorian historical culture 223; first mass medium 18; collaborative enterprise 29, 31-33, 36, 41, 179 (*see also* we-narrator; anonymity); materiality 28, 29, 32. *See also* communal reading; dual texts; ephemeral character; family magazines; media transfer; mixed genre; serialisation

peritext 141n4, 177n57. *See also* media transfer

perspective structure 29, 31, 37, 41, 203-206, 221

Pfennig-Magazin 86n19

»Philadelphia Printer, The« 149

»Pictures from the History and Life of the Early Church« 124-125

»Pictures in Words« 152, 158, 160-162

»Poccahontas« 75, 83-86, 90, 92

popular history, popular, popularisation 15n2, 16n3, 34, 124, 140, 149n20, 184: defending approach, in *Cornhill* 131-132, in *Leisure Hour* 154-156. *See also* history; serialisation

»Popular Literature of the Day« 50

portraits: in *Good Words* 125, 127; *Leisure Hour* 108-110, 125

production 24, 29, 31-34, 41, 55, 57, 63, 65, 92, 129, 141, 223

»Queen of a Literary Coterie, The« 149

Radical press 54

»Ramble in the Tyrol, A« 186, 214-215, 216

re-enactment (as narrative strategy) 199, 202, 210, 211, 215

readership: construction of own version of text 35; cross-class 15, 99; new readerships 19, 51, 54; notices to correspondents 49n9, 65n27; stratification of 48-49, 64-65. *See*
also communal reading; family magazines, readership; family readership

Recollections of a Long Life 187

»Regular Swiss Round, The« 145

regulation 28, 30, 34, 45, 53, 89, 180

religion 30-31, 79-80, 101-102, 103-104, 107, 120-122, 122-127, 182, 184, 185, 188, 192-193, 203-204, 221

religious periodicals, failure of 54-55

Religious Tract Society (RTS) 25; archives 30, 39-40; ideology 28, 47, 51, 71n1, 189; new publishing programme 52, 53; periodicals issued by 46-47, 51, 63; writers for 182. See also *Leisure Hour*, evangelicalism

representation (historical) 18, 23-25, 28, 29, 33-35, 38, 100, 104, 152, 179, 195-186

Reynolds, J. 192, 204, 205

Reynolds's Miscellany 46, 51, 63

»Robert Stephenson« 115-117

role models 84, 109, 111-112, 192, 203-206, 218

»Royal Commission on Historical MSS, The« 186

»Royal Observatory, Greenwich« 184

»Royal Visits to Remarkable Places« 95-98

Russell, W. 192, 205

»Russia« 175

Sala, A. 128

Saturday Magazine 46

science of history 184, 222. *See also* historiography

scissors-and-paste journalism 149n20

Scoffern, J. 144, 182, 184
self-made men 206
serialisation 20-22; binding readers 160; link between single parts 173-175; popularity, indicator for 20, 29; s. of the past: in *Leisure Hour* 31, 76-77, 139-177, in *London Journal* 76-77, and Victorian historical consciousness 21-22, 176, 222; series (Episodenserie) vs. serial (Fortsetzungsserie) 20n16; thematic unity 172-177
Shades and Echoes from Old London 146, 206, 207-209
»Shades of the Departed in Old London« 60, 72, 73, 90, 144n12, 146, 185-186, 192-209, 216, 218
»Shakespeare« 152, 166-171
Shakespeare tercentenary 152, 166-171
Shilling Books for Leisure Hours 208-209
shilling monthlies (new illustrated f.m. of the sixties) 30-31, 45, 65-66, 100, 221
Sieveking, A.W. 127
»Sir Isaac Newton« 148
»Sir John Lawrence« 110-111
»Sketches of the Crimea« 151, 175
Smiles, S. 82
Smith, G. 64, 66, 68, 128
Smith, J.F. 73, 88-92, 198
Stars of the East 190
statues, depiction of: in *Leisure Hour* 113, 200
Stephenson, R. 115
»Story of Ninian, The« 122-124

Stoughton, J. 31, 60, 146, 152, 168-169, 179-180, 182, 184, 185-219
Stowe, H.B. 170
Strahan, A. 66, 68, 122, 145
Stray Leaves of Science and Folk-Lore 144
Strickland, A. 88-89
Sunday at Home 68, 81, 101, 144n12, 188, 189, 190, 208-209
Sunny Memories of Foreign Lands 170

»Tale of a West-End Suburb, The« 186, 210
Thackeray, W.M. 64, 68, 128, 131
Thornbury, W. 147, 182, 184
Tighe, R.R. 212-213
Timbs, J. 151, 182, 184
title-function (periodical) 143-144, 177
Tract Magazine 47
travel writing: in *Leisure Hour* 162-166
Tytler, Sarah 103

Under Egyptian Palms 146

»Vancouver the Voyager« 118-119
Vancouver, G. 117, 118
Victorian Enigmas 158-159
Visitor 47, 52-53

»Walcheren Expedition, The« 150, 175
Walsh(e), E.H. 182, 183
Walton, I. 192, 193-194, 205-206
Ward, E.M. 200-201
Watts, I. 208

we-narrator in periodicals (editorial
we) 37, 41, 179, 194-195, 199,
203-205, 209-210, 211, 214
Whately, M.L. 146-147, 183
»Will and the Way, The« 73
»William Hogarth« 106, 128-131, 135
Wilson, J. 150
»Windsor Castle« 152, 186, 210, 211-
214
*Windsor: A History and Description
of the Castle and the Town* 213

Wivell, A. 113
»Woman's Work, A« 127
»Word With Our Readers, A« 13-14,
60-61, 77-78
»Working Man in the Olden Time,
The« 60, 77-80, 148, 151, 184
worldmaking 38, 41; historical 194-
202, 211